CISCO IOS ESSENTIALS

Cisco IOS Essentials

John Albritton

McGraw-Hill
New York   San Francisco   Washington, D.C.
Auckland   Bogotá   Caracas   Lisbon   London
Madrid   Mexico City   Milan   Montreal   New Delhi
San Juan   Singapore   Sydney   Tokyo   Toronto

Library of Congress Cataloging-in-Publication Data

Albritton, John
   Cisco IOS Essentials / John Albritton.
      p.   cm.
   ISBN 0-07-134743-7
    1. Computer networks. 2. Internetworking (Telecommunication)—
Management. 3. Software configuration management. I. Title.
TK5105.5.A395 1999
005.7′13769—dc21

99-12964
CIP

McGraw-Hill

A Division of The McGraw·Hill Companies

1 2 3 4 5 6 7 8 9 0 DOC/DOC 9 0 4 3 2 1 0 9

ISBN 0-07-134743-7

The sponsoring editor for this book was Michael Sprague, the editing super-
visor was Ruth W. Mannino, and the production supervisor was Claire Stanley.
It was set in New Century Schoolbook by Don Feldman of McGraw-Hill's
Desktop Publishing facility in cooperation with Spring Point Publishing
Services.

Printed and bound by R. R. Donnelley & Sons Company.

McGraw-Hill books are available at special quantity discounts to use as premi-
ums and sales promotions, or for use in corporate training programs. For more
information, please write to the Director of Special Sales, McGraw-Hill, 11
West 19 Street, New York, NY 10011. Or contact your local bookstore.

 This book is printed on recycled, acid-free paper containing a minimum
of 50% recycled de-inked fiber.

CONTENTS

Contents

Acknowledgments

Thanks to:

My wife, Stephannie, for trying (sometimes successfully) to keep me focused.

My daughters—Danielle, Hannah, and Abigail—for their constant interruptions and for helping me to keep my priorities straight.

Darrin Kirby at Al Boenker Computer Services for listening to my ideas and providing real feedback.

Terry Slattery and the rest of the crew at Chesapeake Computer Consultants, Inc. for providing me with great advice and technical support.

Everyone associated with MentorLabs. Most of the configuration examples in this book were done on MentorLabs equipment. By the time this book is published, MentorLabs should be ready for business. Visit their site on the Internet at http://www.mentorlabs.com, and use their vLab product to practice IOS configuration and learn more about the configuration of Cisco routers.

God for all of the above and everything else.

Trademark Acknowledgments

PostScript is a registered trademark of Adobe Systems Incorporated.

Apple, AppleTalk, EtherTalk, LocalTalk, Macintosh, and TokenTalk are registered trademarks of Apple Computer, Inc.

Banyan, StreetTalk, and VINES are registered trademarks of Banyan Systems Incorporated.

Cisco and Cisco IOS are registered trademarks of Cisco Systems, Inc.

DIGITAL, DECnet, VAX are trademarks of Digital Equipment Corporation.

IBM is a registered trademark of International Business Machines Corporation.

Windows is a registered trademark of Microsoft Corporation.

NetWare, Novell, and Novell Directory Services are registered trademarks of Novell, Inc.

IPX, IPX/SPX, NCP, and NDS are trademarks of Novell, Inc.

Other products and services mentioned in this book may be trademarks of their respective owners.

Introduction

Who cares about configuring network routers? Network routers are a major part of the glue that holds all computer networks together. Routers are supposed to configure themselves right? Not really. Routers aren't to the point of being able to configure themselves, yet. They have no artificial intelligence agent so almost everything on them must be done manually. That's where you and I come in. So I guess you and I care about configuring network routers. Since almost every network is different, we as network engineers and administrators must know our networks and configure our routers to become a part of our network infrastructure.

1.1   You Should Read This Book

You are about to find out how all those highly paid (or so they say) network engineers managed to get all of your company's computers talking to each other using Cisco IOS-based routers. The subject matter here is meant for the network administrator or network engineer who understands general computer networking and who needs to configure Cisco routers to provide basic connectivity for networks running multiple protocols. You will see that configuring IOS to perform basic routing and bridging of network messages is pretty easy—it can be done by learning and putting into practice just a few basic commands. Of course, IOS configuration is not always intuitive; that's why you need this book.

1.2   What This Book Is

The purpose of this book is to get you started in configuring Cisco IOS-based routers. This book is meant to be a tutorial for the person new to the Cisco IOS as well as a basic reference for the somewhat experienced IOS person. We cover several hundred IOS commands, so no one expects you to remember all of the commands—however, there are a few you absolutely must know. I will be sure to indicate which ones those are as we go along.

   This book is also a task-oriented programmer's reference for the Cisco IOS. We show the commands in the context in which they are most often used. We cover the very basic configuration of the major routing and bridging features of the Cisco IOS.

1.3 What This Book Is Not

This book is not meant to be a study of computer networking nor is it meant to provide in-depth details on network protocols. Rather it is simply a reference for the basic configuration of Cisco IOS-based routers.

1.4 Game Plan

We're going to start out slowly with a brief description of network routing and how the Cisco IOS fits into the big picture. After the routing description, we cover configuring a brand new Cisco router right out of the box to be installed into an existing network. We're going to use the standard IOS Setup facility to do this the first time. Thereafter, we'll use the IOS Command Line Interface to do the same thing and more. The Cisco 2500-series routers are used in the examples, but the IOS configuration principles that will be shown work for all of the Cisco IOS-based router models from the 1000 to the 12000. There are some minor differences, but we cover those when we get to them.

We use a task-oriented procedure to group the commands for configuring many IOS routing and bridging features. The configuration of each network protocol, such as IP and IPX, is presented as a task. Each protocol is covered with the following steps:

- A brief overview of how the protocol works
- Descriptions of the commands needed to turn on and configure the protocol
- Examples showing the implementation of the commands
- Commands used to make sure everything is working properly

The commands shown are those that I consider to be the most used and most popular. Each IOS command is also explained in the programmer's reference section.

1.5 Chapter Overview

Following is a list of the rest of the chapters along with a brief description of what is covered in each one:

Chapter 2, *Routing and Bridging Overview,* covers router operation and provides an introduction to Cisco IOS.

Chapter 3, *Initial Configuration,* shows the configuration of a Cisco IOS-based router from scratch using the IOS Setup facility. No special command knowledge is required.

Chapter 4, *IOS Command Line Interface,* explains the primary means of configuring the IOS—typing commands into its command line interface.

Chapter 5, *Examining IOS,* could also be called "As long as we're here, we might as well look around." We use the most-used command in IOS—**show**—to examine the main components of the IOS-based router.

Chapter 6, *General IOS Tasks,* provides the first detailed look at IOS configuration before we get into configuring IOS to process network traffic. Other tasks such as managing configuration files and resetting interfaces are also here.

Chapter 7, *Configuring IP,* provides the commands needed to tell our router to start routing IP packets. It covers addressing of interfaces and IP interior routing protocol configuration.

Chapter 8, *Configuring IPX,* provides the commands needed to tell our router to start routing Novell IPX packets.

Chapter 9, *Configuring AppleTalk,* provides the commands to start AppleTalk on our router.

Chapter 10, *Configuring DECnet,* provides the commands necessary to start DECnet on our router. It includes a brief overview of DECnet.

Chapter 11, *Configuring VINES,* provides coverage of the commands for configuring Banyan VINES on our router.

Chapter 12, *Configuring Transparent Bridging,* covers the commands for turning our router into a bridge and why we need them.

Chapter 13, *Configuring Frame Relay,* provides the commands for connecting a Cisco router to a frame relay network.

Chapter 14, *Configuring SRB and DLSw,* provides the commands for doing SRB and DLSw to handle Token Ring network traffic.

Appendix A, *Command Reference,* provides a list of all of the IOS commands used in the book. Each command is cross-referenced to the page where it appears.

Appendix B, *Acronym Glossary,* provides a list of all of the acronyms used in the book. After all, we networking folks do have a tendency to speak our own language of acronyms.

1.6 Conventions

The parts of a command that should be typed as shown will be indicated by **boldface** type. Command arguments that require a value will be shown in *italics*. Optional arguments of a command will be shown within brackets ([ ]). When multiple entries are possible, but only one is allowed, the entries will be separated by a vertical bar (|). When multiple entries are possible, but one is required, the choices will be shown within braces ({ }). These designations can be combined to represent the syntax requirements of a command.

Text produced by the router will also be displayed in lightface `Courier`. Typed text entries—for example, keywords—will also be displayed in **`boldface Courier`**.

For the depiction of multiple keys being pressed simultaneously, the key symbols will be placed together within angle brackets and separated by hyphens; for example, <Ctrl-Shift-6> means that the Ctrl key, the Shift key, and the 6 key should be pressed at the same time.

2

Routing and Bridging Overview

Routing and bridging are the main things that Internetwork Operating System (IOS) does on a Cisco router. You should understand routing and bridging before you begin IOS configuration; therefore, we're going to cover some computer network basics, and then we'll use those basics to do an overview of routing and bridging.

A *computer network* is a broad term meaning a collection of interconnected, autonomous computers; interconnected computers can exchange information with each other (Tanenbaum 2). I refer to a computer network as simply a *network*. Networks are separated by special computers called *routers* or *bridges*. For the purposes of this book, an *internetwork* is a collection of networks separated by routers and/or bridges.

Routing and *bridging* are two different communication mechanisms used to exchange information between computers on different networks, across an internetwork. The mechanism you decide to use will depend on the type of network you have and the protocol that your computers are using to exchange information. Examples of information exchanged on a network and an internetwork are documents, databases, email messages, and World Wide Web (WWW or Web) pages.

Since most routers can perform both routing and bridging, discussion can be pretty confusing so we need some terminology guidelines. When I refer to a *router* in this book, I am talking about a device that is performing routing unless I state otherwise. When I refer to a *bridge,* I am talking about either a bridge or a router performing bridging.

2.1   Networking 101

When your computer sends information on a network, the computer splits the information into little messages called *datagrams,* which get addressed so that, once they get on the network, they arrive at the computer to which your computer is talking. If the other computer is on another network, a router must take the message and get it to the correct network. The router does this by examining the address in the message to determine where the message is supposed to go.

You can think of router operation as being similar to the postal service. When you send a letter to your Aunt Emma in Kansas, you put an address on the outside of the letter's envelope. The postal service examines the address to determine which direction your letter is supposed to go next; in other words, the postal service routes your letter based on the destination address. Of course, the destination address must be correct; otherwise, Aunt Emma will never get the letter. Pretty simple, huh?

To explain routing and bridging, we need to cover some basic concepts of computer networking. The basic concepts of networking that we cover include the Open Systems Interconnection (OSI) Reference Model, encapsulation, and computer address format. We then take these concepts and put them together to describe how routing and bridging work.

2.1.1   OSI Reference Model

The *OSI Reference Model* comes from the International Organization of Standardization (ISO) and provides us with a standard set of terms that we can use to discuss computer networking concepts. The OSI Reference Model describes the functions of a network as layers, seven of them. The layers are stacked and numbered from 1 to 7, bottom to top, like the stories of a building. The seven-layered model is shown in Figure 2-1.

Figure 2-1
OSI reference model.

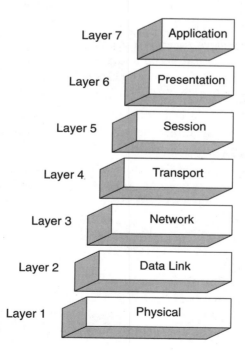

Starting at the top layer, let us briefly review each layer's function. We are, however, going to concentrate on layers 2 and 3 to describe routing and bridging.

Layer 7, the application layer, is where all network applications run. These are the applications that you use to send information, data, across the network, for example, Web browsers and servers and email clients and servers.

Layer 6, the presentation layer, controls the formatting of data for your application's use. For example, if the data are sound from a radio broadcast to which you are listening across the Internet, the presentation layer formats the data for the application that you're using to receive the broadcast.

Layer 5, the session layer, handles the establishment and termination of communication sessions. For example, when you log in to your company's mainframe, a session must be established for you to be able to talk to the mainframe, and when you log out, your session is terminated.

Layer 4, the transport layer, provides source-to-destination connection establishment for data transfer. Over the connection, the transport layer can provide flow control and error checking.

Layer 3, the network layer, is the most important layer in routing. The network layer contains the address that routing software examines to determine where to route a message across a network.

Layer 2, the data link layer, is dependent on the medium to which a host is attached. The data link layer links the data from the network protocol to the physical medium on which it is to be transmitted.

Layer 1, the physical layer, defines the characteristics that belong to the type of physical network connection on a host, for example, the cable type, the connector type, the signal frequency, the signal level, and the maximum cable length. The physical layer determines exactly how bits (binary ones and zeroes) are transmitted and received on a network.

A computing device connected to a network is called a *host.* For example, your computer and a Cisco router are both hosts. To talk to each other, hosts must abide by a set of rules. The rules of communication used between hosts are called *protocols,* and many have been developed. Hosts should use the same protocol to share information. Five protocols are covered in this book.

The data link layer, layer 2, is independent of the protocol being run on a host; it changes only with the network medium, for example, Ethernet and Token Ring. What happens at the upper layers changes from one protocol to the next.

The software implementation of a protocol on a host is called a *stack*, because it's just a "stack" of functional layers. Each individual protocol may have different names and numbers for its layers, but the functionality of the seven layers exists somewhere within the protocol; therefore, we can use the OSI Reference Model to talk about protocols in general.

2.1.2   Encapsulation

Encapsulation is the process of adding headers to data at each layer of a stack. Data that are to be sent over a network start at the application layer and move down a protocol stack until they leave a host at the physical layer. At each layer of a host's stack, a header is placed in front of the data. Your data combined with a header or headers is a *datagram*. A datagram at layer 3 is called a *packet,* which starts with a layer-3 header. A datagram at layer 2 is a *frame,* which starts with a layer-2 header (frame header).

A datagram header provides a path up a stack toward an application. A header must contain a data field that indicates the type of data encapsulated at the layer immediately above the layer that added the header. For example, when your computer receives a Web page from a Web server, the header that immediately precedes the Web-page data must contain a field that indicates to your computer that the data being received are meant for your Web browser. Another example occurs when a host is encapsulating a packet with a frame header at layer 2. The frame header must contain a value that indicates what protocol is being spoken; this value could indicate what type of layer-3 header immediately follows the layer-2 header in the frame.

Let's revisit the postal service analogy. Suppose you are mailing a gift to your Uncle Charlie in Seattle. You put the gift in a box. You then wrap shipping paper around the box. Finally, you write Uncle Charlie's address on the shipping paper so the postal service will know how to route the package. You have just encapsulated the gift twice and put an address on the outer wrapping.

Your process of preparing the gift for shipment is analogous to the process a host goes through when it sends data. The data start off in an application and must move down the stack. As the host is preparing the data for transmission, it encapsulates the data with a header at each layer as the data move down the stack. The last header contains an address that allows the data to reach the correct destination.

The header at layer 2 always contains an address; since this is a data link, or frame, header, the address type changes based on the medium on which the frame is to be transmitted. For some protocols, like IP and AppleTalk, the layer-3 header also has an address. If an internetworking host, like a router, examines a frame's layer-2 address to determine where to send a network message, the internetworking device is bridging frames. If an internetworking device uses a layer-3 address to determine where to send a network message, the internetworking device is routing packets.

When Uncle Charlie receives the package you sent, he checks the destination address on the outside to make sure it's his. He removes the shipping paper and, then, opens the box. He now finds out what the gift is.

A host that receives a network message reads the destination address to determine if the address is its own. If the address matches, the host moves the data up the stack, deencapsulating at each layer. Each layer removes a header that was added by the corresponding layer on the transmitting host until all that is left is the original data that were transmitted.

2.1.3   Layer-2 Addressing

The format of a *layer-2 address* changes by the class of network that is using the address—*Local Area Networks* (LANs) and *Wide Area Networks* (WANs) are the two main classes of networks. A LAN is a network with hosts that are directly connected and close to each other. Control of a LAN usually belongs to a single company. Types of LANs include Ethernet and Token Ring. LANs use a *Medium Access Control* (MAC) address at layer 2. A WAN is a network with hosts a large distance apart. The installation and administration of a WAN usually requires the assistance and facilities of a telecommunications carrier (for example, a phone company). Some examples of WANs are frame relay, leased line, and dial-up. A WAN's layer-2 address depends on the type of WAN.

Layer-2 addresses are important because a host must put a destination address (and sometimes a source address) in the frame header during the encapsulation process before a frame can be transmitted.

2.1.3.1 LAN Addressing

Most LANs use MAC addresses at layer 2. The MAC address identifies a host on a LAN and allows a frame to properly navigate on a LAN. That is, it is used to get a frame from one host to another on the same LAN. Since LANs are usually separated by routers and routers usually base their routing decisions on layer-3 addresses, a MAC address has no bearing on how data are routed. If, however, a router has multiple LAN interfaces and is running bridging, the LANs are treated as one logical, or virtual, LAN. Since bridging causes a router to examine the layer-2 address for message forwarding, MAC addresses become significant in the router's decision to forward a message from one physical LAN to the other.

The format of a MAC address is show in Figure 2-2. As you can see, a MAC address is 48 bits long; that is, 48 binary ones and zeroes. These bits are usually written in hexadecimal (hex). Since a hex digit represents four bits, there are 12 hex digits in a MAC address.

The first half of the MAC address is the *Organizational Unique Identifier* (OUI), which is sometimes referred to as the *vendor code*. For example, the MAC address of my office computer is 00-A0-24-37-8D-9E. The first six hex digits are 00-A0-24, which is the OUI for 3Com. So you can tell I have a 3Com LAN card in my computer.

The second half of the MAC address is the *serial number,* a unique number that a manufacturer assigns to each LAN interface it produces. The combination of OUI and serial number guarantees that MAC addresses are unique to each LAN interface as long as manufacturers follow the guidelines.

Each type of LAN has its own *encapsulations,* or *frame formats.* For Ethernet, there are four encapsulations; for Token Ring, there are three; and for Fiber Distributed Data Interface (FDDI), there are two.

Figure 2-2
MAC address format.

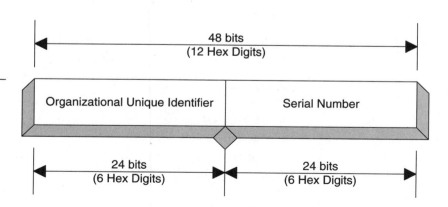

When a LAN host encapsulates a packet with a frame header (in front of the packet) and trailer (at the end of the packet) to create a frame, the host must put both the source MAC address and the destination MAC address into the header. The source MAC address is the host's own MAC address. The destination MAC address is the MAC address of a host on the same physical or logical LAN to which the host is sending the frame.

Since a MAC address is required to send a frame across a LAN, how does a host get the MAC address of another host? There are three ways:

1. Address Resolution Protocol (ARP)

2. Prediction

3. Hello

Using *ARP,* a host broadcasts a request onto a LAN asking for the MAC address of a destination host. If the desired destination host receives the request, it will reply to the source host with a MAC address that can be used to complete the building of a frame. ARP is used in IP and AppleTalk.

With *prediction,* a host runs another host's layer-3 address through a calculation to figure out what the destination MAC address is. Predictable MAC addresses are used in IPX and DECnet.

Some network protocols require that hosts periodically send *Hello* messages that contain their layer-3 address and their layer-2 address. Other hosts listen to these Hello messages and store them in a table for future reference. Hellos are used to acquire MAC addresses in Banyan VINES.

As we cover the configuration of the individual protocols, we go into more detail about how the MAC address acquisition occurs. There are three different types of MAC addresses:

1. Unicast

2. Broadcast

3. Multicast

A *unicast address* is one that is unique to a single host. When one host wants to send a message to a specific host, a unicast address is used. My office computer's MAC address I mentioned earlier is a unicast address.

A *broadcast address* is used when a host wants to send a message to every host on a LAN. The broadcast MAC address is represented by 48 binary ones or 12 hex F's (0xFFFFFFFFFFFF). A message sent to the broadcast address is processed by every host that receives it.

A *multicast address* is one that is meant for multiple hosts, but not all hosts, on a LAN. Multicast addresses are used in lieu of sending multiple unicast messages that would take unnecessary LAN resources and broadcast messages that would take unnecessary host resources.

2.1.3.2 WAN Addressing

WAN addressing involves just one address in the frame header. The reason for this is that most WAN data paths are point to point. In other words, each data path of a WAN has only two hosts. When a host sends a frame directly across a WAN, there's only one place it can go—the host on the other end of the data path. Likewise, according to the host receiving a frame directly from a WAN, there is only one place the frame could have come from—the host on the other end of the path.

WAN data paths can be either physical or logical (virtual). For example, a dedicated T1 leased line is a physical data path, and a frame-relay Permanent Virtual Circuit (PVC) is a logical data path. When one host wants to talk to another, it doesn't have to identify itself in the frame header. Each host already knows who's on the other side of the link.

Addresses in physical point-to-point WANs (for example, leased line and dial-up) are host addresses. Addresses in logical point-to-point WANs like frame relay are data-path addresses.

2.1.4   Layer-3 Addressing

A layer-3 address appears in the layer-3 header built during the encapsulation process—the layer-3 address is the one that a router uses to perform path determination for those protocols being routed. Not all protocols have an address at layer 3; those protocols that don't have layer-3 addresses must be bridged.

An address at layer 3 consists of two parts: network and node. The *network* part is the LAN or WAN address. The *node* part is the address of the host that is attached to the LAN or WAN indicated in the network part of the address.

Consider a building's address consisting of a number and a street name, for example, 1600 Downing Street. The street where the building stands has a name; the street name must be unique in the city. The building has a number; the number doesn't have to be unique in the entire city—it has to be unique only on the street. Think of the street as the network (LAN or WAN) and the building as a node (device) on the network. A network address must be unique in an internetwork, but the

Figure 2-3
Layer-3 address
examples.

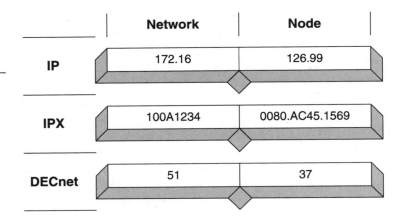

	Network	Node
IP	172.16	126.99
IPX	100A1234	0080.AC45.1569
DECnet	51	37

node part of the address needs to be unique only on the network. The full host address is the combination of the network part and the node part of the layer-3 address. A host address must be unique in an internetwork. Figure 2-3 shows example layer-3 addresses for three protocols.

The network and node parts of a layer-3 address are normally separated by a period ("."); when they are written. The period is verbally communicated with the word *dot*. For example, the IP address in Figure 2-3 would be pronounced, "172 dot 16 dot 126 dot 99."

Each protocol that has layer-3 addressing can be routed; we will see and configure these protocols in the coming chapters. A router bases its path determination on the network portion of the destination address in the layer-3 header. Each protocol capable of being routed (a routed protocol) has a different format for its layer-3 address. We cover each protocol's address format when we cover the protocol.

2.2 The Big Picture

Now that we have gotten some of the little—but very important—stuff out of the way, let's put it all together for the big picture. What do encapsulation and addressing have to do with routing and bridging? Practically everything.

Figure 2-4 shows the Router Operation Flowchart that is used in describing some of what a router does when it's either routing or bridging. We will be going through the steps in a little more detail, but keep in mind this is still very basic and does not cover every possibility.

Before a router can attempt to process a message, the router must receive the message, as a frame, on one of its interfaces (Figure 2-4, Box 1). If the interface that received the frame is a LAN interface, the router examines the frame's destination MAC address to determine if the frame is destined for the router (Figure 2-4, Box 2). If the frame is destined for the router, the router will attempt to route it if the encapsulated data's protocol has been configured on the router (Figure 2-4, Box 3). If the frame is not destined for the router, the router will attempt to bridge it if bridging has been configured on the router (Figure 2-4, Box 4) and if the

Figure 2-4

Router operation flowchart (box numbers are at top left of each box).

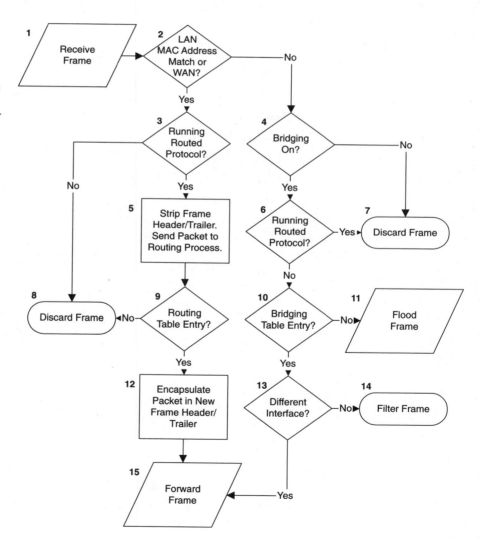

encapsulated data's protocol has not been configured on the router (Figure 2-4, Box 6).

When a host is running a routed protocol and wants to get a message to another host on another network, the host normally sends the frame to the router to be routed. When a host is running a bridged protocol, the host is not aware that a bridge exists; therefore, the host will never send a frame directly to a bridge.

2.2.1   Bridging

Bridging is the process of forwarding a network message based on an address in the message's layer-2 header. There are many types of bridging supported by IOS:

- Transparent Bridging
- Encapsulated Bridging
- Source Route Bridging
- Source Route Transparent Bridging
- Source Route Translational Bridging

To illustrate the bridging process, let us briefly cover transparent bridging. This type of bridging is called *transparent* because a router running it is transparent to the hosts that are attached to its interface LANs. Notice that in the Figure 2-4, Box 4, the router checks for bridging only if it receives a frame not destined for it. If the router receives a frame that is not destined for it and the router is not running bridging, the router just discards the frame (Figure 2-4, Box 7). A router (bridge) running transparent bridging performs the following functions:

- Learns the location of hosts
- Floods, forwards, and filters frames based on layer-2 addresses

A bridge processes all frames on all interfaces and dynamically learns the location of each host. When a bridge receives a frame on an interface, it puts an entry into a bridging table that shows the MAC address of the transmitting host and the interface that received the frame. Using this technique, a bridge populates its bridging table for use in path determination. As the bridge is learning the location of each host, it is performing the three F's: *Flooding, Forwarding,* and *Filtering.*

If the bridge receives a frame with a destination MAC address not in its bridging table, the bridge will flood the frame out every interface except, of course, the one on which it was received (Figure 2-4, Box 11). This will, hopefully, allow the frame to reach its destination regardless of the destination host's location. When the destination host responds back to the originating host, the bridge will update the bridging table with its location.

Figure 2-5 shows a message sent from Host 1 to Host 2. The encapsulation levels and headers are extremely oversimplified so that we can concentrate our coverage on the addressing of network messages and how that affects bridging. MAC addresses are shown as hex digits A through D.

When Host 1 sends a frame to Host 2, the bridge will find Host 2's MAC address in the bridging table and will forward the frame out the appropriate interface if the destination interface is different from the source interface (Figure 2-4, Box 15). Figure 2-5 shows different reception and transmission interfaces.

When frames are forwarded or filtered by a bridge, they are sent exactly as they were received. In Figure 2-5, the frame is forwarded intact out the interface where Host 2 is connected. Note that the bridge is not specifically addressed; it is transparent. Host 1 doesn't know that

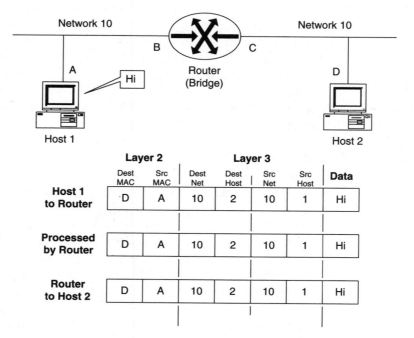

Figure 2-5
Bridged frame flow.

	Layer 2		Layer 3				
	Dest MAC	Src MAC	Dest Net	Dest Host	Src Net	Src Host	**Data**
Host 1 to Router	D	A	10	2	10	1	Hi
Processed by Router	D	A	10	2	10	1	Hi
Router to Host 2	D	A	10	2	10	1	Hi

the bridge is there. Note also that the network address of both LANs is the same. The two physical LANs are treated as a single, logical LAN.

Suppose that two hosts on the same LAN are having a conversation and the bridge has learned that they are both out the same interface. The bridge will filter the frames that it receives from the hosts' conversation (Figure 2-4, Box 14). In other words, the bridge will not transmit the frames out other interfaces. This keeps the conversation traffic local and prevents the local conversation from interfering with conversations on other LAN segments.

Bridging does have some drawbacks. A bridge will always flood a frame the first time a MAC address is referenced. That's not too bad; however, a bridge will also flood all broadcast frames and all multicast frames. If your application relies heavily on broadcast or multicast addressing, this could cause considerable network traffic overhead since all broadcast and multicast frames will appear on all LAN segments.

2.2.2   Routing

Routing is the process of forwarding a network message based on an address in the message's layer-3 header. There's a lot more involved than just reading a layer-3 address, though. Let's walk through the basic steps that a router performs to forward a network message. The Router Operation Flowchart in Figure 2-4 will be used again.

Figure 2-6 shows the flow of a message from Host 1 to Host 2. The encapsulation levels and headers are extremely oversimplified so that we can concentrate our coverage on the addressing of network messages and how that affects routing. Layer-2 addresses are shown as hex digits A through D.

Remember that a MAC address is used for navigation of a LAN. If a host wants to get a message to another host on the same LAN, the originating host puts the MAC address of the other host in the frame header; otherwise, the originating host sends the message to a router for routing to the destination network. When a router receives a frame directly addressed to its own interface, the router knows that it should attempt to route the message within the frame. Notice, in Figure 2-6, that the destination MAC address in the frame transmitted by Host 1 is B, the Router's. Encapsulated inside the frame is a layer-3 header that includes the destination network and host addresses.

If the message is to be processed by the router, the router must figure out what protocol the hosts are speaking so it will know how to handle

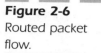

Figure 2-6
Routed packet flow.

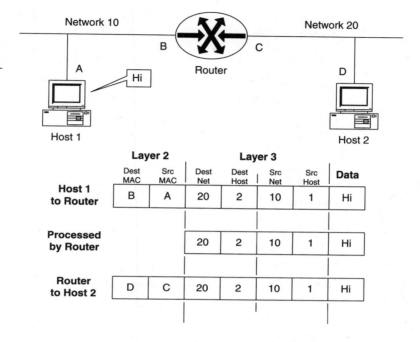

	Layer 2		Layer 3				
	Dest MAC	Src MAC	Dest Net	Dest Host	Src Net	Src Host	**Data**
Host 1 to Router	B	A	20	2	10	1	Hi
Processed by Router			20	2	10	1	Hi
Router to Host 2	D	C	20	2	10	1	Hi

the messages. Remember in Section 2.1.2, I said that each layer's header must contain some value that indicates what is encapsulated at the next layer. The router must check this value in the frame header to find out what protocol is encapsulated in the frame. In the frame header, this could be either a Protocol Type or a Service Access Point (SAP).

If the Protocol Type or SAP field indicates the frame contains data for a protocol that is being routed by the router (Figure 2-4, Box 3), the router removes the frame header and begins processing what's left—the packet that begins with a layer-3 header (Figure 2-4, Box 5). There is a separate program running on the router for each protocol that is being routed; I refer to these programs as routing processes.

The *routing process* examines the destination network address in the packet header (this is layer 3) and looks for a match in a special table, the routing table (Figure 2-4, Box 9). The router maintains a routing table for each protocol that is being routed. The routing table contains a list of all the router's known networks and their direction. If the router doesn't find an entry in its routing table that matches the destination network address, the router discards the packet (Figure 2-4, Box 8). If the router finds a routing table entry that matches the destination network address, the router uses the information in the routing table to determine which interface out which the packet must be forwarded.

Since messages must appear on the network as frames, the router must now create a frame by encapsulating the packet. In other words, the router must put a new frame header and trailer on the packet (Figure 2-4, Box 12). Note in Figure 2-6 that the packet itself does not change. Since there are many different frame header formats, the router uses the interface name and encapsulation found in the routing table entry to determine what the packet's new frame header is supposed to look like.

In Figure 2-6, the packet is supposed to be forwarded out a LAN interface; therefore, the router must place the destination and source MAC addresses in the frame header. In the new frame that is to cross the LAN from the router to Host 2, the destination MAC address is D, Host 2's, and the source MAC address is C, the Router's transmitting interface.

You may be wondering how the router managed to learn about other networks that are used to populate its routing table. The routing table didn't just appear out of thin air. There are three ways that a router can have its routing table populated with destination networks:

1. The router connects directly to networks.

2. We tell the router about networks.

3. The router learns about networks from other routers.

Networks to which a router is directly connected automatically appear in the routing table.

Networks that a router learns from us are normally called *static routes*. These are just manual entries in the routing table. We tell the router which direction we want it to route packets destined for a network.

With the proper configuration, routers will talk to each other and share information about networks. (That's a scary thought: Routers talking to each other.) However, configuring your routers to learn about the network from the other routers takes the building of the routing table out of your hands and puts it into the router's. Your job then becomes the monitoring of the routing tables to make sure that the routers are playing nicely with each other. The protocols that routers use to share network information are called routing protocols.

The protocols that carry real data and are "routed" by a router are called *routed protocols*. Each routed protocol (such as IP) that you can configure on a router has at least one associated *routing protocol* (such as

RIP and OSPF). The configuration of routing protocols is what I call the fun part of configuring IOS. We will see the routing protocols for each of the routed protocols in the configuration chapters.

You can run as many routed protocols and as many routing protocols as you need or want as long as your router has adequate power and memory. The IOS will create a routing table in memory for each routed protocol that is running. There are two main types of routing protocols:

1. Distance Vector

2. Link State

The one that's implemented in your network depends on many things, such as network requirements, business standards, and even personal preferences.

2.2.2.1 Distance Vector Routing Protocols

Routers running a *distance vector* routing protocol learn about other networks directly from their neighboring routers. Distance vector routing is sometimes called "Routing by Rumor" because each router learns about networks from its neighbors' perspective. The routers learn how far away and which direction each network is, that is, each network's distance and vector.

Distance vector routing protocols are pretty easy to spot. The following are some of their characteristics:

- Updates are frequent and periodic.

- Updates are sent to the broadcast address.

- Updates are lists of almost all known networks.

A router running a distance vector routing protocol broadcasts frequent updates out all of its interfaces for its neighboring routers to process, even when nothing has changed in the network. The updates contain all of the networks that the router has in its routing table, unless split horizon is running.

Split horizon is very simple—a router is not to broadcast a path to a network out the same interface in which it learned about the network. In other words, don't repeat to your neighbors what your neighbors just told you.

The updates are transmitted every few seconds. For example, the update period could be every 10 seconds or every 90 seconds. The exact period depends on the individual routing protocol. Routers use an *algorithm,* sometimes called the *Bellman-Ford algorithm,* on all of the information it receives in updates. The Bellman-Ford algorithm produces each network's best path, which is placed in the routing table.

Remember the broadcast address? Frames sent to the broadcast address are processed by all hosts; therefore, all hosts on a LAN—with routers that are running a distance vector routing protocol—will be receiving and processing the updates. The hosts will discard the updates only after they have been interrupted from their normal tasks.

Distance vector routing protocols tend to be preferred in small to medium-sized networks. The frequent, periodic updates tend to take too much bandwidth away from the all-important user traffic as a network grows.

2.2.2.2 Link-State Routing Protocols

Routers running a *link-state routing protocol* learn about networks from the other routers in an internetwork, not just those directly connected to its own networks. Each router transmits a *link-state advertisement packet* (LSA) to a multicast address. The LSA contains information about the individual router and the links, or networks, to which it is connected.

All of the routers receiving the LSA process it and then flood it to other routers. This way, all routers running the link-state routing protocol receive all the LSAs and, thus, learn about all the networks. All the LSAs received by each router are placed into a database. The router runs a special algorithm against the database to create a map of the network. The algorithm is called the *Shortest Path First* (SPF) algorithm. The map shows all of the routers and all of the LANs and WANs. Based on the map, each router can calculate the best path to each network and can update its routing table.

Updates for link state routing protocols are not transmitted at short, periodic intervals. They are instead triggered by state changes in a router's network connections. For example, if a router's LAN interface goes down, the router would transmit a new LSA indicating that the router no longer has a link to the LAN. Each of the routers receiving this LSA would run the SPF algorithm to create a new network map and then update its routing table.

2.2.2.3 Hierarchical Routing

Since routers base their routing decisions on the network portion of the destination layer-3 address, a routing table contains a list of network addresses. Layer-3 addressing is *hierarchical,* which means that the address has a general part and a specific part. The network part is general and the node part is specific. The network part is said to be significant for routing since the node part doesn't play a role in route determination.

Our home addresses usually consist of a street address, a city, a state, and a zip code. Suppose that you lived in Dallas and your Uncle Jimmy Mack has mailed you a package from Lexington, Kentucky. When the postal service wants to route the package to you, imagine that they have to look up your exact street name in a very large database to determine where the package is supposed to go. Finding your street in the database could take a long time. All the postal service in Lexington really needs to know is the path to Dallas. Once the package gets to the Dallas office of the postal service, the package can be routed to your street.

Consider that Dallas is a big network (city) consisting of many LANs and WANs (streets). Each LAN and WAN has some hosts (homes). The routers within Dallas need to know paths to each LAN and WAN, but routers outside Dallas need to know only a general path to the big network.

Maintaining entries for just networks (the general stuff) reduces power and memory load on a router. Routing tables do not normally contain entries for individual hosts.

2.3 IOS

IOS (Internetwork Operating System) is the software that you configure on your Cisco router hardware to either route or bridge your information from one network to another. IOS provides the strength of Cisco's router product line—it's what makes a Cisco router a Cisco router. When you purchase a Cisco router, you must also purchase a license to run IOS. IOS comes in many flavors based on version and feature set. You must make the decision about which flavor you want to run.

There are many versions of IOS. Generally, you decide which version to run based on your comfort with running new software or older, more-tested software, your need to implement a specific IOS feature, or your desire to use a specific Cisco hardware platform.

Cisco uses a special numbering scheme to keep track of IOS versions. The full version number of your IOS has three numbers: (1) major version, (2) minor version, and (3) maintenance release. The major version and minor version numbers are separated by a period (".") and are referred to, collectively, as the *major release*. The maintenance release number is shown in parentheses. For example, the IOS version number

11.2(10) refers to maintenance release 10 of major release 11.2. Cisco releases IOS updates often; when they issue an update for IOS, they generally increment a maintenance release number that's associated with the major release number.

Since there are so many versions of IOS, Cisco issues release notes that contain descriptions of release changes and additions. You should read the release notes if you want to find out what has changed in a release or what has been added to a release.

Cisco uses special release designations to let you know how stable they feel the software is. These release designations are as follows: *General Deployment* (GD), *Limited Deployment* (LD), and *Early Deployment* (ED). As a general rule, GD releases of IOS are the most stable. Cisco puts the GD designation on an IOS release when it has been in the market long enough to have allowed Cisco to fix enough bugs (Yuck!) and Cisco is comfortable with just about anyone using the software.

Feature sets don't change as often as version numbers. You select which feature set you want based on what you want to run on your router. For example, do you want to run just the Internet Protocol (IP) or do you want to run IP, Novell's Internetwork Packet eXchange (IPX), and DECnet? From your requirements, you should pick the feature that includes all of the features that you need for placing the router into operation in your network.

There are many models of routers that run IOS. They vary from the very inexpensive, low-end models to the extremely expensive, high-end models. You determine your model by the router's purpose and its cost. If you need a router for your network backbone, you would probably select from one of Cisco high-end router series: 7000, 7200, 7500, or 12000. These series of routers are meant to be fast and reliable, and you can put many interfaces into them. If your new router is to be used to connect office LANs or WANs to your backbone, then you would select from one of the access-type router series: 1000, 1600, 2500, 2600, 3600, 3800, or 4000. In the examples done in this book, we use Cisco 2520s, one of the 2500-series of routers. (There are over 20 models in the 2500 series.) I'm not going to discuss money here—that changes too fast, but usually the lower the model number, the lower its cost.

The nice thing about IOS configuration is that its commands are consistent across the entire IOS-based router line. This means that you have to learn only one command interface. This interface happens to be a command line interface so it looks the same whether you are talking to a router through a console port, a modem, or a telnet connection.

No matter what type of LAN or WAN interface you want, you can usually find it on at least one of the Cisco router models. After all, a router wouldn't be much good without interfaces, and one of the major components of IOS configuration is interface configuration. Some of the physical interface types that are available on the Cisco routers are as follows:

- Ethernet
- Fast Ethernet
- Token Ring
- FDDI
- Low-Speed Serial
- Fast Serial
- HSSI
- ISDN BRI

Please don't assume the introductory material in this section is definitive since things change rapidly and I'm not a salesperson or a marketing person. I just want to give you some idea of the flexibility and depth of the Cisco router product line. If you really want to get more details about IOS versions, IOS feature sets, and router models, you can either check Cisco's Web site, Cisco Connection Online (CCO), at *http://www.cisco.com* or call your local Cisco sales representative.

IOS configuration principles are consistent across versions, feature sets, and router models. We're going to cover those principles—so let's get started.

3

Initial Configuration

The first time you configure an IOS-based router, you will probably use the IOS Setup facility. We are going to start from the time you take your router out of the box; then we will walk through using the Setup facility to create an internetwork of two routers.

Our steps for initial configuration are as follows:

- Learn the basic router components.
- Develop an implementation plan.
- Connect to the router.
- Turn on the router.
- Run Setup (System Configuration Dialog).

We cover each step in the next few sections.

3.1 Basic Router Components

If we are going to configure a router, we should know a little about what is inside it and what we are configuring.

3.1.1 Processor

Just like any other computer, a Cisco router that runs IOS has a *Central Processing Unit* (CPU). The CPU varies by router series and model. Two examples of processors that Cisco uses are the Motorola 68030 and the Orion/R4600. A router's processor performs work required to process packets such as maintaining all the tables necessary to route and bridge and making routing decisions. The rate at which a router can process packets depends a lot on the type of processor the router has.

3.1.2 Memory

All computers have memory of some type. Cisco routers have four main types of memory:

1. Read-Only Memory (ROM)
2. Flash Memory
3. Random-Access Memory (RAM)
4. Non-Volatile RAM (NVRAM)

Of each of these types of memory, RAM is the only one that loses its contents when the router is booted or power-cycled. The following sections briefly describe the primary purpose of each memory type on Cisco routers.

3.1.2.1 ROM
ROM is where a router's bootstrap software is normally stored. The *bootstrap software* is the first software that runs; it has the responsibility of getting the router going. Some routers have a full IOS stored in ROM for use in emergencies when another source of IOS is not available. ROM is generally on a chip, or multiple chips, on the processor board of a router.

3.1.2.2 Flash
The primary purpose of *flash memory* is to store the IOS software that the router is to run. If a router has flash memory, then flash memory is the default location of the IOS software used to boot the router. With enough flash memory, multiple IOS images can be stored to provide multiple boot options. Flash memory is either on a processor board SIMM or on a PCMCIA card.

Cisco's high-end routers, like those in the 7500 series, have two kinds of flash memory: system flash and boot flash. The IOS image is stored in system flash and the bootstrap software is stored in boot flash.

3.1.2.3 RAM
RAM is used for too many things to list, but two of the things are IOS system tables and buffers. The IOS uses RAM for all of its normal, operational storage requirements.

3.1.2.4 NVRAM
The primary purpose of *NVRAM* is to store the configuration that the IOS reads when a router boots. This configuration is called the *startup configuration*. See Section 3.1.6.

3.1.3 Interfaces

All routers have interfaces. Some of the interface types available on Cisco routers are listed in Section 2.3. On IOS-based routers, interfaces are named and numbered. The full name of an interface consists of its type designation and at least one number. Numbering starts with zero (0).

On those routers with fixed interfaces (most of the 2500 series) or with modular interfaces that cannot be changed without turning off the router (the 4700, for example), the full name of an interface has one number, and interfaces are numbered according to their physical order in the router. For example, Ethernet0 is the name of the first Ethernet interface and Serial2 is the name of the third serial interface.

On routers that support *Online Insertion and Removal* (OIR)—or the capability to change the physical interface configuration (pull cards) while the router is still running—the full name of an interface has at least two numbers separated by a forward slash (/). The first number is a slot number where an interface processor card is installed and the second number is a port number on the interface processor. For example, on a 7507 router, Ethernet5/0 is the name of the first Ethernet interface in slot 5 of the router, assuming that slot 5 had an Ethernet interface processor installed in it.

In the case of a 7500 series router with a *Versatile Interface Processor* (VIP) installed, the name of an interface on a VIP includes three numbers separated by forward slashes (/). The form of the interface number is slot/port adapter/port. For example, Ethernet4/0/1 is the name of the second Ethernet interface on the first port adapter in slot 4.

If this interface numbering stuff sounds confusing, don't worry about it for now. We will see later how to get the router to tell us the full names of all of its interfaces.

3.1.4   Console Port

All Cisco routers have a console port on the back of the router. The *console port* provides an EIA/TIA-232 (formerly called RS-232) asynchronous serial connection that allows us to communicate with the router. The type of physical connection to the console port depends on the model of router. Some routers use a DB25 Female (DB25F) connector and some use an RJ45 connector. As a general rule, the smaller routers have an RJ45 console connector and the larger routers have a DB25 console connector. See Table 3-1 for a list of the connector types for the major series of Cisco routers.

3.1.5   Auxiliary Port

Most Cisco routers have an *auxiliary port,* which, like the console port, provides an EIA/TIA-232 asynchronous serial connection that allows us

TABLE 3-1

*Cisco Router
Console
Connectors*

Router Model Series	Console Connector	Console Cable Type
1000		
1600		
2500	RJ45	Rollover
2600		
3600		
4000		
4500		
4700		
7000	DB25 Female	Straight-Through Serial
7200		
7500		
12000		

to communicate with a router. The auxiliary port is most often used for the connection of a modem for out-of-band router management. An out-of-band path does not carry routed packets; it is primarily used to access a router when a network path or circuit fails.

3.1.6   Configuration Files

There are two types of IOS configurations:

1. Running Configuration
2. Startup Configuration

Both are displayed to us in ASCII text format; therefore, they are easy to read and manipulate. A router can have only one of each type.

3.1.6.1   Running Configuration
The *running configuration,* sometimes called the *active configuration,* resides in RAM and contains the IOS configuration commands that are currently active on a router. When we configure IOS, we are changing a router's running configuration.

3.1.6.2 Startup Configuration

The *startup configuration* resides in NVRAM and contains the IOS configuration commands that are supposed to be executed when a router boots. The commands in the startup configuration essentially become the running configuration.

The startup configuration is sometimes called the *backup configuration* because after we make and verify running configuration changes, we normally copy the running configuration to NVRAM so our changes are backed up and available the next time the router boots.

3.1.7 Processes

An IOS *process* is a software task that is running on the router and performing some function. For example, the routing of IP packets is done with a process; the routing of AppleTalk packets is done with another process. Other examples of IOS processes are routing protocols and memory allocation routines. When we configure IOS by putting commands into the configuration files, we are essentially controlling the behavior of the processes that make up IOS. All of these processes run simultaneously on a router. The number and type of processes we can run on a router are limited by the router's CPU speed and RAM amount, just like the number of programs we can run on a PC is limited by the type of CPU and the amount of RAM it has.

3.2 Planning the Configuration

Before building anything, we must develop a *plan,* which should be documented, sort of like a blueprint, so we can reference it during the implementation of the plan. When modifying an existing internetwork or building a new internetwork, a graphical representation of the layout and configuration of the internetwork comes in handy. To illustrate router configuration, we are going to be building a small internetwork. Figure 3-1 shows the basic infrastructure of the internetwork we will build.

Throughout most of this book, Cisco 2520 routers will be used in the configuration examples; occasionally another model of Cisco router will be used to show a different view. Our two 2520s are connected to each other with a T1 leased line. A *T1* is a point-to-point WAN with a band-

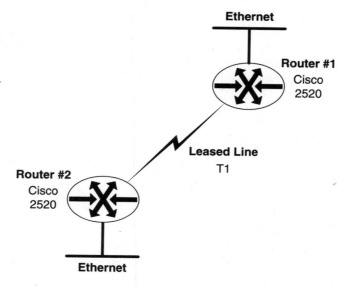

Figure 3-1
Initial configuration
internetwork infra-
structure.

width of 1.544 megabits per second (Mbps). Each of the routers has an Ethernet LAN with a bandwidth of 10 Mbps.

Since we are starting from scratch, we will configure both routers. The following are some of the things that we must know about a new router before its initial configuration:

- Router's name
- Interfaces to be used
- Protocols to run on the router
- Addresses of the interfaces
- Passwords for accessing the router

Knowing and documenting each of these items will make the configuration of a new router easier.

3.2.1   Name

Each router should have a unique *host name* to identify itself. The name should be descriptive; putting the router's location in the name is a common practice.

The name you select can be just about anything you want; however, here are some guidelines from *RFC 1035*. A router's host name should be no longer than 63 characters, and it can contain letters, numeric digits, and hyphens. The name should start with a letter, but it can end with either a letter or a numeric digit. By default, IOS will put the name (up to 29 characters of it) into the IOS command line prompt.

3.2.2 Interfaces

In our example routers, serial interfaces are used to connect to the T1 and Ethernet interfaces are used to connect to 10 Mbps Ethernet LANs.

We need to specify which interfaces we will use to connect to each network. To specify interfaces, we must know what interfaces are available on the router. The Cisco 2520 has one Ethernet interface, two fast serial interfaces, two low-speed serial interfaces, and one ISDN BRI interface. The IOS sees both fast and low-speed serial interfaces as just serial interfaces; therefore, we can say that the 2520 has four serial interfaces. Figure 3-2 shows the names of our routers and the interfaces that will be configured on each router.

The router names are to be *Dallas* and *FortWorth*. On Dallas, the Ethernet0 and Serial1 interfaces will be used. On FortWorth, the Ethernet0 and Serial0 interfaces will be used. We could have connected the Dallas Serial0 to the FortWorth Serial0, but we chose to connect the Dallas Serial1 to the FortWorth Serial0 for this discussion.

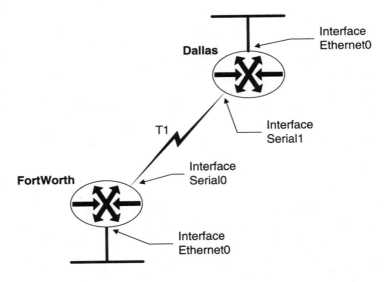

Figure 3-2
Initial configuration router names and interfaces.

3.2.3   Network Protocols

As was covered in Section 2.2.2, there are two major classes of network protocols: routed and routing. We need both.

3.2.3.1   Routed Protocols

The routed protocols that we need are determined by the type of hosts on our internetwork, their operating systems, and their configured protocols. The routed protocols that can be configured on a router are determined by its IOS Feature Set. For example, if your router is running the IP Feature Set, you can start only the IP protocol; if your router has the Enterprise Feature Set, you can start just about any protocol you want.

Our routers are running the IOS Enterprise Feature Set. Let us assume for now that our new network will have the following types of hosts:

- UNIX hosts running TCP/IP
- Novell NetWare servers and clients running IPX
- Apple Macintoshes running AppleTalk

We will build our first internetwork by configuring the IP, IPX, and AppleTalk protocols on the routers.

3.2.3.2   Routing Protocols

For each routed protocol, there should be an associated routing protocol running on all of the routers. To make the initial configuration a little simpler, we are going to run the following routing protocols:

- IP Routing Information Protocol (RIP)
- IPX RIP
- AppleTalk Routing Table Maintenance Protocol (RTMP)

IPX RIP is the default routing protocol for IPX, and RTMP is the default routing protocol for AppleTalk. In other words, when we configure IPX on an interface, IPX RIP also starts on the interface, and when we configure AppleTalk on an interface, RTMP also starts on the interface.

For IP, there is no default routing protocol; therefore, we must manually select one. We will start the simplest IP routing protocol, RIP.

3.2.4   Interface Addresses

Since we are going to initially configure three routed protocols, we need to assign addresses for each of the protocols for each of the routers' interfaces. The specifics of what each protocol requires for address configuration are covered in detail in the protocol configuration sections later; however, for now, here is a basic overview of what we need.

3.2.4.1   IP

We need an IP network, or subnet, address for each of our networks. We have three networks; therefore, we need to choose three network addresses and a network mask for each. The three networks are the Dallas Ethernet LAN, the FortWorth Ethernet LAN, and the WAN between Dallas and FortWorth. For each interface, we should select an IP host address that begins with the chosen network address—for the network to which the interface is connected—and ends with a unique node address. The format of an IP address and its mask is called *dotted decimal,* a format that consists of four decimal numbers between 0 and 255 separated by dots (".").

3.2.4.2   IPX

We need an IPX network number for each of our networks—each network needs a unique IPX network number. The node portion of an IPX host address is automatically assigned when the network number is configured on an interface. The IPX network number is written in hexadecimal (hex) and has from one to eight hex digits.

3.2.4.3   AppleTalk

We need an AppleTalk cable range and zone name for each of the networks. Each network needs a unique cable range which consists of two decimal numbers, the second being larger than the first. The node portion of an AppleTalk host address is selected dynamically when the cable range and zone name are configured on an interface. An AppleTalk zone is a logical group of AppleTalk networks. Each zone has a name that is configured on each of the interfaces that are connected to the zone's networks.

3.2.4.4   Address Plan

For each of the routed protocols briefly described earlier, each interface connected to a network must have the same network address assigned to it. For example, the Dallas Serial1 interface and the FortWorth Serial0 interface are both connected to the same network; therefore, they must have the same network address.

With these addressing principles in mind, the network addresses selected for our internetwork are shown in Figure 3-3.

Using our network addresses, we can assign addresses for the interfaces we are going to use on our routers. Table 3-2 shows the interface information we will need during the initial configuration of each router. (This table will make our routers' initial configuration faster because the table can be referenced during the internetwork implementation.)

3.2.5 Passwords

For initial configuration, we need three passwords:

1. Enable Secret

2. Enable

3. VTY (Virtual Terminal or Virtual Teletype)

All IOS passwords are case-sensitive and can contain any combination of uppercase and lowercase alphanumeric characters (letters, numeric digits, punctuation marks) and spaces; however, a space cannot be the first character in a password. The maximum length of an IOS password is 25 characters. The use of each of the IOS passwords is described in Chapter 6.

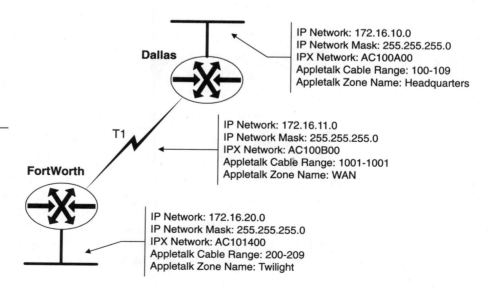

Figure 3-3
Initial
Configuration
Internetwork
Network
Addresses.

TABLE 3-2

Initial
Configuration
Interface
Information

Router Interface	IP Address	IPX Network	AppleTalk Cable Range	AppleTalk Zone Name
Dallas				
Ethernet0	172.16.10.1	AC100A00	100-109	Headquarters
Serial1	172.16.11.1	AC100B00	1001-1001	WAN
FortWorth				
Ethernet0	172.16.20.1	AC101400	200-209	Twilight
Serial0	172.16.11.2	AC100B00	1001-1001	WAN

The passwords we will use during IOS configuration are as follows:

- Enable Secret Password—**itsasecret**
- Enable Password—**enableme**
- VTY Password—**letmein**

Passwords should contain both letters and numeric digits; they should not contain words found in the dictionary and they should not be easily guessed. The passwords selected here violate *all* of these guidelines—please do not use them in a production network.

With all of this planning, we still have not touched a router. The next section describes the connection to the router so we can proceed with our implementation.

3.3   Connecting to the Router

To access and configure IOS on a new router, we must communicate with the router through its console port. Connecting a console terminal to the router's console port enables communication with the router. The terminal can be either a nonintelligent, ASCII terminal, like an old VT100, or a computer, like your Personal Computer (PC). If we are using a PC as a terminal, we have to run terminal emulation software on the PC. Using the terminal's keyboard, we are able to type commands for IOS to execute.

Most people use a PC as their terminal to do IOS configuration. PCs usually have at least two serial ports, called *COM1* and *COM2*. The serial port connectors are normally DB9 Male (DB9M) connectors, but some PCs' serial ports use a DB25 Male (DB25M) connector.

3.3.1   Hardware Connection

The connection between the console port and the terminal is simply a serial cable. See Table 3-2 for the console cable types needed for the two console port connector types.

3.3.1.1   RJ45 Console Connection

An *RJ45 connector* looks like the phone connector in your home, only wider. The phone connector (the little tabbed connector on the end of your phone cable that plugs into your phone jack) has four wires and an RJ45 connector has eight.

A *rollover cable* looks like the cable between your phone and your wall phone jack, only wider, and is so called because its wires are reversed or rolled over, from one end to the other.

For those routers that have an RJ45 console port, Cisco normally provides the rollover cable and at least one adapter in the router shipment box. The adapter allows the connection of the RJ45 plug to the serial port on your terminal. The adapter has a RJ45 jack for the rollover cable's RJ45 plug and a DB9 Female (DB9F) or DB25F connector for your terminal.

If your terminal has a DB9M connector for its serial port, use the RJ45-to-DB9F adapter. Plug one end of the rollover cable into the router's console port. The router's console port will be labeled as Console or an abbreviation of Console. Plug the other end of the rollover cable into the RJ45 jack on the adapter. Then connect the adapter's DB9F connector to your terminal's serial port.

If your terminal has a DB25M connector for its serial port, use the RJ45-to-DB25F adapter. Plug one end of the rollover cable into the router's console port. Plug the other end of the rollover cable into the RJ45 jack on the adapter. Then connect the adapter's DB25F connector to your terminal's serial port.

3.3.1.2   DB25 Console Connection

For those routers that have a DB25F console connector, you will have to provide your own cable. The cable should have a DB25M connector on one end and the appropriate connector on the other end for connection to your terminal's serial port (DB9F or DB25F). The cable should be configured to be straight through. Plug the DB25M end of the straight-through serial cable into the router's console port and plug the other end into your terminal's serial port.

3.3.2 Software Connection

As has already been mentioned, if the terminal to be used for IOS configuration is a PC, we will have to run terminal emulation software to allow us to type IOS commands and see IOS information. Terminal emulation software is readily available from software stores and shareware Web sites. The odds are good that your PC already has terminal emulation software installed on it. Some examples of terminal emulation software are HyperTerminal by Hilgraeve, Procomm by DataStorm Technologies, and Kermit. Usually, availability and personal preference are the deciding factors in the choice of a terminal emulator.

Start the terminal emulation software on your PC. If you are using a nonintelligent, ASCII terminal for console communication, there is no need to run special software. The default speed of a Cisco router's console port is 9600 baud. If you configure your terminal to run at 9600 baud, 8 data bits, no parity, and 2 stop bits (9600-8N2), you should be able to communicate with the router through the console port. (Sometimes using just 1 stop bit, instead of 2, works, also.)

3.4 Turning on the Router

Plug the female end of the router's power cable into the router's power connector on the back of the router. Plug the male end of the power cable into an appropriate power outlet. All IOS-based Cisco routers except the 1000 series have a power switch on the back of the router. If the router has a power switch, set it to the ON (1) position. The cooling fans inside the router should immediately come on and be audible.

For specific instructions on installing and turning on your particular router, please refer to the "Hardware Installation Guide" or "Installation and Configuration Guide" for your router.

Now we are going to walk through the normal boot sequence of a new router.

3.4.1 Run Bootstrap

The first software that runs on the router is called the bootstrap software. Every computer has bootstrap software and, of course, a router is just a special-purpose computer. The initial software is called the *boot-*

strap because it is said to pull a computer up by its bootstraps. The bootstrap software runs a *Power-On Self-Test* (POST) and then locates a boot device that contains a valid copy of IOS, the operating system. The boot device is normally system flash memory.

Within a few seconds after we turn on a router, a bootstrap message is sent to the console. The beginning of the bootstrap message from one of our 2520s—Dallas—is shown in Figure 3-4.

The bootstrap message indicates that the bootstrap software has been located and started. Bootstrap software can be in one of two places on a router: Read-Only Memory (ROM) or boot flash. On a 2500-series router like this one, the bootstrap software is in ROM.

The message states the bootstrap software version number (Line 1) and the amount of main memory in the router (Line 3). The 2520's bootstrap message shows that the 2520's bootstrap software is version 11.0(10c), and the 2520 has 6 megabytes (MB) of main memory. Main memory is the *Random-Access Memory* (RAM) used for IOS operations; it is also called *system RAM* or *system memory*. System RAM is allocated from the total amount of RAM at boot time.

Since the bootstrap software has the responsibility of finding a copy of IOS to load and run so the router can be operational, the bootstrap software checks for any special boot instructions in *Non-Volatile RAM* (NVRAM). NVRAM normally contains the configuration that an IOS-based router loads when it starts IOS; however, since the routers being used in this example are new, NVRAM is empty (Figure 3-4, Line 5). Under normal conditions, the bootstrap software will attempt to find an IOS image in system flash.

3.4.2 Run IOS

In our example, the bootstrap locates a copy of IOS in system flash. The message logged to our 2520's console upon locating and starting IOS is shown in Figure 3-5.

Figure 3-4

Bootstrap message on Dallas.

```
1)   System Bootstrap, Version 11.0(10c), SOFTWARE
2)   Copyright (c) 1986-1996 by Cisco Systems
3)   2500 processor with 6144 Kbytes of main memory
4)
5)   Notice: NVRAM invalid, possibly due to write erase.
```

Figure 3-5

IOS boot message
on Dallas.

```
1)   Cisco Internetwork Operating System Software
2)   IOS (tm) 2500 Software (C2500-JS-L), Version 11.3(5), RELEASE
     SOFTWARE (fc1)
3)   Copyright (c) 1986-1998 by Cisco Systems, Inc.
4)   Compiled Tue 11-Aug-98 04:06 by phanguye
5)   Image text-base: 0x030489A8, data-base: 0x00001000
6)
7)   Cisco 2520 (68030) processor (revision M) with 6144K/2048K
     bytes of memory.
8)   Processor board ID 10353060, with hardware revision 00000003
9)   Bridging software.
10)  X.25 software, Version 3.0.0.
11)  SuperLAT software copyright 1990 by Meridian Technology Corp).
12)  TN3270 Emulation software.
13)  Basic Rate ISDN software, Version 1.0.
14)  1 Ethernet/IEEE 802.3 interface(s)
15)  2 Serial network interface(s)
16)  2 Low-speed serial(sync/async) network interface(s)
17)  1 ISDN Basic Rate interface(s)
18)  32K bytes of non-volatile configuration memory.
19)  16384K bytes of processor board System flash (Read ONLY)
20)
21)  Notice: NVRAM invalid, possibly due to write erase.
```

At the beginning of the logged message, we see that the IOS software is Version 11.3(5) (Line 1). We are told that the router is a 2520 with a total of 8 MB of RAM (Line 7). The text "6144K/2048K bytes of memory" means that 6 MB of the RAM have been allocated for system RAM and the other 2 MB of RAM have been allocated for shared RAM. The 2520 has one Ethernet interface (Line 14), two serial (fast serial) interfaces (Line 15), two low-speed serial interfaces (Line 16), and one ISDN Basic Rate Interface (BRI) (Line 17). This 2520 has 32 kilobytes (kB) of NVRAM (Line 18) and 16 MB of system flash (Line 19).

At the end of the message is another one of those lines telling us that NVRAM is empty (Line 21). When IOS starts, it looks in NVRAM for a configuration to load. The router's configuration contains things such as the router's name, its passwords, the protocols it is running, the interfaces it is using, and the addresses of the interfaces. This type of information should sound familiar; it is what we put in the implementation plan for the routers we are going to install (Section 3.2).

Our routers are new; therefore, there is no configuration for IOS to load. It is now our job to tell IOS what its configuration is. We will use the IOS Setup Facility.

3.5   System Configuration Dialog

The configuration in NVRAM is called the *startup configuration.* When there is no startup configuration for IOS to load at router boot time, the IOS automatically leads us to using the Setup Facility. IOS refers to the Setup Facility as the *System Configuration Dialog,* during which IOS will ask us a few questions that allow us to create a basic configuration on the router. All we have to do, at each question, is type the answer and press <Enter>.

NOTE   *Each question requires that its answer be completed with <Enter>. The sample output will not show the <Enter> key being pressed after each answer.*

The System Configuration Dialog can be divided into four major sections:

1. Introduction
2. Global Parameters
3. Interface Parameters
4. Conclusion

Using the information we put together in Section 3.2, we are going to go through the System Configuration Dialog for both Dallas and FortWorth. The configuration created on each router with the Setup Facility makes our routers operational.

3.5.1   Dallas Setup

We start by configuring Router #1 on our initial infrastructure diagram, Figure 3-1. We named that router Dallas in Figure 3-2.

3.5.1.1   Introduction

The System Configuration Dialog always starts by explaining some things about how to use it and then a very important question as shown in Figure 3-6.

If you are unsure of the meaning of a question during the Initial Configuration Dialog, online help is available (Line 3). Just type ? at the question.

Figure 3-6
Setup mode question on Dallas.

```
1)           -- System Configuration Dialog --
2)
3)  At any point you may enter a question mark '?' for help.
4)  Use ctrl-c to abort configuration dialog at any prompt.
5)  Default settings are in square brackets '[]'.
6)  Would you like to enter the initial configuration dialog?
    [yes]: yes
```

If you start the System Configuration Dialog and then decide that you do not want to finish, you can type <Ctrl-C> to stop the dialog (Figure 3-6, Line 4). If you abort the System Configuration Dialog on a new router, the router will shut down all of its interfaces and wait for you to do something else—like restart the System Configuration Dialog.

If you happen to make a mistake by answering a question with something other than what you want, there is no way to move backward in the dialog. You have two options:

1. Restart the Initial Configuration Dialog either by power-cycling the router to let the router enter the dialog again or by aborting the dialog and restarting it with the **setup** privileged mode command. (We cover privileged mode in Chapter 4.)

2. Complete the current Initial Configuration Dialog, and correct the error manually with IOS configuration mode commands. (We cover configuration mode in Chapter 4.)

The System Configuration Dialog provides a default answer for most questions that it asks. The default answer is shown in square brackets (Figure 3-6, Line 5). If you see a value in square brackets at the end of a question, you can either press <Enter> to accept the value if you want it, or you can type another value and press <Enter>. All answers require the <Enter> key to be pressed after them before they are accepted.

The answer to any question that requires a "Yes" or "No" answer can be abbreviated with just the letter "Y" for "Yes" or the letter "N" for "No." The answer can be in uppercase or lowercase.

The System Configuration Dialog always asks first if we want to continue. In our case, we do want to continue (Figure 3-6, Line 6). The next question and output are shown in Figure 3-7.

The current interface summary allows the router to tell us about all of its interfaces and their full names. Normally we want to see the current interface summary, especially if this is our first time to configure this router.

Figure 3-7
Interface summary
question on Dallas.

```
1)  First, would you like to see the current interface summary?
    [yes]: yes
2)
3)  Any interface listed with OK? value "NO" does not have a valid
    configuration
4)
5)  Interface      IP-Address    OK?   Method  Status   Protocol
6)  BRI0           unassigned    NO    unset   up       down
7)  BRI0:1         unassigned    YES   unset   down     down
8)  BRI0:2         unassigned    YES   unset   down     down
9)  Ethernet0      unassigned    NO    unset   up       down
10) Serial0        unassigned    NO    unset   down     down
11) Serial1        unassigned    NO    unset   down     down
12) Serial2        unassigned    NO    unset   down     down
13) Serial3        unassigned    NO    unset   down     down
```

We want to make sure that the interfaces are numbered as we expected and, what is more, we want to make sure that the router knows about all of its interfaces. On a fixed-configuration router, such as the 2520, this isn't usually an issue; however, on a modular-configuration router, such as one from the 7500-series, the router may not see all of the interfaces that we think have been installed. A modular-configuration router has all of its interfaces on cards that can be added or removed to create a custom interface configuration. Cisco calls these cards *Network Interface Modules* or *Interface Processors,* depending on the type of router in which they are to be installed.

If, when we install an interface card, we somehow do not do it just right, the router may not recognize that the new card has been installed. Examining the current interface summary is a good way of verifying the presence of the interfaces.

3.5.1.2 Global Parameters

Global parameters affect the overall operation of a router and are not specific to an individual interface or individual network protocol. Some examples are the routers' names, their passwords, and their protocols. As shown in Figure 3-8, the first question asked of us is essentially, "What's my name?"

The default name for a new router is **Router**; this should be changed to something that is a little more descriptive. As planned, we will call the first router **Dallas** (Line 3).

Some guidelines for a router's host name are given in Section 3.2.1. The host name is case-sensitive; therefore, the way the name is entered at this question is the way it will appear on the router. In Chapter 4, we

Figure 3-8
Setup mode host
name on Dallas.

```
1)  Configuring global parameters:
2)
3)  Enter host name [Router]: Dallas
```

see that the name appears in the prompt of the IOS command line interface; this allows us to immediately identify which router we are configuring, just in case we forget.

If we have more than one router, the name should be changed to prevent confusion in identifying each of the routers. As an example, most people who have more than one child give each child a different name for that very reason. Of course, if you really do have more than one child, you know that sometimes you call them by the wrong name anyway.

Next, we get asked for some passwords. Using the passwords selected during our planning, we can answer these questions as shown in Figure 3-9.

We must answer each of these questions since they have no default answers on a new router.

The enable secret password is encrypted in the IOS configuration file to help prevent accidental exposure (Line 4). The enable password is shown in clear text (just the way you type it) in the configuration file (Line 9). Both the enable secret password and the enable password have the same purpose: they allow the person configuring the router into IOS privileged mode, which is covered in Chapter 4. The enable secret password overrides the enable password. We must enter both because older versions of IOS software do not support the enable secret password, and if this configuration were ever to be loaded on a router running the older version of IOS, we could want to have an enable password.

Figure 3-9
Setup mode pass-
words on Dallas.

```
1)  The enable secret is a one-way cryptographic secret used
2)  instead of the enable password when it exists.
3)
4)  Enter enable secret: itsasecret
5)
6)  The enable password is used when there is no enable secret
7)  and when using older software and some boot images.
8)
9)  Enter enable password: enableme
10) Enter virtual terminal password: letmein
```

The virtual terminal (VTY) password is the one used to login to the router when we have established a telnet session to the router (Figure 3-9, Line 10).

Now, the System Configuration Dialog will ask which network protocols we are going to run on this router, Dallas. We simply have to answer **yes** or **no.** Our plan states that the only routed protocols we want to run are IP, IPX, and AppleTalk. This part of the dialog is shown in Figure 3-10.

SNMP stands for Simple Network Management Protocol, although it is not really a network protocol. SNMP is an IP application that is used to remotely manage network devices. We are not going to run SNMP (Line 1).

LAT stands for Local Area Transport, a protocol that cannot be routed. LAT must be bridged because it has no layer-3 addressing. LAT is used in terminal servers and print servers in a Digital Equipment Corporation (DEC) environment. We are not going to run LAT (Line 2).

AppleTalk is used on networks with Macintosh hosts. We are going to run it in our example internetwork; therefore, we answered **yes** to the question (Line 3). In an AppleTalk internetwork, networks can be part of more than one zone; each of our networks is in only one. The RTMP routing protocol will automatically be used on the interfaces with AppleTalk enabled.

DECnet is used in DEC internetworks. DEC internetworks typically have host systems from the DEC VAX family. We are not going to run DECnet, yet (Line 5).

Figure 3-10

Setup mode protocols on Dallas.

```
1)  Configure SNMP Network Management? [yes]: no
2)  Configure LAT? [yes]: no
3)  Configure AppleTalk? [no]: yes
4)  Multizone networks? [no]: no
5)  Configure DECnet? [no]: no
6)  Configure IP? [yes]: yes
7)  Configure IGRP routing? [yes]: no
8)  Configure RIP routing? [no]: yes
9)  Configure CLNS? [no]: no
10) Configure IPX? [no]: yes
11) Configure Vines? [no]: no
12) Configure XNS? [no]: no
13) Configure Apollo? [no]: no
14) Configure bridging? [no]: no
15) Enter ISDN BRI Switch Type [none]: none
```

Our internetwork is going to run *IP*; therefore, we answered **yes** to the question (Line 6). IOS has no default routing protocol for IP; we must select one. The System Configuration Dialog asks only about Cisco's Interior Gateway Routing Protocol (IGRP) and RIP. Our plan stated that we are to run RIP. If we wanted to run any other IP routing protocol other than IGRP or RIP, we could not use the System Configuration Dialog to start it.

CLNS stands for Connectionless Network Service, and it is a layer-3 service for the layer-3 OSI protocol Connectionless Network Protocol (CLNP). We are not going to run any OSI protocols (Line 9).

IPX is a Novell protocol that is used most of the time when a network has servers running Novell NetWare or IntraNetWare. We are going to run it in our example internetwork; therefore, we answered **yes** to the question (Line 10). The IPX RIP routing protocol will automatically be used on the interfaces with IPX enabled.

VINES stands for Virtual Integrated Network Services and is a protocol from Banyan. We are not going to run VINES, yet (Line 11).

XNS stands for Xerox Network Systems and is a protocol from Xerox. We are not going to run XNS (Line 12).

The question about *Apollo* refers to the Apollo Domain protocol, which is used in Apollo workstation environments. We are not going to run the Apollo Domain protocol (Line 13).

Since messages from the protocols that we want to start in the initial configuration can be routed by their layer-3 addresses, there is no reason to start bridging during our initial configuration (Line 14).

The Cisco 2520 has an ISDN BRI interface. If we were to use it, we would have to tell IOS what type of ISDN switch to which the BRI is connected. The ISDN switch type is provided by the ISDN service provider. We are not going to use the BRI during the initial configuration (Figure 3-10, Line 15).

3.5.1.3   Interface Parameters

Now we can start telling IOS which interfaces in the router that we want to use. For each interface, the System Configuration Dialog will ask the question, "Is this interface in use?" Our routers are new; therefore, none of our interfaces are in use, yet. We can interpret this question as "Do you want to use this interface now?" Our plan states that we want to use Ethernet0 and Serial1 on Dallas.

For each of the interfaces we want to initially configure, we are asked for basic information about the protocols we said we were going to run in the Global Parameters section. Table 3-2 shows the information we need to configure the interfaces. The dialog for configuring the interfaces is shown in Figure 3-11. Our initial internetwork configuration does not require the use of interface BRI0 (Line 4).

Figure 3-11

Setup mode inter-
face parameters on
Dallas.

```
1)   Configuring interface parameters:
2)
3)   Configuring interface BRI0:
4)     Is this interface in use? [no]: no
5)
6)   Configuring interface Ethernet0:
7)     Is this interface in use? [no]: yes
8)     Configure IP on this interface? [no]: yes
9)       IP address for this interface: 172.16.10.1
10)      Number of bits in subnet field [0]: 8
11)      Class B network is 172.16.0.0, 8 subnet bits; mask is /24
12)    Configure AppleTalk on this interface? [no]: yes
13)      Extended AppleTalk network? [no]: yes
14)      AppleTalk starting cable range [0]: 100
15)      AppleTalk ending cable range [100]: 109
16)      AppleTalk zone name [myzone]: Headquarters
17)    Configure IPX on this interface? [no]: yes
18)      IPX network number [1]: ac100a00
19)
20)  Configuring interface Serial0:
21)    Is this interface in use? [no]: no
22)
23)  Configuring interface Serial1:
24)    Is this interface in use? [no]: yes
25)    Configure IP on this interface? [no]: yes
26)    Configure IP unnumbered on this interface? [no]: no
27)      IP address for this interface: 172.16.11.1
28)      Number of bits in subnet field [8]: 8
29)     Class B network is 172.16.0.0, 8) subnet bits; mask is /24
30)    Configure AppleTalk on this interface? [no]: yes
31)      Extended AppleTalk network? [yes]: yes
32)      AppleTalk starting cable range [2]: 1001
33)      AppleTalk ending cable range [1001]: 1001
34)      AppleTalk zone name [myzone]: WAN
35)    Configure IPX on this interface? [no]: yes
36)      IPX network number [2]: ac100b00
37)
38)  Configuring interface Serial2:
39)    Is this interface in use? [no]: no
40)
41)  Configuring interface Serial3:
42)    Is this interface in use? [no]: no
```

Interface Ethernet0 will be used in our internetwork (Line 7). We planned to run IP, IPX, and AppleTalk on Ethernet0; therefore, we get asked about them.

The IP address 172.16.10.1 (Line 9) is from Table 3-2. The question about the number of bits in the subnet field is rather strange (Line 10). All IP addresses have an associated network mask; we documented the network masks in Figure 3-3. The network mask we defined for this Ethernet is 255.255.255.0. The System Configuration Dialog assumes that an IP address has three fields—network, subnet, and host—and it asks us for only subnet; it can determine the rest on its own.

The combination of the IP address class and network mask defines how many bits of an IP address are in the network and subnet fields. Our planned address is a class B address; therefore, it automatically has 16 bits in its network field. The default network mask for a class B address is 255.255.0.0. We have extended the number of binary ones in that mask by 8 bits to get a network mask of 255.255.255.0; therefore, we have 8 bits in the subnet field. The mask is shown as /24; this is a relatively new way of displaying the mask. All this means is that 24 bits in the network mask are binary ones, or 24 bits of the IP address are used to define the network address; the other 8 bits (out of 32) define an individual node on the network. IP addressing is explained in Chapter 7.

There are two versions of AppleTalk—Phase 1 and Phase 2. Normally, newer networks run Phase 2, which uses extended addressing. Extended addressing uses a cable range to address a network. From Table 3-2, our AppleTalk cable range for Ethernet0 is 100–109. This makes 100 the starting address in the cable range (Line 14) and 109 the ending address in the cable range (Line 15). Ethernet0 is in the Headquarters zone (Line 16). AppleTalk addressing is explained in Chapter 9.

For IPX, all we need for now is a network number. From Table 3-2, the network number for Ethernet0 is AC100A00 (Line 18). IPX addressing is explained in Chapter 8.

Interface Serial0 will not be used in our internetwork's initial implementation (Line 21). Interface Serial1 will be used in our internetwork (Line 24); therefore, we assigned our predetermined IP, IPX, and AppleTalk addressing to it. This information again came from our plan documentation in Figure 3-3 and Table 3-2.

There is one extra question on a serial interface's IP setup. The System Configuration Dialog asks if we want to run IP unnumbered on this interface (Line 26). This question is asked on each serial interface after another interface has been given an IP address. We gave Ethernet0 an IP address; therefore, we got the question. IP unnumbered is a mechanism used to route IP traffic on an interface without actually assigning the interface its own IP address. We have assigned an IP address to Serial1; therefore, we will not use IP unnumbered.

Interface Serial2 will not be used in our internetwork (Line 39) and neither will the Serial3 interface (Line 42).

Figure 3-12
Setup mode conclusion on Dallas.

```
1)   The following configuration command script was created:
2)
3)   hostname Dallas
4)   enable secret 5 $1$S.px$gAcVrJaShGu2x6Rvu/F1C/
5)   enable password enableme
6)   line vty 0 4
7)   password letmein
8)   no snmp-server
9)   !
10)  appletalk routing
11)  no decnet routing
12)  ip routing
13)  no clns routing
14)  ipx routing
15)  no vines routing
16)  no xns routing
17)  no apollo routing
18)  no bridge 1
19)  !
20)  isdn switch-type none
21)  !
22)  interface BRI0
23)  shutdown
24)  no ip address
25)  !
26)  interface Ethernet0
27)  no shutdown
28)  ip address 172.16.10.1 255.255.255.0
29)  appletalk cable-range 100-109
30)  appletalk zone Headquarters
31)  ipx network AC100A00
32)  !
33)  interface Serial0
34)  shutdown
35)  no ip address
36)  !
37)  interface Serial1
38)  no shutdown
39)  ip address 172.16.11.1 255.255.255.0
40)  appletalk cable-range 1001-1001
41)  appletalk zone WAN
42)  ipx network AC100B00
43)  !
44)  interface Serial2
45)  shutdown
46)  no ip address
47)  !
```

Figure 3-12
Setup mode conclusion on Dallas.

```
48) interface Serial3
49) shutdown
50) no ip address
51) !
52) router rip
53) network 172.16.0.0
54) !
55) end
56)
57) Use this configuration? [yes/no]: yes
58) Building configuration...
59) [OK]
60) Use the enabled mode 'configure' command to modify this
    configuration.
61)
62)
63) Press RETURN to get started!
```

3.5.1.4 Conclusion

The conclusion of the System Configuration Dialog consists of a display of the command script created from our answers to the questions and then the last, very important question. All of this is shown in Figure 3-12.

The script shows some of the commands we would have to type if we were not using the System Configuration Dialog to assist us. These are the commands that will be executed by IOS if we accept them.

The last thing the System Configuration Dialog wants to know is if we want to use this configuration or if we want to execute the commands (Line 57). If we answer **no** to this question, the new router would shut down all of its interfaces and wait for us to do something else.

We accepted the configuration by typing **yes.** The System Configuration Dialog then did a couple of things on the router. It executed the commands so they became part of the running configuration, and it saved them to the startup configuration in NVRAM so they would execute the next time the router boots. The messages we get after a **yes** answer are shown next.

The IOS commands in NVRAM are stored in a format that makes them quick and easy to display. Converting them to this format takes a few seconds. The message "Building configuration" indicates that IOS is doing the conversion (Line 58). The **[OK]** indicates completion.

Any configuration changes that need to be done after running the System Configuration Dialog should normally be done manually using configuration mode commands.

Immediately after the completion of the System Configuration Dialog, IOS sends messages to the console about the status of the router's interfaces. After these have stopped, you can press <Enter> for a command line prompt.

3.5.2   FortWorth Setup

Router #2 on our initial infrastructure diagram, Figure 3-1, was named FortWorth in Figure 3-2. We will run the System Configuration Dialog for FortWorth and the answers to the questions will be very similar to those we gave for Dallas. The complete dialog is shown for consistency.

3.5.2.1   Introduction
The introduction for FortWorth looks exactly like the introduction for Dallas.

```
— System Configuration Dialog —

At any point you may enter a question mark '?' for help.
Use ctrl-c to abort configuration dialog at any prompt.
Default settings are in square brackets '[]'.
Would you like to enter the initial configuration dialog? [yes]: yes

First, would you like to see the current interface summary?   [yes]:
yes

Any interface listed with OK? value "NO" does not have a valid
configuration

Interface        IP-Address       OK?    Method   Status     Protocol
BRI0             unassigned       NO     unset    up         down
BRI0:1           unassigned       YES    unset    down       down
BRI0:2           unassigned       YES    unset    down       down
Ethernet0        unassigned       NO     unset    up         up
Serial0          unassigned       NO     unset    up         down
Serial1          unassigned       NO     unset    down       down
Serial2          unassigned       NO     unset    up         down
Serial3          unassigned       NO     unset    down       down
```

We want to run the initial configuration dialog and the interface summary to make sure that all of FortWorth's interfaces are seen by IOS. FortWorth has the same types of interfaces as Dallas.

3.5.2.2   Global Parameters
We will set the name of the router to FortWorth. We will use the same passwords as we did on Dallas so that we do not have to remember so many. FortWorth is also running IP, IPX, and AppleTalk.

```
Configuring global parameters:

  Enter host name [Router]: FortWorth
```

The enable secret is a one-way cryptographic secret used
instead of the enable password when it exists.

```
  Enter enable secret: itsasecret
```

The enable password is used when there is no enable secret
and when using older software and some boot images.

```
  Enter enable password: enableme
  Enter virtual terminal password: letmein
  Configure SNMP Network Management? [yes]: no
  Configure LAT? [yes]: no
  Configure AppleTalk? [no]: yes
    Multizone networks? [no]: no
  Configure DECnet? [no]: no
  Configure IP? [yes]: yes
    Configure IGRP routing? [yes]: no
    Configure RIP routing? [no]: yes
  Configure CLNS? [no]: no
  Configure IPX? [no]: yes
  Configure Vines? [no]: no
  Configure XNS? [no]: no
  Configure Apollo? [no]: no
  Configure bridging? [no]: no
Enter ISDN BRI Switch Type [none]: none
```

Now it is time to tell IOS which interfaces we will be using for the initial internetwork.

3.5.2.3 Interface Parameters

According to our plan documentation in Table 3-2, FortWorth will be using interfaces Ethernet0 and Serial0. Each of these interfaces gets IP, IPX, and AppleTalk information assigned to it.

```
Configuring interface parameters:

Configuring interface BRI0:
  Is this interface in use? [yes]: no

Configuring interface Ethernet0:
  Is this interface in use? [yes]: yes
  Configure IP on this interface? [yes]: yes
    IP address for this interface: 172.16.20.1
    Number of bits in subnet field [0]: 8
    Class B network is 172.16.0.0, 8 subnet bits; mask is /24
  Configure AppleTalk on this interface? [no]: yes
    Extended AppleTalk network? [no]: yes
    AppleTalk starting cable range [0]: 200
    AppleTalk ending cable range [200]: 209
    AppleTalk zone name [myzone]: Twilight
```

```
    Configure IPX on this interface? [no]: yes
      IPX network number [1]: ac101400

    Configuring interface Serial0:
    Is this interface in use? [yes]: yes
    Configure IP on this interface? [yes]: yes
    Configure IP unnumbered on this interface? [no]: no
      IP address for this interface: 172.16.11.2
      Number of bits in subnet field [8]: 8
      Class B network is 172.16.0.0, 8 subnet bits; mask is /24
    Configure AppleTalk on this interface? [no]: yes
      Extended AppleTalk network? [yes]: yes
      AppleTalk starting cable range [2]: 1001
      AppleTalk ending cable range [1001]: 1001
      AppleTalk zone name [myzone]: WAN
    Configure IPX on this interface? [no]: yes
      IPX network number [2]: ac100b00

Configuring interface Serial1:
    Is this interface in use? [yes]: no

Configuring interface Serial2:
    Is this interface in use? [yes]: no

Configuring interface Serial3:
    Is this interface in use? [yes]: no
```

This is almost too easy. We might as well finish it.

3.5.2.4   Conclusion

Examine the command script and answer the final question.

```
The following configuration command script was created:


hostname FortWorth
enable secret 5 $1$LKJD$eQwhzhNEr4LsUFCwrJ8eG0
enable password enableme
line vty 0 4
password letmein
no snmp-server
!
appletalk routing
no decnet routing
ip routing
no clns routing
ipx routing
no vines routing
no xns routing
no apollo routing
no bridge 1
!
isdn switch-type none
!
interface BRI0
```

```
shutdown
no ip address
!
interface Ethernet0
ip address 172.16.20.1 255.255.255.0
appletalk cable-range 200-209
appletalk zone Twilight
ipx network AC101400
!
interface Serial0
ip address 172.16.11.2 255.255.255.0
appletalk cable-range 1001-1001
appletalk zone WAN
ipx network AC100B00
!
interface Serial1
shutdown
no ip address
!
interface Serial2
shutdown
no ip address
!
interface Serial3
shutdown
no ip address
!
router rip
network 172.16.0.0
!
end

Use this configuration? [yes/no]: yes
Building configuration...
[OK]
Use the enabled mode 'configure' command to modify this configuration.

Press RETURN to get started!
```

Now that FortWorth's initial configuration is complete, we can connect the interfaces.

3.6   Router Setup Outcome

Before you turn on a router for the first time, you should have some idea of what you are going to do with it because it is going to ask you to go through an initial configuration dialog and build a *skeletal* configuration on the router. I call the configuration a skeletal configuration because of its bare bones nature. The System Configuration Dialog allows you to turn on interfaces, assign addresses, and assign some passwords; however, it does not allow you to customize IOS configuration things such as routing protocols and filters. With the System Configuration Dialog, we can quickly put a configuration on a router to allow the interfaces to come up and IOS to start routing and/or bridging. From there, we can make modifications. Just remember that a little up-front design work never hurt anybody. Our planning allowed us to very quickly run through the initial configurations of two routers, Dallas and FortWorth.

The process you have just seen is generally what it will look like. Of course, your mileage may vary based on the router model, the IOS version, and the protocols you need.

3.7   Connecting the Interfaces

A router's interface must be connected to a network so messages may be received and routed or bridged from one network to another. This connection is as simple as plugging one end of an appropriate cable into the router's interface and then plugging the other end of the cable into the physical network equipment such as an Ethernet hub or a T1 CSU/DSU (Channel Service Unit/Digital Service Unit). In our internetwork, we are using Ethernet and serial interfaces. These should be connected to their respective networks.

3.8   Completion

Our routers are now configured and operational. The routers' interfaces are connected to their networks and the networks are operational. We now have a working internetwork.

IOS Command Line Interface

Most IOS configuration is done through the *Command Line Interface* (CLI); therefore, to configure IOS-based routers, we need a good understanding of how the CLI works, and we need to feel comfortable with its capabilities. The CLI is very simple; however, just like any other command line interface (remember DOS?), it is not the most intuitive interface for beginners.

In this chapter, we cover the major features of the IOS CLI so you know how it works. We then cover some configuration tasks that are independent of the network protocols that are covered in later chapters.

So far we have done the basic configuration of two routers, but we have not yet typed a command. At the end of the System Configuration Dialog in Chapter 3, we saw the message "Press RETURN to get started!" That is the point from which we are going to start learning about the IOS Command Line Interface.

4.1   Logging In

The most basic way of logging in to an IOS-based router is through a connection to the console port like the one we used for initial configuration. In Chapter 3 we saw that the System Configuration Dialog asked us for three passwords—enable secret, enable, and VTY. We were not asked for a console password; therefore, all we have to do to log in to a router which has a configuration created by the System Configuration Dialog is press <Enter>. As an example, we will log in to Dallas.

```
Press RETURN to get started!

<Enter>
Dallas>
```

When <Enter> is pressed, the command prompt ("Dallas>" in the example) appears. Once we get a prompt, we can start typing commands.

Protecting the console port with a password is good practice; assigning a password to the console port is shown in Chapter 6. If there were a password on the console port, the log in sequence would look slightly different.

```
Press RETURN to get started!

<Enter>
User Access Verification
```

```
Password: noknok
Dallas>
```

When the console port is password protected and <Enter> is pressed, we get a password prompt. We are granted access to the router if we type the correct password. The example shows that the correct password, *noknok*, has been typed and we have been logged in and given the command prompt "Dallas>".

NOTE *When you type a password at the password prompt, the password does not appear on your terminal. The password is shown here only for the purpose of illustrating something being typed.*

Suppose that either the incorrect password is typed or no password is typed. The console output will look like this.

```
Press RETURN to get started!


<Enter>
User Access Verification

Password: knockknock
Password:
% Password: timeout expired!
Password: niknak
% Bad passwords

Press RETURN to get started!

<Enter>
User Access Verification

Password: noknok
Dallas>
```

We get three tries to type the correct password before we are kicked out and have to start over. On the console, this is not really a big deal, since we have to wait only a few seconds before we can press <Enter> and get another password prompt.

If we type the incorrect password on the first or second try, we are simply given another password prompt. The password-prompt timeout period is about 30 seconds; if we do not type anything at a password prompt for the timeout period, the prompt timeout will expire. When the correct password is typed, we are given a user mode command prompt.

We can also log in to IOS by establishing a telnet session to the router and typing the correct password. Once we get a password prompt, the behavior of the IOS command line interface is exactly the same as it is on a console terminal. The password used to log in through a telnet session is the VTY password we entered during the System Configuration Dialog.

4.2   Command Prompts and Modes

The command prompt changes based on the command mode that we are using or the mode in which the router is running. The major command modes are as follows:

- User Mode
- Privileged Mode
- Global Configuration Mode
- Subconfiguration Modes
- ROM Monitor Mode

User, privileged, global configuration, and subconfiguration modes are IOS command modes. These are the modes that we will be moving in and out of as we configure IOS. Figure 4-1 shows these command modes, their default prompts, and the commands or keystrokes that are used to move among them.

The following sections describe each of the modes and their command prompts. All of the modes can be recognized by the default format of their command prompts.

4.2.1   User Mode

When you log in to a router, you are put into *user mode*. You can tell that you are in user mode because the user mode prompt consists of the router's host name followed by the greater-than sign (>). The previous log-in examples in Section 4.1 show that after a successful log in to Dallas, the prompt looks like this:

```
Dallas>
```

User mode can be referred to as the "look but don't touch" mode. In user mode, we can do nothing that would normally affect IOS operation

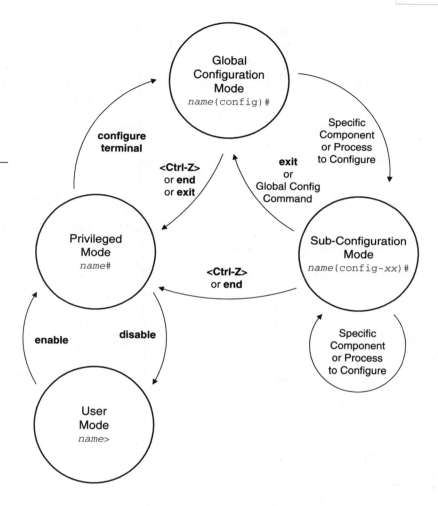

Figure 4-1
IOS command modes. (Prompt shown is default. **name** = router's host name. **XX** varies by subconfiguration mode.)

on the router. All we can do is look. We can look at just about anything on the router except the IOS running configuration and startup configuration.

4.2.2 Privileged Mode

When we want to do something that could potentially affect IOS operation or we want to view either of the configurations, we must move from user mode to *privileged mode,* in which we can do just about anything we want to do. For example, we can examine the configuration files, and we can reboot the router.

The user mode **enable** command tells IOS that we wish to enter privileged mode. The terminal output for this exchange is shown below.

```
Dallas>enable
Password: itsasecret
Dallas#
```

When we type the **enable** command, we are asked for a password before we are granted access to privileged mode. If we type the correct password, we are placed in privileged mode, and our command prompt changes. The command prompt now has the name of the router followed by a number or pound sign (#). At this point, the number sign in the prompt means that we have complete control over the router and we can do whatever we wish. Spending a lot of time in privileged mode can be dangerous for the inexperienced router configuration person; however, sometimes it is necessary.

Let us return to the password that we typed for access to privileged mode. The password we entered was *itsasecret*. This password is the enable secret password that we entered in the System Configuration Dialog on Dallas in Section 3.5.1.2. "Enable secret" is an unusual name for a password used to get into privileged mode. Privileged mode was formerly called enabled mode; thus the command **enable** to get there and the "enable" in enable secret. The word "secret" comes from the way that the password is displayed in the configuration files; it is encrypted with a one-way, cryptographic algorithm.

During the initial configuration of our two routers in Chapter 3, we also entered an enable password. As long as there is an enable secret password, the enable password actually does nothing in our routers as they are currently running. If we were to remove the enable secret password, then the enable password *enableme* would be used to enter privileged mode. The enable password also exists just in case we use the router's configuration file with an old version of IOS that does not support the enable secret password. The regular enable password is sort of the legacy password.

If we want to leave privileged mode and return to user mode, the command is **disable**.

```
Dallas#disable
Dallas>
```

Notice that the last character in the prompt changes from the number sign back to the greater-than sign. To summarize, **enable** gets us into privileged mode, and **disable** gets us out.

Privileged mode commands are a superset of the user mode commands. In other words, all user mode commands are still available to us while we are in privileged mode.

4.2.3   Configuration Modes

The IOS configuration modes are used for entering IOS configuration commands that affect the way IOS runs on a router. The main configuration mode is global configuration mode, or global config mode; it is the one we enter first. From global configuration mode, we can enter the sub-configuration modes. The configuration mode required for a command depends on what is being configured and what command is being entered. All commands that are entered in a configuration mode affect the running configuration, and configuration commands take effect immediately after they are entered.

Since being in a configuration mode implies that we are changing the operation of IOS, we can enter global configuration mode only from privileged mode. User mode and privileged mode commands are not accepted in the configuration modes.

4.2.3.1   Global Configuration Mode
The first configuration mode is *global configuration mode,* in which we can make changes that affect the overall, or global, operation of IOS. For example, we can enter commands that change a router's host name, start processes or services, and set some of the passwords.

The **configure terminal** command is the privileged mode command used to enter global configuration mode if a terminal is being used to enter configuration commands. IOS will accept the command only in privileged mode. (We cover the **configure terminal** command in more detail later.) Terminal output is shown below.

```
Dallas#configure terminal
Enter configuration commands, one per line. End with CNTL/Z.
Dallas(config)#
```

The global configuration mode prompt has the word *config* in parentheses while still maintaining the router's host name and the number sign.

According to the message immediately after the **configure terminal** command, if we want to leave global configuration mode and return to privileged mode, we type <Ctrl-Z>.

```
Dallas(config)#<Ctrl-Z>
Dallas#
```

We could also have typed **end** or **exit** to return to privileged mode. From global configuration, we can move to the other configuration modes. We can enter global configuration commands in any of the configuration modes.

4.2.3.2 Subconfiguration Modes

The *subconfiguration modes* are used to configure individual components such as interfaces and processes. The command to enter a subconfiguration mode varies based on the component that is being configured.

For example, if we want to configure an interface, we must be in interface configuration mode. To get into interface configuration mode, we use the **interface** command in global configuration mode, which requires the full interface name (Section 3.1.3), with type and number, immediately after it.

```
Dallas(config)#interface serial1
Dallas(config-if)#
```

All subconfiguration mode prompts have, within parentheses, the word *config* and a word or abbreviation specifying the subconfiguration mode separated by a hyphen (–). The interface configuration mode prompt has *config-if* in parentheses along with the router's host name and the number sign. The *if* indicates interface configuration mode. Commands to configure interface Serial1 can be typed at this prompt; we could also type any global configuration command here since global configuration commands are accepted in any of the configuration modes.

We can use the **exit** command to return to global configuration mode.

```
Dallas(config-if)#exit
Dallas(config)#
```

If we type a global configuration command that does not cause us to enter another subconfiguration mode, then we will be returned to global configuration mode. For example, suppose we are in interface configuration mode and we decide to change the name of the router.

```
Router(config-if)#hostname Dallas
Dallas(config)#
```

This example reinforces several things that have already been mentioned.

- Global configuration commands can be typed in any configuration mode.

- Entering a global configuration command that does not lead to another subconfiguration mode takes us to global configuration mode.

- Configuration commands take effect immediately. (Notice the name change in the prompt after the global configuration **hostname** command was used to set the router's host name.)

To exit a subconfiguration mode and go all the way to privileged mode, we could press <Ctrl-Z> or type **end** at the subconfiguration mode prompt.

```
Dallas(config-if)#end
Dallas#
```

There are about 20 subconfiguration modes. Some others that we will use in this book are line configuration, router configuration, and IPX-router configuration. They are covered as we get to their configuration commands.

4.2.4 ROM Monitor Mode

ROM monitor mode is not really an IOS mode; it is more of a mode that a router can be in if IOS is not running. If a router attempts to boot and cannot find a good IOS image to run, then the router will enter ROM monitor mode. We can also purposely cause the router to enter ROM monitor mode by sending a Break signal from the console terminal within 60 seconds of the start of the router's boot sequence. Purposely entering ROM monitor mode is usually done only as one of the steps for recovering a lost password.

ROM monitor mode has commands that allow us to manually boot a router by loading a valid IOS image. The exact commands and prompt vary by router model; however, the command prompt is usually just a greater-than sign (>).

4.3 Talking to IOS

Now that we have seen the different modes in which we can enter commands, we can cover the format of those commands and the way that they should be typed. Talking to IOS really is as simple as typing a command and pressing <Enter> or Return, which must be pressed after each command.

Most of the time IOS talks back after a command has been issued. When we type a command asking for information, we usually get information back if it is available. When we type a command that is formatted incorrectly, the IOS command line interpreter tells us where it thinks we made a mistake.

When we type a word at a user mode or privileged mode prompt, IOS checks its command table for the word to see if the word is a valid command. If the single word issued on the command line is not a valid command, the default behavior of IOS is to interpret the word as the name of a host to which a telnet session should be established. The resulting message can be annoying.

```
Dallas>whoops
Translating "whoops"...domain server (255.255.255.255)
% Unknown command or computer name, or unable to find computer address
Dallas>
```

The message is annoying because it indicates that the router is attempting to resolve the host name to an IP address by broadcasting a request to an unknown domain (DNS) server. This translation, which is normally destined for failure, takes about 10 seconds to time out. We cover several ways to change this behavior in Chapter 7.

We can control the way that IOS displays information on our terminal and change other terminal parameters with the user mode command **terminal.** Any terminal parameters we change are effective only for the duration of our current terminal session. If we log out, the terminal parameters return to their original values.

The real skill in talking to IOS comes in knowing which command, or commands, to use. Some IOS tasks require more than one command. Specific commands used to execute IOS tasks are covered in the coming chapters; for now, we will concentrate on how to use the command line interface. Without knowledge of how to effectively use the features of the command line interface, IOS configuration can be a daunting task.

4.3.1 Command Line Editing

IOS allows us to edit a command while we are typing it. We can move the cursor around on the command line, add characters, delete characters, and insert characters. The keystrokes for editing the IOS command line are generally like a subset of those in the Emacs text editor used mostly on Unix hosts. With that in mind, picture the command line as a 10-line text file, or buffer, that we can edit; each line is a command and each command can have 253 characters.

IOS keeps the last 10 commands we typed in a command history buffer. There are two command history buffers. One buffer is for user mode and privileged mode commands; the other is for configuration mode commands.

4.3.1.1 Moving the Cursor Around

The command keystrokes used to move the cursor around on the command line and within the command history buffer are shown in Table 4-1.

The arrow keys are probably the easiest and most straightforward way to move the cursor around; they can be used on ANSI-compliant terminals such as the VT100, the VT220, and the VT320. If your PC's terminal emulation software is emulating a VT-type terminal, the arrow keys can be used for cursor movement.

Pressing the left-arrow key (or <Ctrl-B>) moves the cursor left one character, and pressing the right-arrow key (or <Ctrl-F>) moves the cursor right one character.

Typing <Esc><B> (press and release the <Esc> key and then press and release the <B> key) moves the cursor left to the first character of a word, and typing <Esc><F> moves the cursor right to the end of a word. The command line editor considers words to be bounded by spaces or by hyphens.

Pressing <Ctrl-A> moves the cursor to the beginning of the command line and pressing <Ctrl-E> moves the cursor to the end of the command line.

TABLE 4-1

Cursor Motion Keystrokes

Cursor Motion Desired	Left (Backward)	Right (Forward)
Character	<Ctrl-B> or Left-Arrow Key	<Ctrl-F> or Right-Arrow Key
Word	<Esc><B>	<Esc><F>
Line (to Beginning or End)	<Ctrl-A>	<Ctrl-E>
Command in History Buffer	<Ctrl-P> or Up-Arrow Key	<Ctrl-N> or Down-Arrow Key

Pressing the up-arrow key (or <Ctrl-P>) moves the cursor backward (up) in the command history buffer; in other words, the preceding command entered will be recalled and placed on the command line. Pressing the down-arrow key (or <Ctrl-N>) moves the cursor forward (down) in the command history buffer.

If you want, you can turn off some of the <Ctrl> key and <Esc> key command line editing features with the **terminal no editing** command. To turn the command line editing feature back on, use the **terminal editing** command. The editing features are on by default.

IOS, by default, saves our last 10 commands in the appropriate command history buffer. There are two customizations to command history buffer processing. We can turn off command history and we can change the size of the history buffer. Use the command **terminal no history** to turn off the command history feature and use the command **terminal history** to turn it back on. It is on by default.

To change the number of lines kept in the command history buffers (both of them), use the **terminal history size** command.

```
Dallas>terminal history size 25
Dallas>
```

The preceding command tells IOS to save our last 25 commands in the command history buffer. We can use the user mode command **show history** to see the user mode and privileged mode commands we have typed during the current terminal session.

```
Dallas>show history
  terminal no editing
  terminal editing
  terminal no history
  terminal history
  terminal history size 25
  show history
Dallas>
```

The **show history** command issued in this example shows that the commands covered in this section have been typed on the command line.

4.3.1.2 Deleting Text

Table 4-2 shows the command keystrokes used to delete or kill while editing an IOS command line.

To delete the character immediately left of the cursor, press the <Backspace> key (or <Delete> or <Ctrl-H>). Pressing <Ctrl-D> deletes the character at the cursor.

TABLE 4-2

Deletion Keystrokes

What to Delete	Left (Backward)	Right (Forward)
Character	\<Backspace\> or \<Delete\> or \<Ctrl-H\>	\<Ctrl-D\>
Word	\<Ctrl-W\> or \<Esc\>\<Delete\>	\<Esc\>\<D\>
Line (to Beginning or End)	\<Ctrl-U\> or \<Ctrl-X\>	\<Ctrl-K\>

Pressing \<Ctrl-W\> (or \<Esc\>\<Delete\>) deletes the characters from the one left of the cursor to the beginning of a word to the left. Typing \<Esc\>\<D\> deletes the characters to the right from the cursor to the end of a word.

Pressing \<Ctrl-U\> (or \<Ctrl-X\>) deletes the characters from the cursor to the beginning of the command line. If the cursor is at the end of the command line, pressing \<Ctrl-U\> erases the entire line. Pressing \<Ctrl-K\> deletes the characters from the cursor to the end of the command line.

The characters removed by word and line deletion keystrokes are copied into a deletion buffer. The deletion buffer can contain 10 deleted objects. These objects can be pasted into the command line using keystrokes defined in Section 4.3.1.3.

4.3.1.3 Adding Text

To add characters to the command line, just type them. The characters appear on the command line at the current cursor position.

Pressing \<Ctrl-Y\> pastes the last entry from the deletion buffer into the command line at the cursor position. Typing \<Esc\>\<Y\> without moving the cursor will replace the last object pasted with the next object from the deletion buffer.

4.3.1.4 Other Text Editing Features

Just a few other keystroke commands are useful to us. Table 4-3 shows these.

Pressing \<Ctrl-R\> (or \<Ctrl-L\>) will bring up a fresh command line with all the characters that appear on our current command line. Why would we want that? Every once in a while (especially if we are working on a console terminal), IOS sends a message to our screen that appears right in the middle of our command line that we worked so hard on. Even though the message has no effect on the command itself, the message may cause us to lose our place. Rather than just pressing \<Enter\> to see

TABLE 4-3

Other Editing
Keystrokes

Action	Keystroke
Redisplay current command line.	<Ctrl-R> or <Ctrl-L>
Transpose characters.	<Ctrl-T>
Make word uppercase.	<Esc><U>
Make word lowercase.	<Esc><L>
Capitalize a word.	<Esc><C>

what happens, the safest thing to do is tell IOS to redisplay the current command line so we can make sure that we typed the line correctly and so we can finish typing the command if needed.

Pressing <Ctrl-T> will transpose the character to the immediate left of the cursor with the character at the cursor. This comes in handy if you like to type fast and you occasionally get a couple of characters out of order. Just move the cursor to the rightmost character and press <Ctrl-T>; the characters will switch places.

IOS does not usually care if commands are typed in uppercase, lowercase, or a combination; however, there are a few parameters that are case sensitive. Case-sensitive parameters include passwords, host names, and SNMP community strings.

Typing <Esc><U> will convert to uppercase all the characters from the cursor to the end of a word. The cursor will be moved right to the end of a word.

Typing <Esc><L> will convert to lowercase all the characters from the cursor to the end of a word. The cursor will be moved right to the end of a word.

Typing <Esc><C> will capitalize the character located at the cursor and move the cursor to the end of a word. For example, if the cursor is located at the first character of a word and <Esc><C> is typed, the first character of the word will be made uppercase and the cursor will be moved to the end of the word.

4.3.2 Abbreviations

All interface types, commands, and command arguments can be abbreviated to the number of letters that make them unique on the router. Being able to abbreviate what we type on a command line saves time and reduces mistakes. Once we get used to abbreviating commands, the real power and efficiency of the IOS command line interface becomes evident. Table 4-4 shows some examples of common abbreviations.

Throughout this book, full commands will be shown in the example configurations to help ensure understanding of the commands. The command summary in Appendix A lists the common abbreviations for all of the commands used in this book. The only way to become comfortable with the abbreviations is to use them; once you have used them for a while, you figure out what command abbreviations work best for you. IOS never displays command abbreviations in its configuration files.

4.3.3   Getting Help

Several features or the IOS command line interface assist in typing correct commands. Context-sensitive help can be obtained by typing a question mark (?). IOS determines the context by the command mode and then displays appropriate help text.

Meaningful (once you get used to them) error messages help us determine and correct mistakes in typed commands.

If a question mark is typed at the end of a command line, there is no need to press <Enter>. The question mark is interpreted as the end of the command line, and help is immediately displayed if it is available.

For very high-level help, typing a question mark by itself on a command line tells IOS to display a list of all of the commands allowed on

TABLE 4-4

*Abbreviation
Examples*

Full Name	Abbreviation
show	sh
show protocols	sh prot
terminal length 0	term len 0
enable	en
configure terminal	conf t
ethernet	e
serial	s
tokenring	to
interface ethernet0	int e0
quit	q

the current mode's command line. Here are two examples. The first one is for user mode; the second one is for global configuration mode. Only the first page of the help text is shown.

```
Dallas>?
Exec commands:
  access-enable     Create a temporary Access-List entry
  access-profile    Apply user-profile to interface
  clear             Reset functions
  connect           Open a terminal connection
  disable           Turn off privileged commands
  disconnect        Disconnect an existing network connection
  enable            Turn on privileged commands
  exit              Exit from the EXEC
  help              Description of the interactive help system
  lat               Open a lat connection
  lock              Lock the terminal
  login             Log in as a particular user
  logout            Exit from the EXEC
  mrinfo            Request neighbor and version information from a
                    multicast router
  mstat             Show statistics after multiple multicast
                    traceroutes
  mtrace            Trace reverse multicast path from destination to
                    source
  name-connection   Name an existing network connection
  pad               Open a X.29 PAD connection
  ping              Send echo messages
  ppp               Start IETF Point-to-Point Protocol (PPP)
 —More-
Dallas>enable
Dallas#configure terminal
Enter configuration commands, one per line. End with CNTL/Z.
Router(config)#?
Configure commands:
  aaa               Authentication, Authorization and Accounting.
  access-list       Add an access list entry
  alias             Create command alias
  apollo            Apollo global configuration commands
  appletalk         Appletalk global configuration commands
  arap              Appletalk Remote Access Protocol
  arp               Set a static ARP entry
  async-bootp       Modify system bootp parameters
  autonomous-system Specify local AS number to which we belong
  banner            Define a login banner
  boot              Modify system boot parameters
  bridge            Bridge Group.
  bstun             BSTUN global configuration commands
  buffers           Adjust system buffer pool parameters
  busy-message      Display message when connection to host fails
  call-history-mib  Define call history mib parameters
  cdp               Global CDP configuration subcommands
  chat-script       Define a modem chat script
  clns              Global CLNS configuration subcommands
  clock             Configure time-of-day clock
  config-register   Define the configuration register
 —More—
```

If an abbreviation of a command is typed and then followed immediately by a question mark (no separating space), the IOS help facility displays all of the commands or command arguments that begin with the letters typed. That is, IOS shows the possible ways of completing the word that ends with the question mark.

```
Dallas#se?
send setup

Dallas#se
% Ambiguous command: "se"
Dallas#
```

We typed the letters **se?** in privileged mode because we wanted IOS to tell us all of the commands allowed here that begin with the letters **se**. There are two: **send** and **setup**. After the help text is displayed we are placed on a command line with the letters **se**. The cursor is left in the former position of the question mark. If we press <Enter> there, IOS tells us that **se** is ambiguous. An ambiguous command is an abbreviation that matches more than one command; since IOS does not know which one we want to execute, it executes nothing. We want to execute the **send** command. The **send** command is used to send a message to one or more of a router's terminal line devices.

Since our cursor was left immediately after **se**, we could have just typed **nd** to finish **send**. We can get more help for the **send** command. If a question mark is typed after a command and separated by a space, we are shown the possible arguments for the place in the command held by the question mark.

```
Dallas#send ?
  *          All tty lines
  <0-9>      Send a message to a specific line
  aux        Auxiliary line
  console    Primary terminal line
  tty        Terminal controller
  vty        Virtual terminal
Dallas#send
```

The second argument for the send command can be several things including an asterisk (*), a number from 0 to 9, and the word **console**. Notice that the word **console** is shown in all lowercase letters. When the first word of a help text line is shown in all lowercase letters, this means that the word itself (or a unique abbreviation of it) can be entered at the question mark's place. Once again after the help, the command line is left as we originally typed it with the cursor in the former position of the question mark.

Help is given for the current argument only, not following arguments. If we want help for an argument further into the command, we repeat the process of typing the question mark.

```
Dallas#send console ?
  <0-0> Send a message to a specific line

Dallas#send console
% Incomplete command.

Dallas#
```

Putting a space and a question mark after the command **send console** gives us help text that indicates we need a number between 0 and 0 (that's 0) as the third word of the command. If we just press <Enter> on the resulting command line, IOS tells us that the command is incomplete; this means that the command requires more arguments than we have typed. In this case, the missing argument is the number **0**. However, just to illustrate another IOS command line error message, we will put a **1** as the argument in question.

```
Dallas#send console 1
                    ^
% Invalid input detected at '^' marker.

Dallas#
```

The IOS now tells us that our command has a syntax error. IOS also tells us where it thinks the syntax error is in the command. The caret (^) directly under the **1** indicates that IOS found something invalid there. The **1** is incorrect; according to the help text in the preceding example, the argument must be a **0**.

When the first word of a help text line is shown in all uppercase letters, IOS wants us to type an alphanumeric value in the question mark's place of the command.

```
Dallas#telnet ?
  WORD    IP address or hostname of a remote system
  <CR>

Dallas#telnet
```

The help text WORD, since it is all uppercase letters, means that the first argument for the **telnet** command is an alphanumeric value that we type. The help text <CR> means that we could also just press <Enter> at this point in the **telnet** command.

Value types that can appear in the first column of help text are as follows:

- All lowercase text indicates that the text itself can be typed.

- All uppercase text indicates that alphanumeric text (not a number) can be typed.

- Combination uppercase and lowercase text is usually accompanied by a text pattern in parentheses. The text pattern indicates the format of the text that can be typed.

- A range of numbers in angle brackets (< >) indicates that a numeric value within the range can be typed.

- The text <CR> indicates that no further arguments are required.

Learning to use the context-sensitive help and to interpret the various CLI error messages takes just a little practice. We can be thankful, however—in the old days (software version 8.3), there was no online help, only offline help (the IOS documentation). And we used to have to walk to school barefooted...in the snow...uphill...both ways.

4.3.4   Command Completion

When an abbreviation of a command is typed and then the <Tab> key is pressed, the IOS command line interpreter will complete as much of the command as possible on the command line. The following example illustrates this feature.

```
Dallas#con<Tab>
Dallas#conf<Tab>
Dallas#configure t<Tab>
Dallas#configure terminal
```

The letters **con** were typed and then immediately followed by a <Tab>. The abbreviation "con" is not unique; therefore, IOS simply repeats the letters indicating the no more can be automatically added. If we were to use the question mark, we would see that there are two commands that begin with the letters "con": **configure** and **connect**.

If we type **f** and then <Tab>, IOS uniquely identifies the abbreviation with the **configure** command and gives us a new command line with the word "configure" followed by a space. The cursor is placed at the end of the space so we can just start typing the next word of the command line.

Typing **t** and a <Tab> at the cursor allows the IOS to complete the second word and give us the "configure terminal" command line. Pressing <Enter> here would put us into global configuration mode.

Table 4-4 listed **conf t** as a common abbreviation for the **configure terminal** command. Pressing the <Tab> key after an abbreviated command or command argument is a good way of verifying the abbreviation before pressing <Enter> and possibly receiving an error message for an incorrect or ambiguous command.

4.3.5 Just Say No

We can very easily reverse the effect of IOS configuration commands. To remove a process or to set an IOS parameter to its default value, we can use the word "no" in front of the configuration command we typed to start the process or set the parameter. As a general rule, any IOS configuration command can be undone just by retyping the command with a "no" in front of it. Here are two examples.

EXAMPLE 1

The command to tell IOS to route IPX traffic is the global configuration command **ipx routing**. Putting the word "no" at the beginning of that command has just the opposite effect.

```
Dallas(config)#no ipx routing
```

The global configuration command **no ipx routing** tells IOS to stop routing IPX packets.

EXAMPLE 2

The command to turn off an interface is the interface configuration command **shutdown**. Putting the word "no" in front of the command tells the router to bring up the interface (or at least attempt to bring up the interface).

```
Dallas(config)#interface ethernet0
Dallas(config-if)#no shutdown
```

The first command tells IOS that we want to type commands for configuring interface Ethernet0. The second command, **no shutdown**, tells the router to bring up the interface.

4.3.6   Screen Overload

One of the most used IOS commands is the user mode and privileged mode command **show**. This command is used when we want IOS to tell us information about its configuration or operation. Sometimes the information IOS give us will not fit on one page, and sometimes the IOS separates the information by forcing us to intervene to get more information. In either case, IOS uses its More function to stop the display of information and allow us to read it before it scrolls off our screen. Here is an example of the latter case with the **show protocols** command, which shows us the routed protocols that are running on the router and the interfaces on which the routed protocols have been configured.

```
Dallas>show protocols
Global values:
  Internet Protocol routing is enabled
  Appletalk routing is enabled
  IPX routing is enabled
—More—
```

When the display of information is incomplete and IOS wants to stop the display for emphasis or readability, the More function is used as in the preceding example. The More prompt (**—More—**) on the last line of the display indicates that there is more information to follow.

We have three options for displaying the remaining information:

1. Press <Enter> to see the another line of information.
2. Press <Space> to see the next page or section of information.
3. Press any other printable-character key to stop the information display.

To see the remaining information one line at a time, we can press <Enter> repeatedly since we get one more line for each <Enter>.

The number of lines we get when we press <Space> depends on the number of lines of information left to display and the number of lines IOS is configured to display on our terminal. The default number of lines is 24, normal for a terminal screen. The user mode command **terminal** is used to set terminal parameters. Use the **length** argument to set the number of lines displayed on the screen before the More prompt.

```
Dallas>terminal length 2
Dallas>show protocols
Global values:
  Internet Protocol routing is enabled
  —More—
```

Changing the number of lines to be displayed to two is not a normal thing to do; however, sometimes we want to disable the More function so that IOS sends all the lines of information to the terminal without stopping. This is useful when we are using a PC terminal emulator and we want to log IOS output to a file for later reference. Set the terminal length to zero to disable the More function.

```
Dallas>terminal length 0
Dallas>show protocols
Global values:
   Internet Protocol routing is enabled
   Appletalk routing is enabled
   IPX routing is enabled
BRI0 is administratively down, line protocol is down
BRI0:1 is administratively down, line protocol is down
BRI0:2 is administratively down, line protocol is down
Ethernet0 is up, line protocol is up
   Internet address is 172.16.10.1/24
   AppleTalk address is 100.10, zone Headquarters
   IPX address is AC100A00.0010.7b3a.d4bf
Serial0 is administratively down, line protocol is down
Serial1 is up, line protocol is up
   Internet address is 172.16.11.1/24
   AppleTalk address is 1001.100, zone WAN
   IPX address is AC100B00.0010.7b3a.d4bf
Serial2 is administratively down, line protocol is down
Serial3 is administratively down, line protocol is down
Dallas>
```

IOS displays all of the requested information without us having to type any extra keystrokes when the More function is turned off. This can be annoying when we ask for information that takes more than about 10 screens to display (depending on your pain threshold). For example, suppose our IP routing table contains 1000 routes; at 24 lines per page, 1000 routes will take over 40 pages to display. If you really want to see the whole table, you can leave More on and press <Space> over 40 times, or you can turn More off and capture the output to a file for better viewing. However, if you want to just see a portion of the table and you have More turned off, you will have to wait for the entire table to display because IOS is not going to pause your screen with the More prompt to allow you to stop the display.

There are two ways to set the terminal length back to its default value of 24; both require the **terminal length** command.

```
Dallas>terminal length 24
Dallas>terminal no length
Dallas>
```

Both of the preceding commands do the same thing.

Sometimes we have to type a command that is longer than our terminal screen can handle. For example, suppose our terminal screen is 80 characters wide and the command prompt is seven characters; our command can then be 73 characters before we run out of space on the right side of our terminal display. The current version of IOS has a maximum command length of 253 characters. If we are out of space on the screen, how can we type the long command?

IOS has a special horizontal-scroll feature that allows those long commands to be entered. When we are typing a command and the command exceeds our terminal width, IOS scrolls the command to the left and allows us to continue typing at the end of the command.

When the line is scrolled to the left, IOS puts a dollar sign ($) at the beginning of the command to show us that the command has been scrolled and only some of the command is being displayed. If we move the cursor to the beginning of the long command, IOS scrolls the command to the right and displays a dollar sign ($) at the right side of our screen to inform us that only part of the command line is being displayed. Section 4.3.1.1 shows commands for moving around on a command line.

The default width of a terminal device is 80 characters. The width can be changed for the current session using the user mode command **terminal width**, which has one argument—the number of characters wide the terminal is.

4.4 Logging Out

We have seen plenty about how things look and what to do after we get logged in to an IOS-based router, so we might as well see how to log out. There are three user mode commands that can be used to log out of an IOS terminal session.

1. exit
2. logout
3. quit

Any one of these three commands can be typed in either user mode or privileged mode to stop and exit a terminal session.

By default, all terminal sessions will time out after 10 minutes of inactivity. The terminal session inactivity timeout can be changed with the line configuration command **exec-timeout**, which is covered in Chapter 6.

4.5   Conclusion

- Log in to a router from a console terminal by pressing <Enter> and possibly typing a correct password.

- Complete all commands by pressing <Enter> at the end of them.

- You can check IOS status for most things from user mode.

- If you want to make configuration changes, type **enable** and a correct password to go to privileged mode, and then type **configure terminal** to go to global configuration mode.

- Type the necessary configuration commands to accomplish your objective.

- Remember that if you are configuring an entity such as a process or a device, you must be in the subconfiguration mode appropriate for the entity. For example, you must be in interface configuration mode to configure an interface and you must be in line configuration mode to configure a line.

- Press <Ctrl-Z> (or **end**) to exit configuration mode.

- Abbreviate commands and their arguments whenever possible; abbreviations will save time and reduce typographical errors (typos).

- While in any of the command modes, remember your two little friends: the question mark and the up-arrow. Use the question mark to get context-sensitive help, and use the up-arrow (or <Ctrl-P>) to recall commands from the command history buffer.

- When you are finished with the terminal session, type **exit** (or **logout** or **quit**) to log out.

Examining IOS

Network engineers and administrators do more looking around than configuring on an IOS-based router. We are going to cover some of the things that are useful to look at on a new router and some of the things that are useful to look at regularly on a production router. Some of the things we need to know about a router are as follows:

- What version of IOS is the router running?
- How much RAM does the router have?
- How much of that RAM is IOS using?
- How busy is the router?
- What interfaces does the router have?
- How long has the router been running?
- How did the router last boot?
- What is the status of the interfaces?
- Which protocols are configured on the router?

All of these items can be found by using one of the most used commands in the IOS, the **show** command. The **show** command is used to look at IOS stuff and it can be issued in either user mode or privileged mode. The output of each **show** command used in this chapter is accompanied by a brief description of its contents. From user mode, we can look at just about anything on the router except the configuration files.

For the most part, the IOS examination in the chapter is independent of the routed and routing protocols. The examination of protocol dependent details is covered in the protocol configuration chapters.

5.1 General Router Information

The user mode command **show version** gives us information about the general configuration of the router. Figure 5-1 has the output generated by the **show version** command on our test 2520 router Dallas.

We saw output similar to this in Section 3.4.2. IOS sends this type of system information out the console port when a router boots. On Line 3, there is the router's IOS version, 11.3(5). On Line 5, we see who compiled the image and when; this may not be of immediate interest to you, but it may be of interest to the Cisco Technical Assistance Center (TAC) if you ever have a very weird problem. Lines 8 and 9 show the bootstrap software version, 11.0(10c), stored in both ROM and boot flash.

Figure 5-1

Show version output on 2520.

```
1)  Dallas>show version
2)  Cisco Internetwork Operating System Software
3)  IOS (tm) 2500 Software (C2500-JS-L), Version 11.3(5), RELEASE
    SOFTWARE (fc1)
4)  Copyright (c) 1986-1998 by Cisco Systems, Inc.
5)  Compiled Tue 11-Aug-98 04:06 by phanguye
6)  Image text-base: 0x030489A8, data-base: 0x00001000
7)
8)  ROM: System Bootstrap, Version 11.0(10c), SOFTWARE
9)  BOOTFLASH: 3000 Bootstrap Software (IGS-BOOT-R), Version
    1.0(10c), RELEASE SOFTWARE (fc1)
10)
11) Dallas uptime is 4 hours, 18 minutes
12) System restarted by reload
13) System image file is "flash:c2500-js-l.113-5", booted via
    flash
14)
15) Cisco 2520 (68030) processor (revision M) with 6144K/2048K
    bytes of memory.
16) Processor board ID 10353405, with hardware revision 00000003
17) Bridging software.
18) X.25 software, Version 3.0.0.
19) SuperLAT software copyright 1990 by Meridian Technology
    Corp).
20) TN3270 Emulation software.
21) Basic Rate ISDN software, Version 1.0.
22) 1 Ethernet/IEEE 802.3 interface(s)
23) 2 Serial network interface(s)
24) 2 Low-speed serial(sync/async) network interface(s)
25) 1 ISDN Basic Rate interface(s)
26) 32K bytes of non-volatile configuration memory.
27) 16384K bytes of processor board System flash (Read ONLY)
28)
29) Configuration register is 0x2102
30)
31) Dallas>
```

Figure 5-1, Lines 11 through 13, tell us the router was booted 4 hours 18 minutes ago because someone issued the privileged mode command **reload**. At that time, the IOS image named c2500-js-l.113-5 was loaded from system flash.

Knowing when a router last booted and what initiated the boot is important. If the router had been power cycled, Line 12 would have looked like this:

```
System restarted by power-on
```

If the router had crashed (it happens), Line 12 would have looked something like this.

```
System restarted by bus error at PC 0x384B3DE, address 0xD0D0D0D
```

Line 15 shows that the router is a 2520 and has 8 MB of RAM. The 8 MB is the sum of the values 6144 KB and 2048 KB. On a 2500-series router, the RAM is divided into system RAM, for IOS system functions and tables, and shared RAM, for Input/Output (I/O) operations.

Figure 5-1, Lines 22 through 27, tell us about the physical configuration of the router. Lines 22 through 25 show what interfaces are in the router. The 32 KB of nonvolatile configuration memory mentioned on Line 26 is the amount of NVRAM; so the router has 32 KB of memory to hold its startup configuration. Line 27 says that there are 16 MB of system flash, and we cannot currently write to it. System flash is normally read-only on a 2500-series router that booted from flash because IOS stays in flash while it runs, as opposed to getting completely loaded into RAM to run.

The last line of the **show version** command output (Figure 5-1, Line 29) contains the value of the configuration register. The value is hexadecimal (hex) 2102. The configuration register has many purposes, including controlling how the router boots and setting the console port baud rate. Hex 2102 is the default value for a 2500-series router.

The general information displayed by the **show version** command is consistent from one router model to another; however, the specific information varies. With this one command, we get plenty of good information about the router's hardware and software.

5.2   Input/Output Devices

There are many input/output devices on Cisco routers. Some of those that we can control and configure are flash, controllers, interfaces, and terminal lines. This section covers the basic commands to check these devices.

5.2.1   Flash

We can check the contents of flash memory with the user mode command **show flash**. Figure 5-2 shows the output of the **show flash** command on our test router Dallas.

The **show flash** command displays a directory of the contents of flash memory. On the 2500-series routers, flash is in SIMM form inside the router. On Line 5, we see that there is one file in Dallas's flash; this is an IOS image and is the same image that Dallas is running. The image

Figure 5-2

Show flash output
on 2520.

```
1)   Dallas>show flash
2)
3)   System flash directory:
4)   File   Length    Name/status
5)     1   8945732   c2500-js-1.113-5
6)   [8945796 bytes used, 7831420 available, 16777216 total]
7)   16384K bytes of processor board System flash (Read ONLY)
8)
9)   Dallas>
```

is 8,945,732 bytes in length. Since there are 16 MB of RAM, this leaves 7,831,420 bytes available (Line 6).

On the 7x00-series routers (7000, 7200, 7500), flash memory can either be imbedded internally as a SIMM or installed externally as PCMCIA cards. Normally these routers have two slots for PCMCIA flash cards; the slots are numbered 0 and 1. The **show flash** command works, but to see contents of individual flash devices, we should use the user mode command **dir** (short for directory). Figure 5-3 shows a sample output of the **dir** command from a Cisco 7206 router.

According to Figure 5-3, Line 6, this PCMCIA slot has an 8-MB flash card (1,227,716 bytes available plus 6,767,676 bytes used). The card contains two files shown on Lines 3 and 4.

5.2.1.1 Flash Contents

The files that are in flash are usually IOS images that can be run. We are allowed to put as many files in flash as it can hold. A router will, by default, attempt to boot the first IOS image from flash.

Let us compare the 2520 flash contents from Figure 5-2 with the 7206 flash contents shown in Figure 5-3. The 2520 flash contains one IOS image, and that image is over 8 MB. However, the 7206 flash, which has half the size of the 2520's, has two files, and each is just over 3 MB. The 2520 IOS image would not even fit on the 7206 flash card. The 7206 is

Figure 5-3

Dir output on
7206.

```
1)   Router>dir slot0:
2)   -#- -length- -----date/time------name
3)   1      3375568 Feb 19 1998 08:24:32 c7200-is-mz.112-11.P.bin
4)   2      3391852 Mar 23 1998 11:26:41 c7200-is-mz.112-12.P.bin
5)
6)   1227716 bytes available (6767676 bytes used)
7)   Router>
```

supposed to be one of the high-end routers; one would expect just the opposite. How can this be?

The answer lies in the difference between the way that the 2500-series routers run IOS and the way 7x00-series routers run IOS. In Section 5.1, we stated that the 2500-series routers usually run IOS in flash; that is why flash memory was marked as read-only. Since IOS is running in flash, we cannot write to flash, and the IOS image cannot be compressed. On the 7x00-series router, IOS runs in RAM; therefore, the IOS images can be stored in flash in a compressed form. When a 7x00-series router runs an image from flash, the image is uncompressed into RAM before it runs. This is one of the reasons that the 2520 image is much larger than the 7206 images.

The other reason is the IOS feature set of the images. The 2520 image has the enterprise feature set and the 7206 image has the IP feature set. The enterprise feature set image has most of the possible IOS features included; therefore, it is obviously going to be bigger than an image that has only IP features, compressed or not. How can we tell that just by looking at the image name?

5.2.1.2 Image Names

Cisco uses its own naming convention to name IOS files. The naming convention allows us to look at an image name and determine its router platform, its feature set, its version, where it runs (flash or RAM), and if it is compressed. This naming convention changes occasionally, but here are some recent highlights using the images from Figures 5-2 and 5.3.

The image name is composed of at least two sections separated by periods (.). The first section has three parts separated by hyphens (–). The first part (*c2500* and *c7200*) is the router platform. The second part (*js* and *is*) is the feature set. The *j* represents the enterprise feature set; the *i* represents the IP feature set, and the *s* means that additional features have been added to the images. The third part (*l* and *mz*) tells us where the image is supposed to run and if it is compressed. The *l* means that the image is relocatable; that is, it can run in either flash or RAM. The *m* means that the image runs in RAM, and the *z* means that the image is zip compressed.

The next section contains the version of the image. On the 2520 this is *113-5*, which means IOS version 11.3(5). On the 7206, the second section for the first file is *112-11*, which means IOS version 11.2(11). The 7206 has a third section (*P*) and a fourth section (*bin*). The *P* indicates that this image contains platform-specific features for the 7200-series.

The *bin* means that the image is a binary file; of course, all IOS images are binary files.

5.2.2   Controllers

A controller handles the communication and signaling for router hardware. There are many different types of controllers, and the controllers available on a router depend on the router model and its physical configuration. All interfaces connect to the router through a controller, and on the high-end routers, the communications bus has a controller.

The user mode command **show controllers** with its arguments can be used to display information about the installed controllers or information about an individual controller. The **show controllers** command can provide us with the following information for each controller.

- Hardware type
- Hardware version
- Microcode version
- Statistics

We are going to show examples from several different routers just to show some of the different types of controllers. The output for the **show controllers** command can be rather lengthy; therefore, we are going to show just the first few lines of the output for most of the examples.

To see all of the controllers on a router, the **show controllers** command without any arguments should work. However, if we want information about just one controller in a router, use the question mark to get help and find out what arguments are available.

Each interface on a 2500-series router usually has its own controller. Controllers for interfaces are numbered starting with zero. Figure 5-4 shows part of the output for a BRI controller on a 2520.

Figure 5-4

Show controllers BRI output on 2520.

```
1)  Dallas>show controllers bri
2)  BRI unit 0
3)  D Chan Info:
4)  Layer 1 is ACTIVATED
5)  idb 0xBE604, ds 0xCD2C0, reset_mask 0x8
6)  buffer size 1524
7)  [text omitted]
8)  Dallas>
```

On Line 2, we see that this information is for the first BRI controller, unit 0. A BRI has three channels: two B channels and one D channel. The D channel is used for signaling between the router and the ISDN switch. The message "Layer 1 is ACTIVATED" on Line 4 means that the router's BRI port is connected to an ISDN switch. If the connection to the switch were down, Layer 1 would be "DEACTIVATED"; and it would be "PENDING ACTIVATION" if the connection to the switch were pending.

Figure 5-5 shows part of the output for an Ethernet controller. Line 2 shows that this is the first Ethernet controller, unit 0, and it has a LANCE chip set. Line 4 shows the MAC address for the interface on the controller.

Figure 5-6 shows part of the output for a serial controller. In Line 1, we have put a specific unit number, 0. When a unit number is referenced in the **show controllers** command, there must be a space between it and the controller type. According to Line 3, the type of cable attached to the serial interface on this controller is a V.35 DTE (Data Terminal Equipment) cable. This cable has a V.35 connector on the end not connected to the router. The V.35 connector is meant to be plugged in to a CSU/DSU, which provides the DCE (Data Circuit-terminating Equipment) side of the connection. On Cisco routers, the electrical interface (EIA/TIA-232 DTE, V.35 DCE, etc.) of a serial interface is determined by the type of cable attached to the port.

Figure 5-7 shows the output for a cbus controller on a 7505 router. Line 11 shows that there is a Versatile Interface Processor 2 (VIP2) in

Figure 5-5

Show controllers Ethernet output on 2520.

```
1)  FortWorth>show controllers ethernet
2)  LANCE unit 0, idb 0xB71B0, ds 0xB8900, regaddr = 0x2130000,
    reset_mask 0x2
3)  IB at 0x606E64: mode = 0x0000, mcfilter 0000/0000/0900/2020
4)  station address 0010.7b3a.d4af default station address
    0010.7b3a.d4af
5)  buffer size 1524
6)  [text omitted]
7)  FortWorth>
```

Figure 5-6

Show controllers serial 0 output on 2520.

```
1)  FortWorth>show controllers serial 0
2)  HD unit 0, idb = 0xD7D8C, driver structure at 0xDD028
3)  buffer size 1524 HD unit 0, V.35 DTE cable
4)  cpb = 0x62, eda = 0x408C, cda = 0x40A0
5)  [text omitted]
6)  FortWorth>
```

Figure 5-7

Show controllers
Cbus output on
7505.

```
1)  Router>show controllers cbus
2)  MEMD at 40000000, 2097152 bytes (unused 0, recarves 1,
    lost 0)
3)    RawQ 48000100, ReturnQ 48000108, EventQ 48000110
4)    BufhdrQ 48000128 (2378 items), LovltrQ 48000148 (8 items,
      2016 bytes)
5)    IpcbufQ 48000158 (16 items, 4096 bytes)
6)    IpcbufQ_classic 48000150 (8 items, 4096 bytes)
7)    3570 buffer headers (48002000 - 4800FF10)
8)    pool0: 9 buffers, 256 bytes, queue 48000130
9)    pool1: 1147 buffers, 1536 bytes, queue 48000138
10)   pool2: 4 buffers, 1568 bytes, queue 48000140
11)   slot3: VIP2 R5K, hw 2.0, sw 22.20, ccb 5800FF50, cmdq
      48000098, vps 8192
12)     software loaded from system
13)     IOS (tm) VIP Software (SVIP-DW-M), Version 12.0(1.0.2)S,
        EARLY DEPLOYMENT DEVELOPMENT TEST SOFTWARE
14)     ROM Monitor version 115.0
15)     Ethernet3/0/0, addr 00e0.34b4.a860 (bia 00e0.34b4.a860)
16)       gfreeq 48000138, lfreeq 48000160 (1536 bytes)
17)       rxlo 4, rxhi 860, rxcurr 4, maxrxcurr 5
18)       txq 48001A00, txacc 48001A02 (value 458), txlimit 458
19)     Ethernet3/0/1, addr 00e0.34b4.a861 (bia 00e0.34b4.a861)
20)       gfreeq 48000138, lfreeq 48000168 (1536 bytes)
21)       rxlo 4, rxhi 860, rxcurr 0, maxrxcurr 0
22)       txq 48001A08, txacc 48001A0A (value 458), txlimit 458
23)     Ethernet3/0/2, addr 00e0.34b4.a862 (bia 00e0.34b4.a862)
24)       gfreeq 48000138, lfreeq 48000170 (1536) bytes
25)       rxlo 4, rxhi 860, rxcurr 0, maxrxcurr 0
26)       txq 48001A10, txacc 48001A12 (value 458), txlimit 458
27)     Ethernet3/0/3, addr 00e0.34b4.a863 (bia 00e0.34b4.a863)
28)       gfreeq 48000138, lfreeq 48000178 (1536 bytes)
29)       rxlo 4, rxhi 860, rxcurr 0, maxrxcurr 0
30)       txq 48001A18, txacc 48001A1A (value 458), txlimit 458
31)   Router>
```

slot 3. This 7505 is running IOS version 12.0(1.0.2)S (Line 13). The VIP2
has four Ethernet interfaces as shown on Lines 15, 19, 23, and 27; the
MAC address of each interface is shown. VIP interfaces have unit desig-
nators with three numbers separated by forward slashes: slot, port
adapter, and port.

Most of the information found with the **show controllers** command
is not very useful for day-to-day monitoring of IOS; however, the information may come in handy for in-depth troubleshooting.

5.2.3 Interfaces

We frequently need to check an interface's status or an interface's statistics such as errors and traffic counters. Generally, the first thing we

check on an interface is its status. An interface's status consists of two components:

1. Physical layer status
2. Data link status

The first component is the *physical layer status,* which indicates whether the interface has passed diagnostics and is receiving appropriate signaling. On a serial interface, appropriate signaling could be Carrier Detect (CD) signal or a clocking signal from a WAN. Appropriate signaling on an Ethernet interface could be link signaling from a hub or switch.

The second component, referred to as line protocol, is the *data link status,* which indicates whether the interface is receiving keepalives (if they are enabled). A *keepalive* is a small, layer-2 message that is transmitted by a network device to let directly connected network devices know of its presence.

Keepalives are transmitted out every interface every 10 seconds by default; the time between keepalives is configurable for each interface. On WAN interfaces, the keepalives are meant to be received by a neighboring router or switch, depending on the WAN type; an IOS-based router marks its WAN interface line protocol as up if it is receiving keepalives. On LAN interfaces, the router sends keepalives to itself; an IOS-based router marks its LAN interface line protocol as up if it is receiving its own LAN keepalives.

Table 5-1 shows the common combinations of the two interface status components along with a possible reason that an interface can have the status.

An operational interface is commonly referred to as "up/up" or "up and up," which is a shortcut way of saying or writing the two components of an interface's status. If line protocol (data link status) is up and the interface doesn't receive a keepalive for three keepalive intervals, line protocol will change state to down.

The general way of checking status and statistics is to use a form of the user mode command **show interfaces**. Issuing the **show interfaces** command without any arguments will show information for every interface in a router. This produces more than a terminal screen of information for every interface in a router; this could be a lot of terminal output to wade through to see the very last interface in the router, especially if the router has 30 interfaces. If we know the interface that we want to check, we can put the interface name as an argument to the

Physical Layer Status	Data Link Status	Possible Explanation
Up	Up	Interface is probably operational.
Up	Down	Interface physical connection is OK, but interface is not receiving keepalives. Interface is not operational.
Down	Down	Interface physical connection is bad or not connected.
Administratively Down	Down	Interface has been manually shut down or has never been turned on after initial configuration.
Up	Up (looped)	WAN interface is receiving its own keepalives.
Up	Up (spoofing)	WAN dialer-type interface is artificially marked as operational to maintain its network(s) in the routing table(s).

show interfaces command. Figure 5-8 shows output for an Ethernet interface and Figure 5-9 shows output for a serial interface.

The **show interfaces** output, in Figure 5-8, provides plenty of interesting information about a single interface; we will mention the major items. We can tell that this Ethernet interface is probably on a 7x00-series router because its unit designator has two numbers, slot 4 and port 0. On Line 2 we see the status is up/up. The status is always the first thing shown. Line 3 provides the MAC address. The first one is currently being used; the one in parentheses is the BIA (burned-in-address). The IOS allows one way of documenting an IOS configuration on the router, and that is putting a description on an interface; this interface's description is shown on Line 4. We are given one layer-3 address, the primary IP address on Line 5.

Figure 5-8, Line 6, shows the Ethernet interface's MTU (Maximum Transmission Unit) in bytes, BW (bandwidth) in kbps, DLY (delay) in microseconds, rely (reliability) as a fraction of 255, and load (line utilization) as a fraction of 255. MTU is the maximum size of a packet that can transmitted or received on the interface; 1500 is the default for Ethernet. Some processes require a fixed value for the bandwidth of a network; those processes use the bandwidth parameter—its value has no effect on the speed of an interface. Some processes also require a fixed value for network delay (how long does it take a signal to get from one side of a network to the other); those processes use the delay parameter—its value also has no effect on the speed of an interface. Reliability

Figure 5-8
Show interfaces
Ethernet output.

```
1)   Router>show interfaces ethernet4/0
2)   Ethernet4/0 is up, line protocol is up
3)     Hardware is cyBus Ethernet, address is 0060.3e22.b880 (bia
       0060.3e22.b880)
4)     Description: Third Floor Software Development LAN
5)     Internet address is 10.46.20.1 255.255.255.0
6)     MTU 1500 bytes, BW 10000 Kbit, DLY 1000 usec, rely 255/255,
       load 26/255
7)     Encapsulation ARPA, loopback not set, keepalive set (10
       sec)
8)     ARP type: ARPA, ARP Timeout 4:00:00
9)     Last input 0:00:02, output 0:00:02, output hang never
10)    Last clearing of "show interface" counters 6d18
11)    Output queue 0/40, 9 drops; input queue 0/75, 0 drops
12)    5 minute input rate 1056000 bits/sec, 546 packets/sec
13)    5 minute output rate 1027000 bits/sec, 509 packets/sec
14)      208267944 packets input, 71626541 bytes, 0 no buffer
15)      Received 197995 broadcasts, 0 runts, 0 giants
16)      7 input errors, 7 CRC, 0 frame, 0 overrun, 0 ignored,
       0 abort
17)      0 input packets with dribble condition detected
18)      207558863 packets output, 3056717135 bytes, 0 underruns
19)      0 output errors, 25912392 collisions, 0 interface
       resets, 0 restarts
20)      0 output buffer failures, 236 output buffers swapped out
21)  Router>
```

is the router's judgment call based on interface errors for how stable the interface is. The value *255* indicates 100 percent reliability. Load is the router's measured utilization of the interface; the load of *26* shown on Line 6 represents about 10 percent.

On Line 7 of Figure 5-8, we see that the encapsulation is ARPA (from Advanced Research Projects Agency). This is also referred to as Ethernet_II; it defines the format of the Ethernet frame header. Line 7 also tells us that keepalives are enabled and they are being transmitted every 10 seconds. Conversely, IOS expects to receive keepalives every 10 seconds on this interface.

According to Line 10 of Figure 5-8, the interface counters were cleared six days and 18 hours (*6d18*) ago. The interface counters are those shown in Lines 14 through 20 for input packets, bytes, and errors and output packets, bytes, and errors. We can use these and the 5-minute input and output rates from Lines 12 and 13 to help determine what our interface is doing. The 5-minute rates are just averages from the last 5 minutes of interface activity. Based on the statistics, we can tell that the number of packets being received and transmitted on this interface are about the same; however, the amount of data being trans-

Figure 5-9

*Show interfaces
serial output.*

```
1)   Dallas>show interfaces serial1
2)   Serial1 is up, line protocol is up
3)     Hardware is HD64570
4)     Internet address is 172.16.11.1/24
5)     MTU 1500 bytes, BW 1544 Kbit, DLY 20000 usec, rely
       255/255, load 1/255
6)     Encapsulation HDLC, loopback not set, keepalive set (10
       sec)
7)     Last input 00:00:07, output 00:00:01, output hang never
8)     Last clearing of "show interface" counters never
9)     Input queue: 0/75/0 (size/max/drops); Total output
       drops: 0
10)    Queueing strategy: weighted fair
11)    Output queue: 0/1000/64/0 (size/max total/threshold/drops)
12)    Conversations 0/2/256 (active/max active/max total)
13)    Reserved Conversations 0/0 (allocated/max allocated)
14)  5 minute input rate 0 bits/sec, 0 packets/sec
15)  5 minute output rate 0 bits/sec, 0 packets/sec
16)    71 packets input, 3865 bytes, 0 no buffer
17)    Received 60 broadcasts, 0 runts, 0 giants, 0 throttles
18)    0 input errors, 0 CRC, 0 frame, 0 overrun, 0 ignored,
       0 abort
19)    79 packets output, 4373 bytes, 0 underruns
20)    0 output errors, 0 collisions, 6 interface resets
21)    0 output buffer failures, 0 output buffers swapped out
22)    33 carrier transitions
23)    DCD = up DSR = up DTR = up RTS = up CTS = up
24)  Dallas>
```

mitted is over four times the amount being received (see bytes in Lines
14 and 18). Either transmitting big packets or detecting many collisions
could cause this discrepancy. Line 19 shows that Ethernet4/0 has had
over 25 million collisions; this seems like an unusually large number of
collisions. However, we must compare the collisions with the number of
packets that have been transmitted (see packets output in Line 18).
About 200 million packets have been transmitted; that makes the colli-
sion rate about 12 percent. These are very rough field calculations, but
some network experts may consider that to be excessive.

Figure 5-9 shows similar information for a serial interface. Notice
that a serial interface has no MAC address. Line 5 shows the bandwidth
to be 1544 kbps (1.544 Mbps); 1544 kbps is the bandwidth of a T1 and is
the default for a fast serial interface. Remember that this bandwidth
parameter has no effect on the speed of the interface. On Line 6, the
encapsulation is shown as HDLC (High-level Data Link Control). HDLC
is the default encapsulation for all IOS-based router serial interfaces.

Cisco's implementation of the HDLC standard is proprietary (just like everybody else's). HDLC keepalives are being sent every 10 seconds, and IOS expects to receive an HDLC keepalive from the router on the other end of the WAN every 10 seconds.

The counters have never been cleared according to Line 8 of Figure 5-9. So how do we find out how old they are? Since the counters have never been cleared, they have been counting up since the router booted; therefore, if we find out how long the router has been running, we will know how old the counters are. The **show version** command covered in Section 5.1 provides router uptime. The counters are almost worthless unless we know how old they are so we can put them in perspective.

All of these statistics and pages of information are great, but we just want to find out the status of each of the router's interfaces. One of my personal favorite IOS commands is the user mode command **show ip interface brief**. This command gives the status of all the interfaces on a single page, unless you have more than 20 interfaces. Figure 5-10 has a sample.

This output was done on our test router Dallas. It shows that Ethernet0 and Serial1 are both up/up and all the other interfaces are administratively down. Ethernet0 and Serial1 are the two interfaces we configured on Dallas in Chapter 3.

5.2.4 Terminal Lines

Terminal lines are router devices that allow us to gain access to the IOS command line interface. There are four types of terminal lines:

1. Console (CTY or CON)
2. Asynchronous Serial (TTY)

Figure 5-10

Show IP interface brief output.

```
1)  Dallas>show ip interface brief
2)  Interface   IP-Address    OK? Method Status                Proto
3)  BRI0        unassigned    YES unset  administratively down down
4)  BRI0:1      unassigned    YES unset  administratively down down
5)  BRI0:2      unassigned    YES unset  administratively down down
6)  Ethernet0   172.16.10.1   YES manual up                         up
7)  Serial0     unassigned    YES unset  administratively down down
8)  Serial1     172.16.11.1   YES manual up                         up
9)  Serial2     unassigned    YES unset  administratively down down
10) Serial3     unassigned    YES unset  administratively down down
11) Dallas>
```

3. Auxiliary (AUX)

4. Virtual (VTY)

The *console port* is a line device, and a router has only one. In Chapter 3, we attached a terminal to the console port to perform the initial configuration. The console port provides an EIA/TIA-232 DCE interface and is used for configuration when physical access to the router is available. We could also attach a modem to the console port and dial in to it; however, the console port provides no flow control signaling or modem control signaling. On older routers, the maximum speed of the console port is 9600 baud; Cisco's new series of routers allow speeds of up to 115 kbps.

Asynchronous serial ports are usually used for dial-up access using PPP (Point-to-Point Protocol) or SLIP (Serial Line IP). Not all routers have asynchronous serial ports.

The *auxiliary port* is a line device, and a router has only one (if it has one at all). The auxiliary port provides an EIA/TIA-232 DTE interface and is normally used for dial-up access through a modem since it provides modem control signaling. Older routers have a maximum speed of 38400 baud.

Virtual ports are logical terminal lines used for telnet access to the router. They are commonly referred to as *VTYs*. All IOS-based routers have five VTYs. More can be created if we need the capability of having more than five simultaneous telnet sessions to the router.

The easiest way to check the status of terminal line devices is to issue the user mode command **show line**. Figure 5-11 shows a sample output.

In Figure 5-11, Line 2, the first two columns are labeled **Tty** and **Typ**. The **Tty** column is for the line number; line numbers, just like interface numbers, start at zero (0). The **Typ** column is for the line type. Only three types are shown in this display. If there were any asynchronous serial lines, they would be shown between the console line (CTY on Line

Figure 5-11

Show line output.

```
1)  Dallas>show line
2)  Tty Typ Tx/Rx       A Modem Roty AccO AccI Uses Noise Overruns
3)    0 CTY             -   -    -    -    -    0    0    0/0
4)    1 AUX 9600/9600   -   -    -    -    -    0    0    0/0
5)    2 VTY             -   -    -    -    -   18    0    0/0
6)  * 3 VTY             -   -    -    -    -    7    0    0/0
7)    4 VTY             -   -    -    -    -   37    0    0/0
8)  * 5 VTY             -   -    -    -    -   64    0    0/0
9)    6 VTY             -   -    -    -    -   48    0    0/0
10) Dallas>
```

3) and the auxiliary line (AUX on Line 4). This would affect the line numbering.

There are two types of line numbering schemes: *absolute* and *relative*. The numbering scheme shown in Figure 5-11 is the absolute one. All of the lines are shown, and the first one is line 0. Each type of line also has a number. For example, the five default VTYs are numbered 0 through 4. The numbers 0 through 4 are relative numbers for the VTYs even though their absolute numbers on the router shown are 2 through 6. If we were to add another VTY, its relative number would be 5 and its absolute number would be 7. Lines can be referenced either by their absolute number (Line 2 for example) or by their relative number if the line type is included in the reference (Line VTY 0 for example).

The order that IOS puts the lines for determination of absolute line numbers is as follows:

- The console line is always first; therefore, the console is always Line 0.

- Asynchronous serial lines follow the console line; therefore, the absolute line number for the first asynchronous serial line is 1.

- The auxiliary line follows the asynchronous serial lines if they are present; otherwise, it follows the console. The absolute line number of the auxiliary line is one greater than the last asynchronous serial line number.

- The VTYs follow the auxiliary line. The absolute line number of the first VTY (VTY 0) is one more than the auxiliary line number.

Other important information displayed in Figure 5-11 is whether an inbound access class (**AccI** column) or outbound access classes (**AccO** column) are applied to the lines. An access class is a security mechanism used for limiting access to a line. The **Uses** column shows the number of times a network connection has been established to the line. The **Noise** column shows the number of framing errors received on a line; a framing error, such as a missing stop bit, should occur only on console, asynchronous serial, and auxiliary lines.

Figure 5-11 shows two lines that are in use. In-use lines are designated with an asterisk (*) as the first character of the line display. Lines 3 and 5 (VTY 1 and VTY 3) have a connection established to them. Figure 5-12 shows information about Line 5.

To get detailed information for a specific line, we just put the absolute line number as an argument to the **show line** command as shown in Figure 5-12. On Line 6 of Figure 5-12, we see the terminal length is 24

Figure 5-12

Show line output
for individual line.

```
1)   Dallas>show line 5
2)    Tty Typ Tx/Rx  A  Modem Roty AccO AccI  Uses  Noise Overruns
3)   *  5 VTY    -      -     -    -    -     64      0     0/0
4)
5)   Line 5, Location: "", Type: "vt100"
6)   Length: 24 lines, Width: 80 columns
7)   Baud rate (TX/RX) is 9600/9600
8)   Status: Ready, Active, No Exit Banner
9)   Capabilities: none
10)  Modem state: Ready
11)  Special Chars: Escape Hold Stop Start Disconnect Activation
12)                 ^^x   none  -    -     none
13)  Timeouts: Idle EXEC Idle Session Modem Answer Session Dispatch
14)            00:10:00     never                   none   not set
15)  Modem type is unknown.
16)  Session limit is not set.
17)  Time since activation: never
18)  Editing is enabled.
19)  History is enabled, history size is 10.
20)  Full user help is disabled
21)  Allowed transports are pad v120 telnet. Preferred is telnet.
22)  No output characters are padded
23)  No special data dispatching characters
24)  Dallas>
```

lines and the terminal width is 80 characters. These were described in
Section 4.3.6. On Line 12 of the figure, the Escape character is shown as
^^x; this means <Ctrl-Shift-6><x> is the special sequence of characters
the user of this connection can type to suspend it. Line 14 shows that
the EXEC timeout is 10 minutes; after 10 minutes of inactivity on this
line, IOS will kill the connection.

In Figure 5-12, Line 19, we see that this terminal line has the default
command history settings (see Section 4.3.1.1). Line 21 states that the
preferred transport is telnet. In Section 4.3, we learned that the IOS, by
default, assumes that a single word typed on the command line is the
name of a host to which to telnet if the word is not a command.
Configuring the preferred transport on a terminal line controls this
behavior.

We have seen which terminal lines are in use. Suppose we now want
to see who is connected to them. We can use the user mode command
show users to do just that. See Figure 5-13 for an example.

The **show users** command displays the current terminal line connections and their originating location, if applicable. For VTY connections,
the originating location will be the IP address or name of the host from
which the telnet session was established. On Line 3 of Figure 5-13, we

Figure 5-13
Show users output.

```
1)  Dallas>show users
2)      Line      User        Host(s)        Idle Location
3)    3 vty 1                  idle           3 172.16.11.2
4)  * 5 vty 3                  idle           0 euless.tx.witcon.com
5)  Dallas>
```

see that the connection to VTY 1 originated from the host with the address 172.16.11.2; that address belongs to FortWorth, one of our test routers. On Line 4, we see that the connection to VTY 3 came from the host euless.tx.witcon.com. The asterisk in the first column of Line 4 indicates that this connection is the current session where the **show users** command was typed; that is our session.

To see specific information for our current terminal session, we can issue the user mode command **show terminal**. The output will be similar to that shown in Figure 5-12.

5.3   IOS Status

This section covers a few commands we can use to check the operational status of IOS on a router. IOS has many features and resources, and they should be checked on a regular basis.

5.3.1   CPU Utilization

Use the user mode command **show processes cpu** to find out how busy the CPU is and what IOS processes are running, as shown in Figure 5-14.

Line 2 of Figure 5-14 shows CPU utilization averages over the last five seconds, one minute, and five minutes. On the 5-second utilization, there are two numbers separated by forward slashes. The first number is the average utilization and the second number is the percent of CPU time spent processing interrupts, for example, processing packets.

Starting on Line 4 of Figure 5-14, we are shown all of the processes currently running. The display shows the Process ID (PID), name, and statistics for each process. The **Runtime** for a process is the CPU time it has used in milliseconds (ms). The number of times the processes has been invoked is shown in the **Invoked** column, and the **uSecs** columns

Figure 5-14
Show processes
CPU partial output.

```
1)  Dallas>show processes cpu
2)  CPU utilization for five seconds: 6%/4%; one minute: 8%; five
    minutes: 8%
3)    PID Runtime(ms) Invoked uSecs  5Sec  1Min   5Min TTY Process
4)     1          32     233   137  0.00% 0.00% 0.00% 0  Load
                                                          Meter
5)     2        3556    1601  2221  0.00% 1.25% 1.06% 0  Exec
6)     3        2436      69 35304  0.00% 0.12% 0.16% 0  Check
                                                          heaps
7)     4           0       1     0  0.00% 0.00% 0.00% 0  Pool
                                                          Manager
8)  [text omitted]
9)  Dallas>
```

shows the average amount of CPU time, in microseconds (μsec), each invocation has used. If we multiply the number of invocations by the amount of time for each invocation, the result should be the total amount of CPU time used.

If you believe CPU utilization is too high, check the list of processes to determine which one is using the most CPU time. Much of the output is not shown here; there can be hundreds of processes running on a router.

5.3.2 Memory Utilization

Memory—RAM—is one of those resources that is extremely valuable to IOS. Monitoring memory utilization can be done with the user mode commands **show processes memory** and **show memory**. Figure 5-15 shows part of the output from the **show processes memory** command.

In Figure 5-15, Line 2, we see a couple of things very important to the health of our router—how much RAM is being used and how much RAM is free. IOS does not put many constraints on how much RAM a process can use; therefore, it is up to us to keep track of it. After all, we do not want messages like the one below showing up when we attempt something from the console.

```
%% Low on memory; try again later
```

The output in Figure 5-15 shows the processes and their memory statistics. The amount of RAM currently being used by a process is shown in the **Holding** column. If the free memory is constantly going down for no apparent reason, check to see which process is holding more and more memory. That process may have what is called a *memory leak*;

Figure 5-15
Show processes
memory partial
output.

```
1) Dallas>show processes memory
2) Total: 7791452, Used: 1540688, Free: 6250764
3) PID TTY  Allocated   Freed  Holding  Getbufs  Retbufs Process
4)  0   0      34956     1252  1206092        0        0 *Init*
5)  0   0        912    33520      912        0        0 *Sched*
6)  0   0    2196656   796448    59292   444900        0 *Dead*
7)  1   0        268      268     1740        0        0 Load Meter
8)  2   0     212512   111768    45252        0        0 Exec
9)  3   0          0        0     2740        0        0 Check
                                                         heaps
10) 4   0         96        0     2836        0        0 Pool
                                                         Manager

11) [text omitted]
12) 71  0         96     2736     2836        0        0 RIP Send
13) 72  0       6660        0    11072        0        0 RIP
                                                         Router

14)                           1540488 Total
15 Dallas>
```

memory leaks will eventually cause the IOS to run out of RAM and die. We can normally repair memory leaks by upgrading IOS on a router.

To get detailed statistics on memory utilization, use the **show memory** command to show the characteristics for all of the IOS memory blocks. Part of the output from the **show memory** command is in Figure 5-16.

The output shown in Figure 5-16 has three sections: (1) memory utilization, (2) processor memory, and (3) I/O memory. The information in the processor memory and I/O memory sections may be a little more than we really need for normal IOS monitoring. With that in mind, here is a word of warning. The complete output of the show memory command can be lengthy; the output that was used for Figure 5-16 was over 2400 lines before it was cut down. If we set our terminal length to zero (0) to avoid having to deal with the More prompt, we will be waiting a very long time for the output to be displayed on our terminal screen.

The memory utilization section of the Figure 5-16 output is Lines 2 through 4. Memory has been divided into processor (system) memory and I/O (shared) memory. See the show version explanation in Section 5.1 (Figure 5-1, Line 15). The total amount of processor memory is about 5.7 million bytes, and the total amount of I/O memory is about 2 million bytes. The number of bytes used and free for each type of memory is shown also. The sum of free processor memory and free I/O memory is about 6.25 million bytes (see Figure 5-15, Line 2). The **Head** column shows the hex address of the beginning of each memory type. The head of processor memory matches the address of the first memory block

Figure 5-16
Show memory
partial output.

```
1)   Dallas>show memory
2)              Head Total(b) Used(b) Free(b) Lowest(b) Largest(b)
3)   Processor  90CA4 5694300 1079756 4614544  4606572    4614468
4)        I/O  600000 2097152  460952 1636200  1636200    1636032
5)
6)             Processor memory
7)
8)   Address   Bytes Prev.   Next Ref  PrevF NextF Alloc PC What
9)   90CA4     1064  0       910F8 1               319E578 List
                                                           Elements
10)  910F8     2864  90CA4   91C54 1               319E578 List
                                                           Headers
11)  91C54     2664  910F8   926E8 1               314D6CC TTY data
12)  926E8     2000  91C54   92EE4 1               314FA9A TTY
                                                           Input
                                                           Buf
13)  [text omitted]
14)
15)          I/O memory
16)
17)  Address   Bytes  Prev.   Next   Ref PrevF NextF Alloc PC What
18)  600000    260   0       600130  1               3181060 *Packet
                                                             Data*
19)  600130    260   600000  600260  1               3181060 *Packet
                                                             Data*
20)  [text omitted]
21)  Dallas>
```

shown in the processor memory section (Line 9). The head of I/O memory matches the address of the first memory block shown in the I/O memory section (Line 18).

The processor memory and I/O memory sections of the output in Figure 5-16 shows the beginning address, the size in bytes, and the owning process for each block of memory. Again, this is probably more than the average person needs to know.

5.3.3   Buffer Utilization

IOS uses many types of buffers. The most common buffers that we need to keep an eye on are the network packet buffers. There are six types of network packet buffers, each with a different size; some routers have only five types of packet buffers. IOS keeps a pool for each type of buffer. Monitoring these pools is useful during troubleshooting of lost or dropped packets. We can use the user mode command **show buffers** to check the buffer pools. Figure 5-17 shows a sample output.

Figure 5-17

Show buffers
output.

```
1)   Router>show buffers
2)   Buffer elements:
3)       498 in free list (500 max allowed)
4)       32853792 hits, 0 misses, 0 created
5)
6)   Public buffer pools:
7)   Small buffers, 104 bytes (total 120, permanent 120):
8)       115 in free list (20 min, 250 max allowed)
9)       16890500 hits, 238 misses, 646 trims, 646 created
10)      0 failures (0 no memory)
11)  Middle buffers, 600 bytes (total 90, permanent 90):
12)      81 in free list (10 min, 200 max allowed)
13)      6358828 hits, 292 misses, 386 trims, 386 created
14)      11 failures (0 no memory)
15)  Big buffers, 1524 bytes (total 90, permanent 90):
16)      90 in free list (5 min, 300 max allowed)
17)      87900 hits, 0 misses, 0 trims, 0 created
18)      0 failures (0 no memory)
19)  VeryBig buffers, 4520 bytes (total 10, permanent 10):
20)      10 in free list (0 min, 300 max allowed)
21)      323205 hits, 0 misses, 0 trims, 0 created
22)      0 failures (0 no memory)
23)  Large buffers, 5024 bytes (total 10, permanent 10):
24)      10 in free list (0 min, 30 max allowed)
25)      89441 hits, 0 misses, 0 trims, 0 created
26)      0 failures (0 no memory)
27)  Huge buffers, 18024 bytes (total 0, permanent 0):
28)      0 in free list (0 min, 13 max allowed)
29)      249958 hits, 64 misses, 128 trims, 128 created
30)      0 failures (0 no memory)
31)  Router>
```

Each public packet buffer can hold a network packet that is being processed by IOS. When a packet is received, a buffer from the appropriate pool is allocated and the packet is placed into the buffer. The appropriate pool is selected based on the packet's size. The packets are placed into the smallest buffer in which they will fit. The sizes of buffers are described as *Small, Middle, Big, VeryBig, Large,* and *Huge.* Suppose, for example, that a 450-byte packet were received. IOS would allocate a Middle buffer (600 bytes) because a Small buffer (104 bytes) does not have enough space to hold the packet. On the display's first line for each buffer pool are the size of the buffers in the pool, the number of buffers currently in the pool, and the number of permanent buffers in the pool. Permanent buffers are allocated at boot time and are never removed from the pool.

We now examine the Middle buffers in Figure 5-17 to describe the fields of each pool's description. The number in the free list is the number of buffers that are currently not being used, in other words, the number of buffers that do not contain a packet for processing. On Line

11, we see that the pool contains 90 Middle buffers, and on Line 12, we see that 81 of those are available; therefore, we can calculate that 9 Middle buffers are allocated. Also on Line 12, the minimum and maximum number of free Middle buffers allowed is given. The minimum is shown as 10; therefore, if the Middle buffer free list goes below 10, IOS will create more Middle buffers. The maximum is 200; this means that IOS is allowed to have up to 200 Middle buffers if they are needed for a burst of Middle-buffer-sized packets.

On Line 13 of Figure 5-17, we see counters for the number of buffer hits, the number of buffer misses, the number of buffer trims, and the number of buffers created. A *buffer hit* is a successful attempt to allocate a buffer when a packet needs to be placed in one. A *buffer miss* is an unsuccessful attempt to allocate a buffer; this is the result of not having enough buffers in the free list. A buffer miss usually results in a new buffer being created unless the maximum number of buffers allowed has been reached. The number of *buffer trims* is the number of buffers that are destroyed because they are no longer being used. The number of buffers that are created is the times a buffer was created as a result of a buffer miss. Line 14 shows the number of failures; this is the number of times that a buffer allocation failed as a result of not having had a free buffer and not creating another buffer to accommodate the request. The **no memory** counter shows the number of failures resulting from not having enough memory.

5.3.4   Stacks

The user mode command **show stacks** shows information that only a programmer could love; however, if a router crashes, the **show stacks** command provides information that is valuable for finding out what caused the crash. Figure 5-18 shows a sample output after a crash.

Lines 23 through 35 have information that can be used to trace the cause of the crash. The Cisco TAC will most likely ask for the output of the **show stacks** command if you call them after a router crashes and reboots.

5.3.5   Routing and Bridging Tables

Routing and bridging tables are stored in RAM. IOS maintains a routing table for each routed network protocol that has been configured on a

Figure 5-18
Show stacks output
after a crash.

```
1)   Router>show stacks
2)   Minimum process stacks:
3)   Free/Size   Name
4)   1020/2000   Router Init
5)   2832/4000   Init
6)   1468/2000   RADIUS INITCONFIG
7)   2056/3000   IP-EIGRP Router
8)   1396/2000   IP-EIGRP Hello
9)   2400/4000   Exec
10)  2012/3000   IGRP Router
11)  1968/3000   OSPF Router
12)   848/2000   OSPF Hello
13)  1688/2000   OSPF Scanner
14)
15)  Interrupt level stacks:
16)  Level   Called   Unused/Size   Name
17)   1          0     3000/3000    CL-CD2430 transmit interrupts
18)   2          0     3000/3000    CL-CD2430 receive interrupts
19)   3          6     2772/3000    Serial interface state change
                                    interrupt
20)   4      18305     2476/3000    Network interfaces
21)   5     130161     2872/3000    Console Uart
22)
23)  System was restarted by bus error at PC 0x384B3DE, address
     0xD0D0D0D
24)  2500 Software (C2500-JS-L), Version 11.3(2), RELEASE SOFTWARE
     (fc1)
25)  Compiled Mon 23-Feb-98 22:38 by ccai (current version)
26)  Image text-base: 0x03048154, data-base: 0x00001000
27)
28)
29)  Stack trace from system failure:
30)  FP: 0x19DB50, RA: 0x323F774
31)  FP: 0x19DB6C, RA: 0x31912D6
32)  FP: 0x19DB88, RA: 0x3148F46
33)  FP: 0x19DBA8, RA: 0x31496B8
34)  FP: 0x19DBDC, RA: 0x315BBCE
35)  FP: 0x19DC18, RA: 0x31A7E52
36)
37)  *****************************************************
38)  ******* Information of Last System Crash **********
39)  *****************************************************
40)
41)  Router>
```

router. Without a routing table for a network protocol, IOS cannot route packets for that protocol. If bridging has been configured on a router, IOS maintains a bridging table; without a bridging table, IOS cannot bridge frames. We can examine these tables with the user mode commands **show route** and **show bridge**.

The **show route** command requires a protocol keyword before the word **route**. The protocol keyword tells IOS which routing table it should display. The general form of the command looks like this:

Figure 5-19

Show ip route
output.

```
1)  Dallas>show ip route
2)  Codes: C - connected, S - static, I - IGRP, R - RIP,
           M - mobile, B - BGP
3)         D - EIGRP, EX - EIGRP external, O - OSPF, IA - OSPF
           inter area
4)         N1 - OSPF NSSA external type 1, N2 - OSPF NSSA
           external type 2
5)         E1 - OSPF external type 1, E2 - OSPF external type 2,
           E - EGP
6)         i - IS-IS, L1 - IS-IS level-1, L2 - IS-IS level-2,
           * - candidate default
7)         U - per-user static route, o - ODR
8)
9)  Gateway of last resort is not set
10)
11)     172.16.0.0/24 is subnetted, 3 subnets
12) R      172.16.20.0 [120/1] via 172.16.11.2, 00:00:05, Serial1
13) C      172.16.10.0 is directly connected, Ethernet0
14) C      172.16.11.0 is directly connected, Serial1
15) Dallas>
```

show *protocol* **route**

where *protocol* is the name of a routed protocol such as **ip, ipx, appletalk,** or **decnet**. For example, to examine the IP routing table, the complete command is **show ip route**; Figure 5-19 shows the result.

A routing table shows all of the routes, or networks, that IOS has learned. The routing table display starts with a legend that explains the abbreviations that appear in the first column of each route in the table. This routing table from our router Dallas shows two directly connected routes and one RIP-learned route. The RIP-learned route is the Ethernet LAN on FortWorth (see Figure 3-3). We can get a summary of the IP routing table with the **show ip route summary** command. Figure 5-20 shows a sample output.

Figure 5-20 shows counters for the sources of routes in the IP routing table along with the amount of memory that the routing table is using.

Figure 5-20

Show ip route
summary output.

```
1) Dallas>show ip route summary
2) Route Source   Networks   Subnets   Overhead   Memory (bytes)
3) connected      0          2         104        368
4) static         0          0         0          0
5) rip            0          1         52         184
6) internal       1                               138
7) Total          1          3         156        690
8) Dallas>
```

The routing and bridging tables are described in more detail in the protocol configuration chapters.

5.3.6 Logging

Logging allows IOS to inform us when a system event has taken place by sending a message to defined logging locations. By default, all logged messages are sent to the console port. There is also a buffer in RAM where the most recent messages are stored; however, this buffer is small and will wrap when it fills up. When the buffer wraps, old messages are purged to make room for new messages.

There are eight levels of logging numbered from 0 through 7. The lower the level number, the more serious the condition being reported in the message. The eight levels are normally configured by their names. Table 5-2 shows the logging level numbers and their names.

The level descriptions in Table 5-2 are straight out of the IOS context-sensitive help facility. Logged messages for levels 0 through 6 always start with a percent sign (%) and contain a facility code, the severity level number, a mnemonic code, and the message itself. The facility code identifies the part of the router (process or device) to which the message refers. The severity level number is a level number from 0 to 7 that indicates the severity of the situation being reported by the message. The mnemonic code identifies an individual error message for the facility. The message itself is just a text string that describes what happened or what is happening. If we want, we can have IOS add a timestamp to the message. The timestamp can be either the relative time since the router booted or the absolute time from the router's clock.

TABLE 5-2

Logging Levels

Level Number	Level Name	Level Description
0	Emergencies	System is unusable
1	Alerts	Immediate action needed
2	Critical	Critical conditions
3	Errors	Error conditions
4	Warnings	Warning conditions
5	Notifications	Normal but significant conditions
6	Informational	Informational messages
7	Debugging	Debugging messages

The user mode command **show logging** shows the types of logging that can be configured and displays the logged messages that have been buffered. Figure 5-21 shows logging information from Dallas soon after it booted.

There are several locations to which messages can be logged. Some of these are as follows:

- Syslog server
- Console terminal
- Monitor terminal
- Buffer
- SNMP management station

Syslog logging (Figure 5-21, Line 2) sends message to an IP host running a syslog server; typically this is a UNIX host running syslogd. Messages are logged to the syslog server only if the severity level of the message is less than or equal to the configured trap level (*informational* on Line 5) and if the IP address of the host has been defined in the IOS configuration.

Console logging (Figure 5-21, Line 3) sends messages to the console. By default all messages for all severity levels are logged to the console. If console logging is enabled, the **show logging** command shows the highest level of messages that are to be sent to the console. Line 3 shows this to be *debugging,* the default.

Monitor logging (Figure 5-21, Line 4) sends message to a monitor terminal. There are no monitor terminals until we create them. Monitor terminals can be used to view the console message output on a VTY terminal line. We can give a terminal the monitor functionality by issuing the privileged mode command **terminal monitor**. When a terminal is a monitor, it has the capability of receiving logging output for the message with a severity up to the defined level. The defined monitor logging level on Line 4 is *debugging;* therefore, all logged messages will be sent to a monitor terminal.

Buffer logging (Figure 5-21, Line 6) sends messages to the buffer in RAM as long as the severity level of the messages are less than or equal to the defined level (*debugging* on Line 6).

SNMP logging sends messages to an SNMP management station for processing by a network management application.

On Line 8 of Figure 5-21, we see that the log buffer is 4 kB. In Lines 10 through 33, the router's interfaces changed states until they all ended up as administratively down. The severity level for the LINK

Figure 5-21
Show logging
output.

```
1)  Dallas>show logging
2)  Syslog logging: enabled (0 messages dropped, 0 flushes,
    0 overruns)
3)      Console logging: level debugging, 37 messages logged
4)      Monitor logging: level debugging, 0 messages logged
5)      Trap logging: level informational, 41 message lines
        logged
6)      Buffer logging: level debugging, 37 messages logged
7)
8)  Log Buffer (4096 bytes):
9)
10) %LINK-3-UPDOWN: Interface BRI0, changed state to up
11) %LINK-3-UPDOWN: Interface Ethernet0, changed state to up
12) %LINK-3-UPDOWN: Interface Serial0, changed state to down
13) %LINK-3-UPDOWN: Interface Serial1, changed state to up
14) %LINK-3-UPDOWN: Interface Serial2, changed state to up
15) %LINK-3-UPDOWN: Interface Serial3, changed state to down
16) %LINEPROTO-5-UPDOWN: Line protocol on Interface BRI0, changed
    state to down
17) %LINEPROTO-5-UPDOWN: Line protocol on Interface BRI0:1,
    changed state to down
18) %LINEPROTO-5-UPDOWN: Line protocol on Interface BRI0:2,
    changed state to down
19) %LINEPROTO-5-UPDOWN: Line protocol on Interface Ethernet0,
    changed state to up
20) %LINEPROTO-5-UPDOWN: Line protocol on Interface Serial0,
    changed state to down
21) %LINEPROTO-5-UPDOWN: Line protocol on Interface Serial1,
    changed state to up
22) %LINEPROTO-5-UPDOWN: Line protocol on Interface Serial2,
    changed state to up
23) %LINEPROTO-5-UPDOWN: Line protocol on Interface Serial3,
    changed state to down
24) %LINEPROTO-5-UPDOWN: Line protocol on Interface Serial1,
    changed state to down
25) %LINEPROTO-5-UPDOWN: Line protocol on Interface Serial2,
    changed state to down
26) %LINK-3-UPDOWN: Interface Serial1, changed state to down
27) %LINEPROTO-5-UPDOWN: Line protocol on Interface Ethernet0,
    changed state to down
28) %LINK-5-CHANGED: Interface BRI0, changed state to
    administratively down
29) %LINK-5-CHANGED: Interface Serial0, changed state to
    administratively down
30) %LINK-5-CHANGED: Interface Ethernet0, changed state to
    administratively down
31) %LINK-5-CHANGED: Interface Serial1, changed state to
    administratively down
32) %LINK-5-CHANGED: Interface Serial2, changed state to
    administratively down
33) %LINK-5-CHANGED: Interface Serial3, changed state to
    administratively down
34) %IP-5-WEBINST_KILL: Terminating DNS process
35) %SYS-5-RESTART: System restarted —
36) Cisco Internetwork Operating System Software
37) IOS (tm) 2500 Software (C2500-JS-L), Version 11.3(5), RELEASE
    SOFTWARE (fc1)
```

Figure 5-21

Show logging output (cont.).

```
38) Copyright (c) 1986-1998 by Cisco Systems, Inc.39) Compiled Tue
    11-Aug-98 04:06 by phanguye
40) %LINK-3-UPDOWN: Interface BRI0:1, changed state to down
41) %LINK-3-UPDOWN: Interface BRI0:2, changed state to down
42) %SYS-5-CONFIG_I: Configured from console by console
43) %SYS-5-CONFIG_I: Configured from console by console
44) %LINEPROTO-5-UPDOWN: Line protocol on Interface Ethernet0,
    changed state to up
45) %LINK-3-UPDOWN: Interface Ethernet0, changed state to up
46) %LINK-3-UPDOWN: Interface Serial1, changed state to up
47) %SYS-5-CONFIG_I: Configured from console by console
48) %LINEPROTO-5-UPDOWN: Line protocol on Interface Serial1,
    changed state to up
49) %AT-6-ONLYROUTER: Ethernet0: AppleTalk interface enabled;
    no neighbors found
50) %AT-6-CONFIGOK: Serial1: AppleTalk interface enabled;
    verified by 1001.200
51) Dallas>
```

facility messages is 3, Errors; the LINK facility is used for physical layer status of interfaces. The severity level of the LINEPROTO facility messages is a 5, Notification; this is not as severe as the LINK facility message since LINEPROTO indicates a data link problem rather than a physical problem. At Line 35 is the message about the system restarting; the severity level for the RESTART message is 5, Notification. Lines 49 and 50 have AppleTalk messages with severity level 6, Informational. Before AppleTalk becomes operational on an interface, it must locate neighboring AppleTalk devices and verify the cable range and zone(s) for the network to which the interface is attached.

5.3.7 Time

Every Cisco router has a system clock, and some routers like the high-end, 7x00-series routers have a battery-powered, system calendar. If the router does not have a calendar, the clock is set to midnight (00:00) on March 1, 1993 each time the router boots; otherwise, the clock is set from the calendar time when the router boots.

On a running router, several ways are available for setting the system clock. For example, the clock can be set manually by using the privileged mode **clock** command or automatically by using *Network Time Protocol* (NTP).

To check the system clock, issue the user mode command **show clock**. Figures 5-22 and 5-23 are two samples of the **show clock** command.

Figure 5-22
Show clock output
nonauthoritative.

```
1)  Dallas>show clock
2)  *00:26:09.327 UTC Mon Mar 1 1993
3)  Dallas>
```

Figure 5-22
Show clock output
nonauthoritative.

Figure 5-23
Show clock output
authoritative.

```
1)  Dallas>show clock
2)  12:37:15.901 CST Wed Nov 18 1998
3)  Dallas>
```

Figure 5-23
Show clock output
authoritative.

The hours, minutes, seconds, and milliseconds are shown from the system clock. There is also the time zone, month, day, and year. Since Dallas is a 2520 router, it has no battery-powered calendar; therefore, its system clock was set to midnight of March 1, 1993, when it booted. According to the time on Line 2 of Figure 5-22, Dallas has been running for 26 minutes and 9 seconds. The time zone is shown at *UTC*, which stands for Coordinated Universal Time, and is the default time zone. UTC is sometimes referred to as *Greenwich Mean Time* (GMT) or *Zulu time* in other texts. Any other time zone must be manually configured. The asterisk (*) in Line 2 means that the time is not authoritative; IOS doesn't believe that the time is accurate.

If IOS is configured to get its time from a timing source such as an NTP server, the clock will be shown as authoritative once the router's system clock has synchronized with the time learned through NTP.

Figure 5-23, Line 2, shows the time with no extra character (such as an asterisk) in front of it. This indicates that the time is believed to be accurate (authoritative). An authoritative clock can be used to synchronize clocks on other host systems. The time zone is CST (Central Standard Time); this was set in the configuration file.

5.3.8 Protocols

The easiest way to see what routed protocols have been configured on a router is to issue the user mode command **show protocols**, which tells us all the routed protocols that IOS has been configured to run and all the interfaces' status and primary routed protocol information. Figure 5-24 shows an output of the **show protocols** command from Dallas.

Figure 5-24

Show protocols
output.

```
1)   Dallas>show protocols
2)   Global values:
3)     Internet Protocol routing is enabled
4)     Appletalk routing is enabled
5)     IPX routing is enabled
6)   BRI0 is administratively down, line protocol is down
7)   BRI0:1 is administratively down, line protocol is down
8)   BRI0:2 is administratively down, line protocol is down
9)   Ethernet0 is up, line protocol is up
10)    Internet address is 172.16.10.1/24
11)    AppleTalk address is 100.10, zone Headquarters
12)    IPX address is AC100A00.0010.7b3a.d4bf
13)  Serial0 is administratively down, line protocol is down
14)  Serial1 is up, line protocol is up
15)    Internet address is 172.16.11.1/24
16)    AppleTalk address is 1001.100, zone WAN
17)    IPX address is AC100B00.0010.7b3a.d4bf
18)  Serial2 is administratively down, line protocol is down
19)  Serial3 is administratively down, line protocol is down
20)  Dallas>
```

The output has two main sections: global values and interface values. The *global values* section shows the routed protocols. This is global because the protocols are turned on in global configuration mode. Dallas is running IP, AppleTalk, and IPX (Figure 5-24, Lines 3, 4, and 5, respectively). The *interface values* section begins on Line 6. The status of all interfaces is given; interfaces Ethernet0 and Serial1 are up/up; all others are administratively down. For those interfaces that have been configured with routed protocol parameters, the output includes the primary parameters. As an example, let us examine the Ethernet0 parameters given. Line 10 has the primary IP address and prefix length (network mask); Line 11 has the AppleTalk address and primary zone; Line 12 has the IPX address.

Using the **show protocols** command is a way to get all of the different protocol addresses for a router's interfaces. These come in handy for network documentation and troubleshooting.

To get specific information about a routed protocol on an interface, we can use the **show interface** command that includes a protocol keyword. The command looks like this:

show *protocol* **interface**

where *protocol* is the name of a routed protocol such as **ip, ipx, appletalk**, or **decnet**. For example, to get specific AppleTalk information about all interfaces, the complete command is **show appletalk**

interface. Examples of these commands will be given in the protocol configuration chapters.

5.3.9 Environment

High-end routers like those in the 7x00-series have environmental controllers that monitor things like temperatures and voltage levels in a router; if the temperature gets too high or too low or if voltage levels get too far from normal, the router will be shut down. The user mode commands **show environment** and **show environment all** display information about the environmental conditions on a router that has an environmental controller. Figure 5-25 has output from both commands issued on a 7505 router.

The **show environment** command gives a status of environmental conditions. Line 2 of Figure 5-25 tells us that all measured values are normal. If we add the **all** keyword to the command, we get environmental condition details. Line 14 shows the temperatures taken at the router's RSP4. Air being pulled into the chassis is 78 degrees Fahrenheit (F) and air being blown out is 113 degrees F. Lines 18 through 22 show actual voltage levels of the router's test points.

Figure 5-25

Show environment [all] output.

```
 1)  Router>show environment
 2)  All measured values are normal
 3)  Router>show environment all
 4)  Arbiter type 1, backplane type 7505 (id 1)
 5)  Power supply #1 is 600W AC (id 1)
 6)  Active fault conditions: none
 7)  Active trip points: Restart_Inhibit
 8)  15 of 15 soft shutdowns remaining before hard shutdown
 9)
10)          01234
11) Dbus slots:  XX
12)
13)    card     inlet     hotpoint     exhaust
14) RSP(4)  26C/78F    38C/100F     45C/113F
15)
16) Shutdown  temperature  source  is  'hotpoint'  on  RSP(4),
    requested RSP(4)
17)
18) + 12V measured at 12.21
19) + 5V measured at 5.15
20) -12V measured at -11.98
21) + 24V measured at 23.68
22) + 2.5 reference is 2.49
23)
24) Router>
```

5.4 Configuration Files

All of the **show** commands we have used so far can be issued in user mode; however, sometimes the easiest way to see how a router is configured is to just look at its configuration files. Since the configuration files contain sensitive information like passwords and SNMP community names, we must be in privileged mode to view them.

The two configuration files are the running configuration and the startup configuration. The *running configuration* is the current, active configuration of IOS, and it is kept in RAM. The *startup configuration* is the backup configuration, and it is stored in NVRAM so that IOS can read it into RAM during a boot. We can look at the contents of both files; under normal, stable production conditions the files should be identical.

IOS always has a running configuration, even when all interfaces are disabled (shut down); however, a startup configuration does not always exist. For example, a new router does not have a startup configuration. If a startup configuration is not present in NVRAM, the router will ask to enter the System Configuration Dialog.

5.4.1 Running Configuration

The command to view the running configuration is **show running config**. This is a privileged mode command. Figure 5-26 contains the output of the **show runningconfig** command on Dallas.

On Line 2, there is the message "Building configuration . . . ." To display the running configuration, IOS must examine all of its settings and put them into an easily readable, text format. Depending on a router's processor speed, this configuration file build could take from 1 to 5 seconds. After the build, the file itself is displayed. IOS separates the sections of the file with exclamation points (!) to make the file easier to read.

Line 9 shows the command that set the router's host name to Dallas. This host name appears in the command prompt in Line 1. Notice also that the prompt ends with a number sign (#) signifying privileged mode.

Line 11 has the enable secret password. The enable secret password is used to get into privileged mode. The value we assigned to it during the initial configuration is *itsasecret*; however, that is not what the configuration file shows—not exactly, anyway. The enable secret password is displayed in its encrypted form in an IOS configuration file. Most network managers and administrators make a practice of keeping copies of

Figure 5-26

Show running-config output on Dallas.

```
1)   Dallas#show running-config
2)   Building configuration...
3)
4)   Current configuration:
5)   !
6)   version 11.3
7)   no service password-encryption
8)   !
9)   hostname Dallas
10)  !
11)  enable secret 5 $1$S.px$gAcVrJaShGu2x6Rvu/F1C/
12)  enable password enableme
13)  !
14)  appletalk routing
15)  ipx routing 0010.7b3a.d4bf
16)  !
17)  interface Ethernet0
18)   ip address 172.16.10.1 255.255.255.0
19)   no lat enabled
20)   appletalk cable-range 100-109 100.10
21)   appletalk zone Headquarters
22)   ipx network AC100A00
23)   no mop enabled
24)  !
25)  interface Serial0
26)   no ip address
27)   shutdown
28)  !
29)  interface Serial1
30)   ip address 172.16.11.1 255.255.255.0
31)   appletalk cable-range 1001-1001 1001.100
32)   appletalk zone WAN
33)   ipx network AC100B00
34)  !
35)  interface Serial2
36)   no ip address
37)   shutdown
38)  !
39)  interface Serial3
40)   no ip address
41)   shutdown
42)  !
43)  interface BRI0
44)   no ip address
45)   shutdown
46)  !
47)  router rip
48)   network 172.16.0.0
49)  !
50)  ip classless
51)  !
52)  line con 0
53)  line aux 0
54)  line vty 0 4
55)   password letmein
56)   login
```

```
57)  !
58)  end
59)
60)  Dallas#
```

their routers' running configurations on their PCs, on a TFTP server, or even on hardcopy. Notice the other passwords on Lines 12 and 55; they are easily read in their unencrypted form, which is the default way they are displayed. Without the enable secret password being encrypted, anyone with access to the disk drive files or paper files of the configurations would know all of the passwords. This is not considered to be very secure.

The next major section of the configuration in Figure 5-26 is where the routed protocols get turned on. The command telling IOS to route AppleTalk packets is on Line 14 and the command telling IOS to route IPX packets is on Line 15. We saw in Figure 5-24 that Dallas is also routing IP packets; however, the configuration file does not show a command telling IOS to route IP packets. Most of the time, a running configuration file will not contain commands for default settings. The routing of IP packets is turned on by default in IOS; therefore, the command telling IOS to route IP packets (**ip routing**) is not shown.

As another example of this, look at the configuration sections for interface Ethernet0 (beginning on Line 18) and Serial0 (beginning on Line 26). The **shutdown** command on Line 27 is used to turn off an interface and put it into administratively down state. The opposite of **shutdown** is **no shutdown**. (Remember Section 4.3.5. Just say no.) There is not a **no shutdown** command under the Ethernet0 configuration section. The reason is that, by default, an interface is turned on, and the default setting is not in the configuration file.

According to Lines 47 and 48, Dallas is running the IP RIP routing protocol on its interfaces that have addresses in the 172.16.0.0 network; that is all of them.

5.4.2 Startup Configuration

The *startup configuration* is a text file stored in NVRAM. When a router boots, IOS looks in NVRAM for the file and then loads the file into RAM where its commands are entered into the running configuration. Issue

Figure 5-27
Show startup-
config output with
NVRAM empty on
Dallas.

```
1) Dallas#show startup-config
2) %% Non-volatile configuration memory has not been set up or
   has bad checksum
3) Dallas#
```

the privileged mode command **show startup-config** to view the startup configuration file. If we bypass the System Configuration Dialog on a new router, NVRAM will remain empty. Figure 5-27 shows that output of the **show startup-config** command when NVRAM is empty.

Figure 5-26 shows the running configuration; however, Figure 5-27 shows that we have no startup configuration. The command to create a startup configuration from the running configuration is as follows:

```
Dallas#copy running-config startup-config
Building configuration...
[OK]
Dallas#
```

The **copy running-config startup-config** privileged mode command will create the running configuration text file and then put that file into NVRAM. Figure 5-28 shows part of the output from the **show startup-config** now that there is a startup configuration.

Since the startup configuration is already in text format and ready for display, there is no delay associated with preparing for output. Instead, the first message we get refers to the size of the startup configuration file and the size of NVRAM. According to Line 2 of Figure 5-28, the size of Dallas's startup configuration file is 833 bytes, and Dallas has 32762

Figure 5-28
Show startup-
config partial
output on Dallas.

```
1) Dallas#show startup-config
2) Using 833 out of 32762 bytes
3) !
4) version 11.3
5) no service password-encryption
6) !
7) hostname Dallas
8) [text omitted]
9) Dallas#
```

total bytes of NVRAM (see also Figure 5-1, Line 26, for the amount of Dallas's NVRAM).

5.5   Conclusion

The **show** command in all of its different forms is the most used command in IOS. We have barely scratched the surface of the information available using **show**. More detailed, protocol-specific information is covered in the configuration chapters.

One more general **show** command that you find may useful for fast information gathering is the privileged mode command **show tech-support**, which runs multiple preconfigured **show** commands one after the other. For example, it will issue the **show version, show running-config, show controllers, show interfaces,** and a few other commands in quick succession. The command will also temporarily set you terminal length to zero (0) thus disabling the More prompt and causing the information to scroll very fast. The output of the **show tech-support** command is meant to be captured to a log file by your terminal emulation software and then sent to the Cisco TAC. The resulting file provides them (and us) with an overview of a router's configuration and status.

General
IOS Tasks

This chapter covers those tasks that are not really specific to the configuration of a network protocol. Management and troubleshooting tasks fall into that category. We also need to cover in a little more detail the steps necessary to configure interfaces and terminal lines since there are so many types of them.

6.1 Simple Management Configuration Tasks

Just like on any other network host, a router needs certain items that uniquely identify it and make it easier to manage.

6.1.1 Host Name

All routers must have a host name. The suggested guidelines were covered in Section 3.2.1; basically you can make the host name anything you want, but we suggest that it conform to the rules for Internet domain names specified in *RFC 1035*.

The default host name is *Router*; however, you should always change it to something unique. Use the global configuration command **hostname** to change a router's name. The **hostname** command has a single argument, which is the word the host name should be. Here is an example.

```
Dallas(config)#hostname Philadelphia
Philadelphia(config)#
```

By default, IOS puts the first 29 characters of the host name into the command line prompt of all modes. This allows us to tell immediately which router we are logged in to. When we are administering multiple routers in an internetwork, knowing which router we are looking at is extremely important. We would not want to shut down an interface or change an address on the wrong router, would we?

The default prompt can be no longer than 30 characters; this can cause a problem with the configuration mode prompts if the assigned host is more than about 15 characters. For example, let us set the host name to *PhiladelphiaRouterNumber1*.

```
Philadelphia(config)#hostname PhiladelphiaRouterNumber1
PhiladelphiaRouterNumber1(co)#<Ctrl-Z>
PhiladelphiaRouterNumber1#
```

A normal prompt in global configuration mode has the letters *config* in parentheses. Since the host name is so long, the parentheses now contain only *co*. The will prevent us from determining our specific configuration mode by just looking at the prompt. The new host name is completely shown in the global configuration mode prompt and the privileged mode prompt. Let us change the host name back to its original value.

```
PhiladelphiaRouterNumber1#configure terminal
Enter configuration commands, one per line.  End with CNTL/Z.
PhiladelphiaRouterNumber1(co)#hostname Dallas
Dallas(config)#
```

Remember to give each router a unique name. Even though Internet domain names are not case sensitive when referenced in *Domain Name Service* (DNS), the host name is displayed exactly as you typed it.

6.1.2   Banners

An IOS banner is used to give information to users or administrators when they log in to a router via a terminal line. We are going to cover three types of banners.

1. MOTD (Message Of The Day)
2. Login
3. Exec

An *MOTD* banner is sent to a terminal as soon as the terminal's connection becomes active. A *login* banner is also sent to a terminal when a terminal becomes active; however, the login banner is displayed after an MOTD banner (if there is one). An *exec* banner is displayed to a terminal immediately after a person has successfully logged in.

We use the global configuration mode command banner to create a banner; its general form looks like this.

```
banner {exec | login | motd} dc message dc
```

The argument *dc* is a delimiting character. The delimiting characters surround the message that is to be displayed to the person logging in. Each instance of *dc* must be the same within the entry of the banner. The delimiting character can be any character as long as it is not part of the message. The **banner** command should include one of the arguments

exec, **login**, and **motd**; however, all three types of banners can be created by issuing the **banner** command three times—one for each type.

Banners can have multiple lines. To create a multiple-line banner, type the command up to and including the first delimiting character, and press <Enter>. You will be given a blank line to type the banner message. When you have finished with the banner message, just type the delimiting character and <Enter> again.

Examples of banner creation are shown below.

```
FortWorth(config)#banner motd %
Enter TEXT message.  End with the character '%'.
This is the motd banner.
System maintenance is scheduled for today at 1700 GMT.
%
FortWorth(config)#banner login %
Enter TEXT message. End with the character '%'.
This is the login banner.
You have accessed a private system.
Unauthorized access is prohibited.
If you don't belong here, leave.
%
FortWorth(config)#banner exec %
Enter TEXT message. End with the character '%'.
This is the exec banner.
So, you got in. So what! Who cares!
They're coming to take you away.
%
FortWorth(config)#
```

We have created each type of banner. The percent sign (%) was used as the delimiting character. Everything between the percent signs is the banner. When the configuration is displayed, IOS uses its own standard delimiter. Figure 6-1 shows the part of the running configuration containing the banners.

Notice in Figure 6-1 that the banners are shown in an order different from the one in which we typed them. The configuration file order does not really matter to the banner function. The delimiting character is shown as the character pair ^C, which is IOS's way of displaying <Ctrl-C>. This could be significant if you get into the habit of typing exactly what you see from a configuration file onto the IOS configuration mode command line. Figure 6-2 shows how the banners look when we telnet from Dallas to Fort Worth.

The MOTD banner is displayed first on Line 4. The login banner is sent to the terminal starting on Line 7. We have not logged in yet; however, we have a connection. After typing the correct password (Line 15), the exec banner is displayed on Line 16 before we get a user mode prompt.

Figure 6-1

Banners in configuration file.

```
1) FortWorth#show running-config
2) [text omitted]
3) !
4) banner exec ^C
5) This is the exec banner.
6) So, you got in. So what! Who cares!
7) They're coming to take you away.
8) ^C
9) banner login ^C
10) This is the login banner.
11) You have accessed a private system.
12) Unauthorized access is prohibited.
13) If you don't belong here, leave.
14) ^C
15) banner motd ^C
16) This is the motd banner.
17) System maintenance is scheduled for today at 1700 GMT.
18) ^C
19) !
20) [text omitted]
21) FortWorth#
```

Figure 6-2

Banner output at login.

```
1)  Dallas>telnet 172.16.11.2
2)  Trying 172.16.11.2 ... Open
3)
4)  This is the motd banner.
5)  System maintenance is scheduled for today at 1700 GMT.
6)
7)  This is the login banner.
8)  You have accessed a private system.
9)  Unauthorized access is prohibited.
10) If you don't belong here, leave.
11)
12)
13) User Access Verification
14)
15) Password: letmein
16) This is the exec banner.
17) So, you got in. So what! Who cares!
18) They're coming to take you away.
19)
20) FortWorth>
```

Since there is always a chance that an unauthorized person will gain access to your routers, the banners should contain very strong language that allows you to prosecute them. You may want to get your company's legal department involved in writing a banner that will hold up in a court of law.

There is one caveat about the login banner. It is not displayed unless the **login** command (Sections 6.1.3.1 and 6.3.1) is part of the terminal line configuration.

6.1.3 Passwords

IOS has many passwords—they are all used to protect IOS from unauthorized entry. We are going to cover the ones used to grant access to user mode and privileged mode.

IOS passwords are case-sensitive and can be no longer than 25 characters. The characters can be any combination of uppercase and lowercase letters, numeric digits, punctuation marks, and spaces; however, the first character cannot be a space.

6.1.3.1 User Mode Access

Access to user mode is configured on terminal lines such as the console or the VTYs; therefore the command to enter passwords for user mode access will be entered in line configuration mode. Each terminal line can have its own password; however, assigning a different password to every terminal line may not be in our best interests.

Two line configuration mode commands are required to assign a password to a line and have IOS check the password before granting access. The commands are **password** and **login**. The **login** command entered on a terminal line tells IOS to perform authentication (check for a password). The password itself is an argument of the **password** command. An example is shown below.

```
Dallas(config-line)#password letmein
Dallas(config-line)#login
Dallas(config-line)#
```

This example sets a line's password to *letmein* and tells IOS to authenticate an incoming connection by making the user of the connection type the correct password at a password prompt.

During the System Configuration Dialog in Chapter 3, only the VTY terminal lines were assigned passwords. All five VTYs (0 through 4) were given the same password, *letmein*. Usually, all VTY lines are given the same password. VTYs are allocated in order for incoming telnet connections; we can only guess which VTY will be given to us when we telnet to a router. We get three chances to type a VTY line's correct password before IOS terminates our telnet connection. We then have to establish another telnet connection; we may be given a different VTY than we had the time before. If all VTYs have different passwords, our password guessing exercise could take a long time. The more VTYs the router has, the longer it could take to type the correct password and get in, even if we know all the passwords.

If a router's VTY lines are not password protected, no one will be able to telnet to the router. This effectively disables telnet access completely. IOS attempts to save us from ourselves by not leaving the doors to our router wide open.

The console and auxiliary lines can also be given a password. Protecting a router's console port with a password is a recommended practice, especially if physical access to the router is unsecured. If a modem has been installed on the auxiliary port, the auxiliary port should definitely have a password.

Configuring locally assigned passwords is not the only way of granting user mode access. We can also control user mode access using CiscoSecure (TACACS+) or Radius. These access mechanisms require an external server and are not covered here.

6.1.3.2 Privileged Mode Access

Remember that a person in user mode cannot do much harm to a router; the person can essentially look but not touch. Just about anything except the configuration files can be displayed from user mode. Once someone has been granted access to privileged mode, that person can do whatever he or she wants to do, such as shut down an interface, change a password, or reboot the router. For this reason, IOS has passwords for privileged mode access.

There are two passwords for granting access to privileged mode. Both are forms of the enable password. There is the regular enable password, which is by default shown in clear text in a configuration file, and there is the enable secret password, which is always shown as encrypted in a configuration file.

The commands to set the enable passwords are both global configuration commands. The **enable password** command creates or changes the regular enable password and the **enable secret** command creates or changes the enable secret password. Both commands take the actual password as an argument.

The enable secret password overrides the enable password. If an enable secret password is in the running configuration, it is used to get to privileged mode and the enable password is ignored. The enable password is used only if the enable secret password does not exist or if the IOS image does not support the enable secret password.

If the running configuration contains neither type of the enable password, a user on a console terminal will not be prompted for a password after typing the **enable** command to get to privileged mode. On the other hand, if neither type of enable password exists, a user who has established a telnet session to the router will not be allowed to enter privileged mode unless a password has been assigned to the router's console terminal. In that case, the console password is used to enter privileged mode. If we run the System Configuration Dialog, IOS forces us to set both types of enable passwords but not a console password.

The enable secret and enable passwords should have different values. It does no good to encrypt one of the passwords if you have the unencrypted version of the password right next to it. If you attempt to make the passwords identical, IOS will complain to you and ask you to make them different; however, IOS will allow them to be the same. Look at the following example.

```
Router(config)#enable secret itsasecret
Router(config)#enable password itsasecret
The enable password you have chosen is the same as your enable secret.
This is not recommended. Re-enter the enable password.

Router(config)#
```

The IOS tells us to reenter the enable password if we make it the same as the enable secret password, but if we examine the running configuration, we see that the enable password was accepted. Figure 6-3 shows this.

Lines 4 and 5 of Figure 6-3 show the password *itsasecret* in its encrypted form and its unencrypted (clear text) form. The enable secret password cannot be understood by someone who is looking over your shoulder while you are reading the running configuration file.

Figure 6-3

Enable passwords in configuration file.

```
1)  Router#show running-config
2)  [text omitted]
3)  !
4)  enable secret 5 $1$hEby$WJlwC0Vp/VQEC4Hcxc0Dg/
5)  enable password itsasecret
6)  !
7)  [text omitted]
8)  Router#
```

The three types of passwords that we have talked about so far—line, enable secret, enable—should all have different values.

6.1.3.3 Encryption

IOS allows us to encrypt all of our passwords in the configuration files. The default is to have only the enable secret password encrypted. The encryption algorithm used for the enable secret password is one-way; IOS cannot decrypt the password.

If we would like the other passwords encrypted in the configuration file, we can start the IOS password-encryption service. We use the global configuration command **service password-encryption** to start the service. This service will use a two-way encryption algorithm to encrypt the passwords in the configuration file; IOS can decrypt these passwords, and so can you.

We can tell by looking at a password entry in the configuration file which encryption algorithm has been used. Figure 6-4 shows some configuration file passwords.

The enable and VTY line passwords have been encrypted. The enable secret password maintains is original form; the encryption algorithm is indicated by the numeral that immediately precedes the password. There are several possible values:

- The numeral 7 indicates that the password is encrypted with the two-way algorithm.

- The numeral 5 indicates that the password is encrypted with the one-way, secret algorithm.

- The numeral 0 (or no value) indicates that the password is being displayed in its unencrypted form.

If you turn off password encryption with the command **no service password-encryption**, the passwords will remain encrypted until you enter them again.

Figure 6-4

Encrypted passwords in configuration file.

```
1)  Dallas#show running-config
2)  !
3)  enable secret 5 $1$S.px$gAcVrJaShGu2x6Rvu/F1C/
4)  enable password 7 121C0B16100709092F
5)  !
6)  [text omitted]
7)  line vty 0 4
8)  password 7 011F0310560E0F01
9)  [text omitted]
10) Dallas#
```

6.1.4 Command Prompt

The IOS user mode and privileged mode prompts normally have a router's host name (the first 29 characters of it) and a trailing character, which indicates the command mode. You can change the prompt by using the global configuration command **prompt**.

You can make the prompt whatever you want it to be up to a maximum of about 29 characters. IOS has some escape sequences available for putting special values into the prompt. These are as follows:

- %h—The router's host name.

- %n—The absolute line number that is being used by the user.

- %p—The prompt character that can be either the greater-than sign (>) for user mode or the number sign (#) for privileged mode.

- %s—The space character.

- %t—The tab character.

Setting the prompt will change only the user mode and privileged mode command prompts. The configuration mode prompt will not be affected. The configuration mode prompt always has the host name and as much of the configuration mode indicator text [for example, (*config*) and (*config-if*)] as possible unless you turn it off completely with the global configuration command **no service prompt config.** Figure 6-5 shows an example of changing the command prompt.

Line 1 of Figure 6-5 shows the default, privileged mode prompt. The prompt is changed on Line 3 with the **prompt** command. After the command is entered, the configuration mode prompt does not change. Upon leaving configuration mode, we see that the privileged mode prompt has changed to the configured value that has the host name (*%h*), a space (*%s*), the word *Line*, another space (*%s*), the absolute TTY number (*%n*), and the prompt character (*%p*). We see from the command prompt on

Figure 6-5

Changing the command prompt.

```
1)  Dallas#configure terminal
2)  Enter configuration commands, one per line. End with CNTL/Z.
3)  Dallas(config)#prompt %h%sLine%s%n%p
4)  Dallas(config)#<Ctrl-Z>
5)  Dallas Line 0#
6)  Dallas Line 0#configure terminal
7)  Enter configuration commands, one per line. End with CNTL/Z.
8)  Dallas(config)#no prompt
9)  Dallas(config)#<Ctrl-Z>
10) Dallas#
```

Line 5 that we are using the console terminal (line 0) to configure this router. To set the prompt back to its default value, use the **no prompt** command as shown on Line 8.

6.1.5 Address Resolution

When you type a single word on the user mode or privileged mode command line, IOS assumes that word to be a command. If the word is not a command, IOS will by default assume that the word is the name of a host to which a telnet session should be established. At the network layer, hosts are not identified by names—they are identified by addresses; therefore, there must be a way to get (lookup) the IP address associated with a given host name.

Address resolution is the process of looking up the IP address of a host given its name. There are two ways to perform address resolution.

1. Domain Name Service (DNS)
2. Local host table

DNS is an application that runs on a server. The server accepts a request containing a host name and looks up the IP address associated with the host name. The server replies to the sender with the IP address of the requested host name. The sender can then use the IP address to build a packet for the destination host.

IOS is capable of sending a request to a DNS server asking for the IP address of a host to which it wants to telnet, ping, or traceroute. DNS lookups are turned on by default. Normally, a host that can send DNS requests for address lookups has the address of a DNS server configured. The default DNS server address for IOS is 255.255.255.255, the broadcast IP address. So when you reference a host name that should be looked up, IOS will broadcast a request out all interfaces looking for a DNS server to perform the lookup.

Routers block broadcast packets; therefore, if IOS sends an IP broadcast packet looking for a DNS server, the server will not get the packet unless the server is on a local network directly attached to the requesting router. The resulting message looks like this.

```
Dallas#ping ftp.foo.com
Translating "ftp.foo.com"...domain server (255.255.255.255)
Unrecognized host or address, or protocol not running.

Dallas#
```

The DNS request for the IP address of **ftp.foo.com** was sent to the broadcast address. Since there was no DNS server on a directly connected network, the DNS request failed. This failed DNS lookup takes about 10 seconds to timeout. This can be annoying if you make a mistake typing a command.

```
Dallas#pong
Translating "pong"...domain server (255.255.255.255)
% Unknown command or computer name, or unable to find computer address
Dallas#
```

In the preceding example, we wanted to perform an extended ping, but the word *pong* was typed instead of *ping*. Since *pong* is not a command, IOS assumed that this was the name of a host to which to telnet. The DNS lookup to the broadcast address failed and cost us 10 seconds, which is not very much time unless you are watching and waiting for it to end.

If you are going to depend on DNS for address resolution, you should define the address of a DNS server to which IOS can direct its requests. You can define up to six DNS server addresses. The command to configure them is **ip name-server** followed by the DNS server address, or addresses. The **ip name-server** command is a global configuration command. Figure 6-6 shows the use and effect of the command.

Lines 3 and 4 of Figure 6-6 show the assignment of three DNS servers for lookups. IOS puts these into the running configuration in the

Figure 6-6
DNS server assignment and effect.

```
1)  Dallas#configure terminal
2)  Enter configuration commands, one per line. End with CNTL/Z.
3)  Dallas(config)#ip name-server 192.168.19.61
4)  Dallas(config)#ip name-server 172.16.1.1 10.99.99.99
5)  Dallas(config)#<Ctrl-Z>
6)  Dallas#ping ftp.foo.com
7)  Translating "ftp.foo.com"...domain server (192.168.19.61)
    [OK]
8)  Type escape sequence to abort.
9)  Sending 5, 100-byte ICMP Echs to 172.17.7.130, timeout is 2
    seconds:
10) !!!!!
11) Success rate is 100 percent (5/5), round-trip min/avg/max o =
    80/80/80 ms
12) Dallas#pong
13) Translating "pong"...domain server (192.168.19.61)
    (172.16.1.1) (10.99.99.99)
14) % Unknown command or computer name, or unable to find
    computer address
15) Dallas#
```

order that they are entered. The order that they are entered is also the order in which they are tried. The ping to ftp.foo.com on Line 6 causes a DNS lookup, which succeeds as shown on Line 7. The first DNS server replied with the IP address, which was then pinged on Line 9. On Line 12 is the erroneous entry of the word *pong* instead of *ping*. IOS attempts to find the IP address of the host pong by sending requests to each of the DNS servers in order. All of the requests for pong fail.

If you have a DNS server that you want IOS to use, then you should configure IOS with the address of the server. However, if you do not want to use DNS lookups for address resolution, then you should disable the process to stop IOS from sending the requests to the default DNS server address of 255.255.255.255. The entry of the command that disables DNS lookups is shown below.

```
Dallas(config)#no ip domain-lookup
Dallas(config)#
```

To turn DNS lookups back on (the default), use the command **ip domain-lookup**.

A local host table can be used for address resolution, too. A local host table is just a table containing entries for the names and addresses of hosts that you frequently access. You can put entries into the host table in global configuration mode with the **ip host** command. Here are some examples of host table entries.

```
Dallas(config)#ip host FortWorth 172.16.20.1
Dallas(config)#ip host pong 192.168.1.1 192.168.2.2
Dallas(config)#
```

The **ip host** command's first argument is the name that you use to reference the host. After that, you can put up to eight IP addresses that the host has. When you attempt to telnet to the host by name, IOS will try the IP addresses in order until it finds one that works or they all fail. When you ping or traceroute by name, IOS will use only the first address from the table.

IOS always tries to look up a name in the host table before it tries DNS, if DNS lookups are enabled. To see the contents of the host table, use the user mode command **show hosts** as shown in Figure 6-7.

The table shows the hosts that IOS knows about along with their addresses (up to eight). The *Flags* column shows *temp* if the entry was made by a DNS lookup or *perm* if the entry was made with the **ip host** command. IOS caches host names and their DNS-derived addresses in the host table so it does not have to perform another DNS lookup the

Figure 6-7

Show hosts com-
mand output.

```
 1)  Dallas>show hosts
 2)  Default domain is not set
 3)  Name/address lookup uses domain service
 4)  Name servers are 192.168.19.61, 172.16.1.1, 10.99.99.99
 5)
 6)  Host            Flags       Age  Type  Address(es)
 7)  ftp.foo.com     (temp, OK)  0    IP    172.17.7.130
 8)  www.witcon.com  (temp, OK)  8    IP    192.168.19.61
 9)  FortWorth       (perm, OK)  0    IP    172.16.20.1
10)  pong            (perm, OK)  0    IP    192.168.1.1 192.168.2.2
11)  Dallas>
```

next time that the host name is referenced. The *Age* column shows how
many hours have passed since an entry was last referenced.

If you would like to clear the host table, you can issue the privileged
mode command **clear host**. You can clear a single host table entry by
name as shown below:

```
Dallas#clear host pong
Dallas#
```

or you can clear the entire host table as shown next:

```
Dallas#clear host *
Dallas#
```

The **clear host pong** command removes pong from the host table, and
the **clear host *** command removes all entries from the table.

Configuring a host table entry for each of the routers in your network
will allow you to access those routers easily by name without having to
memorize their addresses.

6.2   Interface Tasks

The configuration of individual interfaces is done from either interface
configuration mode or subinterface configuration mode. The global configuration mode command **interface** is used to get to these modes. The
interface command has two arguments: the interface type and the
interface (or subinterface) number. The interface type and number can
be separated by a space or typed together. The following sections provide
plenty of examples.

6.2.1 Interface Types

The types of interfaces available on a Cisco router come in two major classifications: physical and logical. Physical interfaces have connections on the outside of a router and logical interfaces exist only in router memory; a subinterface is a special type of logical interface. These three types of interfaces are covered in the next sections.

6.2.1.1 Physical Interfaces

Physical interfaces are pretty easy to recognize, as they are the ones that you plug cables into on the outside of a router. All routers have at least two of them. Examples of physical interfaces are as follows:

- Ethernet
- Fast Ethernet
- Token Ring
- Fiber Distributed Data Interface (FDDI)
- Serial
- Basic Rate Interface (BRI)
- High-Speed Serial Interface (HSSI)

The presence of these interfaces depends on the router model and how it is configured. If a router has a physical interface, the interface's configuration commands exist in the running configuration even if you are not using the interface. The commands for configuring physical interfaces must be entered in interface configuration mode. You use the global configuration mode command **interface** to specify which interface you wish to configure, and IOS will put your terminal session into interface configuration mode. Figure 6-8 shows an example of physical interface configuration.

In Figure 6-8, we configured IP addresses on Ethernet0 and Serial1. Since we wanted to configure Ethernet0 first, we typed the command **interface ethernet0** to get into interface configuration mode for

Figure 6-8
Physical interface configuration.

```
1) Dallas(config)#interface ethernet0
2) Dallas(config-if)#ip address 172.16.10.1 255.255.255.0
3) Dallas(config-if)#interface serial1
4) Dallas(config-if)#ip address 172.16.11.1 255.255.255.0
5) Dallas(config-if)#
```

Ethernet0. Notice that the prompt changed to contain *(config-if)*. Once there, we could enter commands specific to Ethernet0 such as the **ip address** command on Line 4. Next we wanted to configure Serial1 so we typed the command **interface serial1** (Line 5). Remember that **interface** is a global configuration mode command and global configuration mode commands can be typed in any of the configuration modes. The **interface serial1** command puts us into interface configuration mode, for Serial1, where we can enter commands specific to Serial1.

IOS does not show us, on the command line, what interface we are configuring. It is up to us to keep track of it.

Usually interfaces are referenced by their abbreviated types. Abbreviating the interface type saves time and typographical errors. For example, Ethernet can be abbreviated with the letter *E*. This would allow us to reference the first Ethernet interface on the router in Figure 6-8 as E0 (or e0). Serial can be abbreviated with the letter *S*; so the second serial interface of the Figure 6-8 router is S1 (or s1).

Occasionally, we will see interface abbreviations in the output of **show** commands and we will use them in some command line examples.

6.2.1.2   Logical Interfaces

Logical interfaces are special-purpose interfaces that we create as we need them. They have no external connections and exist only within router memory. Logical interfaces are neither LAN nor WAN interfaces. IOS treats logical interfaces just like physical interfaces in that they are configured using the same steps, once they are created. The major, common characteristic of logical interfaces is that they do not go down unless someone shuts them down. Here are some examples of logical interfaces:

- Loopback
- Tunnel
- Dialer
- Null
- Bridge-Group Virtual Interface (BVI)

A *loopback interface* is used when we need a dummy interface to reference; it does not connect to anything. A loopback interface can be used for monitoring the router from a network management application, like one that uses SNMP. If you monitor a router based on a single interface and that interface goes down, the network management application will assume that the entire router is down; this may not be true. If you monitor a router based on a loopback interface, which never goes down, the network management application, which was monitoring the physical interface that went down, will now report that the interface, rather than the router, is down as long as the application has any path to the router.

A *tunnel interface* is used when we need to pass protocol traffic across a network that does not normally support the protocol. For example, you might use a tunnel to get IPX traffic across a network that supports only IP traffic. When building a tunnel, there must be two routers with tunnel interfaces referencing each other.

Dialer interfaces are used in dial-on-demand routing (DDR). They can be used to create rotary groups for interfaces that support DDR.

The *null interface* is a special interface that leads nowhere. You can think of it as the bit bucket, the place to throw traffic we do not want.

A *BVI* is used for integrated routing and bridging (IRB). IRB allows IOS to both route and bridge the same protocol, something it cannot normally do.

We create a logical interface by referencing it with the **interface** command. The exception to this is the null interface; we do not have to manually create the null interface. Once we've created a logical interface, the steps to configure it are the same ones used to configure a physical interface. Figure 6-9 shows the creation and configuration of a loopback interface.

Logical interfaces can have any number from 0 to 2,147,483,647 ($2^{31}-1$). Most administrators pick small numbers to make it easy on themselves. On Line 1 of Figure 6-9, we made the loopback interface number zero (0). Since this was the first time that the Loopback0 interface was referenced, IOS created it and immediately brought it up. Just for this example, we assigned an IP address and an IPX network number to the interface. Logical interface configuration is done from interface configuration mode.

Figure 6-9
Loopback interface configuration example.

```
1) Router(config)#interface loopback0
2) %LINEPROTO-5-UPDOWN: Line protocol on Interface Loopback0,
   changed state to up
3) Router(config-if)#ip address 10.1.1.5 255.255.255.252
4) Router(config-if)#ipx network badd00d
5) Router(config-if)#
```

6.2.1.3 Subinterfaces

A *subinterface* is a special logical interface that is bound to a physical interface, yet is referenced as a separate interface. It is kind of a hybrid interface, and it is either a LAN interface or a WAN interface depending on the physical interface from which it was created. A subinterface takes some of its properties from its physical interface, but it can have its own layer-3 properties such as IP address and IPX network number.

The most prevalent use of subinterfaces is found in the configuration of frame relay connections. On a frame relay connection, we typically have many logical (or virtual) connections coming into the router through a single physical serial interface. The frame relay logical connections are called *Permanent Virtual Circuits* (PVCs) and are created by our frame relay service provider to give us a communications channel through the frame relay network to another device. Subinterfaces can be created to service the PVCs coming into a physical interface. In frame relay, there are two kinds of subinterfaces—point-to-point and multipoint. The point-to-point subinterface services one PVC and the multipoint subinterface services multiple PVCs.

Another use of subinterfaces is found in Novell networks. In Novell networks running IPX, LAN interfaces can use multiple encapsulations (layer-2 header formats). For example, Ethernet_II and Ethernet_802.2 are two Novell encapsulations. For each encapsulation on a LAN interface, there must be a unique IPX network number. We can create a subinterface for each encapsulation type since we can give each subinterface its own layer-3 address (IPX network number).

The state of a subinterface follows its associated physical interface down, but not necessarily up. If a physical interface goes down, all of its subinterfaces also go down. A subinterface can be shut down individually even if the physical interface is up. When a subinterface is servicing a single frame relay PVC and the PVC goes down, the subinterface will also go down regardless of the physical interface status.

We create subinterfaces by referencing them with the interface command. When we reference a subinterface with the interface command, IOS puts us into subinterface configuration mode where we can enter commands specific to the subinterface.

Subinterfaces are named with the physical interface type and number followed by a period (.) and another number. The period is pronounced as "dot." For example, Serial0.1 (serial zero dot one) is a subinterface of Serial0. The number after the period can be anything from 0 to 4,294,967,296 ($2^{32}-1$). The number 0 refers to the physical interface;

therefore, the first available number for a subinterface is 1. Figure 6-10 shows the configuration of a frame relay subinterface.

The example of Figure 6-10 assumes that the Serial0 physical interface is running attached to a frame relay network and is running frame relay encapsulation. On Line 1, Serial0.1 is created as a point-to-point subinterface. This places us into subinterface configuration mode where we can enter the subinterface's IP address (Line 2), IPX network number (Line 3), and PVC to service (Line 4). PVCs are addressed with *Data-Link Connection Identifiers* (DLCI).

6.2.2 Interface Numbering

Interface numbering was introduced in Section 3.1.3. Let us review that information now that we are configuring individual interfaces. Probably the biggest difference in IOS configuration across Cisco router platforms is the numbering of interfaces due to hardware configuration. The full specification of an interface is its type followed by its number designation. The type and number designation may, optionally, be separated by a space when referencing an interface.

On the low-end routers (1000 series and 2500 series) to the midrange routers (4000 series), physical interfaces are numbered with a single value, the port number. The first interface of each type is numbered 0, and the numbers for the rest of the same-type interfaces increment from there. For example, the first Token Ring interface on a 4000 series router is TokenRing0, and the second one is TokenRing1.

On the high-end routers (7000 series) that support Online Insertion and Removal (OIR), a physical interface's number designation must include a slot number and a port number separated by a forward slash (/)—numbering for both slots and ports begins with 0. OIR allows us to swap the cards containing interfaces (interface processors) in and out of a router chassis without shutting down the router. For example, the first

Figure 6-10

Frame relay subinterface configuration example.

```
1) Router(config)#interface serial0.1 point-to-point
2) Router(config-subif)#ip address 10.200.200.1 255.255.255.0
3) Router(config-subif)#ipx network badf00d
4) Router(config-subif)#frame-relay interface-dlci 222
5) Router(config-subif)#
```

serial interface in the second slot of a 7507 is Serial1/0 and the second serial interface in the second slot is Serial1/1.

On the high-end routers that have a Versatile Interface Processor (VIP) installed, the interfaces on the VIP have a number designation that contains a slot number, a port adapter number, and a port number all separated by forward slashes (/). Port adapter numbers start at 0. For example, on a 7513, the second Ethernet interface on the first port adapter in the tenth slot is Ethernet9/0/1.

Logical interfaces have a number designation that contains only the single number that we assigned to it. Logical interfaces have no slot number or port adapter number; for example, Tunnel46 could be a tunnel interface on any IOS-based Cisco router.

Subinterface number designations consist of the entire physical interface designation followed by a period (.) and the number that we assigned to the subinterface. For example, Serial1/0.88 could be a subinterface of Serial1/0 on the 7507 mentioned earlier.

6.2.3   Setting the Encapsulation

The concept of encapsulation was covered throughout Chapter 2. The encapsulation method on an interface determines the format of the layer-2 header and trailer in which a packet is encapsulated before it is transmitted out an interface and in which the router expects data to arrive when it is received on an interface.

A LAN interface can support multiple encapsulations, and the encapsulations used are usually protocol-specific. On an Ethernet interface for example, IP traffic uses ARPA encapsulation (ARPA is the IOS keyword for Ethernet_II); Appletalk uses SNAP encapsulation; and IPX can use from one to four different encapsulations. Since LAN interface encapsulations are protocol-specific, we cover them in the protocol configuration chapters.

A WAN interface can support only one encapsulation, and the encapsulation is dependent on the device that the interface communicates with at the data link layer. If the interface communicates with a frame relay switch, the encapsulation must be frame relay. If the interface communicates with an X.25 switch, the encapsulation must be X.25. If the interface communicates directly with another router at layer 2, the encapsulation can be HDLC, PPP, or LAPB.

HDLC is the default encapsulation for all serial interfaces. As a general rule, if your WAN is a dedicated leased line, like a T1, and the router on the other end of it is a Cisco router, you can leave the encapsulation as HDLC. However, since Cisco's implementation of HDLC is proprietary (so is everyone else's), you should use PPP if the router on the other end is a non-Cisco router.

We use the interface configuration mode command **encapsulation** to change an interface's encapsulation.

```
Router(config)#interface serial0
Router(config-if)#encapsulation ppp
Router(config-if)#
```

Some of the keywords that can be accepted by the encapsulation command are *hdlc, ppp, frame-relay,* and *x25.* We come back to a few of these as we progress through the book.

To set an interface's encapsulation back to its default value, even if you do not know the default, issue the command **no encapsulation** in interface configuration mode for the interface.

6.2.4   Setting the Bandwidth

Setting the bandwidth on an interface has nothing to do with the speed of the interface. The *bandwidth* setting is used to communicate the bandwidth of an interface to upper-layer protocols and applications. For example, the EIGRP routing protocol uses the bandwidth to calculate a route's metric, and an SNMP-based network management application may use an interface's bandwidth setting to calculate network utilization. If you are using a protocol or application that uses the bandwidth setting, you should verify that the bandwidth has the correct value.

The interface bandwidth setting is given in kilobits per second (kbps). All interfaces have a default bandwidth setting; however, setting the bandwidth is usually an issue only on WAN interfaces, such as serial interfaces.

The default bandwidth of a fast serial interface is 1544—that is 1544 kbps or 1.544 Mbps—this is the bandwidth of a T1. IOS assumes that all fast serial interfaces are connected to T1 unless we tell it something different. Use the interface configuration mode command **bandwidth** to change the bandwidth setting. An example is shown below.

```
Router(config)#interface serial0
Router(config-if)#bandwidth 56
Router(config-if)#
```

This **bandwidth 56** command in this example tells IOS that Serial0 is connected to a 56-kbps WAN. If the bandwidth setting on an interface is not the same as the actual bandwidth of the directly connected network, you should use the **bandwidth** command to change the setting.

6.2.5   Setting a Description

We can put a text description on each interface. The *description* can be used to tell, or remind, a network administrator something about an interface. This interface description is the only text documentation that IOS saves in the configuration file. We can use the interface configuration mode command **description** to put a descriptive comment on each interface.

```
Dallas(config)#interface serial1
Dallas(config-if)#description T1 to FortWorth. Installed 10-Oct-1998.
                  DHEC123456.
Dallas(config-if)#interface ethernet0
Dallas(config-if)#description Call John at x1 immediately to report
                  problems.
Dallas(config-if)#
```

You can put any information you want in a description. Some useful things to include are a network's location and contact person. For WANs, the interface description is a great place to put circuit IDs and technical support contact information. You can put over 240 characters of text in each interface's description. The description is displayed when the **show interfaces** command is issued. Figure 6-11 shows an example output with an interface description.

The description we entered appears on Line 4 of Figure 6-11. Now a network administrator can use the **show interfaces** command to get the circuit ID of this WAN in case of a problem that involves the service provider.

6.2.6   Clearing

Figure 6-11, Line 9, shows that the counters at the bottom of the **show interfaces** output have never been cleared. We can use the privileged mode command **clear counters** to force the counters back to zero. If we issue the **clear counters** command without any arguments, IOS will clear the counters for all interfaces after it get a confirmation from us that we really want to do it. To clear the counters of an individual inter-

Figure 6-11

Show interfaces output with description.

```
1)   Dallas#show interfaces serial1
2)   Serial1 is up, line protocol is up
3)     Hardware is HD64570
4)     Description: T1 to FortWorth. Installed 10-Oct-1998.
       DHEC123456.
5)     Internet address is 172.16.11.1/24
6)     MTU 1500 bytes, BW 1544 Kbit, DLY 20000 usec, rely 255/255,
       load 1/255
7)     Encapsulation HDLC, loopback not set, keepalive set (10
       sec)
8)     Last input 00:00:04, output 00:00:06, output hang never
9)     Last clearing of "show interface" counters never
10)    Input queue: 0/75/0 (size/max/drops); Total output drops: 0
11)    Queueing strategy: weighted fair
12)    Output queue: 0/1000/64/0 (size/max total/threshold/drops)
13)      Conversations 0/1/256 (active/max active/max total)
14)      Reserved Conversations 0/0 (allocated/max allocated)
15)    5 minute input rate 0 bits/sec, 0 packets/sec
16)    5 minute output rate 0 bits/sec, 0 packets/sec
17)      13953 packets input, 946610 bytes, 0 no buffer
18)      Received 13952 broadcasts, 0 runts, 0 giants,
         0 throttles
19)      0 input errors, 0 CRC, 0 frame, 0 overrun, 0 ignored,
         0 abort
20)      13954 packets output, 957096 bytes, 0 underruns
21)      0 output errors, 0 collisions, 2 interface resets
22)      0 output buffer failures, 0 output buffers swapped out
23)      2 carrier transitions
24)      DCD = up DSR = up DTR = up RTS = up CTS = up
25)    Dallas#
```

face, put the interface type and number designator as the arguments of the **clear counters** command. For example, **clear counters serial1** will clear the *show interface* counters for the Serial1 interface shown in Figure 6-11.

Sometimes, not very often, we may have a use for resetting the hardware of an interface. The privileged mode command **clear interface** will accomplish this purpose. The **clear interface** command takes as its arguments the interface type and number designator for the interface we wish to reset. For example, the command **clear interface serial1/0** will reset the hardware for Serial1/0. Use this command with caution since it will cause any traffic flowing through the interface to be lost while the hardware reinitializes.

6.2.7   Shutting Down

To shut down an interface and place it into administratively down state, use the interface configuration mode command **shutdown**.

```
Dallas(config)#interface ethernet0
Dallas(config-if)#shutdown
%LINEPROTO-5-UPDOWN: Line protocol on Interface Ethernet0, changed
state to down
%LINK-5-CHANGED: Interface Ethernet0, changed state to
administratively down
```

The console messages indicate that Ethernet0 has been shut down. To take an interface out of administratively down state and have IOS attempt to bring it up, issue the **no shutdown** command. (Just say no.)

```
Dallas(config-if)#no shutdown
%LINEPROTO-5-UPDOWN: «Line protocol on Interface Ethernet0, changed
state to up
%LINK-3-UPDOWN: Interface Ethernet0, changed state to up
```

The console messages now indicate that Ethernet0 is again active with an up/up state.

6.3   Terminal Line Tasks

Section 5.2.4 explains the types of terminal lines, the way that they are numbered, and the **show line** command for examining them. To configure a terminal line, we must be in line configuration mode. We use the global configuration command **line** to get there.

We can configure lines by their absolute line number or their relative number. Using the relative number is the most straightforward. When referencing a terminal line by its relative number, we must include the line type such as *con* or *vty*. An example of getting into line configuration mode for the console is shown below.

```
Dallas(config)#line con 0
Dallas(config-line)#
```

There is only one console; therefore, its relative number is always 0. Actually, its absolute number is always 0, too. The *(config-line)* indicates that we are in line configuration mode. We can now enter commands to configure the console.

When configuring a line type that has multiple instances, such as VTYs, we can configure individual lines or a range of lines. Normally, we want all of a router's VTYs to have identical configurations; therefore, we can use range of relative line numbers to get to line configuration mode. Then the commands we type will affect all of the VTYs in the range. The relative line numbers in the range are separated by a space. Here is an example:

```
Dallas(config)#line vty 0 4
Dallas(config-line)#
```

By default, a Cisco router has five VTYs, whose relative numbers are 0, 1, 2, 3, and 4. To configure all of the VTYs simultaneously, we issue the **line vty 0 4** command. The 0 and the 4 represent the range 0 through 4. All of the line configuration mode command typed at the prompt will now affect all five of the VTYs.

We can create more VTYs by referencing new numbers on the **line vty** command. For example, the command **line vty 9** will create five more VTYs with relative numbers 5, 6, 7, 8, and 9.

6.3.1   Setting a Password

Terminal line passwords are set in line configuration line mode. After typing a terminal line password, a user is put into user mode. Enabling the use of terminal line passwords with the **password** command and the **login** command was covered in Section 6.1.3.1.

6.3.2   Setting the Timeout

After 10 minutes of inactivity, IOS will automatically disconnect a terminal line session. This means that if you log in on the console and you do not press any keys for 10 minutes, IOS will log you out. We can change this timeout interval by using the line configuration mode command **exec-timeout**, which has two arguments—*minutes* and *seconds*. The following example removes the console timeout and reduces the VTY timeout.

```
Dallas(config)#line con 0
Dallas(config-line)#exec-timeout 0 0
Dallas(config-line)#line vty 0 4
Dallas(config-line)#exec-timeout 5 0
Dallas(config-line)#
```

Setting the timeout to 0 minutes and 0 seconds disables the timeout; with this setting, the console session will never be disconnected unless someone manually disconnects it. The timeout for all five VTYs has been shortened to 5 minutes and 0 seconds. If someone telnets to this router and leaves their session idle for 5 minutes, IOS will clear the line to disconnect the session.

6.3.3   Clearing

If you want to manually clear a line that does not belong to you, the privileged mode command **clear line** can be used. Figure 5-13 has the output of a **show users** command. Suppose that the user, from host euless.tx.witcon.com, with the telnet session on VTY 3 (absolute line 5) has no business in your router. You can disconnect the session with the **clear line 5** command.

6.4   Managing Configuration Files

Managing the two IOS configuration files, startup and running, is essential to the administration of a router-based internetwork. Here is a quick review of the files. The running configuration contains the configuration that is currently active on the router. When we enter commands from a configuration mode command line during a terminal line session, they are placed into the running configuration file. Since the running configuration is kept in RAM, it disappears when a router goes down.

The startup configuration is stored in NVRAM. The commands from the startup configuration are read and entered into the running configuration when a router boots.

All configuration file management must be done from privileged mode. The operations that we can perform on the configuration files are as follows:

- Display the running configuration.
- Update the running configuration.
- Back up the running configuration.
- Display the startup configuration.
- Replace the startup configuration.
- Back up the startup configuration.

The IOS commands for performing these operations are covered in the next few sections.

6.4.1 Displaying the Running Configuration

IOS displays the running configuration to us when we issue the following command in privileged mode:

```
show running-config
```

The active configuration will be sent in ASCII text format to our terminal line session. If we are running terminal emulation software, capturing the running configuration to a log file is useful. When examining the running configuration file, remember that IOS typically will not display default settings; therefore the configuration file normally contains only those commands that change IOS defaults.

The **show running-config** command was first documented in IOS version 11.0, even though it was available in earlier releases. The original IOS command for displaying the running configuration is

```
write terminal
```

The **write terminal** command is available in all IOS releases and both commands perform the same operation.

6.4.2 Updating the Running Configuration

The only way to actually replace the running configuration is to reboot the router; however, we can update the running configuration with new commands. These commands must be entered in ASCII text and they can be entered from the following sources:

- Terminal Line
- NVRAM
- TFTP Server
- rcp Server
- Flash Memory

Trivial File Transfer Protocol (TFTP) is an application that allows the transfer of files to and from a server without any authentication. TFTP runs over *User Datagram Protocol* (UDP); therefore, it has no windowing or sequencing of packets. It is for use over reliable networks that are not subject to dropped packets. To use TFTP, we must have a host running the server process; IOS by default runs the client process that sends file transfer requests to a server. TFTP server software is available for just about any host operating system.

Remote Copy (rcp) is another application that allows the transfer of files to and from a server; however, rcp runs over *Transmission Control Protocol* (TCP) and requires authentication—rcp is more reliable and secure than TFTP. We can use rcp over networks that are subject to dropped packets, such as frame relay; rcp server software is not as widely available as TFTP server software, but if you look hard enough, you can probably find it for your host operating system.

6.4.2.1 From a Terminal Line

To enter commands from a terminal line session, we must be in configuration mode. The command for getting to configuration mode has already been covered and should be familiar by now. It is

```
configure terminal
```

The **configuration terminal** command will put us into global configuration mode where we can type configuration commands that affect the IOS running configuration.

In addition to typing individual commands at the configuration mode prompt, we can enter commands through the *transmit* and *paste* functions of our terminal emulation software. If we have a text file of configuration commands stored on a local disk drive, we can transmit the file to the router by performing an ASCII file transmit operation if our terminal emulator supports it. The commands in the file will be executed just as if they were typed. If our terminal emulator supports the *copy* and *paste* functions, we can paste text commands directly onto the IOS command line after we have selected and copied them into our copy buffer.

6.4.2.2 From NVRAM

NVRAM, hopefully, contains a startup configuration file, which is a text file of commands that can be entered into the running configuration. The command for updating the running configuration with the commands from the startup configuration is as follows:

```
copy startup-config running-config
```

This command will take the lines of the startup configuration from NVRAM and enter them into the running configuration one at a time just as if we were typing them on a configuration mode command line.

The operation is not really a copy as the command suggests; some people call it a *merge*.

The **copy startup-config running-config** command was first documented in IOS version 11.0, even though it was available in earlier releases. The original IOS command for updating the running configuration from NVRAM is

```
configure memory
```

The **configure memory** command is available in all IOS releases, and both commands perform the same operation.

6.4.2.3   From a TFTP Server

TFTP servers can have text files of commands or running configuration backup files on them. The lines of these files can be entered into a running configuration with the following command:

```
copy tftp running-config
```

The **copy tftp running-config** command will take the lines of a text file from a TFTP server and enter them into the running configuration one at a time just as if we were typing them on a configuration mode command line. Like the other copy operations that have the running configuration as the destination, this operation is more of a merge rather than a copy as the command suggests. Figure 6-12 shows the dialog of the **copy tftp running-config** command. Default answers are given in brackets ([ ]).

The question on Line 2 can be answered with either *host* or *network*. For the purpose of a configuration file copy, a file is a *host file* if it contains commands that are specific to an individual router, and a file is a *network file* if it contains commands common to multiple routers. The answer is used in the generation of the files default name (Line 4). A host file has a default name that contains the router's host

Figure 6-12

Copy TFTP running-config dialog.

```
1)  Dallas#copy tftp running-config
2)  Host or network configuration file [host]? host
3)  IP address of remote host [255.255.255.255]? 172.16.10.2
4)  Name of configuration file [Dallas-confg]? dallas-1.txt
5)  Configure using dallas-1.txt from 172.16.10.2? [confirm] y
6)  Loading dallas-1.txt from 172.16.10.2 (via Ethernet0): !!!!!
7)  [OK - 2035/32723 bytes]
8)  Dallas#
```

name followed by *-confg*, and a network has the default name *network-confg*.

The next question (Figure 6-12, Line 3) asks for the IP address of the TFTP server. This could be an actual address or a host name, if we have DNS enabled or we have a host file entry for the name.

The question on Line 5 just asks for confirmation. If the answer is affirmative, IOS attempts to perform the copy. Line 6 shows the status of the configuration file load; the exclamation points (!) indicate blocks of text that have been successfully copied. Periods (.) indicate failed block copies. Some versions of IOS display the word **Booting** instead of **Loading**; this operation is not a boot—it is merely a merge.

To avoid an error at the end of the copy, we need to make sure that the last command in the text file is the single word *end*. Since IOS is treating the text file commands just like they were being typed into configuration mode, the *end* command is needed to exit configuration mode when the copy is finished.

The **copy tftp running-config** command was first documented in IOS version 11.0, even though it was available in earlier releases. The original IOS command for updating the running configuration from a TFTP server is

```
configure network
```

The **configure network** command is available in all IOS releases and both commands perform the same operation.

6.4.2.4   From an rcp Server

TFTP servers can also have text files of commands or running configuration backup files on them. The lines of these files can be entered into a running configuration with the following command:

```
copy rcp running-config
```

This command will take the lines of a text file from an rcp server and enter them into the running configuration one at a time just as if we were typing them on a configuration mode command line. The last line of the text file should be the command **end**. Similar to the other commands for copying files to the running configuration, this operation is more of a merge rather than a copy. The dialog for the **copy rcp running-config** command is similar to that shown for the TFTP copy in Figure 6-12.

Since rcp requires authentication to perform a copy, there are some additional steps that we must perform to allow the router to access the rcp server's files. There are many variations of the rcp process, but here are the steps for one of the ways to prepare for the copy.

- On the router, define a username, which the router will use to log in to the rcp server. The username for rcp can be defined with the **ip rcmd remote-username** command.

- On the rcp server, define a user with the same username and give the user a home directory. Text files of commands should be stored in the home directory.

- On the rcp server, build a .rhosts file in the user's home directory. The .rhosts file is a text file that contains a line entry for each host and username that is allowed to access the directory. Add an entry for the router and its username.

You may have to experiment with rcp to get it to work—it's not the most intuitive application to use; it is, however, very reliable.

6.4.2.5   From Flash Memory

Text files that have been stored on in flash memory can also be merged with the running configuration. When copying a text file from flash, we should reference the exact flash device and file name on the command line. The command is as follows:

```
copy flashdev:filename running-config
```

In the command, *flashdev:* is the name of a flash device such as flash: or slot0:, and *filename* is the name of the text file, for example, dallas-1.txt.

6.4.3   Backing Up the Running Configuration

We should always maintain backup copies of router configuration files, preferably in multiple locations. From privileged mode, we can back up a router's running configuration to the following locations:

- NVRAM
- TFTP server
- rcp server

- Flash memory
- Local disk drive

When performing a backup of the running configuration file, IOS builds the configuration and formats it as ASCII text; it then copies the entire file to the specified destination. The commands for backing up the running configuration are just the reverse of those used to update the running configuration, but we will go over them anyway.

6.4.3.1   To NVRAM

The command to back up the running configuration to NVRAM is as follows:

```
copy running-config startup-config
```

When this command is executed, IOS replaces the startup configuration with the contents of the running configuration. This operation should always be performed after changes to a router's running configuration have been made and verified to be working properly.

The **copy running-config startup-config** command was first documented in IOS version 11.0, even though it was available in earlier releases. The original IOS command for copying the running configuration to NVRAM is

```
write memory
```

The **write memory** command is available in all IOS releases and both commands perform the same operation.

6.4.3.2   To a TFTP Server

The command used for backing up the running configuration to a TFTP server is

```
copy running-config tftp
```

The **copy running-config tftp** command will copy the running configuration to a specified text file on a specified TFTP server. Figure 6-13 shows the dialog of the **copy running-config tftp** command. Default answers are given in brackets ([ ]).

The dialog begins (Figure 6-13, Line 2) by asking for the address of the TFTP server. This can be either an address or a host name as long as the address associated with the name can be resolved using DNS or a host table.

Figure 6-13
Copy running-config TFTP dialog.

```
1) Dallas#copy running-config tftp
2) Remote host []? 172.16.10.2
3) Name of configuration file to write [Dallas-confg]?
   dallas-2.txt
4) Write file dallas-2.txt on host 172.16.10.2? [confirm] y
5) Building configuration...
6)
7) Writing dallas-2.txt !!!!! [OK]
8) Dallas#
```

The default file name (Line 3) is the router's host name followed by the characters *-confg*. We have changed the file name to agree with our naming standard. There is already a file named dallas-1.txt (see Figure 6-12) so we used dallas-2.txt.

Some TFTP server implementations require that a file exist on the server before a TFTP client can write to it. If your server has this restriction and the server is running UNIX, you can use the UNIX command **touch** to create an empty file with the desired name.

After the affirmative confirmation on Line 4, IOS compiles the configuration into text format and attempts to write the file. On Line 7, the exclamation points (!) indicates successful writes of text blocks.

The **copy running-config tftp** command was first documented in IOS version 11.0, even though it was available in earlier releases. The original IOS command for backing up the running configuration to a TFTP server is

```
write network
```

The **write network** command is available in all IOS releases and both commands perform the same operation.

6.4.3.3   To an rcp Server
Use the following command to backup the running configuration to an rcp server:

```
copy running-config rcp
```

The **copy running-config rcp** command will copy the running configuration to a specified text file on a specified rcp server. The dialog for the rcp copy is similar to that shown for the TFTP copy in Figure 6-13.

An example of the preparation steps for performing an rcp operation is given in Section 6.4.2.4.

6.4.3.4   To Flash Memory

The command for making a backup of the running configuration in flash memory has the following form:

```
copy running-config flashdev:filename
```

In the command, *flashdev:* is the name of a flash device such as flash: or slot0:, and *filename* is the name of the text file, for example, dallas-3.txt.

IOS cannot write to flash memory that has a read-only status. We can use the **show flash** or **show version** command to verify that flash is not read-only.

6.4.3.5   To a Local Disk Drive

To back up the running configuration to a local disk drive, set your terminal emulation software to log screen output to a text file and issue the **show running-config** command.

This technique also can be used to save other IOS output to a text file. You will find it useful for documenting the configuration and operation of your routers if you save the output of your **show** commands in text files.

6.4.4   Displaying the Startup Configuration

IOS displays the startup configuration to us when we issue the following command in privileged mode:

```
show startup-config
```

The startup configuration will be sent in ASCII text format to our terminal line session. On a stable, production router, the startup configuration should contain the same commands as the running configuration.

The **show startup-config** command was first documented in IOS version 11.0, even though it was available in earlier releases. The original IOS command for displaying the startup configuration is

```
show config
```

The **show config** command is available in all IOS releases and both commands perform the same operation.

6.4.5   Replacing the Startup Configuration

The commands for replacing the startup configuration are similar to those in Section 6.4.2 for updating the running configuration. Just replace the keyword *running-config* with the keyword *startup-config* to make the command operate on the startup configuration. The startup configuration can be replaced with the following:

- TFTP server file
- rcp server file
- Flash memory file
- Nothing

The commands that perform startup configuration operations have one major operational difference with those that perform running configuration operations. Where the running configuration commands entered command lines into a preexisting running configuration, the commands that operate on the startup configuration actually replace the contents of NVRAM with the specified source file.

The most common maintenance operations that administrators perform on the startup configuration are replacing it with the running configuration after changes have been made and verified and erasing it (replacing it with nothing) to start from scratch with a router's configuration.

6.4.5.1   With the Running Configuration File

The command to replace the startup configuration with the running configuration is the same one used to back up the running configuration to NVRAM covered in Section 6.4.3.1:

```
copy running-config startup-config
```

This command will replace the contents of NVRAM with the entire running configuration file, assuming that there is enough NVRAM to hold the file.

Remember that the original IOS command for replacing the startup configuration with the running configuration is

```
write memory
```

Both commands perform the same operation.

6.4.5.2   With a TFTP Server File

Use the following command to replace the NVRAM contents with a file from a TFTP server:

```
copy tftp startup-config
```

This command has a dialog similar to that shown in Figure 6-12. We need to tell IOS the IP address of the TFTP server and the name of the file to copy from the server.

IOS will allow any file, even if it does not contain configuration commands, to be copied directly to NVRAM. If you put a file in NVRAM other than a configuration file, IOS will fail during its boot sequence when it tries to load the contents of NVRAM into the running configuration. Therefore, we better have a backup copy of the configuration on a server, in flash memory, or on a local disk drive.

The **copy tftp startup-config** command was first documented in IOS version 11.0, even though it was available in earlier releases. The original IOS command for backing up the running configuration to a TFTP server is

```
configure overwrite-network
```

The **configure overwrite-network** command is available in many IOS releases (even though it was undocumented until recently) and both commands perform the same operation.

6.4.5.3   With an rcp Server File

Use the following command to replace the startup configuration with a file from an rcp server:

```
copy rcp startup-config
```

This command has a dialog that asks for the IP address of the rcp server and the name of the file that is to be copied to NVRAM. Any file can be copied since IOS does no checking of file contents for this copy. (See Section 6.4.2.4 for some of the things that should be done to allow rcp copies from a server.)

6.4.5.4   With a Flash Memory File

We can move a file from flash memory to NVRAM with the following command:

```
copy flashdev:filename startup-config
```

In the command, *flashdev:* is the name of a flash device such as flash: or slot0:, and *filename* is the name of the text file, for example, dallas-3.txt.

As in any other file copy to NVRAM, IOS does not check the contents of a file during the copy.

6.4.5.5 With Nothing

Sometimes it is necessary to start over. When a router boots without a startup configuration, IOS assumes that the router is new and it asks if we want to enter the System Configuration Dialog. Therefore, if we remove the startup configuration from a router and then reboot the router, we can start from scratch with IOS configuration.

The command used to erase the contents of NVRAM is as follows:

```
erase startup-config
```

A router that rebooted after this command is issued is just like a brand new router as far as IOS is concerned. The **erase startup-config** command is not often used in production; however, it is very useful in a lab environment.

The **erase startup-config** command was first documented in IOS version 11.0, even though it was available in earlier releases. The original IOS command for erasing NVRAM is

```
write erase
```

The **write erase** command is available in all IOS releases and both commands perform the same operation.

6.4.6   Backing Up the Startup Configuration

We do not normally have a need to back up the startup configuration, but just in case, here are the commands.

The command for backing up the startup configuration to a TFTP server is

```
copy startup-config tftp
```

The command for backing up the startup configuration to an rcp server is

```
copy startup-config rcp
```

Both of the preceding commands have a dialog that requests the IP address of a server and the name of the backup file on the server.

The command for backing up the startup configuration to flash memory is

```
copy startup-config flashdev:filename
```

where *flashdev:* is the flash device and *filename* is the name of the file on the flash device.

6.5   Accessing Remote Routers

Accessing routers across a network or internetwork can be done using telnet to establish a session to one of the remote router's VTYs. Telnet can be done only across networks running IP. When you want to start a telnet session to a host, use the **telnet** command followed by the host's name or IP address. The **telnet** command can be issued in either user mode or privileged mode. Figure 6-14 shows a telnet session being established and cleared.

On Line 1 of Figure 6-14 a telnet session is being requested to the host **fortworth**. To use host names, we must have some form of address resolution. Dallas's configuration contains a host table entry that associ-

Figure 6-14

Telnet session establishment example.

```
1)  Dallas#telnet fortworth
2)  Trying FortWorth (172.16.20.1)... Open
3)
4)  User Access Verification
5)
6)  Password: letmein
7)  FortWorth>quit
8)
9)  [Connection to fortworth closed by foreign host]
10) Dallas#
```

ates the name FortWorth to the IP address 172.16.20.1. The address that resulted from the lookup is shown on Line 2. If we had remembered the address, we could have used it in place of the host name. Host names in DNS files and host tables are not case-sensitive when they are referenced from a command line. In this example, we just logged in and then, immediately, logged out. Note that the password is not really displayed on our terminal when we log in, and we would not be allowed to log in at all if FortWorth did not have a password configured on the VTY that it allocated for the incoming telnet connection.

If we telnet to a router and want to return to our source and perhaps perform some function or telnet to another router, we can suspend our current telnet session with the standard IOS escape sequence followed by the letter x. Suspending a telnet session leaves it active and allows us to resume the connection without have to log in again. The IOS default escape sequence is <Ctrl-Shift-6>; therefore the full sequence of commands to suspend a telnet session is <Ctrl-Shift-6><x>. This sequence is two keystrokes and requires three fingers. Press the <Ctrl>, <Shift>, and <6> keys simultaneously; then release them and press the <x> key.

Figure 6-15 shows a telnet example with an event sequence that seems illogical; however, we will use it to illustrate several things including a session being established, suspended, resumed, and forcefully disconnected.

On Line 1 of Figure 6-15, we requested a telnet session to **fortworth**. Remember that IOS assumes a noncommand word (or

Figure 6-15

Telnet session suspension example.

```
1)  Dallas#fortworth
2)  Trying FortWorth (172.16.20.1)... Open
3)
4)  User Access Verification
5)
6)  Password: letmein
7)  FortWorth><Ctrl-Shift-6>
8)  Dallas#show sessions
9)  Conn Host            Address        Byte     Idle  Conn Name
10) *  1 fortworth       172.16.20.1       0        0  fortworth
11)
12) Dallas#<Enter>
13) [Resuming connection 1 to fortworth ... ]
14) <Enter>
15) FortWorth><Ctrl-Shift-6> <x>
16) Dallas#disconnect 1
17) Closing connection to fortworth [confirm]y
18) Dallas#
```

address) typed in user mode or privileged mode is the name (or address) of a host to which a telnet session should be established. If you do not like this behavior, you can turn it off on a terminal line with the line configuration mode command **transport preferred none**. Doing this will cause IOS to interpret everything you type as a command, never a host; therefore, when you want to telnet to a host, we must use the **telnet** command.

On Line 2 the address of the host name has been resolved and the telnet session is started. After logging in, we got a command prompt (Line 7) and suspended the telnet session. We were immediately placed back on Dallas (Line 8). The **show sessions** command is used to display suspended telnet connections. Line 10 shows that there is one telnet session, and it is connected to **fortworth**. The connection number is 1.

In the **show sessions** command output, the asterisk to the left of the connection number indicates the next active session. If we press <Enter> on an empty command line of the original router, the session with the asterisk is resumed (Lines 12 and 13). When a session is resumed, we usually do not get a command prompt immediately; therefore, we may need to type something like <Enter> to get to a prompt. Be careful about typing <Enter> when you are not sure about what is on the command line. Suppose that the session to FortWorth had been suspended at the end of a typed command but before <Enter> was pressed to execute the command. Resuming the session would put you back at the end of the original command line, and pressing <Enter> would execute the command that you can no longer see. If you are unsure about the contents of a command line in such a case, consider pressing <Ctrl-U> to erase the command line or <Ctrl-R> to redisplay the command line before pressing <Enter>.

If we had multiple sessions and did not want to resume the one with the asterisk, we could issue the **resume** command followed by the desired connection number or we could just issue the connection number itself, as a command, on the command line.

On Line 15 of Figure 6-15, the telnet session to FortWorth is again suspended to get back to Dallas (Line 16). The command to clear a suspended telnet session, without having to return to the destination host and log out, is **disconnect**. Typing **disconnect** alone on a command line will disconnect the next active session (the one with the asterisk in the **show sessions** output). On Line 16, we elected to reference the specific connection number 1 for disconnection. The session is cleared after an affirmative confirmation.

6.6   Cisco Discovery Protocol

The *Cisco Discovery Protocol* (CDP) is a Cisco-proprietary, data link protocol that runs by default on most Cisco devices, including routers. Cisco devices use CDP to advertise their presence and basic configuration information to neighboring Cisco devices and to learn about the presence and basic configuration of neighboring Cisco devices. Neighboring devices refer to those devices that are on directly connected networks. As noted earlier, CDP is a data link protocol; therefore, CDP communication cannot be routed—it must stay on a device's local networks.

CDP runs on any network (LAN or WAN) that supports SNAP encapsulation; these networks include Ethernet, Token Ring, FDDI, HDLC, PPP, and frame relay (not X.25). At periodic intervals, Cisco devices send a CDP message out each interface which has CDP enabled. The default update interval is 60 seconds. Neighboring Cisco devices hear the CDP messages and update a CDP neighbor table in their RAM. The CDP neighbor table contains the information that each neighbor has advertised and a hold timer. The hold timer is used to tell how much time has elapsed since information about a neighbor device was heard. The default hold timer starts at 180 seconds and counts down. If a device's hold timer reaches zero (0), the device is removed from the table.

A CDP message includes information about the transmitting device and information about the interface from which the message was transmitted. The IOS command to display a summary of the CDP neighbor table is **show cdp neighbors**. Figure 6-16 shows an example of the **show cdp neighbors** command output on Dallas.

```
1)  Dallas#show cdp neighbors
2)  Capability Codes: R - Router, T - Trans Bridge, B - Source Route Bridge
3)                    S - Switch, H - Host, I - IGMP, r - Repeater
4)
5)  Device ID        Local Intrfce   Holdtme    Capability Platform   Port ID
6)  FortWorth          Ser 1           150          R        2520      Ser 0
7)  Dallas#
```

Figure 6-16
Show CDP neighbors command output.

As shown on Line 6 of Figure 6-16, Dallas has one neighbor device, FortWorth. FortWorth's CDP messages are being received on Dallas's Serial1 interface (see *Local Intrfce* column). Since the hold timer started at 180 seconds and is now at 150 seconds (see *Holdtime* column), 30 seconds have elapsed since the last CDP message was received from FortWorth. According to the *Platform* and *Capability* columns, FortWorth is a 2520 router. FortWorth is sending its CDP message, being received by Dallas, out its Serial0 interface (see *Port ID* column). From this display we can deduce that FortWorth's Serial0 interface is directly connected to the same network as Dallas's Serial1 interface.

To view the full contents of the CDP neighbor table, issue the **show cdp neighbors detail** command. Figure 6-17 show an example output from Dallas.

From the table details, we can gather more information about FortWorth. On Lines 5 through 7, we get the IP address, IPX address, and AppleTalk address for FortWorth's Serial0 interface (see *Port ID* on Line 9). Line 14 shows that FortWorth is running IOS version 11.3(5). The interface addresses comes in handy when we need to access a neighboring Cisco router, but we do not know its address. They can also be used to discover the layout of an internetwork that consists of Cisco devices.

To look at an individual entry in the CDP neighbor table, use the command

```
show cdp entry name
```

Figure 6-17
Show CDP neighbors detail command output.

```
1)  Dallas#show cdp neighbors detail
2)  ------------------------
3)  Device ID: FortWorth
4)  Entry address(es):
5)  IP address: 172.16.11.2
6)  Novell address: AC100B00.0010.7b3a.d4af
7)  Appletalk address: 1001.200
8)  Platform: Cisco 2520, Capabilities: Router
9)  Interface: Serial1, Port ID (outgoing port): Serial0
10) Holdtime : 151 sec
11)
12) Version :
13) Cisco Internetwork Operating System Software
14) IOS (tm) 2500 Software (C2500-JS-L), Version 11.3(5), RELEASE
      SOFTWARE (fc1)
15) Copyright (c) 1986-1998 by Cisco Systems, Inc.
16) Compiled Tue 11-Aug-98 04:06 by phanguye
17)
18) Dallas#
```

where *name* is the name of a device from the neighbor table. The name is case-sensitive. This command is useful if the neighbor table is large and you want to get detailed information about a single neighbor without having to view the details of all neighbors.

CDP can be enabled and disabled either on individual interfaces or globally. If you want to turn off CDP on an individual interface, use the interface configuration mode command **no cdp enable**. To turn it back on, issue the **cdp enable** command. To turn off CDP on all interfaces simultaneously, issue the global configuration command **no cdp run**. Issue the **cdp run** command to turn CDP back on.

The CDP timers (update interval and hold time) are global parameters. When they are changed, all interfaces running CDP are changed. The command to change the periodic update interval is

`cdp timer` *seconds*

where *seconds* is the length of the interval. The default value is 60. The command to change the hold timer is

`cdp holdtime` *seconds*

where *seconds* is the starting value of the hold timer. The default value is 180. When timers are changed on one device, they should be changed on all the rest of the devices to help prevent neighbor-table synchronization problems.

The status of CDP on a router can be viewed with the commands **show cdp** and **show cdp interface**. Figure 6-18 shows a sample output of these two commands on Dallas.

The **show cdp** command shows the values of the timers (Lines 3 and 4). The **show cdp interface** command shows the interfaces that have CDP enabled; in this example, all of the interfaces have CDP enabled. We also get the status and encapsulation of each interface. The timers are shown, but they are not interface-specific.

6.7   Sending Messages

We can send text messages from our terminal line session to other terminal line sessions with the privileged mode **send** command. The **show users** command will show us which terminal lines have active sessions

Figure 6-18

Show CDP command output.

```
1)  Dallas#show cdp
2)  Global CDP information:
3)        Sending CDP packets every 60 seconds
4)        Sending a holdtime value of 180 seconds
5)  Dallas#show cdp interface
6)  BRI0 is administratively down, line protocol is down
7)     Encapsulation HDLC
8)     Sending CDP packets every 60 seconds
9)     Holdtime is 180 seconds
10) BRI0:1 is administratively down, line protocol is down
11)    Encapsulation HDLC
12)    Sending CDP packets every 60 seconds
13)    Holdtime is 180 seconds
14) BRI0:2 is administratively down, line protocol is down
15)    Encapsulation HDLC
16)    Sending CDP packets every 60 seconds
17)    Holdtime is 180 seconds
18) Ethernet0 is up, line protocol is up
19)    Encapsulation ARPA
20)    Sending CDP packets every 60 seconds
21)    Holdtime is 180 seconds
22) Serial0 is administratively down, line protocol is down
23)    Encapsulation HDLC
24)    Sending CDP packets every 60 seconds
25)    Holdtime is 180 seconds
26) Serial1 is up, line protocol is up
27)    Encapsulation HDLC
28)    Sending CDP packets every 60 seconds
29)    Holdtime is 180 seconds
30) Serial2 is administratively down, line protocol is down
31)    Encapsulation HDLC
32)    Sending CDP packets every 60 seconds
33)    Holdtime is 180 seconds
34) Serial3 is administratively down, line protocol is down
35)    Encapsulation HDLC
36)    Sending CDP packets every 60 seconds
37)    Holdtime is 180 seconds
38) Dallas#
```

and, for VTYs, from where the connections originated. Figure 6-19 shows the use of the two commands together.

Line 4 of Figure 6-19 indicates that someone has a telnet connection to our router. The person originated the connection from the host at address 172.16.11.2. To send a message to this user, we can reference the connection's absolute line number, 5, on the **send** command (Line 6). We are presented with a blank line (Line 8) for entering the text message. After entering the message, pressing <Ctrl-Z>, and confirming the operation, the message is sent to the specified line. The user with the session receives a message like this:

Figure 6-19
Send command
example.

```
1)  Dallas#show users
2)      Line        User       Host(s)        Idle Location
3)  *   0 con 0                idle       04:14:36
4)      5 vty 0               idle       00:00:05 172.16.11.2
5)
6)  Dallas#send 5
7)  Enter message, end with CTRL/Z; abort with CTRL/C:
8)  Who are you?
9)  Go away!<Ctrl-Z>
10) Send message? [confirm]y
11) Dallas#
```

```
***
***
*** Message from tty0 to tty5:
***
Who are you?
Go away!
```

The **send** command also accepts a relative line number along with the terminal line device type. For the example in Figure 6-19, the command **send vty 0** would have accomplished the same purpose. If you want to send a message to all active terminal lines, issue the command **send ***.

6.8 Debugging

The **debug** command allows us to see what IOS is doing as things happen and is normally used for troubleshooting and experimenting. We can turn on many different types of debug activities. Each one shows us something different about what is going on inside a router. To see the possible variations of the debug command, use the online, context-sensitive help. Start by typing **debug ?**, and extend the command from there.

Debug output, by default, is logged to the console line and to terminal lines that have the monitor capability turned on. See Section 5.3.6 for coverage of message logging. When we want to view debug output in a telnet session, we can give our VTY the monitor capability by issuing the command **terminal monitor** in privileged mode.

Debug output can also be excessive and can overload—and crash—a busy router when the router spends so much trying to tell us what it is doing that it stops doing what it is supposed to be doing—forwarding

▬ ▭ ▬
Figure 6-20
Debug IP RIP output.

```
1)  Dallas#debug ip rip
2)  RIP protocol debugging is on
3)  Dallas#
4)  RIP: sending v1 update to 255.255.255.255 via Ethernet0
    (172.16.10.1)
5)      subnet 172.16.20.0, metric 2
6)      subnet 172.16.11.0, metric 1
7)  RIP: sending v1 update to 255.255.255.255 via Serial1
    (172.16.11.1)
8)      subnet 172.16.10.0, metric 1
9)  RIP: received v1 update from 172.16.11.2 on Serial1
10)     172.16.20.0 in 1 hops
11) Dallas#no debug ip rip
12) RIP protocol debugging is off
13) Dallas#
```

packets. For this reason, the **debug** command should be used with caution. Figures 6-20 and 6-21 give sample outputs from debug commands.

The **debug ip rip** command instructs IOS to log the output and input of the IP RIP process. We see on Line 4 of Figure 6-20 that an update is being sent out the Ethernet0 interface; Lines 5 and 6 show the contents of the update. Line 9 shows an update being received on Serial1, presumably from FortWorth. Line 10 shows that the update contains the subnet address of FortWorth's Ethernet network.

▬ ▭ ▬
Figure 6-21
Debug IPX routing activity output.

```
1)  Dallas#debug ipx routing activity
2)  IPX routing debugging is on
3)  Dallas#
4)  IPXRIP: update from AC100B00.0010.7b3a.d4af
5)      AC101400 in 1 hops, delay 7
6)  IPXRIP: positing full update to AC100B00.ffff.ffff.ffff via
    Serial1 (broadcast)
7)  IPXRIP: Update len 40 src = AC100B00.0010.7b3a.d4bf,
    dst=AC100B00.ffff.ffff.ffff(453)
8)      network AC100A00, hops 1, delay 7
9)  IPXRIP: positing full update to AC100A00.ffff.ffff.ffff via
    Ethernet0 (broadcast
10) IPXRIP: Update len 48 src = AC100A00.0010.7b3a.d4bf,
    dst=AC100A00.ffff.ffff.ffff(453)
11)     network AC101400, hops 2, delay 8
12)     network AC100B00, hops 1, delay 2
13) Dallas#no debug ipx routing activity
14) IPX routing debugging is off
15) Dallas#
```

The **debug ipx routing activity** command shows the information that the IPX routing protocol process (IPX RIP) is transmitting and receiving. Line 4 of Figure 6-21 shows that an IPX RIP update was received on the interface with IPX network number AC100B00 (Serial1), and Line 5 shows that contents of the update (the IPX network number of FortWorth's Ethernet network). Line 10 shows that an update has been transmitted out the Ethernet0 interface, and Lines 11 and 12 show the contents of the update.

We can turn off debug activity by typing the word **no** followed by the command that we used to turn on debug activity—just say no. Examples are shown on Line 11 of Figure 6-20 and Line 13 of Figure 6-21.

We could have run both of the examples' debug activities at the same time; as a matter of fact, we can run as many simultaneous debug activities as we believe we—and our router—can handle. As we turn on more debug activities, the output generated by an individual activity gets interlaced with the output from the other activities and it becomes hard to read and interpret. The easiest way to turn off multiple debug activities is to issue the following command:

```
no debug all
```

The **no debug all** command will turn off all debug activities that have been started. Since the command **no debug all** exists, the opposite command, **debug all**, must also exist. The **debug all** command will turn on all debugging and is practically guaranteed to crash a very busy router and sometimes a not-so-busy router.

6.9   Rebooting

There are two ways to reboot a router.

1. Turn it off and back on.
2. Issue the privileged mode command **reload.**

Turning a router off and back on is the rather obvious way to reboot a router; however, most of the time, the power switch on a router is not accessible to us. Perhaps we want to reboot a router that is in another location. To do that, we have to use the **reload** command. If a power-cycle is a cold boot, then a reload is a warm boot.

When the **reload** command is issued, IOS always asks for confirmation before proceeding. See the following example.

```
Dallas#reload
Proceed with reload? [confirm]y
```

Some IOS releases require that we press <Enter> after we answer the *confirm* question; however, most do not.

If the **reload** command is issued after a configuration command, but the running configuration has not been copied to NVRAM, IOS will ask if it should save the running configuration for us. The following example shows this.

```
Dallas#reload
System configuration has been modified. Save? [yes/no]: y
Building configuration...
Proceed with reload? [confirm]y
```

If we tell IOS to save the configuration, the startup configuration will be replaced with the running configuration (just like the **copy running-config startup-config** command was issued) so the router will come back up with the same configuration it is currently running.

If we tell IOS not to save the configuration, it will proceed with the reload and the router will boot with the current startup configuration, although it may not include our latest changes.

Configuring IP

The *Internet Protocol* (IP) is the only routed protocol that is turned on by default on a Cisco router. The acronym IP is actually an abbreviated way of writing *TCP/IP* (Transmission Control Protocol/Internet Protocol), which is the suite of protocols and applications used on the Internet and many private internetworks.

We begin the coverage of IP configuration with a brief overview of IP and how IOS processes its traffic. Then we delve into the configuration itself and make some modifications to the internetwork that we built in Chapter 3. The only version of IP covered in this book is IP version 4.

7.1 IP Addressing

All hosts that run IP must have a unique *IP address,* which is a logical address that is independent of a host's hardware. IP addressing is perhaps the most mystifying part of IP for people who are new to the networking world; however, it really is very simple. To understand, you just need to use a little bit of binary (base 2) arithmetic and decimal (base 10) arithmetic.

IP addresses are 32 bits long and the normal way of writing them is called *dotted-decimal notation.* To write an address in dotted-decimal notation, we divide the 32 bits of the address into four 8-bit chunks. Each 8-bit chunk is called an *octet* or a *byte.* We then convert the octets from binary to decimal and put dots (.) between them. Figure 7-1 shows four forms of the same IP host address.

The first form in Figure 7-1 is normal binary, just a string of 32 ones and zeros; each one and zero is a bit. This form is difficult for people to read, but it is what a computer, like a router, sees. The decimal representation of the binary address has a rather large value—32 bits can represent decimal numbers between 0 and 4,294,967,295. The second line is

Figure 7-1

IP address notations.

Binary	11000000101010001000000101100011
Decimal	3,232,268,643
Dotted-Binary	11000000.10101000.10000001.01100011
Dotted-Decimal	192.168.129.99

the decimal equivalent of the first line. How would you like to read a number like that every time you wanted to communicate a host address to someone?

The third line of Figure 7-1 is just an intermediate step toward the last line, with the 32 bits divided into four octets. The last form, dotted-decimal notation, is the one that we use, and it is the easiest to read and write.

Since each of the four quarters (octets) of an IP address is eight bits and the decimal values that can be represented with eight bits range from 0 to 255, the value of any one of the numbers in a dotted-decimal IP address cannot exceed 255.

IP addresses have two main parts—a *network part* that identifies the network where a host resides and a *node part* that identifies a specific host on the network (sort of like a street name and a house number). The network and node parts together make up the full IP address of a host. The network part is used by routing software to determine for which network a packet is destined. The node part is used by routing software to send a packet to an individual host once the packet has reached the host's network. Just to make this a little more exciting, the line between network and node moves.

There are three things that can be used to tell which part of an address is network and which part of an address is node. These are as follows:

1. Network Mask
2. Prefix Length
3. Class

The *network mask* explicitly specifies which part of an IP address represents a network. The network mask is 32 bits long and is normally written in dotted-decimal notation just like an address. An IP address and mask are usually written together, with the mask immediately after the address.

A network mask has binary ones in the bit positions that represent the network part of an address and binary zeros in the bit positions that represent the node part of an address. The binary ones must start from the left (most-significant) side of the mask and extend contiguously—they must be side—by side—until the network part ends; the rest of the mask must be all zeros. For example, the mask

```
255.255.255.0
```

when paired with an IP address, would tell us that the first 24 bits of the address is considered network and the last eight bits are node. This becomes clear when the binary equivalent of this mask is examined as shown below:

```
11111111 11111111 11111111  00000000   (Binary)
  255  .  255  .  255  .   0      (Dotted-Decimal)
```

We see that the mask has 24 ones, starting from the left, and eight zeros. Let us apply this mask to the IP address in Figure 7-1.

```
11000000 10101000 10000001 01100011   (Address)
11111111 11111111 11111111 00000000   (Mask)
```

Since the mask indicates that the first 24 bits of the address are the network, the network address must be

```
11000000 10101000 10000001 01100011
  192  .  168  .  129  .   0
```

An IP address that has binary zeros in all of the node bits represents a network, not a host. An IP address that has binary ones in all of the node bits represents all of the hosts on a network; this is called a *broadcast address*. The broadcast address of the 192.168.129.0 network in the previous example is

```
10101100 00010000 10000001 11111111
  192  .  168  .  129  .  255
```

The node values between all zeros and all ones identify individual hosts on a network. Therefore, the 192.168.129.0 255.255.255.0 network can have hosts with addresses between 192.168.129.1 and 192.168.129.254. That is 254 valid host addresses on this particular network. Below is the network hosts formula, the simple formula for calculating the number of valid host addresses on a network.

$(2^{(\text{No. of node bits})}) - 2 = $ No. of valid host addresses on a network (7.1)

Applying this formula to our running example with eight node bits has the following results:

```
2^8−2 = 256−2 = 254 Hosts
```

The answer is the same, 254 hosts on the network 192.168.129.0 255.255.255.0.

Some publications refer to an address's network part, the part that is significant for routing, as a *prefix*; therefore, all we really have to do is specify the length of the prefix to communicate the same information as the network mask. A *prefix length* is written immediately after an IP address as a decimal number preceded by a forward slash (/). In our preceding example, the host address with prefix length would be written as

```
192.168.129.99/24
```

Notice that 24 is the length of the network part (prefix) of the address; this leaves 8 (32 minus 24) node bits. Notice also that the prefix length is the number of binary ones in the network mask.

IOS can use either a network mask or a prefix length when it displays IP addressing information to us. As of version 11.2, prefix length is the default.

In the absence of an explicitly stated network mask, the *class* of an address identifies the network part of an address. There are five classes of IP addresses: A, B, C, D, and E; these are summarized in Table 7-1. Only class A, B, and C addresses are used for host addressing; class D addresses are used for multicast addresses; and class E addresses are reserved. We will be concentrating on class A, B, and C addresses.

Each of the host-address classes has a default-length network part and node part; therefore, each has a default network mask and prefix length. These are shown in Table 7-1.

The easiest way to tell the class of an address is to look at its first octet in decimal. Again, the first octet refers to the most significant one, the one on the left. Table 7-1 shows the range of decimal numbers for each class's first octet. Based on these ranges, the address, 192.168.129.99, used in Figure 7-1 and the network mask examples is a

TABLE 7-1

IP Address Classes

	First Octet Decimal	Network Bits	Node Bits	Default Mask	Default Prefix Length
Class A	1–126	8	24	255.0.0.0	/8
Class B	128–191	16	16	255.255.0.0	/16
Class C	192–223	24	8	255.255.255.0	/24
Class D	224–239			Multicast	
Class E	240–255			Reserved	

class C address. The network mask and prefix length we used in the examples is the default for a class C address.

7.1.1   Subnetting

There is a limited number of IP network addresses and, since each network must have its own address, we sometimes need to artificially increase the number of networks we can address at the cost of reducing the number of hosts on each network.

Suppose, for example, that we have been assigned a class B address to address our network. A class B address has 16 node bits so we can address a single network that has 65,534 hosts. Our internetwork is likely to have many networks and none of them is likely to have that many hosts. Therefore, to efficiently utilize the assigned address space, we can take some of the node bits and use them to address networks (subnets) instead of hosts. A *subnet* is still a network, but it has an address that has been derived from a classful network address such as a class B network address.

Subnetting is the act of taking some of the node bits and using them as network bits. This is accomplished by extending the binary ones of the network mask to the right to include some of the node bits. The length of the mask must still be 32; therefore, to increase the number of network bits, we must decrease the number of node bits.

The extent of the increase in network bits depends on the number of subnets we need and the number of hosts we need on each subnet. Table 7-2 shows some possible ways of subnetting class B networks and Table 7-3 shows some possible ways to subnet class C networks.

The number of hosts per subnet shown in Tables 7-2 and 7-3 was calculated using Eq. (7.1). The number of subnets uses the same formula except subnet bits have been substituted for node bits. The same formulas can be applied to class A addresses, even though they are not shown. The number of subnet bits in Tables 7-2 and 7-3 is the number of bits that the mask has been extended to the right from the default according to the address class.

Once we determine what type of subnetting will be used, addresses for each of the networks (or subnets) should be calculated. We can use decimal arithmetic to do this easily. Let us again take the IP address used in Figure 7-1, 192.168.129.99. Using the default mask for a class C address, we determined that this is the address of a host on the 192.168.129.0 network. Now suppose that we need to use this same network to address six

TABLE 7-2

Class B Network
Subnetting

Network Mask	Prefix Length	Subnet Bits	Node Bits	Subnets	Hosts
255.255.0.0	/16	0	16	0 (1 Net)	65,534
255.255.192.0	/18	2	14	2	16,382
255.255.224.0	/19	3	13	6	8190
255.255.240.0	/20	4	12	14	4094
255.255.248.0	/21	5	11	30	2046
255.255.252.0	/22	6	10	62	1022
255.255.254.0	/23	7	9	126	510
255.255.255.0	/24	8	8	254	254
255.255.255.128	/25	9	7	510	126
255.255.255.192	/26	10	6	1022	62
255.255.255.224	27	11	5	2046	30
255.255.255.240	/28	12	4	4094	14
255.255.255.248	/29	13	3	8190	6
255.255.255.252	/30	14	2	16382	2

TABLE 7-3

Class C Network
Subnetting

Network Mask	Prefix Length	Subnet Bits	Node Bits	Subnets	Hosts
255.255.255.0	/24	0	8	0 (1 Net)	254
255.255.255.192	/26	2	6	2	62
255.255.255.224	/27	3	5	6	30
255.255.255.240	/28	4	4	14	14
255.255.255.248	/29	5	3	30	6
255.255.255.252	/30	6	2	62	2

networks that will have no more than 30 hosts each. Based on Table 7-3, we can use a network mask of 255.255.255.224 (three subnet bits) to accomplish this.

Following these steps to calculate the network addresses of the subnets.

- Locate the last nonzero octet of the network mask.
- Note the octet number and its value.
- Subtract the value from 256 to get the subnet seed.
- Calculate multiples of the seed to get the subnet addresses.

For example, in our mask, the last nonzero octet is the fourth octet and its value is 224. Subtracting 224 from 256 yields 32. The subnet seed is 32, and all of the subnet addresses are multiples of 32 in the fourth octet. The network addresses of our six subnets are as follows:

1. 192.168.129.32
2. 192.168.129.64
3. 192.168.129.96
4. 192.168.129.128
5 192.168.129.160
6. 192.168.129.192

That is six subnets just as Table 7-3 indicated. The first and last combinations of the three subnet bits are not normally used, even though they can be used. These combinations yield subnet addresses 192.168.129.0 and 192.168.129.224. We will call these the *zero subnet* and the *all-ones subnet,* respectively. IOS will support the use of these special subnets, but not all other hosts will; therefore, to be safe, we are not including them here.

The broadcast address of each subnet is the address one less than that of the next higher subnet. For example, the broadcast address of the 192.168.129.96 subnet is 192.168.129.127. Remember that the valid host addresses for a network or subnet are those addresses between the network's address and its broadcast address; therefore, the valid host addresses for the 192.168.129.96 255.255.255.224 network range from 192.168.129.97 through 192.168.129.126; that is 30 hosts, just as we calculated.

Our example IP host address, 192.168.129.99, is in this range; therefore, it is a host on the 192.168.129.96/27 subnet. We could have just calculated this by using a calculation similar to the one we used to calculate the subnet addresses. The last nonzero value in the network mask is 224 in the fourth octet. Dividing the fourth octet of the host address (99) by the subnet seed (32) gives a result of 3 (never mind the remainder). Multiplying the result (3) by the seed (32) yields the subnet address's fourth octet value (96).

7.1.2 Public and Private IP Addresses

Network traffic that traverses a public network such as the Internet must use public addresses. When we connect one of our networks directly to the Internet, we usually have public addresses assigned to us by an *Internet Service Provider* (ISP). ISPs get their public addresses from *American Registry for Internet Numbers* (ARIN).

IP packets with public addresses can be routed on the Internet because the addresses are unique; however, because of a shortage of public addresses, private addresses have been defined for use on networks that are not going to connect directly to the Internet. RFC 1918 defines one class A network address, 16 class B network addresses, and 256 class C network addresses to be private. These addresses are as follows:

- 10.0.0.0
- 172.16.0.0 through 172.31.0.0
- 192.168.0.0 through 192.168.255.0

The IP address, 192.168.129.99, that we have been using in our examples is taken from a private class C network address.

Many companies are using these network addresses to address their internal internetworks (intranetworks), which connect to the Internet through a firewall or some other system that performs *Network Address Translation* (NAT). In these cases, NAT is used to translate the private addresses found in the internal IP packets to public addresses to allow the packets to be routed on the external Internet.

7.2   IP Overview

The TCP/IP protocol suite has been around since the late 1970s—long before the OSI Reference Model (see Section 2.1.1) was developed. However, since the OSI Reference Model is a "reference model," we will refer to it when discussing the layers of the IP stack. The OSI Reference Model and the IP stack are shown side by side in Figure 7-2. The functionality of the OSI Reference Model layers is present even though the IP stack is represented as only four layers instead of seven.

We are going to cover just enough about the basics of IP to allow us to understand what we are doing when we configure it. We will start at the bottom of the stack and work our way up describing each layer and the individual blocks shown in them in Figure 7-2.

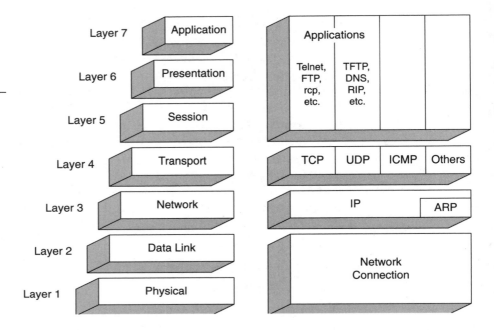

7.2.1   Layers 1 and 2

Layers 1 and 2 deal with the connection of a host to a network. IP running on a host is independent of the type of network connection.

Layer 1 defines the physical medium where a host is attached. A host running IP can be attached to just about any kind of network.

Layer 2 defines the format of the frame header and trailer that a host builds and wraps around a packet before transmitting the packet. The frame header contains a field that indicates the protocol encapsulated between the frame header and the frame trailer. The field is called either *protocol type* or *Service Access Point* (SAP) depending on the encapsulation type configured on the host's interface. For example, with ARPA encapsulation on Ethernet, a protocol type field value of 0x0800 (hexadecimal 0800) indicates that an IP packet is encapsulated within the frame and an IP header immediately follows the frame header. With SAP encapsulation, a SAP field value of 0x06 means the same thing.

The layer-2 header of a frame traveling a LAN contains the addresses that are used to identify the network host that transmitted the frame and the host, or hosts, to whom the frame is destined. These addresses are called *MAC addresses.*. The MAC address of each host on a network must be unique. The layer-2 header gets removed and rebuilt each time that frame is forwarded by a router; therefore, the layer-2 addresses change in the header from one network to the next.

7.2.2 Layer 3

At layer 3, there can be either an IP header or Address Resolution Protocol (ARP) data.

7.2.2.1 Internet Protocol

Internet Protocol (IP) is used for the exchange of data between hosts. At layer 3 of an IP packet is the IP header. The IP header does not contain real data, but it does contain many items that are used by the protocol. Some of these are shown below:

- Source IP Address
- Destination IP Address
- Time to Live
- Protocol Number

The *source IP address* is the 32-bit IP address of the host that originated the packet. The *destination IP address* is the 32-bit IP address that routers examine to determine where to route a packet; the destination IP address can be a unicast host address, a broadcast address, or a multicast address. Neither the source IP address nor the destination IP address normally changes from the time a packet leaves a host to the time the packet arrives at its destination.

The *time to live* (TTL) field in a packet's IP header is decremented each time the packet is routed by a router. The use of TTL keeps a packet from being routed endlessly on an internetwork when its destination cannot be found. When a router decrements a packet's TTL to zero (0), the router must drop the packet. The router can then send an ICMP message to the packet's source indicating the reason the packet was dropped (TTL exceeded). The TTL field has a maximum value of 255; therefore, in theory, if the source host sent a packet with a beginning TTL of 255, the packet could get routed 255 times before it got dropped.

The *protocol number* identifies the next level protocol, that is, what is after the IP header in the packet. Following are some examples of items that could follow the IP header and their associated protocol numbers:

TCP Header—Protocol Number 6

UDP Header—Protocol Number 17

ICMP Message—Protocol Number 1

IGRP Message—Protocol Number 9

Upper-layer applications usually use TCP or UDP, but before a host gets to the application data, it must read a TCP or UDP header. TCP and UDP are probably the most used protocol numbers.

7.2.2.2 Address Resolution Protocol (ARP)

Hosts use *ARP* to acquire the MAC address of another host to which a frame is being transmitted. This is done during the frame encapsulation process. A source host presumably would already know the IP address of a destination host and would be able to build the layer-3 (IP) header containing both source and destination IP addresses. However, the source host also must build a frame header for encapsulation of the packet on a LAN. The frame header contains the source and destination MAC addresses. The source host knows its own MAC address, but it needs to know the destination host's MAC address to complete the frame header.

The source host locates a destination host's MAC address by sending a layer-2 broadcast frame onto the LAN asking for the MAC address associated with a given IP address; this frame is called an *ARP request.* Every host on a network examines a layer-2 broadcast frame. If the destination host is on the network, it will recognize the IP address in the ARP request frame and send an *ARP reply* to the source host. The ARP reply contains the destination host's MAC address that the source host uses to complete the frame header. The source host also puts the destination host's MAC address and IP address into a table, called the *ARP cache.* The next time the source host wants to send a frame to the destination host, it can just look up the destination host's MAC address in the ARP cache and not send the ARP request.

If a router receives an ARP request for a destination host on a network other than the one on which the request was received, the router can reply on behalf of the destination host. The source host receives an ARP reply containing the router interface's MAC address, thus instructing the source host to send its frame to the router to be routed. The feature, called *proxy ARP,* is enabled by default in IOS, but we can disable it if we desire.

ARP is extremely important in IP-based networks. Some textbooks call ARP a layer-2 protocol because its messages are never routed at layer 3. ARP is included at layer 3 here only because the ARP messages follow the layer-2 header.

7.2.3   Layer 4

A router is not normally concerned with information above layer 3 in a packet unless the router is generating its own traffic, receiving traffic destined for it, or performing packet filtering.

IP traffic generated by a router can include ICMP messages and routing protocol updates. A router both receives and generates traffic when a telnet connection is established to it or from it.

7.2.3.1   Transmission Control Protocol

Transmission Control Protocol (TCP) is a connection-oriented protocol. This means that applications can use TCP at layer 4 to establish a connection with each other, and the applications can depend on TCP to perform sequencing, acknowledging, and windowing of their data. TCP is considered to be a reliable transport for application data.

Port numbers in the TCP header identify the upper-layer applications—source and destination—that are using the connection.

7.2.3.2   User Datagram Protocol

User Datagram Protocol (UDP) is a connectionless protocol. Applications that use UDP at layer 4 must do connection establishment themselves if a connection is required. UDP does no data sequencing, acknowledging, or windowing. UDP is used when applications want to handle these tasks themselves or applications want to just send data to other applications without the overhead and delay of connection establishment.

Similarly to TCP, port numbers in the UDP header identify the upper layer application that a message came from and the upper layer application for which a message is destined.

7.2.3.3   Internet Control and Messaging Protocol

Hosts (especially routers) use the Internet Control and Messaging Protocol (ICMP) to communicate network conditions or errors to other hosts. For example, ICMP is used to communicate a packet's exceeded time to live to the host that sent the packet (see Section 7.2.2.1).

ICMP messages are also used to communicate broken routing or non-existent networks to transmitting hosts. ICMP *Destination Unreachable* messages are used for this purpose.

Probably the most recognizable use of ICMP is found within the ping application. The IP implementation of ping uses ICMP *echo* messages to test connectivity. When we want to find out if a host is accessible, we can "ping" the host with an ICMP echo request containing data. If the host receives the request, it should respond by returning an ICMP echo response containing the same data.

7.2.3.4   Others
Other possible protocols that appear at layer 4 of IP include *Interior Gateway Router Protocol* (IGRP), *Enhanced IGRP* (EIGRP), and *Open Shortest Path First* (OSPF). All of these examples are IP routing protocols.

7.2.4   Layers 5, 6, and 7

Layers 5, 6, and 7 are loosely bundled for all IP-based applications. Most of the applications we use everyday run over TCP or UDP. IOS can run many of these applications.

7.2.4.1   TCP Applications
TCP applications that can run on IOS include:

- Telnet (client and server)
- rcp (client)
- HTTP (server)

Telnet is a remote session application that is used when configuring a remote router; *rcp* is a file copy application that can be used to copy files to and from a Cisco router; *HTTP* is the application used to transfer World Wide Web (WWW) pages from Web servers to Web clients (browsers).

7.2.4.2   UDP Applications
UDP applications that can run on IOS include:

- TFTP (client and server)
- SNMP (client)
- DNS (client)

TFTP is a file copy application that is used to copy files to and from a Cisco router; *SNMP* is a network management application used to monitor and manage network devices; and *DNS* is the application used to translate host names to IP addresses and vice versa.

7.3 IP Routing

When a router receives a frame that contains an IP packet, the router removes the frame header and trailer; it then sends the packet to the IP routing process. The IP routing process looks for an entry in the IP routing table that matches the destination IP address in the packet's IP header.

The IP routing table contains a list of the best paths to the networks that IOS knows about. Each network entry includes its address and its prefix length (or network mask). The prefix length tells the router how much of an address is significant for routing, or how much of a destination address to use when a routing decision is being made. If the router finds multiple matches for a destination in the routing table, the router uses the most specific entry, that is, the one with the longest prefix length.

The routing table also contains the name of the interface out of which IOS should transmit a packet to reach the network and, potentially, the address of another router (a next-hop gateway) to which IOS can forward the packet for further routing. Figure 7-3 shows the display of the IP routing table resulting from the entry of the **show ip route** command on our test router Dallas.

Figure 7-3

IP routing table on Dallas.

```
1)  Dallas>show ip route
2)  Codes:  C - connected, S - static, I - IGRP, R - RIP,
            M - mobile, B - BGP
3)          D - EIGRP, EX - EIGRP external, O - OSPF, IA - OSPF
            inter area
4)          N1 - OSPF NSSA external type 1, N2 - OSPF NSSA exter-
            nal type 2
5)          E1 - OSPF external type 1, E2 - OSPF external type 2,
            E - EGP
6)          i - IS-IS, L1 - IS-level-1, L2 - IS-IS level-2,
            * - candidate default
7)          U - per-user static route, o - ODR
8)
9)  Gateway of last resort is not set
10)
11)      172.16.0.0/24 is subnetted, 3 subnets
12) R        172.16.20.0 [120/1] via 172.16.11.2, 00:00:05,
             Serial1
13) C        172.16.10.0 is directly connected, Ethernet0
14) C        172.16.11.0 is directly connected, Serial1
15) Dallas>
```

We will see many versions of IP routing tables throughout this chapter as we make modifications to our test network, but let us start with this very simple one. The display of the IP routing table begins with a legend describing the character notations that appear at the beginning of each network entry. On Line 12 of Figure 7-3, the entry begins with an *R* indicating that the network was learned through RIP. Lines 13 and 14 begin with a *C* indicating networks that are directly connected to this router.

Line 11 shows that we have three subnets, each with a prefix length of /24; that is a network mask of 255.255.255.0 (24 ones, remember). The two entries for directly connected networks are almost self-explanatory. All we are shown is the interface that is used to reach the network.

The RIP entry on Line 12 contains a little more information. We can interpret this the following way. When IOS receives a packet with a destination address matching 172.16.20.0/24, IOS should forward the packet out Serial1 to the router with address 172.16.11.2; network 172.16.20.0/24 is one hop away, and IOS last received an update for it 5 seconds ago. The next hop router, the time, and the interface are easily spotted in the displayed entry. The hop count is not so obvious.

Immediately after the network address itself are two numbers in brackets, *[120/1]*. The second number within the brackets (after the slash) is a metric, *1* in this case. Since RIP's metric is hop count, this must be a number of hops. The first number within the brackets is called the *administrative distance*.

IOS has three primary ways of learning about network routes to put into its routing table. Two of these are displayed in Figure 7-3: a direct network connection and a routing protocol. The third is a static route, which is our manual entry of a route into the routing table.

IOS can run many routing protocols simultaneously; only RIP is being run so far on our test network. Each routing protocol uses a different *metric*, which is used to gauge the length of the paths to the networks it has learned. When IOS learns about multiple paths to a network from a routing protocol, IOS puts the best path, the one with the lowest metric, into the routing table. However, when IOS is running multiple routing protocols and it learns about multiple paths to a network from different routing protocols, how does it compare the different metrics of the protocols? The answer is, "It doesn't."

Each routing protocol and each other way that IOS can get potential routing table entries has an associated administrative distance. We can think of administrative distance as a measure of believability for something heard. The lower the administrative distance for a potential routing table entry, the more believable the entry and, thus, the more likely the learned route will be placed into the routing table as the best route to a network.

A directly connected network has an administrative distance of zero (0). This is the lowest possible distance and the most believable route. A route cannot be any better than directly connected. The next most believable route is a static route; if we manually enter a route into the routing table, IOS assumes that we know what we are doing. A static route has a default administrative distance of one (1). We cover static routes and routing protocols in more detail as we implement them.

When IOS learns about several routes to a network and must select the best one for placement in the routing table, the first measurement IOS uses is administrative distance. The route with the lowest administrative distance is the best one and is placed in the routing table. If IOS has multiple routes with the same administrative distance, the one with the lowest metric is the best one. If multiple routes to a network have the same administrative distance and the same metric, all of the routes—up to six—are placed into the routing table; IOS then load shares traffic across all of the routes.

7.4   Configuring IP on an Interface

The command to tell IOS to route IP packets on an interface is

```
ip address address mask
```

where *address* is the IP address, in dotted-decimal notation, that should be assigned to the interface, and *mask* is the address's network mask in dotted-decimal notation. The **ip address** command is an interface configuration mode and subinterface configuration mode command. This makes sense because we must specify the interface that will get the address before we assign the address.

The address specified with this command becomes the primary IP address for an interface. To change an interface's IP address, we can just type this command again in interface configuration mode with the new IP address and mask.

The **ip address** command is used in the next section when we add a router to our test internetwork.

7.5 Adding a Router

We already have an internetwork configured to route IP traffic. We configured this internetwork of two routers—Dallas and FortWorth—in Chapter 3 using the System Configuration Dialog. Figure 7-4 shows the existing internetwork's IP configuration.

The current routing table for Dallas is shown in Figure 7-3. The two routers are using the RIP routing protocol to exchange information about their networks.

To illustrate the configuration of IP, we are going to add a router to the internetwork and do its configuration from scratch using the IOS command line interface. The new internetwork of three routers is shown in Figure 7-5. We are going to add a router named Austin, and this three-router internetwork will be used for most of the examples throughout the rest of this book.

Austin has a 256-kbps leased line to Dallas and a 56-kbps leased line to FortWorth. Figure 7-5 has the IP addresses of each of the new interfaces that we will be using to connect Austin into the internetwork. Notice that abbreviations for the interfaces are being used to conserve space—Ethernet is *E* and Serial is *S*.

The implementation of Austin will be done using the following steps:

- Configure Serial0 on Dallas.
- Configure Serial1 on FortWorth.

Figure 7-4

Two-router IP internetwork.

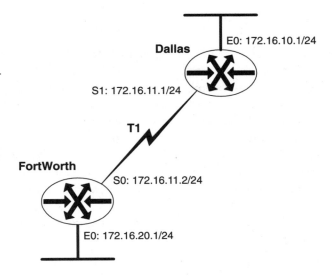

▬▬ ▬▬ ▬▬

Figure 7-5
Three-router IP
internetwork with
interface
addresses.

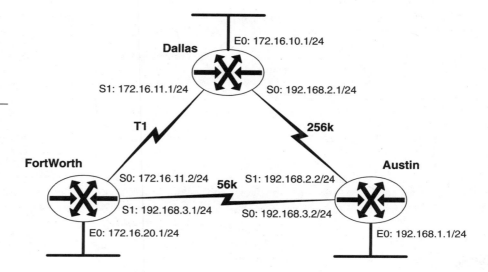

■ Configure miscellaneous items (see Chapter 6) and all active interfaces on Austin.

Dallas and FortWorth already have working configurations; therefore, they each need only one interface configured. Austin will be booted with no startup configuration, and we will answer *No* to the initial configuration dialog question (see Section 3.5.1.1) to avoid entering the System Configuration Dialog.

7.5.1   Configuring IP on Dallas Serial0

We need to give interface Serial0 on Dallas the IP address 192.168.2.1 with a network mask of 255.255.255.0 (prefix length /24), according to Figure 7-5. Since the leased line to which Serial0 connects has a bandwidth of 256 kbps, we should also set the bandwidth for future reference. Figure 7-6 shows the commands for configuring Serial0 on Dallas for connection to Austin.

IOS configuration changes must be made from a configuration mode. The **configure terminal** command (Line 1) is used to get to global configuration mode, and the **interface serial0** command (Line 3) is used to get to interface configuration mode where commands affecting Serial0 can be entered. The **ip address** command is used to assign the IP address to the interface (Line 4) and the bandwidth is set to 256 (Line 5). The bandwidth parameter was described in Section 6.2.4; it does not

Figure 7-6

IP configuration on
Dallas Serial0.

```
1)  Dallas#configure terminal
2)  Enter configuration commands, one per line. End with CNTL/Z.
3)  Dallas(config)#interface serial0
4)  Dallas(config-if)#ip address 192.168.2.1 255.255.255.0
5)  Dallas(config-if)#bandwidth 256
6)  Dallas(config-if)#description 256k Line to Austin
7)  Dallas(config-if)#no shutdown
8)  Dallas(config-if)#<Ctrl-Z>
9)  Dallas#
```

affect the operation of the WAN—we are just putting it here for future informational purposes. The description (Line 6) is just our way of documenting the reason for the link. Since Serial0 was administratively down when we started, we start it with the **no shutdown** command (Line 7). Serial0 will not come up until Austin's Serial1 interface is configured and keepalives are exchanged across the link.

7.5.2   Configuring IP on FortWorth Serial1

According to Figure 7-5, interface Serial1 on FortWorth should be assigned the IP address 192.168.3.1 with a network mask of 255.255.255.0 (prefix length /24). Figure 7-7 shows the commands for configuring Serial1 on FortWorth for connection to Austin.

The commands for FortWorth are very similar to those we just entered for Serial0 of Dallas in Section 7.5.1. The **configure terminal** command (Line 1) is used to get to global configuration mode where we can make changes. Since we are changing the configuration of an interface, we use the **interface serial1** command (Line 3) to get to interface configuration mode for Serial1. The **ip address** command is used to assign the IP address to the interface (Line 4) and the bandwidth is set to 56 (Line 5). The description (Line 6) is just documentation for the link. Serial1 was

Figure 7-7

IP configuration on
FortWorth Serial1.

```
1)  FortWorth#configure terminal
2)  Enter configuration commands, one per line. End with CNTL/Z.
3)  FortWorth(config)#interface serial1
4)  FortWorth(config-if)#ip address 192.168.3.1 255.255.255.0
5)  FortWorth(config-if)#bandwidth 56
6)  FortWorth(config-if)#description 56k Line to Austin
7)  FortWorth(config-if)#no shutdown
8)  FortWorth(config-if)#<Ctrl-Z>
9)  FortWorth#
```

administratively down when we started; we start it with the **no shutdown** command (Line 7). Serial1 will not actually come up (up/up state) until Austin's Serial0 interface is activated and keepalives are exchanged.

7.5.3 Configuring Austin

When we turned on the new router that is to become Austin, it had no startup configuration; therefore, IOS asked us to enter the initial configuration dialog. We answered *No* to the question. It looked like this:

```
Notice: NVRAM invalid, possibly due to write erase.
       — System Configuration Dialog —

At any point you may enter a question mark '?' for help.
Use ctrl-c to abort configuration dialog at any prompt.
Default settings are in square brackets '[]'.
Would you like to enter the initial configuration dialog? [yes]: no

Press RETURN to get started!
```

When we do not run the System Configuration Dialog on a new router, the result is a running configuration that essentially does nothing useful. The router has the default name *Router;* all of the interfaces are shut down (administratively down state) and there are no passwords. We will start from the user mode prompt and configure the host name, the passwords, and the interfaces. All of the commands for accomplishing this are shown in Figure 7-8.

The commands used in Figure 7-8 have been previously covered in this book; we use this context to review them. We cannot make any changes to IOS from user mode; therefore, we must use the **enable** command (Line 1) to get to privileged mode. Notice that the prompt changed (Line 2) and IOS did not ask for a password before allowing us to access privileged mode. At this point there is no enable password and the router's name is *Router* (as indicated by command prompt on Lines 1, 2, and 4). To enter configuration commands, we must enter configuration mode; the **configure terminal** command (Line 2) puts us there.

We use the **hostname** command to name the router Austin (Line 4). The configuration change is immediate; the new host name is entered into the running configuration and the next command prompt has the new name in it (Line 5).

Every router needs passwords; therefore, we will take the opportunity to define them. The two types of enable passwords are configured first.

Figure 7-8

Initial configuration
of Austin with IP.

```
 1)  Router>enable
 2)  Router#configure terminal
 3)  Enter configuration commands, one per line. End with CNTL/Z.
 4)  Router(config)#hostname Austin
 5)  Austin(config)#enable secret itsasecret
 6)  Austin(config)#enable password enableme
 7)  Austin(config)#line vty 0 4
 8)  Austin(config-line)#password letmein
 9)  Austin(config-line)#login
10)  Austin(config-line)#line con 0
11)  Austin(config-line)#password letmein
12)  Austin(config-line)#login
13)  Austin(config-line)#interface ethernet0
14)  Austin(config-if)#ip address 192.168.1.1 255.255.255.0
15)  Austin(config-if)#description Austin Ethernet LAN
16)  Austin(config-if)#no shutdown
17)  Austin(config-if)#interface serial0
18)  Austin(config-if)#ip address 192.168.3.2 255.255.255.0
19)  Austin(config-if)#bandwidth 56
20)  Austin(config-if)#description 56k Line to FortWorth
21)  Austin(config-if)#no shutdown
22)  Austin(config-if)#interface serial1
23)  Austin(config-if)#ip address 192.168.2.2 255.255.255.0
24)  Austin(config-if)#bandwidth 256
25)  Austin(config-if)#description 256k Line to Dallas
26)  Austin(config-if)#no shutdown
27)  Austin(config-if)#<Ctrl-Z>
28)  Austin#
```

The enable secret password is set with the **enable secret** command
(Line 5) and the regular enable password is set with the **enable
password** command (Line 6). The passwords for the five VTY terminal
lines, 0 through 4, must be defined in line configuration mode, so we
issue the **line vty 0 4** command (Line 7) indicating to IOS that the next
commands are to be applied to all of the VTYs. Once in line configuration
mode, we assign the VTY passwords with the **password** command (Line
8) and allow logins with the **login** command (Line 9). If the VTYs do not
have passwords, no one will be able to establish a telnet connection to
Austin. The last password is the one for the console. The console is
another terminal line device so we type the **line con 0** command (Line
10) to go to line configuration mode for the console. The **line** command is
a global configuration command; therefore, it can be typed in any configuration mode. We used the **line** command in line configuration mode,
and IOS just changed the line we were configuring. The command
prompt did not change; it is very important to realize that IOS did not
tell us that we are configuring a different line; we must be aware of what
we are doing. Console password authentication is enabled with the
password command (Line 11) and the **login** command (Line 12).

To configure an interface, we must be in interface configuration mode; the **interface** command is used to put us there. Just like the **line** command, **interface** is a global configuration command and can be used in any configuration mode. The **interface ethernet0** command (Line 13) informs IOS that we wish to enter interface configuration mode and type commands that affect Ethernet0. From there, we assign the IP address (Line 14) and description (Line 15) for Ethernet0. The **no shutdown** command (Line 16) activates the interface.

The configurations of Serial0 (Lines 17 through 21) and Serial1 (Lines 22 through 26) are similar to that of Ethernet0 except for the **bandwidth** commands that set the informational bandwidth parameter to an appropriate value for each interface. The IP addresses for the three interfaces were taken directly from Figure 7-5.

We could have done most of this configuration with the System Configuration Dialog. Typing the commands on the command line is usually faster than answering questions even though the command line may not be quite as intuitive. The command line does not limit what we can do. The System Configuration Dialog cannot be used to set a console password, define an interface's bandwidth, or define an interface's description. Since we wanted to perform those functions, we had to use the command line anyway. So why not just do it all from the command line?

7.5.4 Examining IP Routing Tables

We are going to check connectivity by examining the routing tables. Routing tables are not always a good indication of connectivity in a production network, but we are going to use them for illustration. Figure 7-9 shows our three-router internetwork with the addresses of each of the networks. Figure 7-5 shows the individual interface addresses.

The new IP routing tables for Dallas, FortWorth, and Austin are shown in Figures 7-10, 7-11, and 7-12, respectively.

Much of the specific information displayed was described in Section 7.3. The only difference in the current Dallas routing table and the original one in Figure 7-3 is the addition of the directly connected network 192.168.2.0/24 (Figure 7-10, Line 9). IOS added this to the routing table because we assigned an IP address to Serial0 and Serial0 has an up/up status.

The new Dallas routing table does not show the Austin Ethernet LAN or the serial link between FortWorth and Austin; therefore, Dallas cannot route a packet to those destinations.

Figure 7-9
Three-router IP internetwork with network addresses.

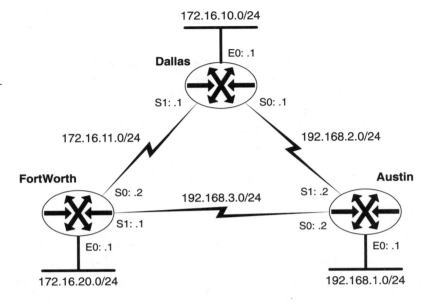

172.16.10.0/24

E0: .1

Dallas

S1: .1   S0: .1

172.16.11.0/24   192.168.2.0/24

FortWorth   **Austin**

S0: .2   192.168.3.0/24   S1: .2

S1: .1   S0: .2

E0: .1   E0: .1

172.16.20.0/24   192.168.1.0/24

Figure 7-10
Dallas IP routing table after Austin installation.

```
1)  Dallas#show ip route
2)  [text omitted]
3)  Gateway of last resort is not set
4)
5)       172.16.0.0/24 is subnetted, 3 subnets
6)  R       172.16.20.0 [120/1] via 172.16.11.2, 00:00:14, Serial1
7)  C       172.16.10.0 is directly connected, Ethernet0
8)  C       172.16.11.0 is directly connected, Serial1
9)  C  192.168.2.0/24 is directly connected, Serial0
10) Dallas#
```

Figure 7-11
FortWorth IP routing table after Austin installation.

```
1)  FortWorth#show ip route
2)  [text omitted]
3)  Gateway of last resort is not set
4)
5)       172.16.0.0/24 is subnetted, 3 subnets
6)  C       172.16.20.0 is directly connected, Ethernet0
7)  R       172.16.10.0 [120/1] via 172.16.11.1, 00:00:08, Serial0
8)  C       172.16.11.0 is directly connected, Serial0
9)  C  192.168.3.0/24 is directly connected, Serial1
10) FortWorth#
```

Figure 7-12
Austin initial IP
routing table.

```
1)  Austin#show ip route
2)  [text omitted]
3)  Gateway of last resort is not set
4)
5)  C    192.168.1.0/24 is directly connected, Ethernet0
6)  C    192.168.2.0/24 is directly connected, Serial1
7)  C    192.168.3.0/24 is directly connected, Serial0
8)  Austin#
```

The FortWorth IP routing table now contains network 192.168.3.0/24 (Figure 7-11, Line 9) because we assigned an IP address to Serial1, which is in an up/up state. The FortWorth routing table does not contain a path to the Austin Ethernet LAN or the serial link between Dallas and Austin; therefore FortWorth cannot route packets destined for either of those networks.

The Austin routing table after the initial configuration shows only the directly connected networks.

Dallas and FortWorth do not have a route to the Austin Ethernet LAN, and Austin does not have a route to either the Dallas Ethernet LAN or the FortWorth Ethernet LAN. All of the routers should have routing table entries that allow IOS to route packets to any network. The reason the routing tables are incomplete is that IOS has not been told of the existence of the additional networks, yet. We need to solve that problem. We are going to partially solve the problem with the brute force method (static routes) and then move on to something a little more elegant (dynamic routing protocols) for complete resolution.

7.6   Static Routes

We need to tell Austin and Dallas of the existence of their Ethernet LANs. We are going to start by manually adding an entry to the Austin IP routing table; this entry is called a *static route*. Adding a static route is done with the global configuration command **ip route**. Figure 7-13 shows the configuration on Austin of a static route to the Dallas Ethernet LAN.

The command to add the static route is on Line 3. The network address of the Dallas Ethernet LAN is 172.16.10.0/24; therefore, the network entry we want to add to the routing table has the address 172.16.10.0 and the network mask 255.255.255.0. The **ip route** command requires the network mask; the prefix length cannot be used. The

Figure 7-13

Austin static route
to Dallas Ethernet.

```
1) Austin#configure terminal
2) Enter configuration commands, one per line. End with CNTL/Z.
3) Austin(config)#ip route 172.16.10.0 255.255.255.0 192.168.2.1
4) Austin(config)#<Ctrl-Z>
5) Austin#
```

last address on the command is the address of the next hop gateway. The *gateway* is the address of the router to which Austin should send packets destined for the indicated network. The gateway address should be on a network that is already in the Austin routing table. In this case, the gateway address is the Dallas Serial0 interface, which is directly connected to Austin. Austin's new routing table is shown in Figure 7-14.

The static route (Line 6) is displayed with the letter *S* in the left column; the static route's administrative distance is 1 and its metric is 0. We can change the administrative distance of a static route by entering the new value of the distance at the end of the **ip route** command. Now when Austin gets a packet destined for the Dallas Ethernet LAN, Austin will forward the packet to 192.168.2.1 out its Serial1 interface.

7.6.1 Testing Connectivity with Ping

The *ping* application is one that uses ICMP echo packets to verify connectivity between two hosts. There are two forms of ping implemented in IOS: simple ping and extended ping. Let us start with simple ping.

A *simple* ping can be done in either user mode or privileged mode and is invoked with the **ping** command. Either an IP address or a host name follows the word **ping**. If a host name is used, some form of address resolution must be used to resolve the name to an IP address. Figure 7-15 shows a simple ping from Austin to Dallas.

Figure 7-14

Austin IP routing
table after static
route
configuration.

```
1)  Austin#show ip route
2)  [text omitted]
3)  Gateway of last resort is not set
4)
5)       172.16.0.0/24 is subnetted, 1 subnets
6)  S       172.16.10.0 [1/0] via 192.168.2.1
7)  C    192.168.1.0/24 is directly connected, Ethernet0
8)  C    192.168.2.0/24 is directly connected, Serial1
9)  C    192.168.3.0/24 is directly connected, Serial0
10) Austin#
```

Figure 7-15
Simple ping from
Austin to Dallas.

```
1)  Austin#ping 172.16.10.1
2)
3)  Type escape sequence to abort.
4)  Sending 5, 100-byte ICMP Echos to 172.16.10.1, timeout is 2
    seconds:
5)  !!!!!
6)  Success rate is 100 percent (5/5), round-trip min/avg/max =
    12/12/12 ms
7)  Austin#
```

On Line 1, we have issued a ping to the address 172.16.10.1, which is the Dallas Ethernet0 interface. The simple ping will send five ICMP echo request packets with 100 bytes of data to the address, and it will expect to receive an ICMP echo reply packet within 2 seconds of each of the requests (Line 4). For each reply received within the timeout period, IOS displays an exclamation point (!). Austin received a reply for all five of the requests (Line 5); this made the success rate 100 percent (Line 6). Each of the replies arrived within 12 milliseconds (ms) of the request.

But what have we really tested here? Any traffic generated by IOS uses the address of the outbound interface as its source address; therefore, what we just tested was connectivity between the Dallas Ethernet0 interface and the Austin Serial1 interface. We would rather test LAN-to-LAN connectivity since our users' host systems are going to be attached to LANs. We can use an *extended* ping to override the source address of the ping packets to check routing between LANs. Figure 7-16 shows an extended ping from Austin's Ethernet0 interface to Dallas's Ethernet0 interface.

To perform an extended ping, just type **ping** in privileged mode. The extended ping application prompts us to change the default ping parameters. The first thing we are prompted for is the protocol (Line 2); the default is IP, which is what we want. Then we are prompted for the destination IP address (Line 3), the number of echo requests to send (Line 4), the size of the requests (Line 5), and the reply timeout (Line 6). Default answers to the questions are shown in brackets; pressing <Enter> accepts the default. The default answers are those that the simple ping uses.

Changing the source address of the ping echoes is an extended command; therefore, we answer *yes* to the Line 7 question indicating that we want to use extended commands. On Line 8, we set the source address to 192.168.1.1. For this test, we took the default answers to all of the rest of the questions.

```
1)  Austin#ping
2)  Protocol [ip]: <Enter>
3)  Target IP address: 172.16.10.1
4)  Repeat count [5]: <Enter>
5)  Datagram size [100]: <Enter>
6)  Timeout in seconds [2]: <Enter>
7)  Extended commands [n]: y
8)  Source address or interface: 192.168.1.1
9)  Type of service [0]: <Enter>
10) Set DF bit in IP header? [no]: <Enter>
11) Validate reply data? [no]: <Enter>
12) Data pattern [0xABCD]: <Enter>
13) Loose, Strict, Record, Timestamp, Verbose[none]: <Enter>
14) Sweep range of sizes [n]: <Enter>
15) Type escape sequence to abort.
16) Sending 5, 100-byte ICMP Echos to 172.16.10.1, timeout is 2 seconds:
17) .....
18) Success rate is 0 percent (0/5)
19) Austin#
```

Figure 7-16 *Extended ping from Austin to Dallas.*

The extended ping fails as indicated by the five periods (.) on Line 17. Using the simple ping, Dallas sends the echo replies to the address of the Austin Serial1 interface, which is on one of Dallas's directly connected networks. However, using the extended ping allows us to change the source address of the echo requests (Line 8) and require that Dallas send the echo replies to the address of the Austin Ethernet0 interface, 192.168.1.1. The Dallas IP routing table (Figure 7-10) does not contain an entry that matches the 192.168.1.0/24 network; therefore, Dallas cannot send the echo replies. LAN-to-LAN connectivity has not been established.

7.6.2 Adding More Static Routes

Dallas needs a static route to Austin's Ethernet LAN; therefore, we will add one. Figure 7-17 shows the configuration of a static route on Dallas.

The Ethernet LAN on Austin has the address 192.168.1.0/24; therefore, the entry for network 192.168.1.0 with the mask 255.255.255.0 is placed into Dallas's routing table. The gateway that Dallas should use to get to the network is 192.168.2.2, Austin's Serial1 interface.

Now if we were to repeat the extended ping from Figure 7-16, it would be successful because Dallas has a route to Austin's Ethernet LAN. But what happens when the serial link between Dallas and Austin goes

Figure 7-17

Dallas static route to Austin Ethernet.

```
1)   Dallas#configure terminal
2)   Enter configuration commands, one per line. End with CNTL/Z.
3)   Dallas(config)#ip route 192.168.1.0 255.255.255.0 192.168.2.2
4)   Dallas(config)#<Ctrl-Z>
5)   Dallas#
```

down? Figure 7-18 shows the broken internetwork and Figure 7-19 shows Austin's routing table during the outage.

Since our connectivity between the Dallas and Austin Ethernet LANs was established with a static route on each router, we would lose connectivity if the serial link between the routers went down, even though there is another potential path through FortWorth. The IP routing table on Austin (Figure 7-19) no longer contains the static route to network 172.16.10.0/24 because the directly connected network where the next hop gateway was located went down.

If we wanted to get full internetwork connectivity, we would have to put several static routes on each router. That is why I called this the *brute force method* of updating the routing tables. Adding static routes and maintaining them during network changes is a major administrative task that can cause problems in large internetworks. Each time that new routers or new networks are added, static routes would have to be added or changed.

Figure 7-18

Broken serial link between Dallas and Austin.

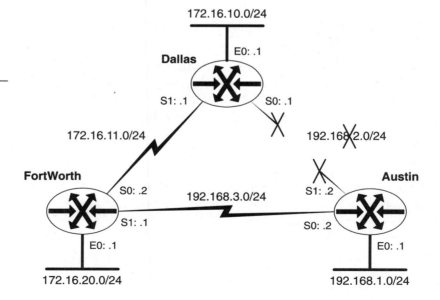

```
1)  Austin#show ip route
2)  [text omitted]
3)  C        192.168.1.0/24 is directly connected, Ethernet0
4)  C        192.168.3.0/24 is directly connected, Serial0
5)  Austin#
```

Dynamic routing protocols allow our routers to share information about the networks that they know about. We are going to configure those next, but we are going to remove the static routes on Dallas and Austin first.

7.6.3 Removing Static Routes

Remember "Just say no." Use the **no ip route** command to remove a static route. Figure 7-20 shows the removal of Austin's static route and Figure 7-21 shows the removal of Dallas's static route.

To remove a static route, just put the keyword **no** in front of the exact command that was used to create the static route. If you do not remember the exact command that created the static route, just display the running configuration and find it.

7.7 Dynamic Routing Protocols

Running a *dynamic routing protocol* will allow our routers to share their network information with each other and recover from a network outage automatically. If an alternate path exists and all of the routers are running properly configured routing protocols, they will eventually locate

Figure 7-20

Removal of static
route on Austin.

```
1)  Austin#configure terminal
2)  Enter configuration commands, one per line. End with CNTL/Z.
3)  Austin(config)#no ip route 172.16.10.0 255.255.255.0
    192.168.2.1
4)  Austin(config)#<Ctrl-Z>
5)  Austin#
```

Figure 7-21

Removal of static route on Dallas.

```
1)  Dallas#configure terminal
2)  Enter configuration commands, one per line. End with CNTL/Z.
3)  Dallas(config)#no ip route 192.168.1.0 255.255.255.0
    192.168.2.2
4)  Dallas(config)#<Ctrl-Z>
5)  Dallas#
```

the alternate path and use it if the primary path goes down. We are going to cover the basic configuration of the following routing protocols, shown in order from simplest to most complex:

- RIP
- IGRP
- EIGRP
- OSPF

These routing protocols are called *interior routing protocols*. They are meant to be run on routers under a common administration.

The first thing that we must do before configuring a routing protocol is to determine which one best suits our needs. If we want a routing protocol that is very simple and supported by just about every IP router on the market, then RIP may be the choice. If we need a routing protocol that will work well in a large internetwork of several hundred routers, then EIGRP or OSPF may be the choice unless some of those routers are not Cisco routers; then OSPF may be the choice.

Regardless of which one is chosen, we should be consistent with its configuration on our routers. IOS can run more than one IP routing protocol, but that usually requires extra configuration and extra maintenance.

The two steps for configuring an IP routing protocol are as follows:

1. Indicate which routing protocol is being configured with the global configuration command **router**.

2. Start the routing protocol on the appropriate interfaces with the router configuration command **network**.

The forms of the **router** and **network** commands differ slightly from one routing protocol to another. We will see those differences in the coming sections as we start with RIP and migrate through each of the routing protocols.

7.7.1 RIP

There are two versions of the Routing Information Protocol (RIP): 1 and 2. The default version of RIP is version 1. Unless we explicitly state that we are referring to RIP version 2 (RIPv2), we are referring to RIP version 1 (RIPv1).

RIP is a distance vector routing protocol that sends updates every 30 seconds. See Section 2.2.2.1 for a summary of distance vector routing protocols. Cisco's implementation of RIP allows the transmission of an update immediately upon the detection of a change in a network's state without waiting for the current 30-second period to expire; this is called a *triggered,* or *flash, update.*

RIP uses a single metric in determining the best path, hop count. The maximum number of hops is 15; anything over that is invalid and indicates an unreachable network. The metric for a network address is carried in the RIP update packets.

7.7.1.1 RIP Version 1

RIP updates are sent to the IP broadcast address that is configured on an interface; the default IP broadcast address is 255.255.255.255. RIP does not include in its updates the network mask or prefix length for a network address being advertised; this makes RIP a *classful* routing protocol. When RIP advertises a subnet of a network out of an interface that is not another subnet of the same network, RIP summarizes the subnets of the network as the classful network address, a feature called *auto-summarization,* which we cannot turn off. Because of these features, one should adhere to the following subnetting rules when addressing networks in an internetwork running RIP.

- All subnets of a major, classful network address should use the same network mask.

- All subnets of a major, classful network address should be contiguous; they should touch each other.

Major, classful network address refers to a class A address, a class B address, or a class C address.

Two of our routers, Dallas and FortWorth, are already running RIP. We will look at their RIP configurations to explain the command and then we will complete the configuration to include Austin. Figure 7-22 shows the RIP configuration on Dallas and Figure 7-23 shows the RIP configuration on FortWorth.

Figure 7-22
Original Dallas RIP
configuration.

```
1)  Dallas#show running-config
2)  [text omitted]
3)  !
4)  router rip
5)   network 172.16.0.0
6)  !
7)  [text omitted]
8)  Dallas#
```

The current RIP configuration of both routers consists of two commands (Lines 4 and 5). The **router rip** command informs IOS that the next commands are to be used on the RIP process. The **network 172.16.0.0** command tells IOS that all of the router's interfaces that have addresses in the 172.16.0.0 network are to send RIP updates and receive RIP updates; this command also tell IOS to include the network addresses of those same interfaces in the RIP updates. The address placed after the network command must be a major, classful network address to which the router has a direct connection. Since Dallas has two interfaces that are part of the 172.16.0.0 network, RIP is started on both of them, Ethernet0 and Serial1. FortWorth also has two interfaces that are part of the 172.16.0.0 network; therefore, RIP is started on both of them, Ethernet0 and Serial0.

We still need to start RIP on Dallas's Serial1 interface, FortWorth's Serial1 interface, and all of Austin's interfaces. Figure 7-24 shows the completion of the RIP configuration on Dallas, Figure 7-25 shows the completion of the RIP configuration on FortWorth, and Figure 7-26 shows the configuration of RIP on Austin.

To verify which routing protocols that IOS is running, we use the user mode command **show ip protocols**. Figure 7-27 shows the output on Dallas.

Figure 7-23
Original FortWorth
RIP configuration.

```
1)  FortWorth#show running-config
2)  [text omitted]
3)  !
4)  router rip
5)   network 172.16.0.0
6)  !
7)  [text omitted]
8)  FortWorth#
```

Figure 7-24
Completion of
Dallas RIP configu-
ration.

```
1)  Dallas#configure terminal
2)  Enter configuration commands, one per line. End with CNTL/Z.
3)  Dallas(config)#router rip
4)  Dallas(config-router)#network 192.168.2.0
5)  Dallas(config-router)#<Ctrl-Z>
6)  Dallas#
```

Figure 7-25
Completion of
FortWorth RIP con-
figuration.

```
1)  FortWorth#configure terminal
2)  Enter configuration commands, one per line. End with CNTL/Z.
3)  FortWorth(config)#router rip
4)  FortWorth(config-router)#network 192.168.3.0
5)  FortWorth(config-router)#<Ctrl-Z>
6)  FortWorth#
```

Dallas is running RIP (Figure 7-27, Line 2). RIP updates are transmitted every 30 seconds, and the next updates are scheduled for transmission in 9 seconds (Line 3). RIP routes that have not been heard in 180 seconds (3 minutes) are marked as invalid and flushed from the routing table after 240 seconds (4 minutes). When IOS is informed by RIP that a route has gone down, IOS places the route in holddown state for 180 seconds. While the route is in holddown, IOS will accept no other route as a replacement until the timer expires unless the replacement route has a better metric than the original. Because of the holddown timer, RIP's convergence time tends to be rather long; however, the holddown timer helps reduce the possibility of routing loops.

RIP is running on interfaces Ethernet0, Serial0, and Serial1 (Lines 10, 11, and 12). On the same lines, we see that IOS is sending RIPv1 updates and is capable of receiving RIPv1 and RIPv2 updates. Lines 14 and 15 show the networks that have been configured for RIP on Dallas. Lines 18 and 19 show the sources of RIP updates received by Dallas—these are

Figure 7-26
Austin RIP configu-
ration.

```
1)  Austin#configure terminal
2)  Enter configuration commands, one per line. End with CNTL/Z.
3)  Austin(config)#router rip
4)  Austin(config-router)#network 192.168.1.0
5)  Austin(config-router)#network 192.168.2.0
6)  Austin(config-router)#network 192.168.3.0
7)  Austin(config-router)#<Ctrl-Z>
8)  Austin#
```

Figure 7-27
Show IP protocols output on Dallas after RIP configuration.

```
1)   Dallas#show ip protocols
2)   Routing Protocol is "rip"
3)      Sending updates every 30 seconds, next due in 9 seconds
4)      Invalid after 180 seconds, hold down 180, flushed after 240
5)      Outgoing update filter list for all interfaces is
6)      Incoming update filter list for all interfaces is
7)      Redistributing: rip
8)      Default version control: send version 1, receive any
        version
9)          Interface           Send  Recv   Key-chain
10)         Ethernet0           1     1 2
11)         Serial0             1     1 2
12)         Serial1             1     1 2
13)     Routing for Networks:
14)         172.16.0.0
15)         192.168.2.0
16)     Routing Information Sources:
17)         Gateway          Distance       Last Update
18)         192.168.2.2         120         00:00:23
19)         172.16.11.2         120         00:00:21
20)     Distance: (default is 120)
21)
22)  Dallas#
```

Austin (Line 18) and FortWorth (Line 19). Since RIP updates are sent to the broadcast address, the sources should always be directly connected neighbor routers. These lines also show a distance of 120, which is the default administrative distance for RIP. The time since an update was received from each source is also given.

Now that RIP is running, we should take a look at the routing tables on our three routers. Figure 7-28 has the IP routing table for Dallas, Figure 7-29 has the IP routing table for FortWorth, and Figure 7-30 shows the IP routing table for Austin.

The Dallas IP routing table prior to the complete RIP configuration is shown in Figure 7-10. Two more RIP routes have been added (Line 15 and Line 17). Dallas has heard an RIP update from Austin about the Austin Ethernet LAN, 192.168.1.0. Since RIP does not put network mask information into its updates, Dallas is using the default network mask for a class C address, 255.255.255.0 for the routing table entry. The serial link between FortWorth and Austin, 192.168.3.0, has been heard from both of the other routers. The metric (second number within the brackets) for both routes is the same, one hop; therefore, IOS places both of them into the routing table. IOS will distribute the traffic destined for the 192.168.3.0 network across the two equal-cost paths. The traffic distribution will most likely not be equal, or balanced; this is called *load*

Figure 7-28
Dallas IP routing table after RIP configuration.

```
1)  Dallas#show ip route
2)  Codes: C - connected, S - static, I - IGRP, R - RIP,
          M - mobile, B - BGP
3)         D - EIGRP, EX - EIGRP external, O - OSPF, IA - OSPF
           inter area
4)         N1 - OSPF NSSA external type 1, N2 - OSPF NSSA
           external type 2
5)         E1 - OSPF external type 1, E2 - OSPF external type 2,
           E - EGP
6)         i - IS-IS, L1 - IS-IS level-1, L2 - IS-IS level-2,
           * - candidate default
7)         U - per-user static route, o - ODR
8)
9)  Gateway of last resort is not set
10)
11)     172.16.0.0/24 is subnetted, 3 subnets
12) R      172.16.20.0 [120/1] via 172.16.11.2, 00:00:02,   Serial1
13) C      172.16.10.0 is directly connected, Ethernet0
14) C      172.16.11.0 is directly connected, Serial1
15) R  192.168.1.0/24 [120/1] via 192.168.2.2, 00:00:00, Serial0
16) C  192.168.2.0/24 is directly connected, Serial0
17) R  192.168.3.0/24 [120/1] via 192.168.2.2, 00:00:00, Serial0
18)                   [120/1] via 172.16.11.2, 00:00:02,   Serial1
19) Dallas#
```

sharing. The first number within the brackets is the administrative distance. The default for RIP routes is 120. This can be changed with the router configuration command **distance**.

The FortWorth IP routing table now shows routes to all of the networks also. Austin's Ethernet LAN is shown as being one hop away (Line 7), and the serial link between Dallas and Austin has two equal-cost

Figure 7-29
FortWorth IP routing table after RIP configuration.

```
1)  FortWorth#show ip route
2)  [text omitted]
3)      172.16.0.0/24 is subnetted, 3 subnets
4)  C      172.16.20.0 is directly connected, Ethernet0
5)  R      172.16.10.0 [120/1] via 172.16.11.1, 00:00:00, Serial0
6)  C      172.16.11.0 is directly connected, Serial0
7)  R  192.168.1.0/24 [120/1] via 192.168.3.2, 00:00:05, Serial1
8)  R  192.168.2.0/24 [120/1] via 172.16.11.1, 00:00:00, Serial0
9)                    [120/1] via 192.168.3.2, 00:00:05,   Serial1
10) C  192.168.3.0/24 is directly connected, Serial1
11) FortWorth#
```

Figure 7-30
Austin IP routing table after RIP configuration.

```
1)    Austin#show ip route
2)    [text omitted]
3)    R    172.16.0.0/16 [120/1] via 192.168.2.1, 00:00:06, Serial1
4)                       [120/1] via 192.168.3.1, 00:00:10, Serial0
5)    C    192.168.1.0/24 is directly connected, Ethernet0
6)    C    192.168.2.0/24 is directly connected, Serial1
7)    C    192.168.3.0/24 is directly connected, Serial0
8)    Austin#
```

paths (Lines 8 and 9). The time shown on each RIP entry indicates how long ago each entry was updated, or how long it has been since an RIP update was received with each entry's information.

The IP routing tables of Dallas and FortWorth each contained six routes; however, Austin's routing table has only four. In the first paragraph of this section, we mentioned autosummarization. Here is an example. There are really three subnets of the 172.16.0.0 network in our internetwork; however, neither Dallas nor FortWorth advertises them. Instead, they advertise the class B network address 172.16.0.0. Since their links to Austin are not subnets of the 172.16.0.0 subnet, the subnets themselves are not sent. Since RIP does not include network mask information in its updates, Austin would not understand them anyway. So Austin gets an update from Dallas containing the summary route 172.16.0.0 and an update from FortWorth with the same summary route. Both updates have the same hop count, 1; therefore, they both go into the routing table. The prefix length used is the default for a class B address, /16. This means that Austin will distribute the traffic for all of the subnets of the 172.16.0.0 subnets across both of its serial interfaces. Traffic may not be sent along the most efficient path. Traffic for Dallas's Ethernet LAN, 172.16.10.0/24, may get routed through FortWorth because Austin has no knowledge of the subnetting.

7.7.1.2   RIP Version 2

RIP version 2 (RIPv2) is just a slight modification of RIPv1. RIPv2 is a distance vector routing protocol with the same timers as those of RIPv1; RIPv1 and RIPv2 also use the same metric, hop count; however, RIPv2 is classless and is capable of doing authentication. RIPv2 updates are sent to the multicast address 224.0.0.9, which is processed only by other routers running RIPv2; therefore, RIPv2 updates do not interrupt the processing of nonrouter hosts.

Being classless, RIPv2 includes the network mask of network addresses in its updates. RIPv2 also does autosummarization by default, but we can turn off autosummarization if we desire. The classless characteristic means that all of the subnets of a major network address do not need to share the same network mask, and they do not have to be contiguous. Using multiple network masks for a single network address is called *variable-length subnet masking* (VLSM), which is essentially the subnetting of subnets—taking a subnet and increasing the number of ones in the network mask for that subnet to get multiple smaller subnets. This can allow us to more efficiently use our network address space, especially in internetworks with many two-host networks such as WANs.

IOS can run both RIPv1 and RIPv2 simultaneously, but both cannot be enabled on the same interface. RIPv1 and RIPv2 can work together within an internetwork; however, there are a few rules we need to remember.

- Interfaces with RIPv1 enabled send RIPv1 updates.

- Interfaces with RIPv1 enabled will receive both RIPv1 and RIPv2 updates by default, but RIPv1 will ignore the network mask and authentication in the RIPv2 updates.

- Interfaces with RIPv2 enabled send RIPv2 updates.

- Interfaces with RIPv2 enabled will receive only RIPv2 updates by default.

The conversion from RIPv1 to RIPv2 can be done one interface at a time or all interfaces at the same time on a router. To completely convert our internetwork from RIPv1 to RIPv2, we need to add just one command to the RIP configuration on each router. The command is the router configuration command **version 2**. We will type this command on each router; since the command sequence is identical on all of the routers, only one is shown. Figure 7-31 shows the configuration of RIPv2 on Dallas.

Figure 7-31

RIP version 2 configuration on Dallas.

```
1)  Dallas#configure terminal
2)  Enter configuration commands, one per line. End with CNTL/Z.
3)  Dallas(config)#router rip
4)  Dallas(config-router)#version 2
5)  Dallas(config-router)#<Ctrl-Z>
6)  Dallas#
```

Typing the sequence of commands on each of our test routers converts them from running RIPv1 to RIPv2. Since we are configuring the RIP process, we must identify it with the **router rip** command (Line 3). The **version 2** command (Line 4) tells IOS that it is to use version 2 on all of the interfaces that currently have RIP enabled unless we explicitly change the version on the interface itself. This command is added to the network commands that we entered when we configured RIPv1 in the preceding section. The RIP configuration on Dallas now looks like this:

```
router rip
 version 2
 network 172.16.0.0
 network 192.168.2.0
```

The RIP configurations on FortWorth and Austin are similar, and the routing tables on the routers appear to be identical to the ones created with RIPv1 shown in Figures 7-28, 7-29, and 7-30.

In Figure 7-32, we saw that Austin has a summary route to 172.16.0.0/16. This means that if Austin gets a packet destined for a subnet of the 172.16.0.0 network that does not really exist, such as 172.16.33.0, Austin will route it toward Dallas or FortWorth. This causes some minor overhead because the packet will cross the WAN just to be dropped at the other side. A side effect of this is that the router that drops the packet will probably send an ICMP destination unreachable

Figure 7-32

Broken serial link between Dallas and FortWorth with autosummarization.

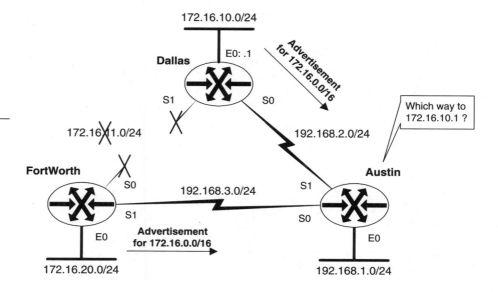

message back across the WAN to the packet's source, thus causing more WAN overhead.

Suppose that the WAN between Dallas and FortWorth were down. Figure 7-32 shows this occurrence. Since Dallas and FortWorth are both summarizing the 172.16.0.0 network to Austin, Austin will maintain the two equal-cost paths to the network, 172.16.0.0/16. When Austin receives a packet with a destination address that exists on the 172.16.10.0 subnet, such as 172.16.10.1, Austin cannot accurately tell which path is valid, and only one path will reach the address. The packet has a 50/50 chance of reaching its destination.

With RIPv2 we can turn off the autosummarization feature that causes the summary route. We use the router configuration command **no auto-summary** to accomplish this. Figure 7-33 shows the disabling of autosummarization on Dallas.

All of the networks are now operational. After a few minutes, an examination of the IP routing tables on FortWorth and Austin reveals something interesting. Figure 7-34 shows the new IP routing table on FortWorth after RIPv2 and Figure 7-35 shows the new IP routing table on Austin.

Dallas is now sending the individual subnets of the 172.16.0.0 network instead of the summary route of 172.16.0.0/16; therefore, Austin has learned about the individual subnets with the /24 prefix length (Figure 7-35, Lines 4 through 6). Austin is summarizing these subnets to FortWorth so now FortWorth's routing table has the summary route (Figure 7-34, Line 7). FortWorth is still sending a summary route for the three subnets to Austin so Austin still has the summary route (Figure 7-35, Line 7).

We need to disable autosummarization on all three routers in order to completely get rid of the summary route. After issuing the **no auto-summary** command under the RIP configurations of FortWorth and Austin and allowing a few minutes for the summary routes to get flushed, the contents of the FortWorth IP routing table return to that displayed in Figure 7-29. Figure 7-36 shows the new Austin routing table.

Figure 7-33

Disabling of RIPv2 autosummarization on Dallas.

```
1)  Dallas#configure terminal
2)  Enter configuration commands, one per line. End with CNTL/Z.
3)  Dallas(config)#router rip
4)  Dallas(config-router)#no auto-summary
5)  Dallas(config-router)#<Ctrl-Z>
6)  Dallas#
```

Figure 7-34
FortWorth IP rout-
ing table after
autosummarization
disabled on Dallas.

```
1)  FortWorth#show ip route
2)  [text omitted]
3)  172.16.0.0/16 is variably subnetted, 4 subnets, 2 masks
4)  C    172.16.20.0/24 is directly connected, Ethernet0
5)  R    172.16.10.0/24 [120/1] via 172.16.11.1, 00:00:17, Serial0
6)  C    172.16.11.0/24 is directly connected, Serial0
7)  R    172.16.0.0/16 [120/2] via 192.168.3.2, 00:00:23, Serial1
8)  R    192.168.1.0/24 [120/1] via 192.168.3.2, 00:00:23, Serial1
9)  R    192.168.2.0/24 [120/1] via 172.16.11.1, 00:00:17, Serial0
10)                    [120/1] via 192.168.3.2, 00:00:23, Serial1
11) C    192.168.3.0/24 is directly connected, Serial1
12) FortWorth#
```

Austin now knows about just the subnets that exist. If Austin receives a packet destined for a nonexistent subnet such as 172.16.33.0, Austin will drop the packet since it has no route that matches the destination address. If the serial link between Dallas and FortWorth goes down as was shown in Figure 7-32 and autosummarization is turned off, Austin would have an accurate, specific path to the 172.16.10.0 subnet even though the subnets of the 172.16.0.0 network would no longer be contiguous.

In most large networks, summarization is a good thing since it reduces the size of the routing table; however, in our small network, we turned it off just to illustrate its effect.

Figure 7-35
Austin IP routing
table after auto-
summarization dis-
abled on Dallas.

```
1)  Austin#show ip route
2)  [text omitted]
3)   172.16.0.0/16 is variably subnetted, 4 subnets, 2 masks
4)  R   172.16.20.0/24 [120/2] via 192.168.2.1, 00:00:01, Serial1
5)  R   172.16.10.0/24 [120/1] via 192.168.2.1, 00:00:01, Serial1
6)  R   172.16.11.0/24 [120/1] via 192.168.2.1, 00:00:01, Serial1
7)  R   172.16.0.0/16 [120/1] via 192.168.3.1, 00:00:15, Serial0
8)  C   192.168.1.0/24 is directly connected, Ethernet0
9)  C   192.168.2.0/24 is directly connected, Serial1
10) C   192.168.3.0/24 is directly connected, Serial0
11) Austin#
```

Figure 7-36
Austin IP routing
table after auto-
summarization dis-
abled on all
routers.

```
 1)  Austin#show ip route
 2)  [text omitted]
 3)      172.16.0.0/24 is subnetted, 3 subnets
 4)  R    172.16.20.0 [120/1] via 192.168.3.1, 00:00:07, Serial0
 5)  R    172.16.10.0 [120/1] via 192.168.2.1, 00:00:00, Serial1
 6)  R    172.16.11.0 [120/1] via 192.168.2.1, 00:00:00, Serial1
 7)                   [120/1] via 192.168.3.1, 00:00:07, Serial0
 8)  C   192.168.1.0/24 is directly connected, Ethernet0
 9)  C   192.168.2.0/24 is directly connected, Serial1
10)  C   192.168.3.0/24 is directly connected, Serial0
11) Austin#
```

7.7.1.3 RIP Interface Customization

Two important *interface customizations* that we can make to RIP are making an interface passive and setting the RIP version.

IOS will not send RIP updates out an interface that we have configured to be passive for RIP. The passive characteristic is routing-protocol specific; it works for the other routing protocols, also. When we make an interface passive, we are telling IOS that no updates are to be transmitted out the interface, but updates are allowed to enter the interface. In other words, the interface will listen but not speak. Why would we want to turn off the updates on an interface?

When we configured RIP, we used the **network** command to indicate which interfaces were to have RIP enabled. The network address that we have to use with the **network** command is a major, classful address, not a subnet address. When we enable RIP on one interface that is connected to a subnet of a network, all of the router's other interfaces in the same network are also enabled for RIP. If there were no other routers on the network to which updates were being sent, the updates would be a waste of network bandwidth. If there were other routers on a network and we did not want them to learn about our networks, we could turn off the updates on the interface that connected our router to the other routers.

We use the router configuration command **passive-interface** to turn off updates on a specific interface. Figure 7-37 shows the command being used to turn off RIP updates to FortWorth's Ethernet LAN.

The **passive-interface** command must be entered in router configuration mode for the routing protocol to which it applies, RIP in this example (Figure 7-37, Line 3). The interface to be passive is specified immediately after the command (Line 4). Because there are no other

Figure 7-37
Passive-interface
command on
FortWorth.

```
1) FortWorth#configure terminal
2) Enter configuration commands, one per line. End with CNTL/Z.
3) FortWorth(config)#router rip
4) FortWorth(config-router)#passive-interface ethernet0
5) FortWorth(config-router)#<Ctrl-Z>
6) FortWorth#
```

routers on FortWorth's Ethernet LAN, we tell IOS to stop sending RIP updates out the Ethernet0 interface. This will stop both RIPv1 and RIPv2 updates from being transmitted.

On the Austin Ethernet LAN, there is a host that our users insist should maintain a routing table similar to our routers. For example, this could be a Unix-based host running *routed*. The host expects to receive RIP updates from Austin, but the host's implementation of *routed* supports only RIPv1. To maintain connectivity to Dallas and FortWorth, Austin should run RIPv2 on its WANs, but we can configure Austin to send RIPv1 updates out its Ethernet0 interface with the interface configuration command **ip rip**. Figure 7-38 shows the configuration of RIPv1 updates on Austin's Ethernet0 interface.

Austin is now running RIPv2, but with the **ip rip send version 1** command (Line 4) issued in interface configuration mode for Ethernet0, we have overridden that to get Austin to send RIPv1 updates onto its Ethernet LAN. Austin will still receive only RIPv2 updates; therefore, it will ignore any RIPv1 updates that it receives from the Ethernet LAN. We could override that also by entering the **ip rip receive version 1** command in interface configuration mode for Ethernet0.

7.7.1.4 RIP Configuration Summary

We configure RIP by entering the **router rip** command in global configuration mode and then the appropriate **network** commands for enabling RIP on the router's interfaces. RIPv1 is the default version; if we want to run RIPv2 on all, or most, of the interfaces, we enter the **version 2** com-

Figure 7-38
Setting RIP version
on an interface.

```
1)  Austin#configure terminal
2)  Enter configuration commands, one per line. End with CNTL/Z.
3)  Austin(config)#interface ethernet0
4)  Austin(config-if)#ip rip send version 1
5)  Austin(config-if)#<Ctrl-Z>
6)  Austin#
```

mand while we are in router configuration mode for RIP. To change the RIP version on an individual interface that has been included in one of the **network** commands, use the **ip rip send version** or the **ip rip receive version** command, with the appropriate RIP version number (1 or 2), in interface configuration mode for the desired interface. To stop updates on an interface, issue the **passive-interface** command, with the interface name, in router configuration mode for RIP.

The RIP-specific configuration commands entered in this chapter for Dallas, FortWorth, and Austin are shown in Figures 7-39, 7-40, and 7-41, respectively.

In Figure 7-41 (Line 4), the **interface Ethernet0** command is shown only to provide context for the **ip rip send version 1** command (Line 5) in context. The **interface** command is not specific to RIP.

7.7.1.5 RIP Removal

Even though the configuration of RIP required quite a few commands, the removal of RIP requires a single global configuration command on each router. Figure 7-42 shows the removal of RIP on Dallas.

The **no router rip** command (Line 3) removes all of the RIP-specific commands from the running configuration. After issuing the command on all three of our test routers, our internetwork is left without an IP routing protocol.

7.7.2 IGRP

IGRP (Interior Gateway Routing Protocol) is a classful, distance vector routing protocol similar to RIP. IGRP does not include network mask information in its periodic updates, and its periodic updates occur every

Figure 7-39

Dallas RIP-specific configuration commands.

```
 1) Dallas#show running-config
 2) [text omitted]
 3) !
 4) router rip
 5)  version 2
 6)  network 172.16.0.0
 7)  network 192.168.2.0
 8)  no auto-summary
 9) !
10) [text omitted]
11) Dallas#
```

Figure 7-40

FortWorth RIP-specific configuration commands.

```
1)  FortWorth#show running-config
2)  [text omitted]
3)  !
4)  router rip
5)  version 2
6)    passive-interface Ethernet0
7)    network 172.16.0.0
8)    network 192.168.3.0
9)    no auto-summary
10) !
11) [text omitted]
12) FortWorth#
```

90 seconds by default. IGRP updates have a destination address of the IP broadcast address configured on the interface out of which the updates are being transmitted; the default IP broadcast address is 255.255.255.255.

The metric used by IGRP is a composite (calculated value) of four parameters that are carried in the update packets. The four parameters are as follows:

1. Bandwidth

2. Delay

3. Reliability

4. Load

All of these parameters are tracked by IOS for each interface in a router. Bandwidth and delay are static; they have default values, and the values

Figure 7-41

Austin RIP-specific configuration commands.

```
1)  Austin#show running-config
2)  [text omitted]
3)  !
4)  interface Ethernet0
5)    ip rip send version 1
6)  [text omitted]
7)  !
8)  router rip
9)    version 2
10)   network 192.168.1.0
11)   network 192.168.2.0
12)   network 192.168.3.0
13)   no auto-summary
14) !
15) [text omitted]
16) Austin#
```

Figure 7-42

Removal of RIP.

```
44)  Dallas#configure terminal
45)  Enter configuration commands, one per line. End with CNTL/Z.
46)  Dallas(config)#no router rip
47)  Dallas(config)#<Ctrl-Z>
48)  Dallas#
```

are configurable. Bandwidth is specified in kbps and is configured with the interface configuration command **bandwidth** as described in Section 6.2.4. Delay is specified in microseconds (μsec) and is configured with the interface configuration command **delay**. The delay is supposed to be the amount of time a bit takes to cross a network. Reliability and load are dynamic. They are each given as a fraction of 255. For example, an interface load of 25 means that interface utilization is at about 10 percent. Figure 7-43 shows that these parameters for an interface are available using the **show interfaces** command. The parameters appear on Line 5.

MTU (Maximum Transmission Unit) is shown for an interface (Line 5, Figure 7-43) and carried in an IGRP update, but it is not part of the composite metric calculation. MTU is given in bytes and is configured with the interface configuration command **mtu**. MTU is the maximum size of a packet, the payload of a frame. A sixth value, hop count, is also carried in the IGRP updates, but, just like MTU, hop count is not included in the composite metric. The default maximum number of hops for an IGRP route is 100; this maximum can be increased or decreased.

IGRP was developed by Cisco. Not many other router vendors have implemented IGRP so it is generally useful only in networks that consist of mostly Cisco routers.

7.7.2.1 IGRP Configuration

The configuration of IGRP is very similar to the configuration of RIP. We just need to specify the IGRP process with the **router igrp** command

Figure 7-43

Five IGRP composite metric parameters in show IP interfaces output.

```
1)  FortWorth#show interfaces ethernet0
2)  Ethernet0 is up, line protocol is up
3)    Hardware is Lance, address is 0010.7b3a.d4af (bia
      0010.7b3a.d4af)
4)    Internet address is 172.16.20.1/24
5)    MTU 1500 bytes, BW 10000 Kbit, DLY 1000 usec, rely
      255/255, load 1/255
6)  [text omitted]
7)  FortWorth#
```

and then enable IGRP on a router's interfaces with **network** commands. IGRP, however, requires that its process be identified with an *autonomous system number* (ASN). There are several definitions of an autonomous system. The one that we use here is a group of routers that are using the same interior routing protocol to share routing information. Our three routers are part of the same autonomous system. All of the routers must have the same ASN in their IGRP configuration for them to be able to share routing information with IGRP. IOS can support multiple IGRP autonomous systems by running multiple IGRP processes, each with a different ASN.

Let us put IGRP on the three routers. Figure 7-44 shows the configuration of IGRP on Dallas, Figure 7-45 shows the configuration of IGRP on FortWorth, and Figure 7-46 shows the configuration of IGRP on Austin.

The ASN that we have chosen is 100 (Line 3 of Figures 7-44, 7-45, and 7-46). All of the routers must use the same ASN if we expect them to be able to exchange route information. The ASN is a 16-bit variable; therefore, its maximum value is 65,535. The **network** commands that we used to enable IGRP for ASN 100 are identical to the ones we used when we configured RIP in Section 7.7.1.1.

If we have a need to stop the transmission of IGRP updates on an individual interface, we can use the **passive-interface** command, with the interface name, in router configuration mode for the IGRP process. The function and use of the command are the same as was explained for RIP in Section 7.7.1.3.

Figure 7-44
IGRP configuration on Dallas.

```
1) Dallas#configure terminal
2) Enter configuration commands, one per line. End with CNTL/Z.
3) Dallas(config)#router igrp 100
4) Dallas(config-router)#network 172.16.0.0
5) Dallas(config-router)#network 192.168.2.0
6) Dallas(config-router)#<Ctrl-Z>
7) Dallas#
```

Figure 7-45
IGRP configuration on FortWorth.

```
1) FortWorth#configure terminal
2) Enter configuration commands, one per line. End with CNTL/Z.
3) FortWorth(config)#router igrp 100
4) FortWorth(config-router)#network 172.16.0.0
5) FortWorth(config-router)#network 192.168.3.0
6) FortWorth(config-router)#<Ctrl-Z>
7) FortWorth#
```

Figure 7-46
IGRP configuration
on Austin.

```
1) Austin#configure terminal
2) Enter configuration commands, one per line. End with CNTL/Z.
3) Austin(config)#router igrp 100
4) Austin(config-router)#network 192.168.1.0
5) Austin(config-router)#network 192.168.2.0
6) Austin(config-router)#network 192.168.3.0
7) Austin(config-router)#<Ctrl-Z>
8) Austin#
```

Figure 7-46
IGRP configuration
on Austin.

7.7.2.2 IGRP Verification

Now that we have IGRP running, we need to examine its status. Figure 7-47 shows the output of the **show ip protocols** command on Dallas.

We see that IGRP for ASN 100 is running (Line 2); IOS always includes the ASN when referencing an IGRP process because there can be multiple IGRP processes. The values of the main IGRP timers are given on Lines 3 and 4; these values are much greater than those for RIP. (See Figure 7-27 for the RIP timer values.) Notice that IGRP's flush timer value is over 10 minutes. Convergence time for an internetwork running IGRP can be much longer then that for one running RIP; however, IGRP uses a little less bandwidth than RIP because the periodic interval for the IGRP update broadcasts is three times longer (90 seconds

Figure 7-47
Show IP protocols
output after IGRP
configuration.

```
1)  Dallas#show ip protocols
2)  Routing Protocol is "igrp 100"
3)    Sending updates every 90 seconds, next due in 32 seconds
4)    Invalid after 270 seconds, hold down 280, flushed after 630
5)    Outgoing update filter list for all interfaces is
6)    Incoming update filter list for all interfaces is
7)    Default networks flagged in outgoing updates
8)    Default networks accepted from incoming updates
9)    IGRP metric weight K1 = 1, K2 = 0, K3 = 1, K4 = 0, K5 = 0
10)   IGRP maximum hopcount 100
11)   IGRP maximum metric variance 1
12)   Redistributing: igrp 100
13)   Routing for Networks:
14)      172.16.0.0
15)      192.168.2.0
16)   Routing Information Sources:
17)      Gateway          Distance          Last Update
18)      192.168.2.2          100          00:00:24
19)      172.16.11.2          100          00:00:24
20)   Distance: (default is 100)
21)
22)  Dallas#
```

as opposed to 30 seconds). Dallas is receiving IGRP updates from Austin (Line 18) and FortWorth (Line 19). The default administrative distance for IGRP is 100 (Line 20). If we were running both RIP and IGRP in our internetwork, IOS would prefer the routes learned from IGRP because IGRP's administrative distance is lower than RIP's (120).

The IP routing tables created by IGRP have the exact same routes as the tables created by RIPv1. The only differences are the values of the administrative distance and the metric given for each route. Figure 7-48 shows the IP routing table on Dallas, Figure 7-49 shows the IP routing table on FortWorth, and Figure 7-50 has Austin's IP routing table.

Just in all the other displays of the IP routing table, the numbers in brackets are the administrative distance followed by the metric. For the IGRP-learned routes indicated by the letter *I* in the left column, the distance is 100, and the metric is the composite metric. We cannot get a real perspective on how far away a network is from a router except that a very large metric generally indicates the presence of a low-bandwidth WAN.

In Figure 7-50 (Line 3), the summary route of 172.16.0.0/16 is evidence that IGRP does autosummarization just like RIP does. We cannot turn off autosummarization for IGRP; therefore, we have the same issues with noncontiguous subnets and static network masking as we did with RIPv1. When the routers were running RIP, the IP routing table showed two equal-cost paths to the summary network address; however, with IGRP, there is only one path—the metric is the reason for this. IGRP's composite metric takes into account the bandwidth of a network in determining best path. The link from Austin to Dallas has a bandwidth of 256 kbps and the link from Austin to FortWorth has a band-

```
 1)  Dallas#show ip route
 2)  [text omitted]
 3)       172.16.0.0/24 is subnetted, 3 subnets
 4)  I       172.16.20.0 [100/8576] via 172.16.11.2, 00:00:30, Serial1
 5)  C       172.16.10.0 is directly connected, Ethernet0
 6)  C       172.16.11.0 is directly connected, Serial1
 7)  I    192.168.1.0/24 [100/41162] via 192.168.2.2, 00:00:09, Serial0
 8)  C    192.168.2.0/24 is directly connected, Serial0
 9)  I    192.168.3.0/24 [100/182571] via 172.16.11.2, 00:00:30, Serial1
10)                      [100/182571] via 192.168.2.2, 00:00:09, Serial0
11) Dallas#
```

Figure 7-48   Dallas IP routing table after IGRP configuration.

```
 1) FortWorth#show ip route
 2) [text omitted]
 3)      172.16.0.0/24 is subnetted, 3 subnets
 4) C       172.16.20.0 is directly connected, Ethernet0
 5) I       172.16.10.0 [100/8576] via 172.16.11.1, 00:00:53, Serial0
 6) C       172.16.11.0 is directly connected, Serial0
 7) I     192.168.1.0/24 [100/43162] via 172.16.11.1, 00:00:53, Serial0
 8) I     192.168.2.0/24 [100/43062] via 172.16.11.1, 00:00:53, Serial0
 9) C     192.168.3.0/24 is directly connected, Serial1
10) FortWorth#
```

Figure 7-49   FortWorth IP routing table after IGRP configuration.

width of 56 kbps. The higher bandwidth link is preferred, but we had to configure the bandwidth of each interface with the **bandwidth** command (Figure 7-8, Lines 19 and 24).

7.7.2.3   Verifying Connectivity with Trace

Trace is a utility that we use to check connectivity to a destination by finding the route that packets take to get to the destination. We see in Figure 7-50 that Austin's path to the 172.16.0.0 network is via Dallas. The Ethernet LAN on FortWorth is part of the 172.16.0.0 network and we can use trace to verify that packets to FortWorth actually go through Dallas. Figure 7-51 shows the output of a trace to FortWorth's Ethernet0 interface from Austin.

We can specify either an IP address or a host name in the **trace** command. We have issued a trace to the IP address 172.16.20.1 (Line 1), which is the address of FortWorth's Ethernet0. The trace output tells us the routers (hops) that our traffic to the IP address is going through. The first router in the path to the address has the IP address 192.168.2.1 (Line 6), which is Dallas. Trace tries each router in the path three times and returns a round-trip time in milliseconds for each try. The second,

Figure 7-50

Austin IP routing table after IGRP configuration.

```
 1)  Austin#show ip route
 2)  [text omitted]
 3)  I 172.16.0.0/16 [100/41162] via 192.168.2.1, 00:00:27, Serial1
 4)  C 192.168.1.0/24 is directly connected, Ethernet0
 5)  C 192.168.2.0/24 is directly connected, Serial1
 6)  C 192.168.3.0/24 is directly connected, Serial0
 7)  Austin#
```

Figure 7-51
Trace from Austin
to FortWorth.

```
1)  Austin#trace 172.16.20.1
2)
3)  Type escape sequence to abort.
4)  Tracing the route to 172.16.20.1
5)
6)    1 192.168.2.1 4 msec 4 msec 8 msec
7)    2 172.16.11.2 12 msec * 8 msec
8)  Austin#
```

and last, router in the path has the IP address 172.16.11.2 (Line 7), which is FortWorth.

If Austin had a host table with entries for the IP addresses returned by the trace, IOS would return the name of the router after it resolved the address to a host name. The same would be true if we were using DNS, and the IP addresses had reverse lookup entries in the DNS database.

7.7.2.4 IGRP Configuration Summary

IGRP is configured by entering the **router igrp** command with an ASN in global configuration mode and then the appropriate **network** commands for enabling IGRP on the router's interfaces. All of the routers that are to share information with IGRP must use the same ASN. To stop updates on an interface, issue the **passive-interface** command, with the interface name, in router configuration mode for the IGRP process.

The IGRP-specific configuration commands entered in this chapter for Dallas, FortWorth, and Austin are shown in Figure 7-52, Figure 7-53, and Figure 7-54, respectively.

With the exception of specifying IGRP and an ASN with the **router** command, the configuration of IGRP is practically identical to the configuration of RIPv1.

Figure 7-52
Dallas IGRP-specific
configuration com-
mands.

```
1)  Dallas#show running-config
2)  [text omitted]
3)  !
4)  router igrp 100
5)   network 172.16.0.0
6)   network 192.168.2.0
7)  !
8)  [text omitted]
9)  Dallas#
```

▪▪ ▪▪▪ ▪

Figure 7-53
FortWorth IGRP-specific configuration commands.

```
1)  FortWorth#show running-config
2)  [text omitted]
3)  !
4)  router igrp 100
5)   network 172.16.0.0
6)   network 192.168.3.0
7)  !
8)  [text omitted]
9)  FortWorth#
```

7.7.2.5 IGRP Removal

The removal of IGRP requires a single global configuration command on each router. Figure 7-55 shows the removal of IGRP on Dallas.

The **no router igrp 100** command (Line 3) removes all of the IGRP-specific commands from the running configuration. After issuing the command on all three of our test routers, our internetwork is left without an IP routing protocol.

Remember that whenever IGRP is referenced in configuration mode, we must include the ASN with it.

7.7.3 EIGRP

EIGRP (Enhanced IGRP) is a classless routing protocol that is neither distance vector nor link state. EIGRP does include prefix length of network addresses in its update packets. We can use VLSM in an internetwork that is using EIGRP; however, since EIGRP does autosummarization by default, we could run into the same issues with noncontiguous subnets that we saw with RIPv2 in Figure 7-32. EIGRP also supports password authentication like RIPv2 does.

▪▪ ▪▪▪ ▪

Figure 7-54
Austin IGRP-specific configuration commands.

```
1)  Austin#show running-config
2)  [text omitted]
3)  !
4)  router igrp 100
5)   network 192.168.1.0
6)   network 192.168.2.0
7)   network 192.168.3.0
8)  !
9)  [text omitted]
10) Austin#
```

Figure 7-55

Removal of IGRP.

```
1) Dallas#configure terminal
2) Enter configuration commands, one per line. End with CNTL/Z.
3) Dallas(config)#no router igrp 100
4) Dallas(config)#<Ctrl-Z>
5) Dallas#
```

EIGRP was developed by Cisco and its internal workings are proprietary to Cisco; therefore, EIGRP has been implemented only in Cisco IOS. EIGRP is rather complicated so we will briefly summarize how it works before we get into its basic configuration. IOS can use EIGRP to exchange information for IPX and AppleTalk, also; the configurations of IPX EIGRP and AppleTalk EIGRP are covered in Chapters 8 and 9, respectively.

7.7.3.1 Comparison with IGRP

EIGRP requires the use of an ASN just like IGRP. All routers that are to share route information with EIGRP must have the same ASN. If IGRP and EIGRP are running on the same router with the same ASN, routes are automatically redistributed between them. *Redistribution* means that the routing processes will advertise routes learned from each other. Routes learned through EIGRP will also be advertised in IGRP updates and routes learned through IGRP will also be advertised in EIGRP updates. IOS includes this handy feature to make the transition from IGRP to EIGRP a little easier.

EIGRP uses the same composite metric parameters as IGRP—bandwidth, delay, reliability, and load. (MTU and hop count are also carried in the updates.) However, the metric calculated for EIGRP is 8 bits longer, so the EIGRP metric is 256 times bigger than the one for IGRP.

7.7.3.2 EIGRP Terminology and Operation

A special algorithm called *Diffusing Update Algorithm* (DUAL) is used by EIGRP to perform its major functions.

Before any updates are exchanged, a router must discover any other routers that are its neighbors. A *neighbor router* is one that is attached to a directly connected network and is running EIGRP with the same ASN. Neighbors are discovered using *Hello* packets that are sent to the multicast address 224.0.0.10 about every 5 seconds by default (60 seconds by default on nonbroadcast networks such as X.25). Routers running EIGRP listen for Hello packets. Upon hearing a Hello packet from a neighbor router, a router will place the neighbor router's address into a *neighbor table.* The neighbor routers then form an *adjacency* with each other. The adjacency formation requires that the routers exchange routing information with each other.

EIGRP Hello packets are sent out every interface that is enabled for EIGRP at periodic intervals. If a router does not hear a Hello packet from a neighbor router within a *hold time,* the neighbor router will be removed from the neighbor table. The default value of the hold time is three times the Hello interval. On a LAN, the default Hello interval is 5 seconds; therefore, the default hold time is 15 seconds. Because of the fast discovery of down routers, EIGRP convergence after a network change can be very fast.

EIGRP does not send periodic updates, rather updates are sent only during the establishment of an adjacency and after a network change. Updates sent after a network change contain partial information about routes, that is, they contain only what is necessary to be communicated, not the entire routing table.

Information about networks learned from neighbor routers is placed into a *topology table,* which contains all of the routes learned from each neighbor and two metrics for each route. The first metric is the composite metric as advertised by a neighbor router. The composite metric as advertised by a neighbor router is actually the neighbor router's metric to the destination network address—this is called the *advertised distance* of a route. The second metric is the local router's composite metric of the route through the neighbor router that advertised the network address—this is called the *feasible distance* of a route. The feasible distance is just the normal metric that is calculated when a route is learned.

All of the routes to a destination network address are compared and the one with the best feasible distance is placed into the routing table. If there is a tie for the best feasible distance, up to six routes to the same destination can be maintained in the routing table. The neighbor router through which the best path flows is called the *successor.* The neighbor router through which the second to the best path flows is called the *feasible successor* for a route if its advertised distance to the destination network address is less than the successor's feasible distance to the destination network address. Once all of the routes to a destination have been placed into the topology table and the successor and feasible successor, if any, have been selected, the route is said to be in *passive* state.

When the successor goes down and there is a feasible successor, the feasible successor immediately becomes the successor and is installed as the preferred path; the route stays in passive state. If there is no feasible successor when the successor goes down, a new successor must be located. The route changes to *active* state and the router sends a query to its neighbors requesting new information about the route. The neighbors send replies with the information, which the router acknowledges. Once all neighbors have responded and an alternate path is available, a new successor and feasible successor, if any, are selected, and the route is changed back to passive state. While the route is active, no traffic will be routed to it. If there is no alternate path, the route is removed from the topology table.

7.7.3.3 EIGRP Configuration

Turning on EIGRP on IOS is practically identical to turning on IGRP, as we did in Section 7.7.2.1, with the exception of the addition of the letter *e*. We configure the EIGRP process by referencing EIGRP with an ASN after the **router** command. Then we need to enable EIGRP on the appropriate interfaces with the **network** command. The network commands used to configure EIGRP on our test network are the exact same ones that we used to configure RIP and IGRP. For consistency, we will show the entering of the commands. Figure 7-56 shows the configuration of EIGRP on Dallas; Figure 7-57 shows the configuration of EIGRP on FortWorth, and Figure 7-58 shows the EIGRP configuration on Austin.

We chose the ASN 100 to use on all of the routers (Line 3). The **network** commands enable EIGRP on all of the active interfaces of the routers. For example, the **network 172.16.0.0** command (Line 4, Figure 7-57) tells IOS on FortWorth that EIGRP should be enabled on all of the

Figure 7-56
EIGRP configuration on Dallas.

```
1)   Dallas#configure terminal
2)   Enter configuration commands, one per line. End with CNTL/Z.
3)   Dallas(config)#router eigrp 100
4)   Dallas(config-router)#network 172.16.0.0
5)   Dallas(config-router)#network 192.168.2.0
6)   Dallas(config-router)#<Ctrl-Z>
7)   Dallas#
```

Figure 7-57
EIGRP configuration on FortWorth.

```
1)   FortWorth#configure terminal
2)   Enter configuration commands, one per line. End with CNTL/Z.
3)   FortWorth(config)#router eigrp 100
4)   FortWorth(config-router)#network 172.16.0.0
5)   FortWorth(config-router)#network 192.168.3.0
6)   FortWorth(config-router)#<Ctrl-Z>
7)   FortWorth#
```

Figure 7-58
EIGRP configura-
tion on Austin.

```
1)  Austin#configure terminal
2)  Enter configuration commands, one per line. End with CNTL/Z.
3)  Austin(config)#router eigrp 100
4)  Austin(config-router)#network 192.168.1.0
5)  Austin(config-router)#network 192.168.2.0
6)  Austin(config-router)#network 192.168.3.0
7)  Austin(config-router)#<Ctrl-Z>
8)  Austin#
```

interfaces that have addresses in the 172.16.0.0 network address space; these are Ethernet0 and Serial0.

As soon as EIGRP is enabled on an interface, the EIGRP process starts sending Hello packets and listening for Hello packets to determine the neighbor routers. Once the neighbor routers are discovered, their addresses are placed into a neighbor table and adjacencies are formed.

To turn off EIGRP on a single interface that is included in one of the network statements, we can use the router configuration command **passive-interface**. Since there are no other routers running EIGRP on the Ethernet LANs, we can make the Ethernet interfaces passive to stop the Hello packets from being transmitted every 5 seconds out of them. Figure 7-59 shows the **passive-interface** command being issued on FortWorth.

Whenever the EIGRP process is referenced on the command line, the ASN must be included since there may be multiple EIGRP processes. The latest version of IOS supports up to 30 EIGRP processes. With Ethernet0 on FortWorth now passive, EIGRP will send no Hello packets or updates to the Ethernet LAN.

Autosummarization is on by default for EIGRP. It can be turned off with the router configuration command **no auto-summary**. This command will perform the same function as it did for RIPv2 as described in Section 7.7.1.2.

Figure 7-59
Passive-interface
command for
EIGRP.

```
1)  FortWorth#configure terminal
2)  Enter configuration commands, one per line. End with CNTL/Z.
3)  FortWorth(config)#router eigrp 100
4)  FortWorth(config-router)#passive-interface ethernet0
5)  FortWorth(config-router)#<Ctrl-Z>
6)  FortWorth#
```

7.7.3.4 EIGRP Verification

Now that EIGRP has been started, there are a few commands that we can use to check its operation. The commands are as follows:

- `show ip protocols`
- `show ip eigrp neighbors`
- `show ip eigrp topology`
- `show ip route`
- `show ip eigrp traffic`

We will display the output for these just to see the type of information available from each. The **show ip protocols** command is extremely useful for getting general information about which IP routing protocols IOS is running and how they are configured. Figure 7-60 shows the output of the **show ip protocols** command on Dallas.

The output shows that process EIGRP 100 is running (Line 2); that is EIGRP with ASN 100. EIGRP has the same default maximum hop count as IGRP, 100 (Line 8). As has already been mentioned, autosummariza-

Figure 7-60

Show IP protocols output after EIGRP configuration.

```
1)   Dallas#show ip protocols
2)   Routing Protocol is "eigrp 100"
3)     Outgoing update filter list for all interfaces is
4)     Incoming update filter list for all interfaces is
5)     Default networks flagged in outgoing updates
6)     Default networks accepted from incoming updates
7)     EIGRP metric weight K1 = 1, K2 = 0, K3 = 1, K4 = 0, K5 = 0
8)     EIGRP maximum hopcount 100
9)     EIGRP maximum metric variance 1
10)    Redistributing: eigrp 100
11)    Automatic network summarization is in effect
12)    Automatic address summarization:
13)      192.168.2.0/24 for Ethernet0, Serial1
14)      172.16.0.0/16 for Serial0
15)       Summarizing with metric 281600
16)    Routing for Networks:
17)      172.16.0.0
18)      192.168.2.0
19)    Routing Information Sources:
20)      Gateway          Distance      Last Update
21)      (this router)           5      00:00:30
22)      192.168.2.2            90      00:00:30
23)      172.16.11.2            90      00:00:30
24)    Distance: internal 90 external 170
25)
26)   Dallas#
```

tion is in effect by default; this is reported on Line 11 and the summary routes being advertised by Dallas are shown on Lines 13 and 14.

The sources of EIGRP 100 routing information are shown near the bottom of the output. We see that Dallas is one of its own sources (Line 21). This occurs because of the autosummarization of the 172.16.0.0 network address. As we will see in the routing table (Figure 7-63), Dallas installs a local summary route for the 172.16.0.0/16 address that leads to the Null0 interface. The administrative distance for an EIGRP summary is 5 (Line 21). The other two sources are Austin (Line 22) and FortWorth (Line 23). The administrative distance for routes learned via EIGRP from those sources is 90. Routes that originate within the EIGRP autonomous system are called *internal* routes, and those that come from outside the EIGRP autonomous system but are included in EIGRP updates are called *external* routes. The default administrative distance for EIGRP internal routes is 90 (Line 24); this is lower than IGRP's, thus EIGRP-learned internal routes are preferred over IGRP-learned routes. The default administrative distance for EIGRP external routes is 170 (Line 24).

Dallas is receiving route information from FortWorth and Austin; therefore, they must be neighbor routers. We can check that by issuing the **show ip eigrp neighbors** command on Dallas to check the contents of Dallas's EIGRP neighbor table. Figure 7-61 shows the result of this command.

The two neighbor routers are shown on Line 5 (FortWorth) and Line 6 (Austin). The *H* column shows a sequence number indicating the order in which the neighbors were discovered; Austin was discovered first. The *Interface* column shows the local interface out which the neighbor can be reached. The *Hold* column shows the value of the hold timer, in seconds, which by default started counting down at 15 seconds (the Hold Time). This timer for a neighbor router gets set to its maximum value each time that a Hello packet is received from the neighbor. Remember that Hello packets should be received every 5 seconds. If the hold timer ever

Figure 7-61

Show IP EIGRP neighbors output.

```
1) Dallas#show ip eigrp neighbors
2) IP-EIGRP neighbors for process 100
3) H   Address         Interface   Hold  Uptime   SRTT   RTO   Q   Seq
4)                                 (sec)          (ms)         Cnt Num
5) 1   172.16.11.2     Se1         12  00:03:53   324  1944   0    5
6) 0   192.168.2.2     Se0         10  00:04:35   797  4782   0    6
7) Dallas#
```

reaches the zero, the neighbor is assumed to be down. The *Uptime* column contains the elapsed time since a router became a neighbor. *SRTT* is smooth round-trip time; this is the average time that a query response sequence takes to a neighbor router. *RTO* is the retransmission timeout after which a query or update will be retransmitted when a response or acknowledgment has not been received from a neighbor. In the Figure 7-61 example, the RTO is six times the SRTT. The number of packets queued for transmission to a neighbor router is given in the *Q Cnt* column. All of the information packets between neighbor routers have sequence numbers, and the *Seq Num* column shows the sequence number of the last packet received from each neighbor.

We have established that EIGRP is running, and Dallas has discovered that FortWorth and Austin are neighbors. Now we should look at what information has been exchanged between the neighbors. The EIGRP topology table shows the information in a raw format. Figure 7-62 shows Dallas's EIGRP topology table.

The **show ip eigrp topology** command displays a summary of the EIGRP topology table. The topology table on Dallas shows that all of the routes are in passive state, as indicated by the letter *P* in the left column

```
1)   Dallas#show ip eigrp topology
2)   IP-EIGRP Topology Table for process 100
3)
4)   Codes: P - Passive, A - Active, U - Update, Q - Query, R - Reply,
5)          r - Reply status
6)
7)   P 192.168.1.0/24, 1 successors, FD is 10537472
8)          via 192.168.2.2 (10537472/281600), Serial0
9)   P 192.168.2.0/24, 1 successors, FD is 10511872
10)         via Connected, Serial0
11)  P 192.168.3.0/24, 2 successors, FD is 46738176
12)         via 192.168.2.2 (46738176/46226176), Serial0
13)         via 172.16.11.2 (46738176/46226176), Serial1
14)  P 172.16.20.0/24, 1 successors, FD is 2195456
15)         via 172.16.11.2 (2195456/281600), Serial1
16)  P 172.16.10.0/24, 1 successors, FD is 281600
17)         via Connected, Ethernet0
18)  P 172.16.11.0/24, 1 successors, FD is 2169856
19)         via Connected, Serial1
20)  P 172.16.0.0/16, 1 successors, FD is 281600
21)         via Summary (281600/0), Null0
22)  Dallas#
```

Figure 7-62   Show IP EIGRP topology output.

of each route. The successor (or successors) is shown for each route along with the feasible distance (FD) for the route. Remember that the feasible distance is the composite metric as calculated from the local router's (Dallas) perspective through a neighbor router. Those routes that are learned from a neighbor show two numbers separated by a slash (/) in parentheses (Line 8, for example). The first number is the feasible distance through the neighbor, and the second number is the advertised distance of the route from the neighbor.

The successor for each route is placed into the IP routing table. We will look at the IP routing tables for each of our routers. Figure 7-63 shows the IP routing table for Dallas, Figure 7-64 shows the IP routing table for FortWorth, and Figure 7-65 shows the IP routing table for Austin.

When EIGRP is running, the EIGRP-learned routes have a D displayed in the left column of their routing table entries (for example, Line 4). The first number within the brackets, on the entries for routes that are not directly connected, shows that the EIGRP-learned routes have an administrative distance of 90. Whenever a router is running EIGRP and summarization is being done, IOS creates a local summary route for the route being summarized (Line 7). The local summary route points to the Null0 interface. The Null0 interface is a logical interface that goes nowhere; some people may refer to this as the *bit bucket*. If Dallas were to get a packet destined for a nonexistent subnet of the 172.16.0.0 network—for example, 172.16.33.0—the packet would be routed to the Null0 interface and dropped, even if a default route existed. Dallas would also send an ICMP destination (host) unreachable message back to the

```
1) Dallas#show ip route
2) [text omitted]
3)      172.16.0.0/16 is variably subnetted, 4 subnets, 2 masks
4) D       172.16.20.0/24 [90/2195456] via 172.16.11.2, 00:02:29, Serial1
5) C       172.16.10.0/24 is directly connected, Ethernet0
6) C       172.16.11.0/24 is directly connected, Serial1
7) D       172.16.0.0/16 is a summary, 00:02:29, Null0
8) D    192.168.1.0/24 [90/10537472] via 192.168.2.2, 00:02:29, Serial0
9) C    192.168.2.0/24 is directly connected, Serial0
10) D   192.168.3.0/24 [90/46738176] via 192.168.2.2, 00:02:29, Serial0
11)                    [90/46738176] via 172.16.11.2, 00:02:29, Serial1
12) Dallas#
```

Figure 7-63   IP routing table on Dallas after EIGRP configuration.

```
1)  FortWorth#show ip route
2)  [text omitted]
3)          172.16.0.0/16 is variably subnetted, 4 subnets, 2 masks
4)  C       172.16.20.0/24 is directly connected, Ethernet0
5)  D       172.16.10.0/24 [90/2195456] via 172.16.11.1, 00:00:56, Serial0
6)  C       172.16.11.0/24 is directly connected, Serial0
7)  D       172.16.0.0/16 is a summary, 00:00:56, Null0
8)  D     192.168.1.0/24 [90/11049472] via 172.16.11.1, 00:00:56, Serial0
9)  D     192.168.2.0/24 [90/11023872] via 172.16.11.1, 00:00:56, Serial0
10) C     192.168.3.0/24 is directly connected, Serial1
11) FortWorth#
```

Figure 7-64 IP routing table on FortWorth after EIGRP configuration.

source of the original packet. If we were to turn off autosummarization, the local summary route would be removed.

FortWorth's new IP routing table also contains the local summary route to the Null0 interface (Line 7). With the exception of the summary route, the network addresses in the routing table are the same as the ones we saw when the routers were running IGRP (Figure 7-49). In Figure 7-49, the metric for the IGRP-learned route to the 172.16.10.0/24 network is 8576. The metric for the EIGRP-learned route is 2195456 (Line 5). When we multiply the value 8576 by 256, the result is 2195456. Remember the EIGRP composite metric uses the same parameters as the IGRP metric multiplied by 256.

Austin's IP routing table contains the summary route, 172.16.0.0/16, that is being advertised by Dallas (Figure 7-65, Line 3). FortWorth is also advertising the summary route, but the path to Dallas has a lower metric and, thus, is preferred. Austin has no local summary route to the Null0 interface because Austin is not directly connected to any subnets of major network addresses and is not actively summarizing its routes to Dallas and FortWorth.

```
1)  Austin#show ip route
2)  [text omitted]
3)  D     172.16.0.0/16 [90/10537472] via 192.168.2.1, 00:02:09, Serial1
4)  C     192.168.1.0/24 is directly connected, Ethernet0
5)  C     192.168.2.0/24 is directly connected, Serial1
6)  C     192.168.3.0/24 is directly connected, Serial0
7)  Austin#
```

Figure 7-65 IP routing table on Austin after EIGRP configuration.

Figure 7-66

Show IP EIGRP
traffic output.

```
1)   Dallas#show ip eigrp traffic
2)   IP-EIGRP Traffic Statistics for process 100
3)     Hellos sent/received: 303/154
4)     Updates sent/received: 13/10
5)     Queries sent/received: 1/0
6)     Replies sent/received: 0/1
7)     Acks sent/received: 5/6
8)     Input queue high water mark 1, 0 drops
9)
10) Dallas#
```

We use the **show ip eigrp traffic** command to check the number of packets being processed by EIGRP. Figure 7-66 shows the output of the **show ip eigrp traffic** command on Dallas.

The number of times each type of EIGRP packet was transmitted and received is given in the output. The packet types were covered in Section 7.7.3.2. In a stable network, the number of Hello packets (Line 3) should steadily increase since they are transmitted and received periodically. The other counters should not change very much unless a network is in transition.

7.7.3.5 EIGRP Configuration Summary

EIGRP configuration, at least getting it started, is very similar to that of RIP and IGRP. EIGRP is configured by entering the **router eigrp** command with an ASN in global configuration mode and then the appropriate **network** commands for enabling EIGRP on the interfaces. Just as with IGRP, all of the routers that use EIGRP to share information must have the same ASN. In order to stop updates on an interface, issue the **passive-interface** command, with the interface name, in router configuration mode for the EIGRP process. The router configuration command **no auto-summary** can be used to turn off autosummarization for an EIGRP process.

The EIGRP-specific configuration commands, from the running configurations, entered for Dallas, FortWorth, and Austin are shown in Figures 7-67, 7-68, and 7-69, respectively.

EIGRP is very easy to turn on. IOS hides most of its complexity from us.

7.7.3.6 EIGRP Removal

The removal of an IP routing protocol is almost too easy. It requires a single global configuration command on each router. Figure 7-70 shows the removal of EIGRP on Dallas.

Figure 7-67
Dallas EIGRP-specific configuration commands.

```
1)  Dallas#show running-config
2)  [text omitted]
3)  !
4)  router eigrp 100
5)   network 172.16.0.0
6)   network 192.168.2.0
7)  !
8)  [text omitted]
9)  Dallas#
```

Figure 7-68
FortWorth EIGRP-specific configuration commands.

```
1)  FortWorth#show running-config
2)  [text omitted]
3)  !
4)  router eigrp 100
5)   passive-interface Ethernet0
6)   network 172.16.0.0
7)   network 192.168.3.0
8)  !
9)  [text omitted]
10) FortWorth#
```

Figure 7-69
Austin EIGRP-specific configuration commands.

```
1)  Austin#show running-config
2)  [text omitted]
3)  !
4)  router eigrp 100
5)   network 192.168.1.0
6)   network 192.168.2.0
7)   network 192.168.3.0
8)  !
9)  [text omitted]
10) Austin#
```

Figure 7-70
Removal of EIGRP.

```
1)  Dallas#configure terminal
2)  Enter configuration commands, one per line. End with CNTL/Z.
3)  Dallas(config)#no router eigrp 100
4)  Dallas(config)#<Ctrl-Z>
5)  Dallas#
```

The **no router eigrp 100** command (Line 3) removes all of the EIGRP-specific commands from the running configuration. After issuing the command on all three of our test routers, our internetwork is once again left without an IP routing protocol and is awaiting the configuration of another.

Remember that whenever EIGRP is referenced in configuration mode, the ASN must be included with it to uniquely identify the EIGRP process.

7.7.4 OSPF

OSPF (Open Shortest Path First) is an open standard, link state routing protocol. (See Section 2.2.2.2 for an overview of link state routing protocols.) OSPF was developed by the *Internet Engineering Task Force* (IETF) and its latest version, 2, is defined in RFC 2328.

Similar to EIGRP, OSPF is classless, has a very fast convergence time, and is complicated, both in operation and in configuration, just as one would expect from something developed by a committee. The following coverage provides just a glimpse into its complexity.

7.7.4.1 OSPF Terminology and Operation

The nature of OSPF practically requires that some type of hierarchy be designed into an internetwork. The hierarchy can be either physical or logical.

We build a hierarchy of an internetwork running OSPF by defining *areas*. An area is a logical group of routers and networks. Each area has its own numeric identifier (ID). An area ID is a 32-bit value that can be written as either a decimal number or a dotted-decimal value, like an IP address. A router can be attached to multiple areas, but a network should be a part of only one area. If an OSPF network has multiple areas, one of the areas must be area 0 (or 0.0.0.0). Area 0 is the *backbone* area, and interarea traffic (traffic between areas) flows through the backbone area. The backbone area should consist of stable networks. The areas of an OSPF internetwork are collectively referred to as an *autonomous system.*

A router with connections to multiple areas is called an *Area Border Router* (ABR). A router with connections to a single area is called an *internal router,* and a router that connects to another autonomous system is called an *Autonomous System Boundary Router* (ASBR).

Each router running OSPF gets a dynamically assigned *router ID* (RID); the router ID is derived from the IP address of one of a router's active interfaces and is assigned when OSPF is started. If a router has a *loopback* interface with an IP address configured, the router ID is the IP address of loopback interface, or the highest loopback interface IP address if there are multiple loopback interfaces. If there are no loopback interfaces, the router ID is the highest IP address that is assigned to one of the other router's active interfaces. An active interface is one that is in an up/up state. Loopback interfaces are logical interfaces that we create; they do not go down unless we manually shut them down. A router's OSPF RID will change if the interface from which it was derived goes down.

All routers running OSPF transmit and save *Link State Advertisements* (LSA) in a *link state database.* There are many types of LSAs; the most basic ones are described in the next few paragraphs. All of the routers within an area must contain identical LSAs in their database for the area, or areas, to which they are connected. Routers transmit LSAs when a network changes state and periodically at 30-minute intervals. The retransmission every 30 minutes happens because each LSA in the link state database must be refreshed every 90 minutes. Routers must acknowledge all valid LSAs that they receive.

A *router LSA* is one that is generated by each router in an OSPF autonomous system; it contains information about an individual router such as its RID and the links (for example, networks) to which it is attached. Router LSAs are propagated, or flooded, to every router that is connected to the area in which the LSA originated.

Routes to networks within an area are called *intra-area* routes, and routes to networks in another area of the same OSPF autonomous system are called *interarea* routes. Interarea routes are advertised by ABRs by using *summary LSAs,* which propagate within area borders. Routes to networks in another autonomous system are called *external* routes; external routes are injected into the OSPF autonomous system by ASBRs by using *external LSAs,* which propagate throughout an entire OSPF autonomous system except as indicated below.

Several types of OSPF areas are defined; we cover the following types:

- Normal Area
- Stub Area
- Totally Stubby Area

A *normal* area is an area that can contain internal routers, ABRs, and ASBRs. Area 0 must be a normal area.

A *stub* area is one that does not allow the propagation of external routes. The ABR that connects a stub area to the backbone area blocks the propagation of external LSAs and transmits a default route along with the normal interarea routes (by summary LSAs) into the stub area. The default route is used by all of the stub area's internal routers to get to networks that are not a part of the OSPF autonomous system. The interarea routes are used to get to networks that are a part of the autonomous system. A stub area cannot contain an ASBR. Stub areas are defined in the OSPF standard.

A *totally stubby* area is a Cisco-proprietary area type that extends the definition of a stub area. A totally stubby area does not allow the propagation of external routes (external LSAs) or interarea routes (normal summary LSAs); instead, the ABR that connects a totally stubby area to the backbone area transmits only a default route into the totally stubby area. The default route is used by all of the totally stubby area's internal routers to get to networks that are not a part of the local totally stubby area. Internal routers in totally stubby areas tend to have very small routing tables relative to the routers in normal areas.

Similarly to EIGRP, OSPF discovers neighbor routers by transmitting *Hello* packets and listening for Hello packets. OSPF routers transmit Hello packets to the multicast address designated for all OSPF routers, 224.0.0.5. Once neighbors are discovered, their information is placed into a *neighbor table.* In order for two routers to become OSPF neighbors, they must agree on five OSPF parameters that are contained in the Hello packets:

1. Area ID
2. Hello Interval
3. Dead Interval
4. Stub Area Flag
5. Authentication Password (if applicable)

The *hello interval* is the length of time between hello packets. The default hello interval is 10 seconds. The *dead interval* is the amount of time that must elapse without a router hearing a Hello from a neighbor before the router will remove the neighbor's information from its table. This is similar to the Hold Time that was covered for EIGRP. The default dead interval is four times the hello interval, 40 seconds.

The *stub area flag* is set in the hello packets transmitted by a router into an area when we define the area to be a stub area or a totally stubby area. The flag is actually just a single bit within the packet. All of the routers that connect to any kind of stub area must know that the area is a stub area.

OSPF provides password authentication just like RIPv2 and EIGRP, so it is reasonable that two routers cannot be neighbors and share information if they do not know each other's password.

On multiaccess networks such as LANs and frame relay multipoint WANs, a *Designated Router* (DR) and a *Backup Designated Router* (BDR) are elected based on OSPF *priority* and router ID. The router with the highest OSPF priority on a multiaccess network is selected to be DR; the router with the second-highest OSPF priority is selected to be the BDR. The default OSPF priority of an IOS-based router is 1 (one). If multiple routers have the same priority, the RID is used as the tiebreaker. The router with the highest RID wins. Once a router has been elected DR for a network, the router continues to be DR until its connection to the network goes down. When a network loses its DR, the BDR immediately becomes the DR, and there is an election for a new BDR.

The DR is responsible for advertising the network to the rest of the OSPF routers using a *network LSA,* which contains the network's address and mask along with the RIDs of all of the routers attached to the network. The propagation of network LSAs is bounded by an area's border, just as that of router LSAs and summary LSAs are.

Each multiaccess network gets its own DR and BDR. All routers on the multiaccess network build *adjacencies* only with the DR and the BDR; this usually reduces the number of adjacencies that must be maintained by all of the routers except the DR and BDR. When routers transmit LSAs meant for the DR and BDR, the routers send the LSAs to the multicast address designated for all DRs and BDRs, 224.0.0.6. An adjacency is the synchronization of the routers' link state databases so that they have identical LSAs for the area in which the network exists.

There is no DR and BDR election on point-to-point networks; the routers on each end do, however, establish an adjacency with each other.

OSPF uses a single metric called *cost,* which is calculated from the bandwidth assigned to an interface; this bandwidth is defined the same way as the bandwidth used in the composite metric for IGRP and EIGRP. The cost of a link is included in the LSA that is being used to advertise the link. OSPF costs are additive. To get the total metric from one network to another, routers simply add the costs of the individual networks that must be crossed to get to a destination. The default formula for calculating the outbound cost of an interface is as follows:

```
10⁸ / bandwidth (in bps) = cost
```

For example, the default cost of a 10 Mbps Ethernet interface is 10 as shown below.

```
10⁸ / bandwidth = 10⁸ / 10,000,000 = 10⁸ / 10⁷ = 10
```

So now there are all of these types of LSAs being transmitted and collected by different types of routers within different types of areas. We still have not reached the point where a router running OSPF can route packets using the information it has gathered in its link state database.

The OSPF process runs a special algorithm called the *Shortest Path First* (SPF) algorithm against the link state database; the algorithm is also called the *Dijkstra* algorithm. The running of the SPF algorithm produces a map of an internetwork in the form of a tree with the local router as the root. From the network tree, the router takes the shortest path to each network and places that path into the IP routing table.

When the link state database is updated, a router must run the SPF algorithm, produce another network tree, and then update the routing table. Because of this three-step process, routers running OSPF use more CPU time than those running the other routing protocols we have covered. The existence of the neighbor table, the link state database, and the network tree requires a little more RAM, also.

7.7.4.2 OSPF Basic Configuration

The configuration of OSPF requires the designation of an OSPF process with the **router ospf** command along with a *process ID* (PID). The PID identifies the local OSPF process only, and does not have to be the same on all of the routers running OSPF. OSPF is enabled on a router's interfaces by using the **network area** command. The **network area** command associates a wildcard mask with an address and specifies the area to which interfaces that match the address and wildcard mask pair are connected. This gives us control over exactly which interfaces have OSPF enabled and which area each interface is in. The command syntax looks like this:

```
network address wildcard-mask area area-ID
```

The *address* is the dotted-decimal address of a network, a subnet, or an interface. The *wildcard-mask* is a 32-bit, dotted-decimal value sometimes called an *inverse mask* because the meanings of its bits are inverted from their meanings in a network mask.

We covered network masks when we did IP address subnetting. In a *network mask,* a binary one in a bit position means that the bit position is important in routing, and a binary zero in a bit position means that the bit position has no significance in routing. The opposite is true for a wildcard mask. In a *wildcard mask,* a binary zero means that the bit position should be checked in matching an address, and a binary one means that the bit position should be ignored during the matching process. A wild-card mask of 255.255.255.255 is used to match any address, and a wild-card mask of 0.0.0.0 is used to match only the specific address with which it is paired. Those are the two extremes of the wildcard mask; the configuration examples will provide more insight. The *area-ID* is the number that we have assigned to the area to which all interfaces with addresses matching the address/wildcard-mask pair are connected.

The OSPF internetwork that we are going to configure is shown in Figure 7-71. There are two areas, 0 and 1. The area boundaries are highlighted. Area 0 will contain Dallas's Ethernet0 and Serial1 interfaces and FortWorth's Ethernet0 and Serial0 interfaces. Area 1 will contain Dallas's Serial0 interface, FortWorth's Serial1 interface, and all of Austin's interfaces. Dallas and FortWorth will be ABRs, and Austin will be an internal router.

Figure 7-72 shows the configuration of our OSPF design on Dallas, Figure 7-73 shows the OSPF configuration on FortWorth, and Figure 7-74 has the configuration of OSPF on Austin.

Figure 7-71
OSPF area diagram.

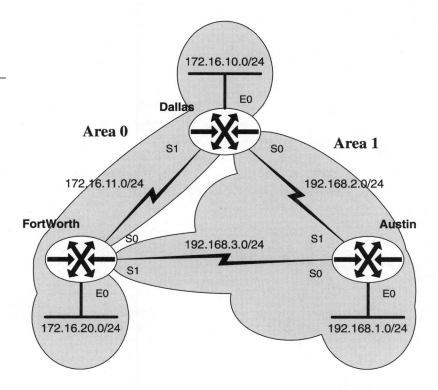

Figure 7-72
OSPF configuration
on Dallas.

```
1)  Dallas#configure terminal
2)  Enter configuration commands, one per line. End with CNTL/Z.
3)  Dallas(config)#router ospf 100
4)  Dallas(config-router)#network 172.16.10.1 0.0.0.0 area 0
5)  Dallas(config-router)#network 172.16.11.1 0.0.0.0 area 0
6)  Dallas(config-router)#network 192.168.2.1 0.0.0.0 area 1
7)  Dallas(config-router)#<Ctrl-Z>
8)  Dallas#
```

The configuration of OSPF is initiated on Dallas with the **router ospf 100** command (Line 3). The PID is 100; this identifies the OSPF process on Dallas. This number does not have to be the same on the other routers. As a matter of fact, we purposely used a different PID on each router to illustrate this. Under normal circumstances, we would have used the same PID on all the routers just to be consistent and to avoid having to figure out which PID we used each time that we wanted to configure OSPF on a router. On the Line 4 **network area** command, we have an address of 172.16.10.1 with a wildcard mask of 0.0.0.0. The interfaces with addresses matching this address/mask pair are to run OSPF for area 0. Since the wildcard mask is all zeros, there can be only one matching address. This particular command enables OSPF on Dallas's Ethernet0 interface and places the Ethernet LAN in area 0 because the Ethernet0 interface has the exact address 172.16.10.1. The next **network area** command (Line 5) enables OSPF on the Serial1 interface for area 0. The last **network area** command (Line 6) enables OSPF on the Serial0 interface for area 1.

The **network area** commands are processed from top to bottom so the order in which they are typed is important when an interface's address matches multiple statements. When using the 0.0.0.0 wildcard mask, the order does not really matter since each statement can possibly match only one address.

Figure 7-73
OSPF configuration
on FortWorth.

```
1) FortWorth#configure terminal
2) Enter configuration commands, one per line. End with CNTL/Z.
3) FortWorth(config)#router ospf 200
4) FortWorth(config-router)#network 172.16.0.0 0.0.255.255 area 0
5) FortWorth(config-router)#network 192.168.3.0 0.0.0.255 area 1
6) FortWorth(config-router)#<Ctrl-Z>
7) FortWorth#
```

Figure 7-74

OSPF configuration on Austin.

```
1) Austin#configure terminal
2) Enter configuration commands, one per line. End with CNTL/Z.
3) Austin(config)#router ospf 300
4) Austin(config-router)#network 192.0.0.0 0.255.255.255 area 1
5) Austin(config-router)#<Ctrl-Z>
6) Austin#
```

We used the PID 200 on FortWorth (Line 3, Figure 7-73). The first **network area** command (Line 4) enables OSPF on both the Ethernet0 and the Serial0 interfaces and places them both in area 0. The address of 172.16.0.0 paired with the wildcard mask of 0.0.255.255 means that the interfaces with addresses beginning with 172.16 match the statement; those are Ethernet0 and Serial0. The Line 5 command puts Serial1 into area 1 because the address of Serial1 starts with 192.168.3.

Austin gets another different PID, 300 (Line 3, Figure 7-74). We used a single **network area** command (Line 4) to put all of Austin's interfaces into OSPF area 1. With the wildcard mask of 0.255.255.255, only the first octet of an interface's address is checked in the statement. All of Austin's addresses begin with 192; therefore, all of them get placed into area 1.

7.7.4.3   OSPF Verification

The commands we will use to verify the operation of OSPF are as follows:

- show ip protocols
- show ip route
- show ip ospf
- show ip ospf neighbor
- show ip ospf interface
- show ip ospf database

Since we started the verification of all the other routing protocols with the **show ip protocols** command, we will do the same thing here. Figure 7-75 shows the output of the **show ip protocols** command on Dallas.

As shown on Line 2, OSPF with the PID of 100 is running. OSPF updates are triggered, not periodic; that is why the timers are all 0 (Lines 3 and 4). The addresses that match our address/wildcard mask pairs on the **network area** commands are specified on Lines 9, 10, and 11. Dallas is receiving routing from both FortWorth (Line 15) and Austin

Figure 7-75

Show ip protocols output after OSPF configuration.

```
1)   Dallas#show ip protocols
2)   Routing Protocol is "ospf 100"
3)     Sending updates every 0 seconds
4)     Invalid after 0 seconds, hold down 0, flushed after 0
5)     Outgoing update filter list for all interfaces is
6)     Incoming update filter list for all interfaces is
7)     Redistributing: ospf 100
8)     Routing for Networks:
9)       172.16.10.1/32
10)      172.16.11.1/32
11)      192.168.2.1/32
12)    Routing Information Sources:
13)      Gateway          Distance      Last Update
14)      192.168.3.2          110       00:01:24
15)      192.168.3.1          110       00:01:34
16)    Distance: (default is 110)
17)
18)  Dallas#
```

(Line 14). The addresses shown are the RIDs for the routers. OSPF's default administrative distance of 110 (Line 16) is lower than that of RIP but higher than that of IGRP and EIGRP.

The IP routing tables are an indication of the type of connectivity our internetwork has. Figure 7-76 shows the IP routing table for Dallas, Figure 7-77 has FortWorth's IP routing table, and Figure 7-78 has Austin's IP routing table.

Dallas's routing shows the usual routes. The routes learned via OSPF have the letter *O* in the left column of their entries. The administrative distance of 110 is shown in the brackets for the OSPF-learned routes. As usual, the second number within the brackets is the metric. The metric for these routes is the OSPF cost. Let us do a quick calculation of a

Figure 7-76

Dallas IP routing table after OSPF configuration.

```
1) Dallas#show ip route
2) [text omitted]
3)    172.16.0.0/24 is subnetted, 3 subnets
4) O    172.16.20.0 [110/74] via 172.16.11.2, 00:02:31, Serial1
5) C    172.16.10.0 is directly connected, Ethernet0
6) C    172.16.11.0 is directly connected, Serial1
7) O 192.168.1.0/24 [110/400] via 192.168.2.2, 00:01:43, Serial0
8) C 192.168.2.0/24 is directly connected, Serial0
9) O 192.168.3.0/24 [110/2175] via 192.168.2.2, 00:01:43, Serial0
10) Dallas#
```

```
1)  FortWorth#show ip route
2)  [text omitted]
3)       172.16.0.0/24 is subnetted, 3 subnets
4)  C    172.16.20.0 is directly connected, Ethernet0
5)  O    172.16.10.0 [110/74] via 172.16.11.1, 00:04:49, Serial0
6)  C    172.16.11.0 is directly connected, Serial0
7)  O 192.168.1.0/24 [110/1795] via 192.168.3.2, 00:03:59, Serial1
8)  O 192.168.2.0/24 [110/2175] via 192.168.3.2, 00:03:59, Serial1
9)  C 192.168.3.0/24 is directly connected, Serial1
10) FortWorth#
```

Figure 7-77   FortWorth IP routing table after OSPF configuration.

route's metric. The route to network address 172.16.20.0 has a cost of 74 (Figure 7-76, Line 4). This is a route to FortWorth's Ethernet LAN across the T1. The cost for the T1 is 64 and the cost for FortWorth's Ethernet0 interface is 10; the total cost is 74.

The IP routing table on FortWorth shows the same basic routes as the one on Dallas.

The IP routing table of Austin shows some differences from what we saw with the other routing protocols. Austin knows about each of the 172.16.0.0 subnets (Lines 4, 5, and 6). OSPF does not do autosummarization; OSPF summarization must be manually configured. The subnets have the additional letters *IA* after the *O* in the left column. The IA indicates that these are interarea routes; the networks are in another area to which Austin is not connected. According to Figure 7-71 and our configuration, they are in area 0 while Austin is entirely within area 1.

```
1)  Austin#show ip route
2)  [text omitted]
3)       172.16.0.0/24 is subnetted, 3 subnets
4)  O IA    172.16.20.0 [110/464] via 192.168.2.1, 00:05:15, Serial1
5)  O IA    172.16.10.0 [110/400] via 192.168.2.1, 00:05:15, Serial1
6)  O IA    172.16.11.0 [110/454] via 192.168.2.1, 00:05:15, Serial1
7)  C    192.168.1.0/24 is directly connected, Ethernet0
8)  C    192.168.2.0/24 is directly connected, Serial1
9)  C    192.168.3.0/24 is directly connected, Serial0
10) Austin#
```

Figure 7-78   Austin IP routing table after OSPF configuration.

General information about OSPF operation can be obtained with the **show ip ospf command.** Figure 7-79 shows the output of the **show ip ospf** command on Dallas.

The only OSPF process running has PID 100 and the RID selected for that process is 192.168.2.1 (Line 2). The address 192.168.2.1 is the highest IP address assigned to an active interface on Dallas. Dallas is connected to two areas—0 (Line 10) and 1 (Line 20). Being connected to two areas makes Dallas an ABR (Line 4). Dallas has two interfaces in area 0 (Line 11) and one interface in area 1 (Line 21). We also see the number of times that the SPF algorithm has been run for each of the areas (Lines 13 and 23). This is a good statistic to monitor. If it starts increasing rapidly, we probably have an unstable network somewhere.

Figure 7-79

Show IP OSPF output.

```
1)  Dallas#show ip ospf
2)  Routing Process "ospf 100" with ID 192.168.2.1
3)  Supports only single TOS(TOS0) routes
4)  It is an area border router
5)  Summary Link update interval is 00:30:00 and the update due
    in 00:26:24
6)  SPF schedule delay 5 secs, Hold time between two SPFs 10 secs
7)  Number of DCbitless external LSA 0
8)  Number of DoNotAge external LSA 0
9)  Number of areas in this router is 2. 2 normal 0 stub 0 nssa
10)    Area BACKBONE(0)
11)        Number of interfaces in this area is 2
12)        Area has no authentication
13)        SPF algorithm executed 4 times
14)        Area ranges are
15)        Link State Update Interval is 00:30:00 and due in
           00:26:23
16)        Link State Age Interval is 00:20:00 and due in
           00:16:23
17)        Number of DCbitless LSA 0
18)        Number of indication LSA 0
19)        Number of DoNotAge LSA 0
20)    Area 1
21)        Number of interfaces in this area is 1
22)        Area has no authentication
23)        SPF algorithm executed 4 times
24)        Area ranges are
25)        Link State Update Interval is 00:30:00 and due in
           00:26:22
26)        Link State Age Interval is 00:20:00 and due in
           00:16:22
27)        Number of DCbitless LSA 0
28)        Number of indication LSA 0
29)        Number of DoNotAge LSA 0
30)
31) Dallas#
```

Figure 7-80

Show IP OSPF
neighbor output.

```
1) Dallas#show ip ospf neighbor
2)
3) Neighbor ID   Pri   State     Dead Time   Address        Interface
4) 192.168.3.2    1    FULL/ -   00:00:31    192.168.2.2    Serial0
5) 192.168.3.1    1    FULL/ -   00:00:35    172.16.11.2    Serial1
6) Dallas#
```

The OSPF neighbor table contains the RIDs for all of the routers that the local router has discovered as neighbors. Figure 7-80 shows the neighbor table displayed on Dallas after issuing the **show ip ospf neighbor** command.

Dallas's two neighbor routers are Austin (Line 4) and FortWorth (Line 5). The *Neighbor ID* column shows the RIDs for the routers, not the addresses of their directly connected interfaces. The neighbors' directly connected interface addresses are given in the *Address* column, and the interface to which the neighbor is connected is shown in the **Interface** column. The *State* column shows the status of the neighbor relationship. A full state indicates that an adjacency has been established with a neighbor. The *Dead Time* column indicates the amount of time left in the dead interval either to receive a Hello packet from a neighbor or to remove the neighbor from the table.

Figure 7-81 shows the output of the **show ip ospf interface** command on Dallas. The **show ip ospf interface** command shows the status of OSPF on a router's interfaces. Figure 7-81 shows that Dallas has OSPF enabled on interfaces Ethernet0, Serial0, and Serial1 (Lines 9, 19, and 28). We will look at some of the information given for the Serial1 interface (starting on Line 27). The Serial1 interface is connected to area 0 (Line 28) for Dallas's OSPF PID 100 (Line 29). Dallas's RID is 192.168.2.1 (Line 29). The network to which Serial1 is connected is a point-to-point network with a cost of 64. The cost of 64 is based on the bandwidth of the Serial1 interface being set to the fast-serial interface default value of 1544—that is, 1544 kbps or 1,544,000 bps—to plug into the formula for calculating OSPF cost. The OSPF timers are given on Line 31. Dallas has one neighbor out its Serial1 interface (Line 33) and an adjacency has been established with that neighbor (Line 33). The neighbor's RID (192.168.3.1) is given on Line 34; the neighbor is Austin.

The link state database is another useful item to examine when verifying the operation of OSPF. Figure 7-82 shows the output of the **show ip ospf database** command on Dallas.

Since Dallas is an ABR with connections to both area 0 and area 1, there are two sets of link state information in the database. There are

Figure 7-81

Show IP OSPF
interface output.

```
1) Dallas#show ip ospf interface
2) BRI0 is administratively down, line protocol is down
3)   OSPF not enabled on this interface
4) BRI0:1 is administratively down, line protocol is down
5)   OSPF not enabled on this interface
6) BRI0:2 is administratively down, line protocol is down
7)   OSPF not enabled on this interface
8) Ethernet0 is up, line protocol is up
9)   Internet Address 172.16.10.1/24, Area 0
10)  Process ID 100, Router ID 192.168.2.1, Network Type
     BROADCAST, Cost: 10
11)  Transmit Delay is 1 sec, State DR, Priority 1
12)  Designated Router (ID) 192.168.2.1, Interface address
     172.16.10.1
13)  No backup designated router on this network
14)  Timer intervals configured, Hello 10, Dead 40, Wait 40,
     Retransmit 5
15)     Hello due in 00:00:01
16)  Neighbor Count is 0, Adjacent neighbor count is 0
17)  Suppress hello for 0 neighbor(s)
18) Serial0 is up, line protocol is up
19)  Internet Address 192.168.2.1/24, Area 1
20)  Process ID 100, Router ID 192.168.2.1, Network Type
     POINT_TO_POINT, Cost: 390
21)  Transmit Delay is 1 sec, State POINT_TO_POINT,
22)  Timer intervals configured, Hello 10, Dead 40, Wait 40,
     Retransmit 5
23)     Hello due in 00:00:08
24)  Neighbor Count is 1, Adjacent neighbor count is 1
25)     Adjacent with neighbor 192.168.3.2
26)  Suppress hello for 0 neighbor(s)
27)  Serial1 is up, line protocol is up
28)  Internet Address 172.16.11.1/24, Area 0
29)  Process ID 100, Router ID 192.168.2.1, Network Type
     POINT_TO_POINT, Cost: 64
30)  Transmit Delay is 1 sec, State POINT_TO_POINT,
31)  Timer intervals configured, Hello 10, Dead 40, Wait 40,
     Retransmit 5
32)     Hello due in 00:00:05
33)  Neighbor Count is 1, Adjacent neighbor count is 1
34)     Adjacent with neighbor 192.168.3.1
35)  Suppress hello for 0 neighbor(s)
36) Serial2 is administratively down, line protocol is down
37)  OSPF not enabled on this interface
38) Serial3 is administratively down, line protocol is down
39)  OSPF not enabled on this interface
40 Dallas#
```

two routers with connections to area 0; therefore, there must be two router link states for area 0: one for Dallas (Line 9) and one for FortWorth (Line 10). There are two ABRs between area 0 and area 1; therefore, each of them generated summary LSAs into area 0 indicating the routes in area 1 (Lines 15 through 20). There are three routers with

```
1)  Dallas#show ip ospf database
2)
3)          OSPF Router with ID (192.168.2.1) (Process ID 100)
4)
5)
6)                  Router Link States (Area 0)
7)
8)  Link ID         ADV Router      Age    Seq#         Checksum   Link count
9)  192.168.2.1     192.168.2.1     280    0x80000003   0x36B3     3
10) 192.168.3.1     192.168.3.1     279    0x80000002   0x7668     3
11)
12)              Summary Net Link States (Area 0)
13)
14) Link ID         ADV Router      Age    Seq#         Checksum
15) 192.168.1.0     192.168.2.1     222    0x80000001   0x5B79
16) 192.168.1.0     192.168.3.1     224    0x80000001   0x358
17) 192.168.2.0     192.168.2.1     232    0x80000001   0xEBF1
18) 192.168.2.0     192.168.3.1     225    0x80000001   0xDDFE
19) 192.168.3.0     192.168.2.1     222    0x80000001   0xD903
20) 192.168.3.0     192.168.3.1     235    0x80000001   0x89D9
21)
22)                 Router Link States (Area 1)
23)
24) Link ID         ADV Router      Age    Seq#         Checksum   Link count
25) 192.168.2.1     192.168.2.1     232    0x80000003   0x668D     2
26) 192.168.3.1     192.168.3.1     237    0x80000003   0x3FB      2
27) 192.168.3.2     192.168.3.2     229    0x80000003   0xCB3B     5
28)
29)              Summary Net Link States (Area 1)
30)
31) Link ID         ADV Router      Age    Seq#         Checksum
32) 172.16.10.0     192.168.2.1     323    0x80000001   0xD926
33) 172.16.10.0     192.168.3.1     276    0x80000001   0x5569
34) 172.16.11.0     192.168.2.1     281    0x80000001   0xECDB
35) 172.16.11.0     192.168.3.1     277    0x80000001   0xE5E1
36) 172.16.20.0     192.168.2.1     272    0x80000001   0xEDC7
37) 172.16.20.0     192.168.3.1     277    0x80000001   0x6490
38) Dallas#
```

Figure 7-82   Show IP OSPF database output.

connections to area 1 so there must be three router link states for area 1: one for Dallas (Line 25), one for FortWorth (Line 26), and one for Austin (Line 27). The two ABRs each generated summary LSAs into area 1 indicating the routes in area 0 (Lines 32 through 37).

7.7.4.4   OSPF Stub Area Configuration
Stub areas were covered in Section 7.7.4.1. We use the router configuration command **area stub** to convert an area into a stub area. The **area stub** command must be entered under the OSPF process for every router

Figure 7-83

Conversion of a normal area to a stub area.

```
1)  Dallas#configure terminal
2)  Enter configuration commands, one per line. End with CNTL/Z.
3)  Dallas(config)#router ospf 100
4)  Dallas(config-router)#area 1 stub
5)  Dallas(config-router)#<Ctrl-Z>
6)  Dallas#
7)  ———
8)  FortWorth#configure terminal
9)  Enter configuration commands, one per line. End with CNTL/Z.
10) FortWorth(config)#router ospf 200
11) FortWorth(config-router)#area 1 stub
12) FortWorth(config-router)#<Ctrl-Z>
13) FortWorth#
14) ———
15) Austin#configure terminal
16) Enter configuration commands, one per line. End with CNTL/Z.
17) Austin(config)#router ospf 300
18) Austin(config-router)#area 1 stub
19) Austin(config-router)#<Ctrl-Z>
20) Austin#
```

that has a connection to the area that is to be a stub area. Figure 7-83 shows the conversion of area 1 from a normal area to a stub area.

The configurations of our three test routers were grouped together to show that the same command must by typed for the OSPF process on each router. The ID of the area being made a stub area must be referenced in the **area stub** command. The area ID goes between the **area** keyword and the **stub** keyword in the command (Lines 4, 11, and 18).

After converting area 1 to a stub area, the IP routing tables of Dallas and FortWorth are unchanged since they are ABRs for area 1. However, the Austin routing table now contains a default route as shown in Figure 7-84.

The default route is shown on Line 18 as a network 0.0.0.0 with a prefix length of /0. The prefix length of /0 will cause any destination address to match this route. Austin will route all IP packets with this route unless there is another routing table match with a longer prefix length. As a general rule, the default route is used if no other match for a destination address can be found in the routing table. The default route also appears as the gateway of last resort (Line 9). The OSPF interarea routes to the 172.16.0.0 subnets are still in the routing table. We can get rid of those by making area 1 a totally stubby area.

To convert an area from a stub area to a totally stubby area, we need to reissue the **area stub** command, on the ABRs, with the keyword **no-summary** at the end of it. Figure 7-85 shows the conversion of area 1 from a stub area to a totally stubby area.

Figure 7-84
IP routing table of
Austin after stub
area conversion.

```
1)  Austin#show ip route
2)  Codes: C - connected, S - static, I - IGRP, R - RIP,
    M - mobile, B - BGP
3)         D - EIGRP, EX - EIGRP external, O - OSPF, IA - OSPF
           inter area
4)         N1 - OSPF NSSA external type 1, N2 - OSPF NSSA exter-
           nal type 2
5)         E1 - OSPF external type 1, E2 - OSPF external type 2,
           E - EGP
6)         i - IS-IS, L1 - IS-IS level-1, L2 - IS-IS level-2,
           * - candidate default
7)         U - per-user static route, o - ODR
8)
9)  Gateway of last resort is 192.168.2.1 to network 0.0.0.0
10)
11)      172.16.0.0/24 is subnetted, 3 subnets
12) O IA    172.16.20.0 [110/464] via 192.168.2.1, 00:00:13,
             Serial1
13) O IA    172.16.10.0 [110/400] via 192.168.2.1, 00:00:13,
             Serial1
14) O IA    172.16.11.0 [110/454] via 192.168.2.1, 00:00:13,
             Serial1
15) C     192.168.1.0/24 is directly connected, Ethernet0
16) C     192.168.2.0/24 is directly connected, Serial1
17) C     192.168.3.0/24 is directly connected, Serial0
18) O*IA 0.0.0.0/0 [110/391] via 192.168.2.1, 00:00:13, Serial1
19) Austin#
```

Since Austin is not an ABR for area 1, the configuration of Austin remains as it is with the original **area 1 stub** command. The **no-summary** keyword (Lines 4 and 11) indicates that the usual summary LSAs containing interarea routes are not to be injected into the area. Instead only a default route is injected. Figure 7-86 shows Austin's routing table after area 1 becomes a totally stubby area.

Figure 7-85
Conversion of a
stub area to a
totally stubby area.

```
1)  Dallas#configure terminal
2)  Enter configuration commands, one per line. End with CNTL/Z.
3)  Dallas(config)#router ospf 100
4)  Dallas(config-router)#area 1 stub no-summary
5)  Dallas(config-router)#<Ctrl-Z>
6)  Dallas#
7)  ─────
8)  FortWorth#configure terminal
9)  Enter configuration commands, one per line. End with CNTL/Z.
10) FortWorth(config)#router ospf 200
11) FortWorth(config-router)#area 1 stub no-summary
12) FortWorth(config-router)#<Ctrl-Z>
13) FortWorth#
```

Figure 7-86
IP routing table of Austin after totally stubby area conversion.

```
1)  Austin#show ip route
2)  Codes: C - connected, S - static, I - IGRP, R - RIP,
           M - mobile, B - BGP
3)         D - EIGRP, EX - EIGRP external, O - OSPF, IA - OSPF
           inter area
4)         N1 - OSPF NSSA external type 1, N2 - OSPF NSSA exter-
           nal type 2
5)         E1 - OSPF external type 1, E2 - OSPF external type 2,
           E - EGP
6)         i - IS-IS, L1 - IS-IS level-1, L2 - IS-IS level-2,
           * - candidate default
7)         U - per-user static route, o - ODR
8)
9)  Gateway of last resort is 192.168.2.1 to network 0.0.0.0
10)
11) C    192.168.1.0/24 is directly connected, Ethernet0
12) C    192.168.2.0/24 is directly connected, Serial1
13) C    192.168.3.0/24 is directly connected, Serial0
14) O*IA 0.0.0.0/0 [110/391] via 192.168.2.1, 00:00:09, Serial1
15) Austin#
```

Austin's IP routing table no longer contains any interarea routes. Instead there is a default route, which will be used to route packets to any network that is not in area 1.

7.7.4.5 OSPF Configuration Summary

We start OSPF by entering the **router ospf** command, with a process id, in global configuration mode and then the appropriate **network area** commands for enabling OSPF on the interfaces. The **network area** command, through the use of a wildcard mask, allows us to accurately control which interfaces get OSPF enabled and which area an interface is connected to.

To convert a normal area to a stub area, we use the **area stub** command—in router configuration mode for the OSPF process—on every

Figure 7-87
Dallas OSPF-specific configuration commands.

```
1)  Dallas#show running-config
2)  [text omitted]
3)  !
4)  router ospf 100
5)   network 172.16.10.1 0.0.0.0 area 0
6)   network 172.16.11.1 0.0.0.0 area 0
7)   network 192.168.2.1 0.0.0.0 area 1
8)   area 1 stub no-summary
9)  !
10) [text omitted]
11) Dallas#
```

Figure 7-88
FortWorth OSPF-
specific configura-
tion commands.

```
1)  FortWorth#show running-config
2)  [text omitted]
3)  !
4)  router ospf 200
5)    network 172.16.0.0 0.0.255.255 area 0
6)    network 192.168.3.0 0.0.0.255 area 1
7)    area 1 stub no-summary
8)  !
9)  [text omitted]
10) FortWorth#
```

router that has a connection to the area. We create a totally stubby area by using the **area stub** command on every router that has a connection to the area, but, on the area's ABRs, we include the **no-summary** keyword on the **area stub** command

The current, OSPF-specific configuration commands, from the running configurations of Dallas, FortWorth, and Austin are shown in Figures 7-87, 7-88, and 7-89, respectively.

Since OSPF is the last IP routing protocol we will be covering, we will be leaving the configuration in this state.

7.7.4.6 OSPF Removal

Removing an OSPF process on a Cisco router requires a single global configuration command. Just put the keyword **no** in front of the command that was used to configure OSPF. For example, the command to remove the current OSPF process from Dallas would be as follows:

```
no router ospf 100
```

When OSPF is referenced in configuration mode, the PID must be included with it to uniquely identify the OSPF process, since there could be multiple OSPF processes running on the router.

Figure 7-89
Austin OSPF-
specific configura-
tion commands.

```
1)  Austin#show running-config
2)  [text omitted]
3)  !
4)  router ospf 300
5)    network 192.0.0.0 0.255.255.255 area 1
6)    area 1 stub
7)  !
8)  [text omitted]
9)  Austin#
```

Configuring IPX

Internetwork Packet eXchange (IPX) is a layer-3 network protocol developed by Novell originally for file and printer sharing in small, desktop environments. IPX is based on a client-server model in which a client cannot do anything on an internetwork until it attaches to a server.

Our coverage of IPX begins with an overview of IPX host addressing and protocol operation. The IOS commands for configuring IPX are illustrated as we make modifications to our test internetwork.

8.1 IPX Addressing

IPX host addresses are 80 bits long and we normally write them in hexadecimal (hex). An IPX address has a 32-bit network part and a 48-bit node part. The *network part* identifies a single network and the *node part* identifies a single host on the network. We must assign a unique network address to every network (physical and logical) that is to carry IPX traffic. There is no common registry to obtain IPX network addresses as there is with IP. Instead, we can use any IPX address we want as long as it is unique within the entire internetwork where it is located. Network addresses are defined only on Novell servers and routers. All servers and routers on the same network must have the same network address defined. Clients figure out the network address of a network dynamically when they start.

Network administrators use many ways of determining IPX network addresses to assign to networks. Some of these are as follows:

- Start with Novell's default address of 1 and increment from there.
- Use the hex form of the IP subnet address of a network; this usually leaves some digits at the end, which can be used for internal server addresses on the network—the method used in this chapter.
- Use the area code and exchange for a network's location as the first six digits of the address; this leaves two digits at the end of the address to be used sequentially.
- Make up words using the available hex digits 0 through 9 and A through F. For example, BADCAFE and DEADBEEF are common.
- Make up addresses at random.

The node portion of an IPX address is defined automatically to be the MAC address of an IPX host's interface. On Cisco router interfaces that do not have MAC addresses, such as serial interfaces, the MAC address of the first LAN interface in the router is used as the node portion of the IPX address. If there are no LAN interfaces in the router, IOS just makes up the node part of the address.

The network number can have from one to eight hex digits; writing leading zeros is not required. A period separates the network and node portion, and the node portion is written in three 4-digit sections separated by periods. For example, AC100A00.0010.7B3A.D4BF is the IPX address of the Ethernet0 interface on our test router Dallas. AC100A00 is the network number we assigned to the network and 0010.7B3A.D4BF is the interface's MAC address.

Novell servers have logical internal networks that contain a single host, the server itself. We define the network number for the internal network, and Novell defines the node address to be 1. In hex, the node portion is 0000.0000.0001.

Since a host's layer-2 address (MAC address) is part of its layer-3 address (IPX address), a host using IPX can determine the destination address to put in the frame header directly from the IPX address without using any network overhead. In Section 2.1.3.1, we defined this method of acquiring a host's MAC address as *prediction*.

8.2   IPX Overview

We are going to use the OSI Reference Model to help discuss the components that make up the IPX protocol suite. Figure 8-1 shows the IPX stack as compared to the seven layers of the OSI Reference Model.

Our goal is be able to configure IPX on an IOS-based router; therefore, this overview is meant to provide enough background information for us to understand what is happening on a router that is routing IPX packets.

8.2.1   Layers 1 and 2

We can run IPX over just about any physical medium. On LAN interfaces, the frame header and trailer format (encapsulation) of IPX packets is defined separately from that of other protocols. LAN interfaces can support multiple frame encapsulation types for IPX. There are four Ethernet encapsulation types, two Token Ring encapsulation types, and two FDDI encapsulation types defined. Table 8-1 shows the defined encapsulation types for Ethernet and Token Ring interfaces. The Novell

Figure 8-1
IPX stack compared
to OSI reference
model.

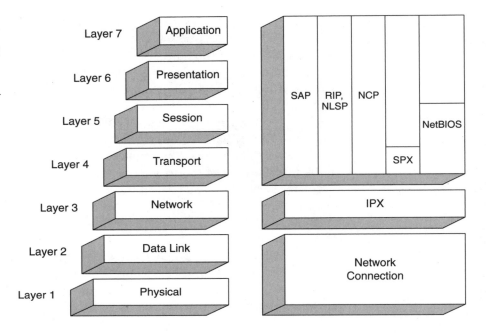

names for the major encapsulation types are shown with their corresponding Cisco IOS names. We are concerned with the Cisco names because they are used in IOS commands.

IOS uses NOVELL-ETHER as its default Ethernet interface encapsulation and SAP as its default Token Ring interface encapsulation for IPX packets. The encapsulation of a router's WAN interface is used for all of the protocols that are being processed on that interface, including IPX. The default encapsulation for a Cisco-router serial interface is HDLC.

TABLE 8-1

Ethernet and
Token Ring IPX
Encapsulation
Types.

LAN Type	Novell's Encapsulation Name	Cisco's Encapsulation Name
Ethernet	Ethernet_II	ARPA
	Ethernet_802.3	NOVELL-ETHER
	Ethernet_802.2	SAP
	Ethernet_SNAP	SNAP
Token Ring	Token-Ring	SAP
	Token-Ring_SNAP	SNAP

8.2.2   Layer 3

IPX appears at layer 3. The first thing in an IPX packet is the layer-3 IPX header. The IPX header contains the IPX destination address and source address. The IPX header also contains a packet type and source and destination socket numbers, which help a host determine the type of data being carried in the packet.

8.2.3   Layers 4, 5, 6, and 7

The top four layers are bundled together into a mixed bag of applications and transport mechanisms.

The *Service Advertisement Protocol* (SAP) runs over IPX and is the application used by servers and routers to learn about services available on a Novell network. Each service is uniquely identified with a combination of type, name, and address. A *service type* is a number given for a particular service provided by a server, such as a file service, a print service, or a database service. The name of the service is a descriptive text string usually defined by a network administrator; the address is the IPX address of the host that is offering the service.

Novell servers use SAP to tell the devices on their local network about their presence. SAP advertisements are transmitted periodically every 60 seconds to the IPX broadcast address of a network. File servers and routers collect the advertised services into a *service table* (sometimes called a *SAP table*) and advertise all of the services, using SAP, out all of their IPX-enabled interfaces every 60 seconds. SAP uses split horizon to avoid advertising a service to the same network from which a service was learned.

Clients ignore the information in the SAP broadcasts; however, since a client cannot perform any internetwork activity until it attaches to a server, the client needs some way of locating servers. Clients use either *Get Nearest Server* (GNS) requests to find a server or *Novell Directory Services* (NDS) tree to which it can attach. File servers, NDS servers, and routers can respond to these requests. Once attached, the client can access Novell services.

The *Routing Information Protocol* (RIP) and *Novell Link Services Protocol* (NLSP) are IPX routing protocols. IPX RIP is very similar to IP RIP. RIP is the default routing protocol for IPX; it is enabled on an interface as soon as an IPX network number is assigned to the interface. IPX RIP is a distance vector routing protocol that uses 60-second periodic updates. RIP uses two metrics: *ticks* and *hop count*. A tick is about 1/18th of a second and is meant to be a measurement of delay across a network. The preferred path to a network is the one with the lowest number of ticks; if ticks are the same, the route with the lowest hop count is preferred. If both ticks and hop count are equal, IOS will just pick one to use unless we have configured IPX load sharing. NLSP is a Novell-developed, link state routing protocol, similar to OSPF. IOS also supports using EIGRP for the exchange of IPX routes and services.

Servers use *NetWare Core Protocol* (NCP) to provide services such as file and print operations.

Sequenced Packet eXchange (SPX) is similar to TCP in IP. SPX provides connection-oriented communication for applications that require it—for example, rconsole and IPX SNA gateways use SPX.

IPX NetBIOS is Novell's implementation of IBM's NetBIOS. Some IPX network applications are written to run over IPX NetBIOS. IPX NetBIOS uses type-20 IPX packets. These must be handled separately in the IOS configuration of IPX.

8.3   IPX Routing

IOS strips the frame header and trailer from IPX packets received on an interface. The IPX packet is then sent to the IPX routing process, which searches the IPX routing table for an entry matching the network part of the destination IPX address. Two of the routers, Dallas and FortWorth, in our test internetwork already have IPX enabled on two of their interfaces. Figure 8-2 shows the existing internetwork with the already configured IPX network addresses. We did this initial configuration in Chapter 3.

We added Austin in Chapter 7, but we have not configured IPX communication for it yet. The FortWorth Ethernet LAN has a NetWare file server attached. The internal IPX address of the server is AC101401.

The IPX routing table can be displayed by issuing the command **show ipx route** in user mode or privileged mode. Figure 8-3 shows the IPX routing table on Dallas.

Just like the displays of all IOS routing tables, the IPX routing table display starts with a legend describing the letters that appear in the left column of each table entry. We see that there are four routes in the table (Line 7). Line 7 also reports that 1 parallel path is supported; this means that equal-cost route load sharing is effectively disabled. For the directly connected networks (Lines 11 and 12), the table has the IPX network

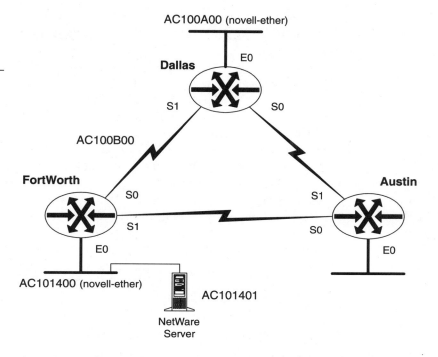

Figure 8-2
Current IPX inter-network.

Figure 8-3
Show IPX route output on Dallas.

```
1)  Dallas#show ipx route
2)  Codes: C - Connected primary network, c - Connected secondary
           network
3)         S - Static, F - Floating static, L - Local
           (internal), W - IPXWAN
4)         R - RIP, E - EIGRP, N - NLSP, X - External, A -
           Aggregate
5)         s - seconds, u - uses, U - Per-user static
6)
7)  4 Total IPX routes. Up to 1 parallel paths and 16 hops
    allowed.
8)
9)  No default route known.
10)
11) C AC100A00 (NOVELL-ETHER), Et0
12) C AC100B00 (HDLC),        Se1
13) R AC101400 [07/01] via AC100B00.0010.7b3a.d4af,  15s, Se1
14) R AC101401 [07/01] via AC100B00.0010.7b3a.d4af,  16s, Se1
15) Dallas
```

address and the IPX encapsulation. Ethernet0 is using NOVELL-ETHER encapsulation, the default. There are two RIP-learned routes (Lines 13 and 14), and for each route, there is the IPX address of the next hop gateway to reach a network, the elapsed time since the route was updated, and the interface out of which packets are to be routed to reach the network. The numbers in brackets are the two metrics used by RIP in determining the best path to the network. The first value is the number of ticks and the second value is the number of hops.

We will be using the **show ipx route** command a few more times in this chapter to check the effects of our configuration changes. Since there is a server on the FortWorth side of the internetwork, there should be something in the service tables of the routers. The **show ipx servers** command tells IOS to display the router's Novell service table shows the output of the show ipx servers command on Dallas.

Figure 8-4 shows that there are five services in Dallas's service table (Line 4). The letter *P* in the left column of each of the five entries indicates that the entries were learned through a periodic SAP advertisement. The *Type* column contains the identification of the service being described by an entry. Service types are written in hex, and the ones shown here are described as follows:

- Type 4—File Service
- Type 47—Print Service
- Type 107—Rconsole
- Type 26B—NDS Time Synchronization
- Type 278—NDS

Figure 8-4
Show IPX servers output on Dallas.

```
1)  Dallas#show ipx servers
2)  Codes: S - Static, P - Periodic, E - EIGRP, N - NLSP,
        H - Holddown, + = detail
3)  U - Per-user static
4)  5 Total IPX Servers
5
6)  Table ordering is based on routing and server info
7)
8)  Type Name            Net Address Port Route Hops Itf
9)  P     4 FW_Server    AC101401.0000.0000.0001:0451 7/01 2 Se1
10) P    47 FW_Printer   AC101401.0000.0000.0001:8060 7/01 2 Se1
11) P   107 FW_Server    AC101401.0000.0000.0001:8104 7/01 2 Se1
12) P   26B FW_Server    AC101401.0000.0000.0001:0005 7/01 2 Se1
13) P   278 FW_Server    AC101401.0000.0000.0001:4006 7/01 2 Se1
14) Dallas#
```

The name assigned to each service is displayed in the *Name* column. The *Net* and *Address* columns combine to give the IPX address of the host that is providing the service. The *Port* column defines the upper layer socket number at which the service can be reached. The *Route* column gives the metrics (ticks and hops) for reaching a service's local network. The *Hops column* shows the number of router hops away the service resides, and the *Itf* column shows which local interface is used to reach a service.

8.4   IPX Configuration

IOS does not route IPX traffic by default; therefore, we must first turn on IPX routing. We use the global configuration command **ipx routing** to do this. We then configure the assigned IPX network numbers on the interfaces that are to transmit and receive IPX packets. On LAN interfaces, we can set an IPX encapsulation if we do not want to use the default encapsulation. The interface configuration command **ipx network** is used to configure the network number and, if applicable, the encapsulation for an interface. As soon as we enter a valid **ipx network** command on an interface, IPX RIP and SAP start processing on the interface.

Figure 8-5 shows an updated internetwork diagram showing the network addresses to be used for Austin IPX connectivity. IPX is already enabled on Dallas and FortWorth so we will start our configuration example on Austin then move to the Dallas and FortWorth interfaces that are connected to Austin.

The commands for configuring IPX on Austin, based on Figure 8-5, are shown in Figure 8-6.

The **ipx routing** command (Line 3) tells IOS to start the process that will be used to route IPX packets. To start IPX processing on an interface, we need to be in interface configuration mode. Starting with Ethernet0 (Line 4), we entered the **ipx network** command (Line 5) assigned for the IPX network number. According the Figure 8-5, the desired encapsulation on the Ethernet LAN is SAP (or Novell Ethernet_802.2). Since this is different from the default of NOVELL-ETHER, we added the keywords **encapsulation sap** to the command. Now IPX packets can be routed through Ethernet0; they will be transmitted with a SAP-formatted frame header, and they will be received and processed if a host on the Ethernet LAN transmitted them with a SAP-formatted frame header. The second interface on Austin is Serial0

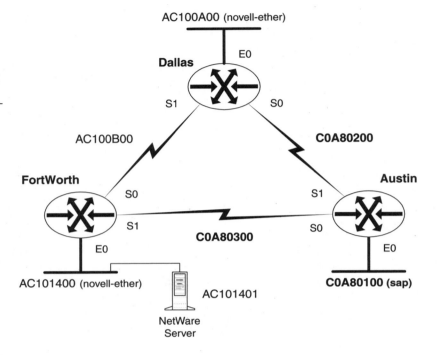

Figure 8-5
Internetwork dia-
gram showing
Austin IPX network
addresses.

Figure 8-6
IPX configuration
on Austin.

```
1)  Austin#configure terminal
2)  Enter configuration commands, one per line. End with CNTL/Z.
3)  Austin(config)#ipx routing
4)  Austin(config)#interface ethernet0
5)  Austin(config-if)#ipx network c0a80100 encapsulation sap
6)  Austin(config-if)#interface serial0
7)  Austin(config-if)#ipx network c0a80300
8)  Austin(config-if)#interface serial1
9)  Austin(config-if)#ipx network c0a80200
10) Austin(config-if)#<Ctrl-Z>
11) Austin#
```

(Line 6) and its IPX network address is assigned on Line 7. The third
interface is Serial1 (Line 8) and its IPX network address is assigned on
Line 9. The encapsulation for the serial interfaces is HDLC, the default.

We still do not have IPX communication from Dallas and FortWorth to
Austin. We need to enable IPX on the other routers' serial interfaces that
are connected to Austin. Figure 8-7 shows Dallas's Serial0 IPX configuration, and Figure 8-8 shows FortWorth's Serial1 IPX configuration.

Now that all of our IPX network addresses have been assigned to the appropriate interfaces, let us take a look at one of the router's IPX routing table. Figure 8-9 shows the IPX routing table on Dallas.

Dallas now has three directly connected IPX networks (Lines 7, 8, and 9) and four RIP-learned IPX routes (Lines 10 through 13). Notice that the number of ticks for the routes is the same for each of the serial links regardless of their bandwidth. Figure 8-5 shows seven IPX networks so this must be all of them.

Now we want to examine Dallas's path to the serial link between FortWorth and Austin, C0A80300 (Line 13). The preferred path goes through Austin, but from looking at our diagram, we can see that there

Figure 8-7

IPX configuration on Dallas Serial0.

```
1)  Dallas#configure terminal
2)  Enter configuration commands, one per line. End with CNTL/Z.
3)  Dallas(config)#interface serial0
4)  Dallas(config-if)#ipx network c0a80200
5)  Dallas(config-if)#<Ctrl-Z>
6)  Dallas#
```

Figure 8-8

IPX configuration on FortWorth Serial1.

```
1)  FortWorth#configure terminal
2)  Enter configuration commands, one per line. End with CNTL/Z.
3)  FortWorth(config)#interface serial1
4)  FortWorth(config-if)#ipx network c0a80300
5)  FortWorth(config-if)#<Ctrl-Z>
6)  FortWorth#
```

Figure 8-9

IPX routing table on Dallas after IPX configuration.

```
1)  Dallas#show ipx route
2)  [text omitted]
3)  7 Total IPX routes. Up to 1 parallel paths and 16 hops
    allowed.
4)
5)  No default route known.
6)
7)  C  AC100A00 (NOVELL-ETHER),   Et0
8)  C  AC100B00 (HDLC),        Se1
9)  C  C0A80200 (HDLC),        Se0
10) R  AC101400 [07/01] via AC100B00.0010.7b3a.d4af,  27s, Se1
11) R  AC101401 [07/01] via AC100B00.0010.7b3a.d4af,  27s, Se1
12) R  C0A80100 [07/01] via C0A80200.0010.7b3a.d204,  52s, Se0
13) R  C0A80300 [07/01] via C0A80200.0010.7b3a.d204,  52s, Se0
14) Dallas#
```

are actually two equal-cost paths (as far as IPX RIP is concerned) from Dallas to the network. We can configure IPX load sharing with the global configuration command **ipx maximum-paths**. Figure 8-10 shows the configuration of load sharing for IPX on Dallas.

Figure 8-11 shows the new IPX routing table. Two parallel (equal-cost) paths to a destination are now allowed in the routing table (Line 3). The new routing table shows the two equal-cost paths (Lines 12 and 13). As far as IPX RIP knows, the two serial links have the same metric even though we know from our original implementation that one is a T1 and one is a 256-kbps line. Turning on load sharing in this case may not be such a good idea, because it increases the likelihood of IPX packets arriving at a host out of order.

8.5   IPX Verification

We have already used the **show ipx route** command to view one of the IPX routing tables. Other commands that we can use for IPX configuration verification are as follows:

Figure 8-10
IPX load sharing configuration.

```
1) Dallas#configure terminal
2) Enter configuration commands, one per line. End with CNTL/Z.
3) Dallas(config)#ipx maximum-paths 2
4) Dallas(config)#<Ctrl-Z>
5) Dallas#
```

Figure 8-11
IPX routing table after load sharing configuration.

```
1)  Dallas#show ipx route
2)  [text omitted]
3)  7 Total IPX routes. Up to 2 parallel paths and 16 hops
    allowed.
4)
5)  No default route known.
6)  C    AC100A00 (NOVELL-ETHER),    Et0
7)  C    AC100B00 (HDLC),            Se1
8)  C    C0A80200 (HDLC),            Se0
9)  R    AC101400 [07/01] via AC100B00.0010.7b3a.d4af,  12s, Se1
10) R    AC101401 [07/01] via AC100B00.0010.7b3a.d4af,  12s, Se1
11) R    C0A80100 [07/01] via C0A80200.0010.7b3a.d204,  37s, Se0
12) R    C0A80300 [07/01] via C0A80200.0010.7b3a.d204,  37s, Se0
13)                      via AC100B00.0010.7b3a.d4af,  12s, Se1
14) Dallas#
```

- show protocols
- show ipx interface
- show ipx interface brief
- show ipx traffic
- ping

The **show protocols** command shows us the protocols that IOS is configured to route, the status of each interface, and the primary address of each protocol on each interface. Figure 8-12 shows the output of the **show protocols** command on Austin.

We see that Austin is routing IP packets (Line 3) and IPX packets (Line 4). The IPX addresses of the configured interfaces are given on Lines 10, 13, and 16. The node part of all of the IPX addresses is the same. Serial0 and Serial1 have no MAC addresses that IOS can use in the IPX address completion; therefore, IOS uses the MAC address of the first Ethernet interface, Ethernet0, in the IPX addresses of both the serial interfaces. The addition of the assigned network address to the node part makes each of the IPX addresses unique. The Ethernet0 IPX address (Line 10) contains the MAC address of the Ethernet0 interface.

The IPX address of an interface can also be obtained from the output of the **show ipx interface** command. Issuing this command without any arguments will display information for all of the interfaces that have been assigned an IPX network address. Figure 8-13 shows the output on Austin when information for a single interface is requested.

Figure 8-12

Show protocols output on Austin.

```
1)  Austin#show protocols
2)  Global values:
3)    Internet Protocol routing is enabled
4)    IPX routing is enabled
5)  BRI0 is administratively down, line protocol is down
6)  BRI0:1 is administratively down, line protocol is down
7)  BRI0:2 is administratively down, line protocol is down
8)  Ethernet0 is up, line protocol is up
9)    Internet address is 192.168.1.1/24
10)   IPX address is C0A80100.0010.7b3a.d204
11) Serial0 is up, line protocol is up
12)   Internet address is 192.168.3.2/24
13)   IPX address is C0A80300.0010.7b3a.d204
14) Serial1 is up, line protocol is up
15)   Internet address is 192.168.2.2/24
16)   IPX address is C0A80200.0010.7b3a.d204
17) Serial2 is administratively down, line protocol is down
18) Serial3 is administratively down, line protocol is down
19) Austin#
```

The output includes both the IPX address and the encapsulation for the interface (Line 3). The delay, in ticks, for Ethernet0 is 1 (Line 4). By default, IOS assigns one tick to LAN interfaces and six ticks to WAN interfaces. The SAP update interval on Ethernet0 is set to its default of 60 seconds (Line 6). This is shown because it can be changed on a per-interface basis. Ethernet0 is not currently propagating type-20 IPX packets. Type-20 packets are transmitted by applications that use Novell's NetBIOS over IPX. RIP updates are being sent every 60 seconds (Line 22), and routes and services learned via RIP/SAP are marked as down if they are not updated within 180 seconds. Ethernet0 has received no RIP updates (Line 28), but has transmitted seven. Since there are not other IPX routers on Austin's Ethernet LAN, we expect that Ethernet0 will never receive any updates.

For a quick summary of IPX interface information, we can add the **brief** keyword to the end of the **show ipx interface** command. Figure

Figure 8-13

Show IPX interface output.

```
1)   Austin#show ipx interface ethernet0
2)   Ethernet0 is up, line protocol is up
3)     IPX address is C0A80100.0010.7b3a.d204, SAP [up]
4)     Delay of this IPX network, in ticks is 1 throughput 0 link
       delay 0
5)     IPXWAN processing not enabled on this interface.
6)     IPX SAP update interval is 60 seconds
7)     IPX type 20 propagation packet forwarding is disabled
8)     Incoming access list is not set
9)     Outgoing access list is not set
10)    IPX helper access list is not set
11)    SAP GNS processing enabled, delay 0 ms, output filter list
       is not set
12)    SAP Input filter list is not set
13)    SAP Output filter list is not set
14)    SAP Router filter list is not set
15)    Input filter list is not set
16)    Output filter list is not set
17)    Router filter list is not set
18)    Netbios Input host access list is not set
19)    Netbios Input bytes access list is not set
20)    Netbios Output host access list is not set
21)    Netbios Output bytes access list is not set
22)    Updates each 60 seconds aging multiples RIP: 3 SAP: 3
23)    SAP interpacket delay is 55 ms, maximum size is 480 bytes
24)    RIP interpacket delay is 55 ms, maximum size is 432 bytes
25)    RIP response delay is not set
26)    IPX accounting is disabled
27)    IPX fast switching is configured (enabled)
28)    RIP packets received 0, RIP packets sent 7
29)    SAP packets received 0, SAP packets sent 6
30)    Austin#
```

```
1)  Austin#show ipx interface brief
2)  Interface          IPX Network Encapsulation Status IPX State
3)  BRI0               unassigned not config'd administratively down n/a
4)                     BRI0:1 unassigned not config'd administratively down n/a
5)  BRI0:2             unassigned not config'd  administratively down n/a
6)  Ethernet0          C0A80100    SAP         up        [up]
7)  Serial0            C0A80300    HDLC        up        [up]
8)  Serial1            C0A80200    HDLC        up        [up]
9)  Serial2            unassigned not config'd administratively down n/a
10) Serial3            unassigned not config'd administratively down n/a
11) Austin#
```

Figure 8-14 Show IPX interface brief output.

8-14 shows the output of the **show ipx interface brief** command on Austin. For each interface, IOS displays the IPX network number, the encapsulation, and the status. We do not get the full IPX addresses.

Statistics for IPX packets can be viewed by using the **show ipx traffic** command. We issued the command on Austin; Figure 8-15 shows the output.

The output of **show ipx traffic** divided into sections. Each section has statistics for a particular type of IPX traffic. The *Rcvd* section shows the number of IPX packets that have been received by IOS (Lines 3 and 4) and the *Sent* section shows the number of IPX packets transmitted (Lines 6 and 7). The number of IPX broadcast packets received and transmitted is given in the *Bcast* section (Line 5). SAP statistics are shown in the SAP section and the number of entries in the service table is also given. There are five entries in Austin's IPX service table (Line 8). Line 13 of the *RIP* section shows that there are seven entries in Austin's IPX routing table. Austin is not yet running EIGRP; therefore, the counters in the *EIGRP* section (Lines 26 through 30) are all still zero.

The **show** commands described previously are good ways of verifying the configuration of IPX; however, they do not do much for making sure that IPX connectivity has been established. For that we need to use the *IPX ping* application. The IPX ping application transmits IPX echo request packets to an IPX destination address and expects to receive IPX echo replies. Three ways of doing an IPX ping are as follows:

Figure 8-15

Show IPX traffic
output.

```
1)  Austin#show ipx traffic
2)  System Traffic for 0.0000.0000.0001 System-Name: Austin
3)  Rcvd:    89 total, 0 format errors, 0 checksum errors, 0 bad
             hop count,
4)           0 packets pitched, 79 local destination,
             0 multicast
5)  Bcast:   54 received, 87 sent
6)  Sent:    116 generated, 10 forwarded
7)           0 encapsulation failed, 0 no route
8)  SAP:     2 SAP requests, 1 SAP replies, 5 servers
9)           0 SAP Nearest Name requests, 0 replies
10)          0 SAP General Name requests, 0 replies
11)          25 SAP advertisements received, 25 sent
12)          4 SAP flash updates sent, 0 SAP format errors
13) RIP:     2 RIP requests, 2 RIP replies, 7 routes
14)          25 RIP advertisements received, 45 sent
15)          7 RIP flash updates sent, 0 RIP format errors
16) Echo:    Rcvd 25 requests, 0 replies
17)          Sent 0 requests, 25 replies
18)          0 unknown: 0 no socket, 0 filtered, 0 no helper
19)          0 SAPs throttled, freed NDB len 0
20) Watchdog:
21)          0 packets received, 0 replies spoofed
22) Queue lengths:
23)          IPX input: 0, SAP 0, RIP 0, GNS 0
24)          SAP throttling length: 0/(no limit), 0 nets pending
             lost route reply
25)          Delayed process creation: 0
26) EIGRP: Total received 0, sent 0
27)          Updates received 0, sent 0
28)          Queries received 0, sent 0
29)          Replies received 0, sent 0
30)          SAPs received 0, sent 0
31) Austin#
```

1. Use the normal **ping** command with an IPX address.

2. Use the **ping ipx** command with an IPX address.

3. Use an extended ping, and type **ipx** when prompted for a protocol.

The normal ping and the ping ipx commands can be used to check connectivity to Cisco routers. Cisco uses its own proprietary IPX ping mechanism by default, and NetWare servers will not respond to it. If you want to ping a NetWare server, use the extended ping and select the Novell echo option. Figure 8-16 shows examples of all three options. The IPX pings are being done from Dallas, and the destination address is that of Austin's Ethernet0 interface as obtained with the **show ipx interface** in Figure 8-13.

When the normal ping is used to performing the IPX ping (Line 1), we are counting on IOS's recognizing that the address we have typed is an

Figure 8-16
IPX ping examples.

```
1)  Dallas#ping C0A80100.0010.7b3a.d204
2)  Translating "C0A80100.0010.7b3a.d204"...domain server
    (255.255.255.255)
3)
4)  Type escape sequence to abort.
5)  Sending 5, 100-byte IPX cisco Echoes to
    C0A80100.0010.7b3a.d204, timeout is 2 seconds:
6)  !!!!!
7)  Success rate is 100 percent (5/5), round-trip min/avg/max =
    12/13/20 ms
8)  ———
9)  Dallas#ping ipx C0A80100.0010.7b3a.d204
10)
11) Type escape sequence to abort.
12) Sending 5, 100-byte IPX cisco Echoes to
    0A80100.0010.7b3a.d204, timeout is 2 seconds:
13) !!!!!
14) Success rate is 100 percent (5/5), round-trip min/avg/max =
    8/11/12 ms
15) ———
16) Dallas#ping
17) Protocol [ip]: ipx
18) Target IPX address: C0A80100.0010.7b3a.d204
19) Repeat count [5]: <Enter>
20) Datagram size [100]: <Enter>
21) Timeout in seconds [2]: <Enter>
22) Verbose [n]: <Enter>
23) Novell Standard Echo [n]: <Enter>
24) Type escape sequence to abort.
25) Sending 5, 100-byte IPX cisco Echoes to
    0A80100.0010.7b3a.d204, timeout is 2 seconds:
26) !!!!!
27) Success rate is 100 percent (5/5), round-trip min/avg/max =
    8/11/12 ms
28) Dallas#
```

IPX address. IOS first thinks that the address is an IP host name and attempts to perform address resolution. When that fails, IOS correctly does the IPX ping by sending five IPX echoes to Austin's Ethernet0 interface and receiving five replies. The success rate and response time information is given on the last line (Line 7).

Using the **ping ipx** command (Line 9) tells IOS that the address in the command is an IPX address so that IOS does not have to guess. The result is the same as that of the normal ping.

We invoke an extended ping by typing the **ping** command without an address (Line 16), and then IOS prompts us for the protocol (Line 17). Entering **ipx** at the protocol prompt will cause IOS to ask for an IPX destination address (Line 18). The extended ping gives us the opportunity to change the number of echoes sent, the size of the echoes, and the reply timeout. Since we are pinging another Cisco router, we answered with **no** (the default) at the *Novell Standard Echo* prompt (Line 23). If we were sending the echoes to a NetWare server, we would answer with **yes**. Cisco routers will respond to both types of echoes.

8.6   IPX EIGRP Configuration

IPX EIGRP has the same basic operation as IP EIGRP, which we described in Section 7.7.3.2. IPX EIGRP is Cisco-proprietary and is supported only on Cisco routers for the sharing of IPX routes and services. IPX EIGRP can replace IPX RIP and SAP on networks that have only Cisco IPX routers and no local Novell services; these networks are usually WANs.

The implementation of IPX EIGRP can save WAN bandwidth since EIGRP performs incremental updates for routes and services. This means that updates are transmitted only when a change occurs, not at the usual 60-second interval.

We will configure IPX EIGRP on the WANs of our internetwork and leave IPX RIP and SAP on the LANs. The configuration of IPX EIGRP is similar to the configuration of an IP routing protocol. We use the **ipx router eigrp** command along with an *Autonomous System Number* (ASN). We then enable IPX EIGRP on interfaces by using **network** commands, with the IPX network numbers of the interfaces that are to have IPX EIGRP enabled. We need at least one **network** command for each interface. Turning on IPX EIGRP on an interface does not automatically turn off IPX RIP on the interface; therefore, we should disable IPX RIP on the interface to avoid running two IPX routing protocols and using network bandwidth needlessly. IPX RIP is disabled on an interface with the **ipx router rip** command along a **no network** command for each interface.

Figure 8-17 shows the configuration of IPX EIGRP on Dallas; Figure 8-18 shows the configuration of IPX EIGRP on FortWorth; and Figure 8-19 shows the configuration on Austin.

The ASN for IPX EIGRP must the same on all of the router sharing information; we chose to use ASN 500 here. When both IPX EIGRP and IPX RIP are running on the same router, IOS automatically redistributes routes between them. Routes learned from RIP are included in EIGRP

Figure 8-17
IPX EIGRP configu-
ration on Dallas.

```
1)  Dallas#configure terminal
2)  Enter configuration commands, one per line. End with CNTL/Z.
3)  Dallas(config)#ipx router eigrp 500
4)  Dallas(config-ipx-router)#network ac100b00
5)  Dallas(config-ipx-router)#network c0a80200
6)  Dallas(config-ipx-router)#ipx router rip
7)  Dallas(config-ipx-router)#no network ac100b00
8)  Dallas(config-ipx-router)#no network c0a80200
9)  Dallas(config-ipx-router)#<Ctrl-Z>
10) Dallas#
```

Figure 8-18
IPX EIGRP configu-
ration on
FortWorth.

```
1)  FortWorth#configure terminal
2)  Enter configuration commands, one per line. End with CNTL/Z.
3)  FortWorth(config)#ipx router eigrp 500
4)  FortWorth(config-ipx-router)#network ac100b00
5)  FortWorth(config-ipx-router)#network c0a80300
6)  FortWorth(config-ipx-router)#ipx router rip
7)  FortWorth(config-ipx-router)#no network ac100b00
8)  FortWorth(config-ipx-router)#no network c0a80300
9)  FortWorth(config-ipx-router)#<Ctrl-Z>
10) FortWorth#
```

updates and routes learned from EIGRP are included in RIP updates.
The same redistribution also performed for services. Figure 8-20 shows
the IPX routing table on Dallas after the configuration on all three
routers.

The routing table on Dallas still shows seven routes (Line 3), but the
routes that are learned from across the WANs have the letter *E* in the
left column of the displayed entry.

IOS maintains a neighbor table and a topology table for IPX EIGRP.
These can be displayed with the **show ipx eigrp neighbors** and **show**

Figure 8-19
IPX EIGRP
Configuration on
Austin.

```
1)  Austin#configure terminal
2)  Enter configuration commands, one per line. End with CNTL/Z.
3)  Austin(config)#ipx router eigrp 500
4)  Austin(config-ipx-router)#network c0a80300
5)  Austin(config-ipx-router)#network c0a80200
6)  Austin(config-ipx-router)#ipx router rip
7)  Austin(config-ipx-router)#no network c0a80300
8)  Austin(config-ipx-router)#no network c0a80200
9)  Austin(config-ipx-router)#<Ctrl-Z>
10) Austin#
```

```
1)  Dallas#show ipx route
2)  [text omitted]
3)  7 Total IPX routes. Up to 2 parallel paths and 16 hops allowed.
4)
5)  No default route known.
6)
7)  C    AC100A00 (NOVELL-ETHER),    Et0
8)  C    AC100B00 (HDLC),            Se1
9)  C    C0A80200 (HDLC),            Se0
10) E    AC101400 [2195456/1]   via AC100B00.0010.7b3a.d4af, age 00:02:05, 1u, Se1
11) E    AC101401 [2297856/1]   via AC100B00.0010.7b3a.d4af, age 00:02:05, 26u, Se1
12) E    C0A80100 [10537472/1] via C0A80200.0010.7b3a.d204, age 00:00:30, 1u, Se0
13) E    C0A80300 [46738176/0] via AC100B00.0010.7b3a.d4af, age 00:00:41, 1u, Se1
14)                           via C0A80200.0010.7b3a.d204, age 00:00:41, 0u, Se0
15) Dallas is
```

Figure 8-20   IPX routing table after IPX EIGRP configuration.

ipx eigrp topology commands, respectively. The structure of the IPX versions of the tables is similar to that of the IP versions we described in Section 7.7.3.4.

8.7 Multiple IPX Encapsulation Configuration

A LAN interface can support multiple IPX encapsulations. When an interface needs multiple encapsulations, we must assign a unique IPX network number for each one—this effectively creates a logical IPX network for each encapsulation type. There are two ways of configuring multiple encapsulations on a LAN interface: *secondary addresses* and *subinterfaces*. We use both methods in configuring multiple encapsulation types on Austin's Ethernet0 interface. Austin's Ethernet0 interface currently is using SAP encapsulation. We will pretend that some hosts just got installed on the Ethernet. These hosts were preconfigured with Novell Ethernet_802.3 encapsulation and the administrator did not want to change them; therefore, we must compensate by adding the second encapsulation to the router. The new internetwork diagram showing the additional encapsulation and network number for Austin is shown in Figure 8-21.

Implementing a secondary IPX address on an interface requires the addition of the keyword **secondary** to the end of another **ipx network** command in interface configuration mode. Figure 8-22 shows the configuration of a secondary IPX address on Austin's Ethernet0 interface.

The **ipx network** command (Line 4) does not affect the existing IPX network number (entered in Figure 8-6, Line 5); however, if we had typed this command without the **secondary** keyword, the original network number and encapsulation would have been replaced with the newly specified values. The hosts that were added to Austin's Ethernet LAN were configured to use Novell's Ethernet_802.3 encapsulation. The IOS keyword for that encapsulation type is **novell-ether** (see Table 8-1).

The second way of doing multiple encapsulations uses subinterfaces. A *subinterface* is a logical interface that is coupled with a physical interface. IOS treats a subinterface just as it does a physical interface as far as routing packets is concerned. We are going to create two subinterfaces

Figure 8-21

Internetwork diagram showing multiple encapsulations on Austin Ethernet.

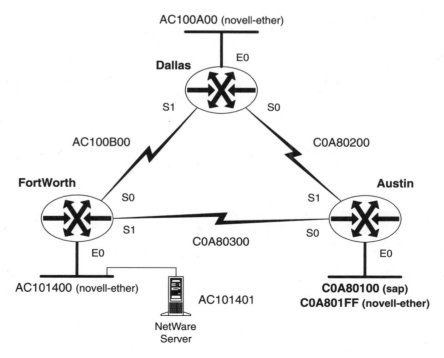

Figure 8-22

Secondary IPX address configuration on Austin.

```
1)  Austin#configure terminal
2)  Enter configuration commands, one per line. End with CNTL/Z.
3)  Austin(config)#interface ethernet0
4)  Austin(config-if)#ipx network c0a801ff encapsulation
                      novell-ether secondary
5)  Austin(config-if)#<Ctrl-Z>
6)  Austin#
```

on Austin's Ethernet0 and give each its own IPX network number and encapsulation.

The subinterface method will be used instead of the secondary address method in our internetwork. Figure 8-23 shows the configuration of subinterfaces on Austin to provide multiple encapsulations on its Ethernet0 interface.

Each of our subinterfaces is to have its own IPX network number; therefore, the physical interface, Ethernet0, no longer needs its network number. The **no ipx network** command removes the IPX network number from an interface (Line 4). To create a subinterface, we just have to reference the subinterface's name with the global configuration command **interface**. Subinterface names always begin with the name of their associated physical interface and end with a period and a decimal number, which is the subinterface number. Subinterface numbers do not have to start with zero and they do not have to be sequential. Our first subinterface is Ethernet0.1 (Line 5). The Ethernet0.1 subinterface is assigned the Ethernet0's original IPX network number (Line 6) and IPX encapsulation (Line 7). The second subinterface is Ethernet0.2 (Line 8). The second IPX network number for the Ethernet LAN is assigned to subinterface Ethernet0.2 (Line 9). Ethernet0.2 is using NOVELL-ETHER encapsulation (Line 10). Since NOVELL-ETHER is the default encapsulation for an Ethernet interface, we do not really have to type this command. It is shown here just for consistency.

Figure 8-23

Configuration of subinterfaces for multiple encapsulation types on Austin.

```
1)   Austin#configure terminal
2)   Enter configuration commands, one per line. End with CNTL/Z.
3)   Austin(config)#interface ethernet0
4)   Austin(config-if)#no ipx network c0a80100
5)   Austin(config-if)#interface ethernet0.1
6)   Austin(config-subif)#ipx network c0a80100
7)   Austin(config-subif)#ipx encapsulation sap
8)   Austin(config-subif)#interface ethernet0.2
9)   Austin(config-subif)#ipx network c0a801ff
10)  Austin(config-subif)#ipx encapsulation novell-ether
11)  Austin(config-subif)#<Ctrl-Z>
12)  Austin#
```

```
1)  Austin#show ipx interface brief
2)  Interface   IPX Network  Encapsulation Status                    IPX State
3)  BRI0        unassigned   not config'd  administratively down n/a
4)  BRI0:1      unassigned   not config'd  administratively down n/a
5)  BRI0:2      unassigned   not config'd  administratively down n/a
6)  Ethernet0   unassigned   not config'd  up                        n/a
7)  Ethernet0.1 C0A80100     SAP           up                        [up]
8)  Ethernet0.2 C0A801FF     NOVELL-ETHER  up                        [up]
9)  Serial0     C0A80300     HDLC          up                        [up]
10) Serial1     C0A80200     HDLC          up                        [up]
11) Serial2     unassigned   not config'd  administratively down n/a
12) Serial3     unassigned   not config'd  administratively down n/a
13) Austin#
```

Figure 8-24 Show IPX interface brief output after subinterface configuration.

Figure 8-24 shows the output of the **show ipx interface brief** command on Austin after the subinterface configuration. The two subinterfaces with their addresses and encapsulations are displayed (Lines 7 and 8).

Subinterfaces can be deleted from the running configuration with the global configuration command **no interface;** however, IOS will not remove a deleted subinterface's *Interface Descriptor Block* (IDB) from RAM until the router is rebooted.

8.8 IPX Configuration Summary

IPX configuration requires that the IOS IPX routing process be started with the **ipx routing** command. Then we must go to each interface that is to be involved in routing IPX packets and assign it an IPX network number and, possibly, an IPX encapsulation. The network numbers and encapsulations are assigned with the **ipx network** command in interface configuration mode.

The internetwork that we now have for IPX connectivity is shown in Figure 8-25. All of the IPX network numbers and encapsulations are shown. The boundary of the IPX EIGRP autonomous system is also displayed.

Figure 8-26 shows the IPX-specific commands from Dallas's running configuration. Figure 8-27 shows FortWorth's IPX-specific commands taken from the running configuration. Figure 8-28 shows the IPX-specific commands from Austin.

Figure 8-25
Final IPX internet-work diagram.

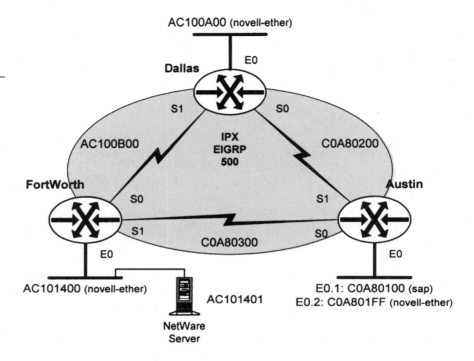

Figure 8-26
Dallas IPX configuration commands.

```
1)   Dallas#show running-config [Some text has been omitted.]
2)   !
3)   ipx routing 0010.7b3a.d4bf
4)   ipx maximum-paths 2
5)   !
6)   interface Ethernet0
7)    ipx network AC100A00
8)   !
9)   interface Serial0
10)   ipx network C0A80200
11)  !
12)  interface Serial1
13)   ipx network AC100B00
14)  !
15)  ipx router eigrp 500
16)   network AC100B00
17)   network C0A80200
18)  !
19)  ipx router rip
20)   no network AC100B00
21)   no network C0A80200
22)  !
23)  Dallas#
```

Figure 8-27
FortWorth IPX configuration commands.

```
1)  FortWorth#show running-config [Some text has been omitted.]
2)  !
3)  ipx routing 0010.7b3a.d4af
4)  !
5)  interface Ethernet0
6)   ipx network AC101400
7)  !
8)  interface Serial0
9)   ipx network AC100B00
10) !
11) interface Serial1
12)  ipx network C0A80300
13) !
14) ipx router eigrp 500
15)  network AC100B00
16)  network C0A80300
17) !
18) ipx router rip
19)  no network AC100B00
20)  no network C0A80300
21) !
22) FortWorth#
```

Figure 8-28
Austin IPX configuration commands.

```
1)  Austin#show running-config [Some text has been omitted.]
2)  !
3)  ipx routing 0010.7b3a.d204
4)  !
5)  interface Ethernet0.1
6)   ipx encapsulation SAP
7)   ipx network C0A80100
8)  !
9)  interface Ethernet0.2
10)  ipx network C0A801FF
11) !
12) interface Serial0
13)  ipx network C0A80300
14) !
15) interface Serial1
16)  ipx network C0A80200
17) !
18) ipx router eigrp 500
19)  network C0A80300
20)  network C0A80200
21) !
22) ipx router rip
23)  no network C0A80300
24)  no network C0A80200
25) !
26) Austin#
```

The address shown at the end of the **ipx routing** command (Line 3, Figures 8-26, 8-27, and 8-28) is the address that IOS uses as the node part of IPX addresses of WAN interfaces. IOS chooses this address itself. On each of our routers, this is the MAC address of the router's Ethernet0 interface. We can change this address to something more easily remembered by including a static address on the **ipx routing** command when we enter it.

8.9   IPX Removal

We are going to leave IPX running on our test internetwork; however, if we want to stop the IPX routing process on a router, we can enter the following global configuration command.

```
no ipx routing
```

The **no ipx routing** command will remove, from the running configuration, the commands dealing with IPX routing. These commands include those that define IPX network numbers, encapsulations, and routing protocols. If we were to type this command on our test router, Austin, the Ethernet subinterfaces would remain, but they would have no addresses.

Configuring AppleTalk

AppleTalk is a layer-3 network protocol developed by Apple. AppleTalk is a protocol suite for peer-to-peer communication, which allows any host to share its files, devices, and services. AppleTalk has two versions—Phase 1 and Phase 2. All references to AppleTalk in this chapter are to Phase 2.

As with the other network protocols, our coverage of AppleTalk begins with a brief overview of host addressing and protocol operation. We then cover the IOS commands for the basic configuration of AppleTalk as we make modifications to our three-router internetwork.

9.1   AppleTalk Addressing

An AppleTalk layer-3 address is 24 bits long and—just as with any other layer-3 address—has a network part and a node part. The *network part* of the address is 16 bits long and is written in decimal form. The *node part* is the last 8 bits and is also written in decimal. The full address is written with the network part and the node part separated by a period (.).

A range of network numbers identifies an AppleTalk network—we call this range of network numbers a *cable range*. A host on the network has a network address within the cable range; a cable range is normally written as two decimal numbers separated by a hyphen. A host's node address must be between 1 and 254. For example, a host on a network with the cable range 300–309 could have an address of 304.219 or 300.1; AppleTalk identifies both addresses as being on the same network.

AppleTalk uses the *AppleTalk Address Resolution Protocol* (AARP) to map AppleTalk addresses to MAC addresses on LANs. When an AppleTalk host needs to send a packet, it sends an AARP request packet to the broadcast address of its network. The AARP request packet contains the AppleTalk address of a desired destination host. When the destination host receives the AARP broadcast and finds its address, the host sends an AARP reply to the source host. The AARP reply contains the MAC address that is placed into the frame header during the encapsulation process on the source host. The source host also caches the information in the reply for later use. This entire process is practically the same one that is performed by IP ARP.

We assign AppleTalk addresses to AppleTalk routers. Other AppleTalk hosts dynamically acquire an address when they start. An AppleTalk host, such as a Macintosh computer, determines the cable range of the network to which it is attached by asking the local routers for it. The host then randomly picks a network number from within the cable range and a node number from 1 to 254. The address must be verified to be unique on the network; therefore, the host uses AARP to see if another host on the network has the same address. The host sends AARP request packets onto the network asking for the MAC address corresponding to its own randomly selected AppleTalk address. If no other host responds, the host is assured of having a unique address. If the host receives an AARP reply to its requests, the address is not unique, and another address is randomly selected. The process repeats until a unique address is acquired.

9.2   AppleTalk Overview

In an AppleTalk internetwork, each network has a cable range and networks are logically grouped into zones. A *zone* is a collection of networks that can be searched for services. Zones have alphanumeric text names that we make up when we build an AppleTalk internetwork. Normally, zone names are descriptive of the services offered by the hosts on its networks. For example, Headquarters and Dallas Sales Office are both valid zone names. An AppleTalk network must be a part of at least one zone. If a network is in multiple zones, the first zone defined for the network is its primary zone.

All of the routers connected to a network must agree on the cable range and zone name(s) for the network. When AppleTalk packet processing is started on a router interface, the AppleTalk routing process checks for other AppleTalk routers on the interface's network, and, if it finds any, it verifies that the other routers have the same cable range and zone(s) defined. If a discrepancy is found, AppleTalk processing stops on the interface until the discrepancy is corrected.

We are going to use the OSI Reference Model to help discuss the components that make up AppleTalk protocol suite. Figure 9-1 shows the AppleTalk stack as compared to the seven layers of the OSI Reference Model.

This chapter's goal is to show the commands for configuring AppleTalk on an IOS-based router; therefore, this overview is meant only to provide enough background information for us to understand what is happening when we configure AppleTalk on a router.

Figure 9-1
AppleTalk stack
compared to OSI
reference model.

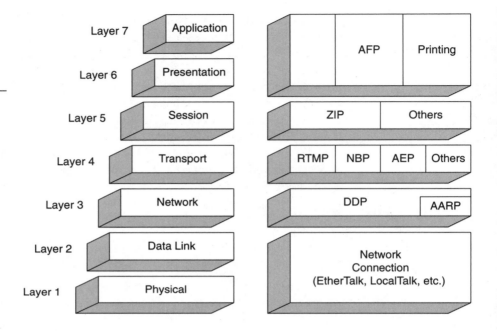

9.2.1 Layers 1 and 2

An AppleTalk hosts access to the network medium happens at layers 1 and 2 with link access protocols such as EtherTalk, TokenTalk, and LocalTalk. *LocalTalk* is an Apple-developed LAN type; *EtherTalk* is used for AppleTalk over Ethernet; and *TokenTalk* is used for AppleTalk over Token Ring.

AppleTalk hosts on Ethernet or TokenRing networks always use a *SubNetwork Access Protocol* (SNAP) encapsulated frame header.

9.2.2 Layer 3

Layer 3 has the *Datagram Delivery Protocol* (DDP), which provides connectionless, end-to-end connectivity between two hosts. The DDP header of a packet contains the source and destination AppleTalk addresses. Upper-layer protocols and applications are identified by a socket number within the DDP header.

9.2.3   Layer 4

Figure 9-1 shows *Routing Table Maintenance Protocol* (RTMP), *Name Binding Protocol* (NBP), and *AppleTalk Echo Protocol* (AEP).

RTMP is the default AppleTalk routing protocol. RTMP is a distance vector routing protocol that uses hop count as its metric and does periodic updates every 10 seconds. As with IPX, IOS also supports the use of EIGRP to share route information among routers. NBP provides a form of AppleTalk host name to address resolution. It allows AppleTalk hosts to locate services by their name, type, or zone. AppleTalk hosts use AEP for connectivity testing.

9.2.4   Layer 5

ZIP allows routers to discover the zones defined in an internetwork. All routers maintain a *Zone Information Table* (ZIT), which contains the names of the zones and the cable ranges of the networks in each zone.

9.2.5   Layers 6 and 7

Layers 6 and 7 contain the *AppleTalk Filing Protocol* (AFP) and the *AppleTalk printing protocol*. AFP is used for host file sharing and PostScript is used for printing.

9.3   AppleTalk Routing

When IOS receives a frame containing an AppleTalk packet, IOS strips the frame header and trailer from around the packet and sends the packet to the AppleTalk routing process. The routing process searches the AppleTalk routing table for an entry matching the network part of the destination AppleTalk address in the DDP header.

During our initial configuration in Chapter 3, we enabled AppleTalk on two of our routers, Dallas and FortWorth. Figure 9-2 shows the existing internetwork with the already-configured AppleTalk cable ranges and zones.

AppleTalk is running on Dallas's Ethernet0 and Serial1 interfaces and on FortWorth's Ethernet0 and Serial0 interfaces. Figure 9-2 shows the

Figure 9-2
Current AppleTalk
internetwork.

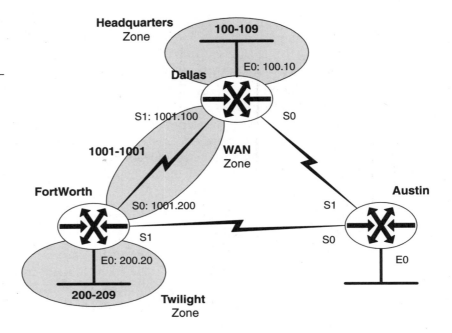

Figure 9-2
Current AppleTalk
internetwork.

AppleTalk addresses for the active interfaces. AppleTalk connectivity has
not been established to Austin, yet.

Figure 9-3 shows the current AppleTalk routing table on Dallas as displayed with the **show appletalk route** command.

The routing table display tells that there are three entries (Line 4).
Dallas has two directly connected AppleTalk networks—each is identified with the letter *C* in left column of the entry (Lines 8 and 10). The let-

Figure 9-3
Show AppleTalk
route output on
Dallas.

```
1)  Dallas#show appletalk route
2)  Codes: R - RTMP derived, E - EIGRP derived, C - connected, A
    - AURP
3)        S - static P - proxy
4)  3 routes in internet
5)
6)  The first zone listed for each entry is its default
    (primary) zone.
7)
8)  C Net 100-109 directly connected, Ethernet0, zone
    Headquarters
9)  R Net 200-209 [1/G] via 1001.200, 1 sec, Serial1, zone
    Twilight
10) C Net 1001-1001 directly connected, Serial1, zone WAN
11) Dallas#
```

ter *R* in the left column of an entry signifies an RTMP-learned route (Line 9). The network with cable range 200-209 is the Ethernet LAN on FortWorth. Dallas's next hop gateway to reach FortWorth's Ethernet is 1001.200, which is the AppleTalk address of FortWorth's Serial0 interface. The values shown in the brackets indicate the route's hop count and status, respectively. For the entry on Line 9 the contents of the brackets are *1/G*. The network is 1 hop away and its status is Good—that is correct; *G* stands for Good. Other status possibilities are *B* for Bad and *S* for Suspect (maybe bad). Each entry in the AppleTalk routing table includes the name of the primary zone for the network described.

Since we have seen the routing table, we should take a look at the ZIT (zone information table). Figure 9-4 shows the output of the **show appletalk zone** command on Dallas.

Dallas's ZIT has three zones (Line 6). Each zone contains one network. In the next section we build onto our AppleTalk internetwork by configuring AppleTalk on Austin and the links that connect it.

9.4 AppleTalk Configuration

The only protocol whose traffic IOS routes by default is IP; therefore, we must first turn on the routing of AppleTalk traffic. We use the global configuration command **appletalk routing** to do that. We then configure the assigned AppleTalk cable range and zone(s) to each interface that is to transmit and receive AppleTalk packets. The interface configuration command **appletalk cable-range** is used to configure the network number and the interface configuration command **appletalk zone** is used to configure the zone name.

The AppleTalk cable range must be entered as two decimal numbers separated by a hyphen; the first number must be less than the second number. Cable ranges are not allowed to overlap in the internetwork. We

Figure 9-4

Show AppleTalk zone output on Dallas.

```
1)   Dallas#show appletalk zone
2)   Name                                      Network(s)
3)   Headquarters                              100-109
4)   WAN                                       1001-1001
5)   Twilight                                  200-209
6)   Total of 3 zones
7)   Dallas#
```

can specify a specific AppleTalk address to be assigned to an interface or we can allow IOS to find a unique address on its own.

If an interface's network is in more than one zone, multiple **appletalk zone** commands can be entered. The zone specified in the first command becomes the primary zone.

As soon as we enter a valid cable range and zone on an interface, IOS attempts to locate other routers on the interface's network and verify the information. If there is no other router on the network or the information from other routers matches the local router, AppleTalk is enabled on the interface.

Figure 9-5 shows an updated internetwork diagram with the cable ranges and zones to be used for Austin AppleTalk connectivity. We will reference this information in the configuration below.

AppleTalk is already enabled on Dallas and FortWorth, so we will start our configuration example on Austin then move to the Dallas and FortWorth interfaces that are connected to Austin. The commands for configuring AppleTalk on Austin, based on the Figure 9-5 information, are shown in Figure 9-6.

The routing of AppleTalk packets is enabled on Austin (Line 3). We have three interfaces on which we want to process AppleTalk traffic; the first one is Ethernet0 (Line 4). The cable range for Austin's Ethernet

Figure 9-5

Internetwork Diagram showing Austin AppleTalk cable ranges and zones.

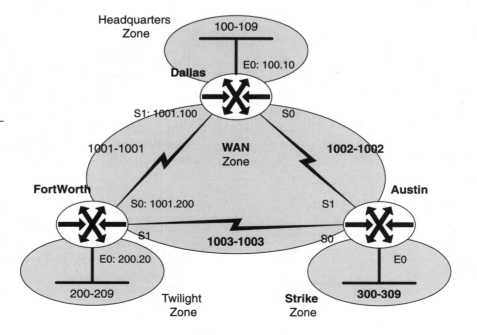

Figure 9-6
AppleTalk configuration on Austin.

```
1)  Austin#configure terminal
2)  Enter configuration commands, one per line. End with CNTL/Z.
3)  Austin(config)#appletalk routing
4)  Austin(config)#interface ethernet0
5)  Austin(config-if)#appletalk cable-range 300-309
6)  Austin(config-if)#appletalk zone Strike
7)  Austin(config-if)#interface serial0
8)  Austin(config-if)#appletalk cable-range 1003-1003 1003.2
9)  Austin(config-if)#appletalk zone WAN
10) Austin(config-if)#interface serial1
11) Austin(config-if)#appletalk cable-range 1002-1002 1002.2
12) Austin(config-if)#appletalk zone WAN
13) Austin(config-if)#<Ctrl-Z>
14) Austin#
```

LAN is 300–309 (Line 5). Since we did not include a specific AppleTalk address, IOS will locate a unique address in the cable range with the selection process that uses AARP as was described in Section 9.1. Once IOS acquires a unique address, it will include the address on the **appletalk cable-range** command that becomes part of the running configuration. The Ethernet LAN is in the zone named Strike (Line 6). On Serial0 (Line 7), we have assigned a specific AppleTalk address, 1003.2 (Line 8). Since Serial0 is connected to a point-to-point WANs and point-to-point WANs have only two hosts, the cable range is a range of one, 1003–1003. Austin's two serial interfaces are part of the same AppleTalk zone, WAN, that the serial link between Dallas and FortWorth is. The WAN zone will contain three networks, all WANs.

We now need to do the configuration on Dallas and FortWorth that will provide AppleTalk connectivity to Austin. Figure 9-7 shows the completion of AppleTalk configuration on the Dallas Serial0 interface that will be used for Austin connectivity and Figure 9-8 shows the completion of AppleTalk configuration on the FortWorth Serial1 interface.

Both of the WANs that connect to Austin have been defined to be part of the WAN zone, and we have specified the AppleTalk addresses on the Dallas and FortWorth interfaces.

Figure 9-7
AppleTalk configuration on Dallas Serial0.

```
1)  Dallas#configure terminal
2)  Enter configuration commands, one per line. End with CNTL/Z.
3)  Dallas(config)#interface serial0
4)  Dallas(config-if)#appletalk cable-range 1002-1002 1002.1
5)  Dallas(config-if)#appletalk zone WAN
6)  Dallas(config-if)#<Ctrl-Z>
7)  Dallas#
```

Figure 9-8
AppleTalk configu-
ration on
FortWorth Serial1.

```
1)  FortWorth#configure terminal
2)  Enter configuration commands, one per line. End with CNTL/Z.
3)  FortWorth(config)#interface serial1
4)  FortWorth(config-if)#appletalk cable-range 1003-1003 1003.1
5)  FortWorth(config-if)#appletalk zone WAN
6)  FortWorth(config-if)#<Ctrl-Z>
7)  FortWorth#
```

RTMP is the default routing protocol for AppleTalk and, if we are going to use it, there is no routing protocol configuration necessary. As soon as AppleTalk processing is enabled on an interface, RTMP is enabled on the interface.

9.5 AppleTalk Verification

AppleTalk has been configured on all of the routers in our internetwork. Now we will use some of the commands that show us the status of AppleTalk. The outputs of the following commands are shown in this section:

- **show protocols**
- **show appletalk route**
- **show appletalk zone**
- **show appletalk interface**
- **ping**

The **show protocols** command shows us the protocols that IOS is configured to route, the status of each interface, and the primary characteristic(s) of each protocol on each interface. For AppleTalk, the primary characteristics are the cable range and the primary zone. Figure 9-9 shows the output of the **show protocols** command on Austin after AppleTalk addresses have been verified by the neighbor routers.

The routing of AppleTalk packets is enabled on Austin (Line 4). IOS has acquired the AppleTalk address 304.219 for use on Ethernet0 (Line 11). We see also that IOS has accepted the AppleTalk address that we specified for Serial0 and Serial1 (Lines 18 and 22).

The **show appletalk route** command shows the contents of the AppleTalk routing table. We first covered this command in Figure 9-3.

Figure 9-9

Show protocols output on Austin after AppleTalk configuration.

```
1)   Austin#show protocols
2)   Global values:
3)     Internet Protocol routing is enabled
4)     Appletalk routing is enabled
5)     IPX routing is enabled
6)   BRI0 is administratively down, line protocol is down
7)   BRI0:1 is administratively down, line protocol is down
8)   BRI0:2 is administratively down, line protocol is down
9)   Ethernet0 is up, line protocol is up
10)    Internet address is 192.168.1.1/24
11)    AppleTalk address is 304.219, zone Strike
12)  Ethernet0.1 is up, line protocol is up
13)    IPX address is C0A80100.0010.7b3a.d204
14)  Ethernet0.2 is up, line protocol is up
15)    IPX address is C0A801FF.0010.7b3a.d204
16)  Serial0 is up, line protocol is up
17)    Internet address is 192.168.3.2/24
18)    AppleTalk address is 1003.2, zone WAN
19)    IPX address is C0A80300.0010.7b3a.d204
20)  Serial1 is up, line protocol is up
21)    Internet address is 192.168.2.2/24
22)    AppleTalk address is 1002.2, zone WAN
23)    IPX address is C0A80200.0010.7b3a.d204
24)  Serial2 is administratively down, line protocol is down
25)  Serial3 is administratively down, line protocol is down
26)  Austin#
```

The new AppleTalk routing table on Dallas is shown in Figure 9-10 and that on Austin in Figure 9-11.

The routing tables now show six routes each—three that are directly connected and three that are learned from RTMP. Dallas's AppleTalk path to reach Austin's Ethernet LAN is via Austin Serial1 interface, which is out its own Serial0 interface (Line 10, Figure 9-10). The routing tables show the primary zone for each cable range. To view the cable ranges that are a part of each zone, we use the **show appletalk zone** command, which we first showed in Figure 9-4. The new ZIT on Dallas is shown in Figure 9-12.

The WAN zone now contains three networks, all of the WANs (Line 4), and the Strike zone has been added to the table (Line 5).

The **show appletalk interface** command returns information about the AppleTalk configuration of each interface. The output of the command on Dallas is in Figure 9-13. The output contains the AppleTalk cable range, address, and zone for each interface that has AppleTalk enabled. For Ethernet0 (Line 8), the cable range is the one we configured (Line 9). The AppleTalk address is 100.10 and it is valid (Line 10). IOS considers an AppleTalk address to be valid once it has been verified to be

Figure 9-10
AppleTalk routing
table on Dallas
after AppleTalk
configuration.

```
 1)  Dallas#show appletalk route
 2)  Codes: R - RTMP derived, E - EIGRP derived, C - connected,
            A - AURP
 3)         S - static P - proxy
 4)  6 routes in internet
 5)
 6)  The first zone listed for each entry is its default
     (primary) zone.
 7)
 8)  C Net 100-109 directly connected, Ethernet0, zone
     Headquarters
 9)  R Net 200-209 [1/G] via 1001.200, 7 sec, Serial1, zone
     Twilight
10)  R Net 300-309 [1/G] via 1002.2, 0 sec, Serial0, zone Strike
11)  C Net 1001-1001 directly connected, Serial1, zone WAN
12)  C Net 1002-1002 directly connected, Serial0, zone WAN
13)  R Net 1003-1003 [1/G] via 1002.2, 1 sec, Serial0, zone WAN
14)  Dallas#
```

unique and the cable range and zone(s) assigned to the interface have been verified to be the same as any other routers connected to the same network. In the case of Ethernet0, there are no other routers on the same network. AppleTalk gleaning (Line 12) is the process by which IOS processes all of the AppleTalk traffic being received by an interface and dynamically builds an AARP cache based on the information in the frames. The gleaning process is disabled by default.

There are two routers on each of the serial links; therefore, each of the routers must go through the verification process once the neighbor

Figure 9-11
AppleTalk routing
table on Austin
after AppleTalk
configuration.

```
 1)  Austin#show appletalk route
 2)  Codes: R - RTMP derived, E - EIGRP derived, C - connected,
            A - AURP
 3)         S - static P - proxy
 4)  6 routes in internet
 5)
 6)  The first zone listed for each entry is its default
     (primary) zone.
 7)
 8)  R Net 100-109 [1/G] via 1002.1, 5 sec, Serial1, zone
     Headquarters
 9)  R Net 200-209 [1/G] via 1003.1, 5 sec, Serial0, zone
     Twilight
10)  C Net 300-309 directly connected, Ethernet0, zone Strike
11)  R Net 1001-1001 [1/G] via 1003.1, 5 sec, Serial0, zone WAN
12)  C Net 1002-1002 directly connected, Serial1, zone WAN
13)  C Net 1003-1003 directly connected, Serial0, zone WAN
14)  Austin#
```

Figure 9-12

AppleTalk Zone information table on Dallas after AppleTalk configuration.

```
1)  Dallas#show appletalk zone
2)  Name                          Network(s)
3)  Headquarters                  100-109
4)  WAN                           1003-1003 1002-1002 1001-1001
5)  Strike                        300-309
6)  Twilight                      200-209
7)  Total of 4 zones
8)  Dallas#
```

router on the other end of the serial link is discovered. On the Serial0 interface (Line 14), the address we entered has been validated (Line 16), and it was verified by the other host on the network, 1002.2 (Line 18).

The **show** commands described here are good ways of verifying the configuration of AppleTalk; however, they do very little for making sure that AppleTalk connectivity has been established. For that we need to

Figure 9-13

Show AppleTalk interface output on Dallas.

```
1)  Dallas#show appletalk interface
2)  BRI0 is administratively down, line protocol is down
3)    AppleTalk protocol processing disabled
4)  BRI0:1 is administratively down, line protocol is down
5)    AppleTalk protocol processing disabled
6)  BRI0:2 is administratively down, line protocol is down
7)    AppleTalk protocol processing disabled
8)  Ethernet0 is up, line protocol is up
9)    AppleTalk cable range is 100-109
10)   AppleTalk address is 100.10, Valid
11)   AppleTalk zone is "Headquarters"
12)   AppleTalk address gleaning is disabled
13)   AppleTalk route cache is enabled
14) Serial0 is up, line protocol is up
15)   AppleTalk cable range is 1002-1002
16)   AppleTalk address is 1002.1, Valid
17)   AppleTalk zone is "WAN"
18)   AppleTalk port configuration verified by 1002.2
19)   AppleTalk address gleaning is not supported by hardware
20)   AppleTalk route cache is enabled
21) Serial1 is up, line protocol is up
22)   AppleTalk cable range is 1001-1001
23)   AppleTalk address is 1001.100, Valid
24)   AppleTalk zone is "WAN"
25)   AppleTalk port configuration verified by 1001.200
26)   AppleTalk address gleaning is not supported by hardware
27)   AppleTalk route cache is enabled
28) Serial2 is administratively down, line protocol is down
29)   AppleTalk protocol processing disabled
30) Serial3 is administratively down, line protocol is down
31)   AppleTalk protocol processing disabled
32) Dallas
```

use the *AppleTalk ping* application, which uses AEP to transmit AppleTalk echo request packets to an AppleTalk destination address and receive AppleTalk echo replies. Three ways of doing an AppleTalk ping in IOS are as follows:

1. Use the normal **ping** command with an AppleTalk address.
2. Use the **ping appletalk** command with an AppleTalk address.
3. Use an extended ping, and type **appletalk** when prompted for a protocol.

Figure 9-14 shows examples of all three options. The AppleTalk pings are being done from Dallas, and the destination address is that of Austin's Ethernet0 interface as obtained with the **show protocols** command in Figure 9-9.

When the normal ping is used to performing the AppleTalk ping (Line 1), we depend on IOS's recognizing that the address we have typed is an

Figure 9-14

AppleTalk ping examples.

```
1)  Dallas#ping 304.219
2)
3)  Type escape sequence to abort.
4)  Sending 5, 100-byte AppleTalk Echos to 304.219, timeout is
    2 seconds:
5)  !!!!!
6)  Success rate is 100 percent (5/5), round-trip min/avg/max =
    16/16/16 ms
7)  Dallas#ping appletalk 304.219
8)
9)  Type escape sequence to abort.
10) Sending 5, 100-byte AppleTalk Echos to 304.219, timeout is
    2 seconds:
11) !!!!!
12) Success rate is 100 percent (5/5), round-trip min/avg/max =
    16/17/20 ms
13) Dallas#ping
14) Protocol [ip]: appletalk
15) Target AppleTalk address: 304.219
16) Repeat count [5]: <Enter>
17) Datagram size [100]: <Enter>
18) Timeout in seconds [2]: <Enter>
19) Verbose [n]: <Enter>
20) Sweep range of sizes [n]: <Enter>
21) Type escape sequence to abort.
22) Sending 5, 100-byte AppleTalk Echos to 304.219, timeout is
    2 seconds:
23) !!!!!
24) Success rate is 100 percent (5/5), round-trip min/avg/max =
    16/18/24 ms
25) Dallas#
```

AppleTalk address. IOS correctly interprets the address as AppleTalk based on its format, and then IOS does the AppleTalk ping by sending five AppleTalk echoes to Austin's Ethernet0 interface and receiving five replies. An exclamation point (!) indicates the successful reception of a ping reply from the target host (Line 5); if no reply were received, IOS would display a period (.) instead. The success rate and response time information is given on the last line (Line 6).

Using the **ping appletalk** command (Line 7) tells IOS that the address in the command is an AppleTalk address so that IOS does not have to figure it out. The result is the same as that of the normal ping.

We invoke an extended ping by typing the **ping** command without an address (Line 13), and then IOS prompts us for the protocol (Line 14). Entering **appletalk** at the protocol prompt will cause IOS to ask for an AppleTalk destination address (Line 15). The extended ping gives us the opportunity to change the number of echoes sent, the size of the echoes, and the reply timeout before actually performing the ping operation. With the default parameters, the extended ping process is the same as the one for the first two pings.

9.6 AppleTalk EIGRP Configuration

AppleTalk EIGRP has the same basic operation as IP EIGRP, which we described in Section 7.7.3.2. AppleTalk EIGRP is Cisco-proprietary, and is supported only on Cisco routers for the sharing of AppleTalk routes. AppleTalk EIGRP can replace RTMP on networks that have only Cisco AppleTalk routers; these networks are usually WANs.

The implementation of AppleTalk EIGRP can save WAN bandwidth since EIGRP performs incremental updates for routes. This means that updates are transmitted only when a change occurs, not at the usual 10-second interval of RTMP.

We will configure AppleTalk EIGRP on the WANs of our internetwork and leave RTMP on the LANs. The configuration of AppleTalk EIGRP is different from the configuration of other routing protocols we have seen; the enabling and disabling of an AppleTalk routing protocol are done in interface configuration mode rather than a routing process configuration mode.

Before we can enable AppleTalk EIGRP on an interface, we must enable it in global configuration mode. The **appletalk routing eigrp** command along with a router identification number will enable us to start AppleTalk EIGRP on an interface. Unlike IP EIGRP and IPX EIGRP, which require a common ASN on all of the routers running them, AppleTalk EIGRP requires a unique router identification number on each of the routers using it to exchange routes.

We enable AppleTalk EIGRP on an interface by using the interface configuration mode command **appletalk protocol eigrp**. Turning on AppleTalk EIGRP on an interface does not automatically turn off RTMP on the interface; therefore, we should disable RTMP on the interface to avoid running two AppleTalk routing protocols and using network bandwidth needlessly. RTMP is disabled on an interface with the **no appletalk protocol rtmp**.

To configure the redistribution of routes between RTMP and AppleTalk EIGRP, we use the global configuration command **appletalk route-redistribution**. Issuing this command will allow the AppleTalk EIGRP process to send RTMP-learned networks in its updates, and it will allow RTMP to send EIGRP-learned networks in its updates. In some older versions of IOS, this command appeared in the running configuration automatically when AppleTalk EIGRP was enabled. We will enter it manually just in case IOS does not do it automatically.

Figure 9-15 shows the implementation of AppleTalk EIGRP on Dallas. Figure 9-16 shows the configuration of AppleTalk EIGRP on FortWorth. Figure 9-17 has the configuration commands on Austin.

We selected the followed router IDs: 100 for Dallas (Figure 9-15, Line 3), 200 for FortWorth (Figure 9-16, Line 3), and 300 for Austin (Figure 9-17, Line 3). We have enabled AppleTalk EIGRP on the Serial0 and Serial1 interfaces of all three routers. For each WAN interface we entered two commands: **appletalk protocol eigrp** to enable AppleTalk EIGRP and **no appletalk protocol rtmp** to disable RTMP since it was

Figure 9-15

AppleTalk EIGRP configuration on Dallas.

```
 1)  Dallas#configure terminal
 2)  Enter configuration commands, one per line. End with CNTL/Z.
 3)  Dallas(config)#appletalk routing eigrp 100
 4)  Dallas(config)#appletalk route-redistribution
 5)  Dallas(config)#interface serial0
 6)  Dallas(config-if)#appletalk protocol eigrp
 7)  Dallas(config-if)#no appletalk protocol rtmp
 8)  Dallas(config-if)#interface serial1
 9)  Dallas(config-if)#appletalk protocol eigrp
10)  Dallas(config-if)#no appletalk protocol rtmp
11)  Dallas(config-if)#<Ctrl-Z>
12)  Dallas#
```

Figure 9-16
AppleTalk EIGRP
configuration on
FortWorth.

```
1)  FortWorth#configure terminal
2)  Enter configuration commands, one per line. End with CNTL/Z.
3)  FortWorth(config)#appletalk routing eigrp 200
4)  FortWorth(config)#appletalk route-redistribution
5)  FortWorth(config)#interface serial0
6)  FortWorth(config-if)#appletalk protocol eigrp
7)  FortWorth(config-if)#no appletalk protocol rtmp
8)  FortWorth(config-if)#interface serial1
9)  FortWorth(config-if)#appletalk protocol eigrp
10) FortWorth(config-if)#no appletalk protocol rtmp
11) FortWorth(config-if)#<Ctrl-Z>
12) FortWorth#
```

enabled by default. As an example, these two commands are shown on Lines 6 and 7 of Figure 9-17.

Just as with the other versions of EIGRP, IOS maintains a neighbor table and a topology table for AppleTalk EIGRP. These can be displayed with the **show appletalk eigrp neighbors** and **show appletalk eigrp topology** commands, respectively. The structure of the AppleTalk versions of the tables is similar to that of the IP versions we described in Section 7.7.3.4.

9.7 AppleTalk Configuration Summary

AppleTalk configuration requires that the IOS AppleTalk routing process be started with the **appletalk routing** command. Then we must go to

Figure 9-17
AppleTalk EIGRP
configuration on
Austin.

```
1)  Austin#configure terminal
2)  Enter configuration commands, one per line. End with CNTL/Z.
3)  Austin(config)#appletalk routing eigrp 300
4)  Austin(config)#appletalk route-redistribution
5)  Austin(config)#interface serial0
6)  Austin(config-if)#appletalk protocol eigrp
7)  Austin(config-if)#no appletalk protocol rtmp
8)  Austin(config-if)#interface serial1
9)  Austin(config-if)#appletalk protocol eigrp
10) Austin(config-if)#no appletalk protocol rtmp
11) Austin(config-if)#<Ctrl-Z>
12) Austin#
```

each interface that is to be involved in routing AppleTalk packets and assign it an AppleTalk cable range and at least one AppleTalk zone. The **appletalk cable-range** command is used to assign an AppleTalk cable range to an interface, and the **appletalk zone** command is used place an interface into an AppleTalk zone.

The internetwork that we now have for AppleTalk connectivity is shown in Figure 9-18. The final internetwork diagram shows all of the cable ranges, zones, and interface addresses. The boundary of AppleTalk EIGRP processing is the same as that of the WAN zone.

Figure 9-19 shows the AppleTalk-specific commands from Dallas's running configuration. Figure 9-20 shows FortWorth's AppleTalk-specific commands taken from the running configuration. Figure 9-21 shows the AppleTalk-specific commands from Austin's running configuration.

We have enabled AppleTalk routing on the three active interfaces of each router in the internetwork. We also enabled AppleTalk EIGRP and disabled RTMP on the WAN interfaces while leaving RTMP on the LAN interfaces. If we have a mixed-vendor router environment, we probably would have left RTMP without EIGRP on all interfaces.

Figure 9-18

Final AppleTalk internetwork diagram.

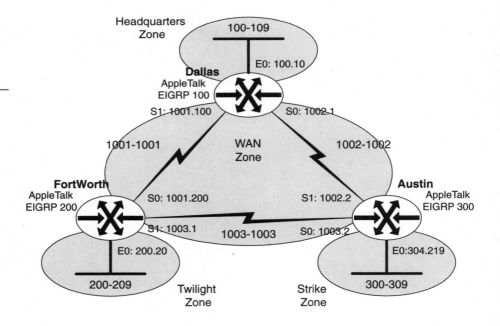

Figure 9-19
Dallas AppleTalk configuration commands.

```
1)  Dallas#show running-config [Some text has been omitted.]
2)  !
3)  appletalk routing eigrp 100
4)  appletalk route-redistribution
5)  !
6)  interface Ethernet0
7)   appletalk cable-range 100-109 100.10
8)   appletalk zone Headquarters
9)  !
10) interface Serial0
11)  appletalk cable-range 1002-1002 1002.1
12)  appletalk zone WAN
13)  appletalk protocol eigrp
14)  no appletalk protocol rtmp
15) !
16) interface Serial1
17)  appletalk cable-range 1001-1001 1001.100
18)  appletalk zone WAN
19)  appletalk protocol eigrp
20)  no appletalk protocol rtmp
21) !
22) Dallas#
```

Figure 9-20
FortWorth AppleTalk configuration commands.

```
1)  FortWorth#show running-config [Some text has been omitted.]
2)  !
3)  appletalk routing eigrp 200
4)  appletalk route-redistribution
5)  !
6)  interface Ethernet0
7)  appletalk cable-range 200-209 200.20
8)  appletalk zone Twilight
9)  !
10) interface Serial0
11) appletalk cable-range 1001-1001 1001.200
12) appletalk zone WAN
13) appletalk protocol eigrp
14) no appletalk protocol rtmp
15) !
16) interface Serial1
17) appletalk cable-range 1003-1003 1003.1
18) appletalk zone WAN
19) appletalk protocol eigrp
20) no appletalk protocol rtmp
21) !
22) FortWorth#
```

Figure 9-21

Austin AppleTalk configuration commands.

```
1)  Austin#show running-config [Some text has been omitted.]
2)  !
3)  appletalk routing eigrp 300
4)  appletalk route-redistribution
5)  !
6)  interface Ethernet0
7)    appletalk cable-range 300-309 304.219
8)    appletalk zone Strike
9)  !
10) interface Serial0
11)   appletalk cable-range 1003-1003 1003.2
12)   appletalk zone WAN
13)   appletalk protocol eigrp
14)   no appletalk protocol rtmp
15) !
16) interface Serial1
17)   appletalk cable-range 1002-1002 1002.2
18)   appletalk zone WAN
19)   appletalk protocol eigrp
20)   no appletalk protocol rtmp
21) !
22) Austin#
```

9.8   AppleTalk Removal

We are going to leave AppleTalk running on our test internetwork; however, if we want to stop the AppleTalk routing process on a router, we can enter the following global configuration command.

no appletalk routing

The **no appletalk routing** command will remove, from the running configuration, the commands dealing with AppleTalk routing. These commands include those that define AppleTalk cable ranges, zones, and routing protocols.

CHAPTER 10

Configuring DECnet

DECnet is the name of products from Digital Equipment Corporation (DEC or DIGITAL) that support networking according to the *Digital Network Architecture* (DNA). For the purposes of this text, we refer to DECnet as the protocol that hosts in a DIGITAL internetwork use to communicate. DIGITAL internetworks generally contain DIGITAL host systems, such as VAX computers. (Note that DIGITAL is now part of Compaq.)

DECnet versions are called *phases*. In this chapter, we cover the configuration of DECnet Phase IV (4).

After a brief overview of DECnet addressing and protocol operation, we go on to cover the IOS commands for the basic configuration of DECnet as we make modifications to our three-router internetwork.

10.1   DECnet Addressing

A *DECnet address* is 16 bits long; it consists of a 6-bit area number and a 10-bit node number. Both numbers are written in decimal and are separated by a period (.). An *area* is a logical grouping of DECnet *nodes*. A DECnet internetwork can have up to 63 areas (numbered 1 to 63), and each area can have up to 1023 nodes (numbered 1 to 1023).

In DECnet, there is no address applied to a network, or a wire. The address is applied to a node rather than to a specific interface of a node. This means that we will be assigning a DECnet address to a router during our configuration.

DECnet uses a special algorithm for mapping DECnet addresses to MAC addresses on a LAN. DECnet addresses are actually translated into MAC addresses. Starting with the full 16-bit address in binary, the two bytes are swapped and converted to four hexadecimal digits. The four hexadecimal digits become the low-order digits of a node's MAC address when combined with the eight high-order digits assigned by DIGITAL to be AA000400.

Figure 10-1 shows an example of this translation algorithm in operation. We start with a DECnet address of 2.1. That is a 6-bit decimal two and a 10-bit decimal one. Converting these decimal values to 16 binary bits, we get 0000.1000.0000.0001. When we swap the bytes and convert them to hexadecimal, we get 0108. The MAC address of the node with DECnet address 2.1 is AA0004000108.

Wait a minute. We already established that a LAN interface has a MAC address assigned to it by its manufacturer. DECnet overrides a

DECnet Address	2.1
Dotted-Binary	000010.0000000001
Binary	00001000 00000001
Swapped Bytes	00000001 00001000
Hexadecimal	01 08
MAC Address	AA00.0400.0108

LAN interface's burned-in MAC address whenever DECnet is enabled on the interface. When we configure DECnet on a router, the MAC addresses of all of the LAN interfaces that have DECnet enabled are going to have their MAC addresses changed to the value calculated with the DECnet algorithm. All of a node's interfaces, which have DECnet enabled, have the same MAC address; this is fine as long as the interfaces are never connected to the same network. These software-defined MAC addresses are called *locally administered addresses* (LAAs).

10.2   DECnet Overview

This overview of DECnet should provide enough information for us to understand what is happening when we configure DECnet on a router. Figure 10-2 shows the DNA layers as compared to the OSI Reference Model. The functionality of the DNA layers maps very closely to that of the OSI layers. The only most obvious exception is Network Management, which extends from layer 2 through layer 6. Network Management provides statistics and controls to DECnet processes running at the included layers.

There are two types of DECnet nodes: routing nodes and endnodes. *Endnodes* are those hosts that run DECnet upper-layer processes, like user applications, and can neither send nor receive information on behalf of another node. A *routing node* learns about the presence of endnodes and other routing nodes so it can help provide communication paths among them. Routing nodes can perform endnode functions.

Figure 10-2
DECnet stack compared to OSI Reference Model.

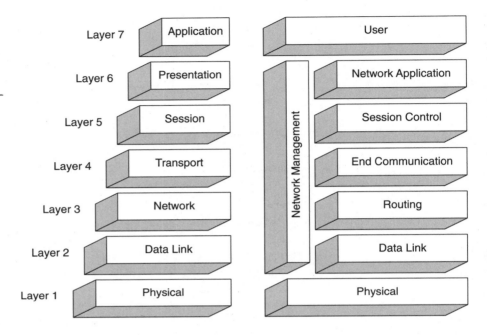

There are two types of DECnet routing nodes: Level 1 and Level 2. A *Level-1* routing node learns about all of the nodes within its area, and provides routing among nodes within the area. A *Level-2* routing node learns about all of the areas in an internetwork so that it can provide interarea routing. A Level-2 routing node also performs the functions of a Level-1 routing node.

DECnet routing nodes use the *DECnet Routing Protocol* (DRP) to communicate information about the presence of nodes and areas. DRP updates are transmitted to a multicast address every 40 seconds by default. Level-1 routing updates contain the addresses of endnodes within an area. Level-1 routing nodes learn about endnodes by listening to Hello packets sent by the endnodes. Level-2 routing updates contain a list of the areas within a DECnet internetwork. Routing nodes also communicate with each other with Hello packets; Hello packets are transmitted by default every 15 seconds.

DRP uses *cost* as a metric to determine the best path between two nodes. Cost is not automatically calculated—it must be set manually. The cost for an outbound interface is a value from 1 to 63. The value of the cost should be inversely proportional to the bandwidth of a link. For example, if we decide to assign a cost of 5 to our 10-Mbps Ethernet LANs, we might assign a cost of 1 to our 100-Mbps Ethernet LANs and a cost of

15 to our T1 WANs. Routing nodes also maintain a *hop count*, in addition to the cost, for each destination.

A *Designated Router* (DR) is selected on each broadcast network such as an Ethernet LAN; this DR is completely different from the one we covered during OSPF configuration. In order for an endnode to speak to another node, it must first speak to the DR of its network. The DR knows which endnodes are connected to the local network because an endnode advertises its presence by sending periodic Hello packets. The DR collects these Hellos and builds an endnode database, which is sent to other routing nodes in DRP updates.

We will use the internetwork diagram of Figure 10-3 to describe the operation of DECnet. The figure shows four endnodes: 1.86, 1.99, 2.60, and 2.61; and three routing nodes: 1.1 (Dallas), 1.2 (FortWorth), and 2.1 (Austin). It is pretty obvious from the addresses that the internetwork has two areas—1 and 2.

Dallas and Austin must be Level-2 routing nodes in order to allow interarea communication. Dallas will inform Austin about a path to area

Figure 10-3

DECnet internetwork diagram with areas and nodes.

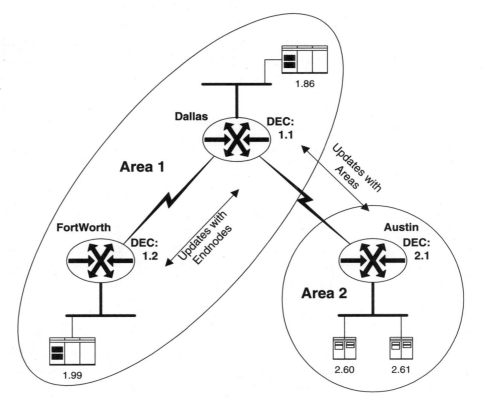

1, and Austin will inform Dallas about a path to area 2. FortWorth can be either a Level-1 or Level-2 routing node; for this example, we will make FortWorth a Level-1 routing node.

Endnode 1.99 will start sending Hello packets when it boots. FortWorth will hear these and advertise the presence of itself and 1.99 to Dallas. Endnode 1.86 will start sending Hello packets when it boots, and Dallas will advertise the presence of itself and 1.86 to FortWorth. Now both Dallas and FortWorth know about all of the nodes within area 1.

Endnodes 2.60 and 2.61 start sending Hellos when they boot, also. Austin hears these and just keeps them locally since there are no other routing nodes in area 2.

Austin and Dallas discover each other's presence through their own Hellos, and since they are both Level-2 routing nodes, they send DRP updates containing a list of known areas. Now Dallas and Austin have a path to each other's area.

Using the figure, let us walk through some communication scenarios.

1. *Scenario One—node 1.99 communicating with node 1.86.*   Since FortWorth is the only routing node on the Ethernet LAN, it is the DR for the LAN. Node 1.99 sends a packet, destined for node 1.86, to FortWorth, which, in turn, looks up node 1.86 in its routing database (routing table). Node 1.86 has been learned from Dallas; therefore, the path has a next hop node of 1.1 (Dallas). FortWorth forwards the packet to Dallas, and Dallas looks in its own routing table for the destination address 1.86. Node 1.86 is locally attached; therefore, Dallas forwards the packet onto the Ethernet LAN.

2. *Scenario Two—node 2.60 communicating with node 2.61.*   Austin is the only routing node on its Ethernet LAN; therefore, it becomes the LAN's DR. Endnodes have no initial knowledge of other endnodes; therefore, node 2.60 sends a packet destined for 2.61 to Austin. Austin looks up 2.61 in its routing table and finds it on the same Ethernet LAN from which the packet was received. Austin forwards the packet back onto the LAN while setting a special intra-Ethernet bit in the packet. The intra-Ethernet bit informs 2.61 that the source node is on the same LAN. When 2.61 receives the packet, it recognizes the intra-Ethernet bit and responds directly back to 2.60 without going through Austin, while also setting the intra-Ethernet bit. Further communication between 2.60 and 2.61 does not have to make use of the DR, Austin.

3. *Scenario Three—node 1.99 communicating with node 2.61.*   Node 1.99 sends a packet to its DR, FortWorth. The packet has a destination address of 2.61. FortWorth is a Level-1 routing node and does not have paths to other areas; therefore, FortWorth forwards the packet to its closest Level-2 routing node, Dallas. Dallas has entries in its routing table for other areas; therefore, Dallas looks up a path to area 2. The path to area 2 has a next hop node of 2.1 (Austin); therefore, Dallas routes the packet across the serial link to Austin. Austin has the area 2 endnodes in its routing table; therefore, Austin forwards the packet onto the Ethernet LAN after a lookup.

10.3 DECnet Configuration

To enable the routing of DECnet packets on a Cisco router, we must perform the following operations:

- Enable DECnet packet routing.
- Assign a DECnet address to the router.
- Define the routing node type (Level 1 or Level 2).
- Assign a cost to each of the interfaces to be used for DECnet packet routing.

We are going to implement DECnet on the same three-router internetwork that we have been using in the examples. Figure 10-4 shows the node addresses and interface costs that we will be configuring in the DECnet examples. Our example configuration uses the same routers and

Figure 10-4
DECnet internetwork diagram for configuration.

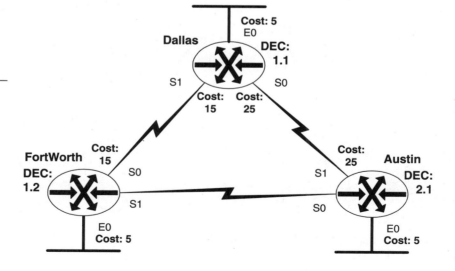

addresses from Figure 10-3, which we described in the communication scenarios. However, our sample internetwork has no endnodes, only routing nodes. Note that we are not going to configure DECnet on the serial link between FortWorth and Austin.

To enable the routing of DECnet packets and assign a DECnet address to a router, we issue the **decnet routing** global configuration command. We use the **decnet node-type** global configuration command to define the routing node type. The keywords for the possible types are **routing-iv**, for a Level-1 routing node, and **area**, for a Level-2 routing node. A DECnet cost is assigned to an interface with the **decnet cost** interface configuration command.

Figure 10-5 shows the configuration of DECnet on Dallas; Figure 10-6 shows the configuration of DECnet on FortWorth; and Figure 10-7 shows the configuration of DECnet on Austin.

After entering the configuration commands, DECnet traffic is being routed on our test internetwork. Dallas and Austin are Level-2 routing nodes and FortWorth is a Level-1 routing node. All of the Ethernet interfaces have a cost of 5. The serial interfaces connected to the T1 between

Figure 10-5

DECnet configuration on Dallas.

```
1)  Dallas#configure terminal
2)  Enter configuration commands, one per line. End with CNTL/Z.
3)  Dallas(config)#decnet routing 1.1
4)  Dallas(config)#decnet node-type area
5)  Dallas(config)#interface ethernet0
6)  Dallas(config-if)#decnet cost 5
7)  Dallas(config-if)#interface serial0
8)  Dallas(config-if)#decnet cost 25
9)  Dallas(config-if)#interface serial1
10) Dallas(config-if)#decnet cost 15
11) Dallas(config-if)#<Ctrl-Z>
12) Dallas#
```

Figure 10-6

DECnet configuration on FortWorth.

```
1)  FortWorth#configure terminal
2)  Enter configuration commands, one per line. End with CNTL/Z.
3)  FortWorth(config)#decnet routing 1.2
4)  FortWorth(config)#decnet node-type routing-iv
5)  FortWorth(config)#interface ethernet0
6)  FortWorth(config-if)#decnet cost 5
7)  FortWorth(config-if)#interface serial0
8)  FortWorth(config-if)#decnet cost 15
9)  FortWorth(config-if)#<Ctrl-Z>
10) FortWorth#
```

Figure 10-7
DECnet configuration on Austin.

```
1)  Austin#configure terminal
2)  Enter configuration commands, one per line. End with CNTL/Z.
3)  Austin(config)#decnet routing 2.1
4)  Austin(config)#decnet node-type area
5)  Austin(config)#interface ethernet0
6)  Austin(config-if)#decnet cost 5
7)  Austin(config-if)#interface serial1
8)  Austin(config-if)#decnet cost 25
9)  Austin(config-if)#<Ctrl-Z>
10) Austin#
```

Dallas and FortWorth each have a cost of 15, and the serial interfaces connected to the 256-kbps leased line between Dallas and Austin each have a cost of 25. These costs assigned to the interfaces are arbitrary, and could have been just about anything. As mentioned before, it is usually a good idea to choose a DECnet cost scheme that allows the costs to be inversely proportional to the bandwidth of the networks.

As soon as we enabled DECnet on an interface by assigning a DECnet cost to the interface, IOS started sending DECnet Hellos. When a router discovered another DECnet routing node, the routers started exchanging Hellos, formed an adjacency, and started exchanging the appropriate types of DRP updates.

10.4 DECnet Verification

Now that DECnet has been configured on the routers, we need to observe and verify its operation. We can use **show** commands to observe the effects of our configuration, and we can use the ping application to test DECnet connectivity. The output of the following commands is shown in this section:

- **show protocols**
- **show decnet route**
- **show decnet neighbors**
- **show decnet interface**
- **ping**

The **show protocols** command shows us the protocols that IOS is configured to route, the status of each interface, and the primary characteristic(s) of each protocol on each interface. For DECnet, the primary interface characteristic is a cost. Remember that the interfaces themselves do not have a DECnet address; we enabled DECnet on an interface by assigning the interface a cost. Figure 10-8 shows the output of the **show protocols** command on Austin.

From the output, we can see that DECnet traffic can be routed (Line 5). We also see that IP, AppleTalk, and IPX routing are still enabled. DECnet has been enabled on Ethernet0 with a cost of 5 (Line 13) and Serial1 with a cost of 25 (Line 25). Turning on DECnet when IPX is already running has a very important side effect (Lines 15 and 17). Since assigning a DECnet cost to the Ethernet0 interface caused the interface to get a new MAC address, and since the node part of an IPX address is the interface's MAC address, the IPX addresses of Ethernet subinterfaces changed. (See Figure 8-12.) This caused a temporary loss of IPX connectivity. The node part of the IPX addresses on the Ethernet subinterfaces is the MAC address we calculated in Figure 10-1 from the DECnet address 2.1 (Austin's address). Some folks follow the rule of thumb that states when configuring both IPX and DECnet on a router,

Figure 10-8

Show protocols output on Austin.

```
1)   Austin#show protocols
2)   Global values:
3)      Internet Protocol routing is enabled
4)      Appletalk routing is enabled
5)      DECNET routing is enabled
6)      IPX routing is enabled
7)   BRI0 is administratively down, line protocol is down
8)   BRI0:1 is administratively down, line protocol is down
9)   BRI0:2 is administratively down, line protocol is down
10)  Ethernet0 is up, line protocol is up
11)     Internet address is 192.168.1.1/24
12)     AppleTalk address is 304.219, zone Strike
13)     Decnet cost is 5
14)  Ethernet0.1 is up, line protocol is up
15)     IPX address is C0A80100.aa00.0400.0108
16)  Ethernet0.2 is up, line protocol is up
17)     IPX address is C0A801FF.aa00.0400.0108
18)  Serial0 is up, line protocol is up
19)     Internet address is 192.168.3.2/24
20)     AppleTalk address is 1003.2, zone WAN
21)     IPX address is C0A80300.0010.7b3a.d204
22)  Serial1 is up, line protocol is up
23)     Internet address is 192.168.2.2/24
24)     AppleTalk address is 1002.2, zone WAN
25)     Decnet cost is 25
26)     IPX address is C0A80200.0010.7b3a.d204
27)  Serial2 is administratively down, line protocol is down
28)  Serial3 is administratively down, line protocol is down
29)  Austin#
```

Figure 10-9
Show DECnet route output on Austin.

```
1)  Austin#show decnet route
2)    Area     Cost   Hops    Next Hop to Node     Expires  Prio
3)  *1         25     1          Serial1 -> 1.1        37     64 A+
4)  *2          0     0          (Local) -> 2.1
5)    Node     Cost   Hops    Next Hop to Node     Expires  Prio
6)  *(Area)     0     0          (Local) -> 2.1
7)  *2.1        0     0          (Local) -> 2.1
8)  Austin#
```

configure DECnet first; this allows the interfaces to get their final IPX addresses upon initial configuration.

Now let us take a look at the DECnet routing table. We use the **show decnet route** command to view it; Figure 10-9 shows the output of the command on Austin and Figure 10-10 shows the output of the command on FortWorth.

Austin is a Level-2 routing node; therefore, the Austin DECnet routing table output contains two sections: *Area* (Line 2) and *Node* (Line 5). The Area section has a list of all of the areas in the DECnet internetwork and the Node section has a list of all of the nodes in the local area; Austin is in area 2. Austin's route to area 1 (Line 3) has a next hop of 1.1 (Dallas), which is out of the Serial1 interface. The cost to get to area 1 is 25 and it is 1 hop away. The *A+* at the end of the entry indicates that the node 1.1 is an adjacent Level-2 routing node. Area 2 is local to Austin (Line 4). There is one node in area 2; this node is the local node, 2.1 (Line 7). The asterisk (*) at the beginning of each entry indicates that the entry is the selected path for the destination given.

The FortWorth DECnet routing table output shows only a *Node* section since FortWorth is a Level-1 routing node. The Node section shows two nodes in area 1—1.1 and 1.2. Node 1.1 is 1 hop away out from Serial0 (Line 4); the *V+* at the end of the entry indicates that 1.1 is an adjacent Level-1 routing node. Dallas is actually a Level-2 routing node, but remember that a Level-2 routing node is also a Level-1 routing node. Node 1.2 is the local node (Line 5). The nearest Level-2 routing node is shown in the *(Area)* entry; it is Dallas.

Figure 10-10
Show DECnet route output on FortWorth.

```
1)  FortWorth#show decnet route
2)    Node     Cost   Hops    Next Hop to Node     Expires  Prio
3)  *(Area)    15     1          Serial0 -> 1.1
4)  *1.1       15     1          Serial0 -> 1.1        31     64 A+
5)  *1.2        0     0          (Local) -> 1.2
6)  FortWorth#
```

We see from the routing tables that Austin and FortWorth have adjacencies with Dallas. This makes the routers neighbors. We can use the **show decnet neighbors** command to see the routing node adjacencies. Figure 10-11 shows the output of the **show decnet neighbors** command on Dallas.

Dallas's DECnet neighbors include 2.1 (Line 3) and 1.2 (Line 4). Node 2.1 is Austin and node 1.2 is FortWorth. Austin is connected to the Serial0 interface of Dallas, and Austin's directly connected interface has no MAC address since serial interfaces do not have MAC addresses. The *A* flag indicates that this is a Level-2 adjacency. FortWorth is connected to the Serial1 interface of Dallas; the *V* flag indicates that this is a Level-1 adjacency.

We can examine further details of the DECnet configuration with the **show decnet interface** command. Figure 10-12 shows the output of this command on Austin.

The output of the **show decnet interface** command begins with global parameters and then continues with interface-specific parameters. Austin is an area (Level-2) router with the address 2.1 (Line 3). The maximum cost to a destination is 1022, and the maximum number of hops to a destination is 30 (Lines 7 and 8). DECnet has been enabled on Ethernet0 with a cost of 5 (Line 17). Austin is the DR for its Ethernet LAN (Line 18). The Hello interval and the update interval for Ethernet0 are at their default values of 15 seconds and 40 seconds, respectively (Line 19). DECnet has also been enabled on Serial1 with a cost of 25 (Line 34). Austin has one Level-2 (*PhaseIV+*) router adjacency (Line 42).

Using the **show** commands, we have established that the DECnet internetwork has been built according to our original specifications in Figure 10-4. We can now use the DECnet ping application to test DECnet connectivity. The command to test for good DECnet routing paths is **ping decnet**. A sample output is shown in Figure 10-13.

This DECnet ping was done from Austin with the destination of FortWorth, node 1.2. By default, five DECnet echo requests are sent with the expectation of receiving a corresponding echo reply for each. In this example, five replies were received as indicated by the five exclamation

Figure 10-11

Show DECnet neighbors output on Dallas.

```
1)  Dallas#show decnet neighbors
2)  Net Node    Interface     MAC address      Flags
3)  0   2.1     Serial0       0000.0000.0000   A
4)  0   1.2     Serial1       0000.0000.0000   V
5)  Dallas#
```

Figure 10-12
Show DECnet
interface output on
Dallas.

```
 1)  Austin#show decnet interface
 2)  Global DECnet parameters for network 0:
 3)    Local address is 2.1, node type is area
 4)    Level-2 'Attached' flag is TRUE
 5)    Maximum node is 1023, maximum area is 63, maximum visits is
      63
 6)    Maximum paths is 1, path split mode is normal
 7)    Local maximum cost is 1022, maximum hops is 30
 8)    Area maximum cost is 1022, maximum hops is 30
 9)    Static routes *NOT* being sent in routing updates
10) BRI0 is administratively down, line protocol is down,
      encapsulation is HDLC
11)    DECnet protocol processing disabled
12) BRI0:1 is administratively down, line protocol is down,
      encapsulation is HDLC
13)    DECnet protocol processing disabled
14) BRI0:2 is administratively down, line protocol is down,
      encapsulation is HDLC
15)    DECnet protocol processing disabled
16) Ethernet0 is up, line protocol is up, encapsulation is ARPA
17)    Interface cost is 5, priority is 64, DECnet network: 0
18)    We are the designated router
19)    Sending HELLOs every 15 seconds, routing updates 40 seconds
20)    Smallest router blocksize seen is 1498 bytes
21)    Routing input list is not set, output list is not set
22)    Access list is not set
23)    DECnet fast switching is enabled
24)    Number of L1 router adjacencies is : 0
25)    Number of non-PhaseIV+ router adjacencies is : 0
26)    Number of PhaseIV+ router adjacencies is : 0
27) Ethernet0.1 is up, line protocol is up, encapsulation is ARPA
28)    DECnet protocol processing disabled
29) Ethernet0.2 is up, line protocol is up, encapsulation is ARPA
30)    DECnet protocol processing disabled
31) Serial0 is up, line protocol is up, encapsulation is HDLC
32)    DECnet protocol processing disabled
33) Serial1 is up, line protocol is up, encapsulation is HDLC
34)    Interface cost is 25, priority is 64, DECnet network: 0
35) Sending HELLOs every 15 seconds, routing updates 40 seconds
36)    Smallest router blocksize seen is 1498 bytes
37)    Routing input list is not set, output list is not set
38)    Access list is not set
39)    DECnet fast switching is enabled
40)    Number of L1 router adjacencies is : 0
41)    Number of non-PhaseIV+ router adjacencies is : 0
42)    Number of PhaseIV+ router adjacencies is : 1
43) Serial2 is administratively down, line protocol is down,
      encapsulation is HDLC
44)    DECnet protocol processing disabled
45) Serial3 is administratively down, line protocol is down,
      encapsulation is HDLC
46)    DECnet protocol processing disabled
47) Austin#
```

```
1)  Austin#ping decnet 1.2
2)
3)  Type escape sequence to abort.
4)  Sending 5, 100-byte DECnet echos to 1.2, timeout is 5 seconds:
5)  !!!!!
6)  Success rate is 100 percent (5/5), round-trip min/avg/max = 8/8/12 ms
7)  Austin#
```

Figure 10-13   Ping DECnet sample output.

points (Line 5). We can use an extended ping to change the number of echo requests, the size of the requests, and/or the timeout.

10.5   DECnet Configuration Summary

To configure DECnet on a Cisco router, we use the **decnet routing** command to start the DECnet routing process and assign a DECnet address to the router. We then must define the routing node type to be either **area** (Level 1) or **routing-iv** (Level 2) with the **decnet node-type** command. Then to enable DECnet on individual interfaces, we assign a cost to each one with the **decnet cost** command.

Figure 10-14
Dallas DECnet configuration commands.

```
1)  Dallas#show running-config [Some text has been omitted.]
2)  !
3)  decnet routing 1.1
4)  decnet node-type area
5)  !
6)  interface Ethernet0
7)    decnet cost 5
8)  !
9)  interface Serial0
10)   decnet cost 25
11) !
12) interface Serial1
13)   decnet cost 15
14) !
15) Dallas#
```

■■■ ■■■■ ■■

Figure 10-15
FortWorth DECnet
configuration com-
mands.

```
1)  FortWorth#show running-config [Some text has been omitted.]
2)  !
3)  decnet routing 1.2
4)  decnet node-type routing-iv
5)  !
6)  interface Ethernet0
7)   decnet cost 5
8)  !
9)  interface Serial0
10)  decnet cost 15
11) !
12) FortWorth#
```

Figure 10-14 shows the DECnet-specific commands from Dallas's running configuration, Figure 10-15 shows FortWorth's DECnet-specific
commands taken from the running configuration, and Figure 10-16
shows the DECnet-specific commands from Austin.

We chose during the configuration examples not to configure DECnet
on the WAN between FortWorth and Austin. We did this so that we could
illustrate the difference between a Level-1 routing node and a Level-2
routing node. Because FortWorth and Austin have addresses from
different DECnet areas, we would have to make FortWorth a Level-2
router if we wanted DECnet traffic to flow across the FortWorth-to-
Austin WAN.

■■■ ■■■■ ■■

Figure 10-16
Austin DECnet con-
figuration com-
mands.

```
1)  Austin#show running-config [Some text has been omitted.]
2)  !
3)  decnet routing 2.1
4)  decnet node-type area
5)  !
6)  interface Ethernet0
7)   decnet cost 5
8)  !
9)  interface Serial1
10)  decnet cost 25
11) !
12) Austin#
```

10.6 DECnet Removal

We are going to leave DECnet running on our test internetwork; however, if we wanted to stop the DECnet routing process on a router, we could enter the following global configuration command:

```
no decnet routing
```

The **no decnet routing** command will remove, from the running configuration, the commands dealing with DECnet routing. These commands include those that define DECnet node type, costs, and timer intervals.

CHAPTER 11

Configuring VINES

The *Virtual Networking System* (VINES) is a protocol suite that was developed by Banyan. It is probably the simplest protocol to configure on Cisco routers.

After a brief overview of VINES addressing and protocol operation, we cover the IOS commands for the basic configuration of VINES as we make modifications to our three-router internetwork.

11.1   VINES Addressing

A VINES address is 48 bits long; it consists of a 32-bit *network number* and a 16-bit *subnetwork number*—for our purposes, we refer to the subnetwork number as a *host number*. Both numbers are written in hexadecimal and separated by a colon (:).

A *VINES network* is a logical network consisting of a server and its client hosts. Banyan servers have their own network numbers. A server's network number is determined from its server key (or serial number). VINES clients are assigned addresses by their local server. A client address consists of the local server's network number and a host number. Servers assign host numbers sequentially starting at 8001 and ending at FFFE. A server's own host number is always 1.

When a VINES client boots, it sends a VINES ARP request for the assignment of an address. The first server that receives the request responds with an address that includes its own server (network) number and its next available host number.

A Cisco router functions just like a Banyan server in a VINES internetwork. The router gets its own network number that is derived from the MAC address of its first LAN interface, and it gets a host number of 1 just like a real Banyan server. The router can also assign VINES client addresses by responding to VINES ARP requests when the local network does not contain a Banyan server.

Figure 11-1 shows an example of a VINES internetwork consisting of three VINES networks. The three VINES networks originate at the Dallas router (301AD4BF), the FortWorth router (301AD4AF), and the Banyan server (100). The host addresses of each of the routers and the server are 1.

The Banyan server is attached to the FortWorth Ethernet LAN. There are also two clients on the LAN. The two clients received addresses from the Banyan server as a result of sending VINES ARP requests when they booted. The first client has an address of 100:8001, which is the network

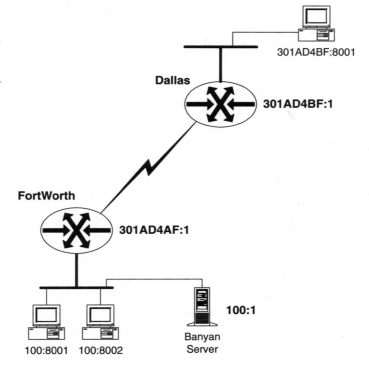

address of the server and the server's first available host number. The second client received the address 100:8002.

There are no Banyan servers on the Dallas Ethernet LAN; therefore, the router is responsible for responding to the VINES ARP requests and assigning client addresses. Figure 11-1 shows one client. The Dallas router assigned the address 301AD4BF:8001 to the client.

Cisco routers get their VINES network numbers by concatenating the 11-bit, binary prefix 0011.0000.000 (hex 300) and the low-order 21 bits of an Ethernet or Token Ring interface's MAC address. For example, the MAC address of the Dallas router's Ethernet0 interface is 0010.7B3A.D4BF; combining the low-order 21 bits of this MAC address with Cisco's VINES prefix yields a VINES network number of 301AD4BF, as shown in Figure 11-1.

VINES routers and servers use keepalives (or hellos) to perform VINES address to MAC address resolution. Every 90 seconds, VINES devices send a keepalive packet. A keepalive contains a device's VINES address and MAC address. VINES routers and servers collect the keepalive information into a VINES neighbor table that can be used for address resolution. A VINES client gets the MAC address of its local server or router from the reply to the VINES ARP, which was used to get a VINES address assigned.

11.2 VINES Overview

When a host boots and loads the VINES client software, it sends a VINES ARP request to find a local server and obtain a VINES address. When a user attempts to log in, the username specifies a group name. Via StreetTalk, all servers maintain a list of all user groups and the servers where they reside; the server that has a user's group is called the *user's home server.* If the local server is not the user's home server, the local server looks up the home server's name and address in its service table and then routes the authentication request to the home server.

Once a user is authenticated to a home server, the local server sends a redirect to the client so that client communication to the home server no longer has to be routed through the local server. Once the client receives the redirect, the client can talk directly to its home server, if it is attached to the same network (wire), or directly to a router, if the home server is on a different network.

VINES uses RTP (routing update protocol) and SRTP (sequenced routing update protocol) as routing protocols. RTP is the original VINES routing protocol and is the default on a Cisco router. SRTP is actually a new version of RTP and was introduced in VINES 5.5. RTP and SRTP send periodic, 90-second updates; however, RTP updates always contain the full list of VINES networks, and SRTP updates are empty unless a network change has occurred. An empty update is called a *null routing update,* which just happens to be the same thing as a VINES keepalive. RTP and SRTP both use delay as a metric for determining the best path to a VINES network.

11.3 VINES Configuration

To enable the routing of VINES packets on a Cisco router, we must perform the following operations:

■ Enable VINES packet routing.

■ Assign a VINES metric to each of the interfaces to be used for VINES packet routing.

As was mentioned at the beginning of this chapter, VINES is very simple to configure. All it takes is one global configuration command, **vines routing**, and one interface configuration command, **vines metric**, on each interface. We are going to configure VINES on Dallas (see Figure 11-2), FortWorth (see Figure 11-3), and Austin (see Figure 11-4).

VINES has now been enabled on all of our test routers and their active interfaces. We used the default form of the **vines routing** and **vines metric** commands.

When we entered the **vines routing** command, IOS automatically selected a VINES network address using the Ethernet0 interface's MAC address. We could have manually specified a VINES network address on the command. Generally, manually specifying a VINES network address is not necessary unless a router has no LAN interfaces or the automatically selected address already exists in the internetwork.

Figure 11-2
VINES
Configuration on
Dallas

```
1)   Dallas#configure terminal
2)   Enter configuration commands, one per line. End with CNTL/Z.
3)   Dallas(config)#vines routing
4)   Dallas(config)#interface ethernet0
5)   Dallas(config-if)#vines metric
6)   Dallas(config-if)#interface serial0
7)   Dallas(config-if)#vines metric
8)   Dallas(config-if)#interface serial1
9)   Dallas(config-if)#vines metric
10)  Dallas(config-if)#<Ctrl-Z>
11)  Dallas#
```

Figure 11-3
VINES configuration on FortWorth.

```
1)   FortWorth#configure terminal
2)   Enter configuration commands, one per line. End with CNTL/Z.
3)   FortWorth(config)#vines routing
4)   FortWorth(config)#interface ethernet0
5)   FortWorth(config-if)#vines metric
6)   FortWorth(config-if)#interface serial0
7)   FortWorth(config-if)#vines metric
8)   FortWorth(config-if)#interface serial1
9)   FortWorth(config-if)#vines metric
10)  FortWorth(config-if)#<Ctrl-Z>
11)  FortWorth#
```

Figure 11-4
VINES configuration on Austin.

```
1)  Austin#configure terminal
2)  Enter configuration commands, one per line. End with CNTL/Z.
3)  Austin(config)#vines routing
4)  Austin(config)#interface ethernet0
5)  Austin(config-if)#vines metric
6)  Austin(config-if)#interface serial0
7)  Austin(config-if)#vines metric
8)  Austin(config-if)#interface serial1
9)  Austin(config-if)#vines metric
10) Austin(config-if)#<Ctrl-Z>
11) Austin#
```

When VINES is enabled on an interface with the **vines metric** command, IOS enables RTP on the interface. If SRTP is needed, the **vines srtp-enabled** global configuration command should be issued. When SRTP is enabled, updates for both routing protocols are sent until IOS determines which one is actually being used by the VINES stations on the network. It is generally a good idea to run only one of the routing protocols at a time on a network since running both of them doubles the normal number of routing updates.

The VINES delay for an interface is automatically calculated from an interface's bandwidth when the **vines metric** command is entered. The metric selected is a value that, when multiplied by 200 milliseconds, equals the delay in seconds. For example, the default value for an Ethernet interface is 2, which yields a delay of 0.4 seconds (400 milliseconds). We can manually override the automatically selected VINES metric by specifying a value on the **vines metric** command.

11.4 VINES Verification

Now that VINES has been configured on the routers, we need to observe and verify its operation. We can use **show** commands to observe the effects of our configuration, and we can use the ping application to test VINES connectivity. The outputs of the following commands are shown in this section:

- **show protocols**
- **show vines route**
- **show vines neighbor**

■ **show vines interface**

■ **ping**

The **show protocols** command always shows the protocols that IOS is configured to route, the status of each interface, and the primary characteristic(s) of each protocol on each interface. For VINES, the primary interface characteristic is the *metric*. Remember that the interfaces themselves do not have a VINES address; we enabled VINES on an interface by assigning a metric to the interface. Figure 11-5 shows the output of the **show protocols** command on Dallas.

We see that the routing of VINES traffic is enabled on Dallas (Line 7). IP, AppleTalk, DECnet, and IPX routing are still enabled, also. VINES is enabled on Ethernet0 with a metric of 2 (Line 16), Serial0 with a metric of 45 (Line 22), and Serial1 with a metric of 45 (Line 28). The metrics are given in three forms:

Figure 11-5

Show protocols output on Dallas.

```
1)  Dallas#show protocols
2)  Global values:
3)    Internet Protocol routing is enabled
4)    Appletalk routing is enabled
5)    DECNET routing is enabled
6)    IPX routing is enabled
7)    Vines routing is enabled
8)  BRI0 is administratively down, line protocol is down
9)  BRI0:1 is administratively down, line protocol is down
10) BRI0:2 is administratively down, line protocol is down
11) Ethernet0 is up, line protocol is up
12)   Internet address is 172.16.10.1/24
13)   AppleTalk address is 100.10, zone Headquarters
14)   Decnet cost is 5
15)   IPX address is AC100A00.aa00.0400.0104
16)   Vines metric is 0020 [2] (0.4000 seconds)
17) Serial0 is up, line protocol is up
18)   Internet address is 192.168.2.1/24
19)   AppleTalk address is 1002.1, zone WAN
20)   Decnet cost is 25
21)   IPX address is C0A80200.0010.7b3a.d4bf
22)   Vines metric is 02D0 [45] (9.0000 seconds)
23) Serial1 is up, line protocol is up
24)   Internet address is 172.16.11.1/24
25)   AppleTalk address is 1001.100, zone WAN
26)   Decnet cost is 15
27)   IPX address is AC100B00.0010.7b3a.d4bf
28)   Vines metric is 0230 [35] (7.0000 seconds)
29) Serial2 is administratively down, line protocol is down
30) Serial3 is administratively down, line protocol is down
31) Dallas#
```

1. Hexadecimal

2. Decimal in brackets

3. Seconds in parentheses (Multiply the decimal value by 200 milliseconds.)

The VINES routing table contains a list of all of the VINES networks. Remember the VINES networks are the VINES servers and routers. We use the **show vines route** command to view the routing table; Figure 11-6 shows the output of the command on Dallas.

The Dallas VINES routing table shows three entries (Figure 11-5, Line 2); the table version is 5; and a routing protocol update is scheduled to be sent in 36 seconds. The table version number changes each time that a network is added or removed from the table. The VINES network number for the entries is shown in the *Network* column, and the next-hop neighbor to reach each network is shown in the *Neighbor* column. The *Flags* column tells us how a route was learned: the letter *R* indicates an RTP-learned route (Lines 6 and 7) and the letter *C* indicates a connected route. Other possible letters are *S* for a static route and *D* for one learned by RTP redirect. The number after the letter tells us the version of RTP used to learn the route; version 0 is RTP and version 1 is SRTP. The asterisk indicates a selected route to reach a VINES network or server. Each entry also contains its age in seconds and the metric in hexadecimal. The first three digits of the metric are the whole number part, and the fourth digit is for a fractional metric.

The VINES neighbors of a router can be listed with the **show vines neighbor** command. Figure 11-7 shows the output of the command on Dallas. Dallas has two zero-hop (directly connected) neighbors—301AD204:1 (Austin) and 301AD4AF:1 (FortWorth). The output also shows Dallas as its own neighbor. The VINES neighbor table shows the interface out from which the neighbor can be reached and the same *Flag*,

Figure 11-6

Show VINES route output on Dallas.

```
1)  Dallas#show vines route
2)  3 servers, 3 routes, version 5, next update 36 seconds
3)
4)  Network          Neighbor         Flags   Age    Metric   Uses
5)
6)  301AD204         301AD204:0001    R0*     51     02D0        0
7)  301AD4AF         301AD4AF:0001    R0*      3     0230        0
8)  301AD4BF         -                C1      -      -           -
9)  Dallas#
```

Figure 11-7

Show VINES neighbor output on Dallas.

```
1)  Dallas#show vines neighbor
2)  3 neighbors, 3 paths, version 3, next update 76 seconds
3)
4)  Address         Hardware Address   Type Int Flag Age Metric Uses
5)
6)  301AD204:0001 HDLC                 HDLC Se0 R0*  25  02D0   0
7)  301AD4AF:0001 HDLC                 HDLC Se1 R0*  53  0230   0
8)  301AD4BF:0001 -                    -    -   C    -   -      -
9)  Dallas#
```

Age, and *Metric* columns that the VINES routing table has. If a neighbor were connected to a LAN interface (none shown here), the neighbor table would show the neighbor's MAC address as learned from its keepalives.

To get detailed information about the operation of VINES on a router, we can use the **show vines interface** command. The output of the command on Dallas is shown in Figure 11-8. The output starts with global parameters and then moves to interface parameters. The VINES address of Dallas is 301AD4BF:0001 (Line 2). The next client that sends a VINES ARP received by Dallas will get assigned the address of 301AD4BF:8001; we know from this address that Dallas has not yet assigned any VINES addresses.

We will use the Ethernet0 interface to cover the VINES interface parameters (Figure 11-8, Line 35). VINES packets are being encapsulated with ARPA (Ethernet_II) frame headers and trailers (Line 36); this is the same encapsulation used by IP. The metric for Ethernet0 is 2 (Line 37). Dallas will respond to VINES ARP requests received on this interface (Line 39), and Dallas will behave like a server if no server exists on the network (Line 40). The routing update interval is 90 seconds (Line 45). Our test internetwork has no real VINES nodes (Lines 46 and 47), and there are no VINES neighbors connected to the Ethernet LAN (Line 48).

The **show** commands described here are good ways of verifying the configuration of VINES; however, they do very little for verifying VINES connectivity—for that we need to use the VINES ping application. Three ways of doing an IOS VINES ping are as follows:

1. Use the normal **ping** command with a VINES address.
2. Use the **ping vines** command with a VINES address.
3. Use an extended ping, and type **vines** when prompted for a protocol.

Figure 11-8
Show VINES interface output on Dallas.

```
1)   Dallas#show vines interface
2)   VINES address is 301AD4BF:0001
3)     Next client will be 301AD4BF:8001
4)     Addresses are displayed in hexadecimal format.
5)     Slowest update interval is 90 seconds
6)     Roll Call timer queue:
7)  Serial1 up, line protocol up, network layer up
8)     Interface metric is 0230 [35] (7.0000 seconds)
9)     Split horizon is enabled
10)    ARP processing is dynamic, currently active, state is serv-
       ice
11)    Serverless is dynamic, currently active
12)    Redirect interval is 1000 ms.
13)    Special propagation of broadcasts is dynamic, currently
       active
14)    Outgoing access list is not set
15)    Fast switching is enabled
16)    Routing updates every 90 seconds. Next in 30 seconds.
17)    Nodes present: 0 5.5x servers, 0 5.5x routers, 0 5.5x
                      clients
18)                  0 4.11 servers, 1 4.11 routers, 0 4.11
                      clients
19)    Neighbors:
20)      0 301AD4AF:0001
21) Serial0 up, line protocol up, network layer up
22)    Interface metric is 02D0 [45] (9.0000 seconds)
23)    Split horizon is enabled
24)    ARP processing is dynamic, currently active, state is serv-
       ice
25)    Serverless is dynamic, currently active
26)    Redirect interval is 1000 ms.
27)    Special propagation of broadcasts is dynamic, currently
       active
28)    Outgoing access list is not set
29)    Fast switching is enabled
30)    Routing updates every 90 seconds. Next in 29 seconds.
31)    Nodes present: 0 5.5x servers, 0 5.5x routers, 0 5.5x
                      clients
32)                  0 4.11 servers, 1 4.11 routers, 0 4.11
                      clients
33)    Neighbors:
34)      0 301AD204:0001
35) Ethernet0 up, line protocol up, network layer up
36)    VINES broadcast encapsulation is ARPA
37)    Interface metric is 0020 [2] (0.4000 seconds)
38)    Split horizon is enabled
39)    ARP processing is dynamic, currently active, state is serv-
       ice
40)    Serverless is dynamic, currently active
41)    Redirect interval is 1000 ms.
42)    Special propagation of broadcasts is dynamic, currently
       active
43)    Outgoing access list is not set
44)    Fast switching is enabled
45)    Routing updates every 90 seconds. Next in 28 seconds.
```

Figure 11-8

Show VINES interface output on Dallas.

```
46)    Nodes present: 0 5.5x servers, 0 5.5x routers, 0 5.5x
               clients
47)               1 0 4.11 servers, 0 4.11 routers, 0 4.11
               clients
48)    Neighbors: none.
49) Dallas#
```

Figure 11-9 shows examples of all three options for doing an IOS VINES ping. The VINES pings are being done from Dallas, and the destination address is that of Austin as shown with the **show vines neighbor** command in Figure 11-7.

When the normal ping is used for the VINES ping (Line 1), we depend on IOS recognizing that the address that we have typed is a VINES

Figure 11-9

VINES ping examples.

```
1)  Dallas#ping 301ad204:1
2)
3)  Type escape sequence to abort.
4)  Sending 5, 100-byte Vines Echoes to 301AD204:0001, timeout is
    2 seconds:
5)  !!!!!
6)  Success rate is 100 percent (5/5), round-trip min/avg/max =
    36/36/36 ms
7)  Dallas#ping vines 301ad204:1
8)
9)  Type escape sequence to abort.
10) Sending 5, 100-byte Vines Echoes to 301AD204:0001, timeout is
    2 seconds:
11) !!!!!
12) Success rate is 100 percent (5/5), round-trip min/avg/max =
    36/37/44 ms
13) Dallas#ping
14) Protocol [ip]: vines
15) Target Vines address: 301ad204:1
16) Repeat count [5]: <Enter>
17) Datagram size [100]: <Enter>
18) Timeout in seconds [2]: <Enter>
19) Pacing interval in seconds (0 = no pacing) [0]: <Enter>
20) Verbose [n]: <Enter>
21) Type escape sequence to abort.
22) Sending 5, 100-byte Vines Echoes to 301AD204:0001, timeout is
    2 seconds:
23) !!!!!
24) Success rate is 100 percent (5/5), round-trip min/avg/max =
    36/36/36 ms
25) Dallas#
```

address. IOS correctly interprets the addresses as VINES based on its format, and then IOS does the VINES ping by sending five VINES echoes to Austin and receiving five replies. An exclamation point (!) indicates the successful reception of a ping reply from the target host (Line 5); if no reply were to be received, IOS would display a period (.) instead. The success rate and response time information is given on the last line (Line 6).

Using the **ping vines** command (Line 7) tells IOS that the address in the command is a VINES address so that IOS does not have to figure it out. The result is the same as that of the normal ping.

We invoke an extended ping by typing the **ping** command without an address (Line 13), and then IOS prompts us for the protocol (Line 14). Entering **vines** at the protocol prompt will cause IOS to ask for a VINES destination address (Line 15). The extended ping gives us the opportunity to change the number of echoes sent, the size of the echoes, and the reply timeout before actually performing the ping operation. With the default parameters, the extended ping process is the same as the one for the first two pings.

11.5   VINES Configuration Summary

In order to configure VINES on a Cisco router, we first use the **vines routing** command to start the VINES routing process. We must then enable VINES on individual interfaces with the **vines metric** command.

The VINES internetwork created by our configuration effort is shown in Figure 11-10.

Figure 11-11 shows the VINES-specific commands from Dallas's running configuration; Figure 11-12 shows FortWorth's VINES-specific commands taken from the running configuration; and Figure 11-13 shows the VINES-specific commands from Austin.

The VINES address shown after each of the **vines routing** commands was selected automatically by IOS; we did not enter it, but we could have. The VINES metric shown after each of the **vines metric** commands was selected automatically by IOS based on the bandwidth. We did not enter the metric either, but we could have.

Figure 11-10
VINES three-router
internetwork.

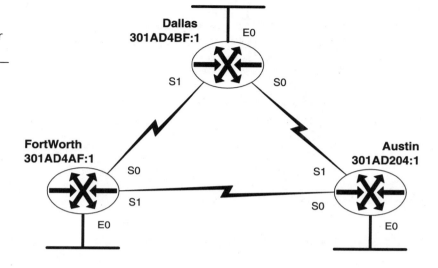

Figure 11-11
Dallas VINES con-
figuration com-
mands.

```
1)  Dallas#show running-config [Some text has been omitted.]
2)  !
3)  vines routing 301AD4BF:0001
4)  !
5)  interface Ethernet0
6)   vines metric 2
7)  !
8)  interface Serial0
9)   vines metric 45
10) !
11) interface Serial1
12)  vines metric 35
13) !
14) Dallas#
```

Figure 11-12
FortWorth VINES
configuration com-
mands.

```
1)  FortWorth#show running-config [Some text has been omitted.]
2)  !
3)  vines routing 301AD4AF:0001
4)  !
5)  interface Ethernet0
6)   vines metric 2
7)  !
8)  interface Serial0
9)   vines metric 35
10) !
11) interface Serial1
12)  vines metric 45
13) !
14) FortWorth#
```

Figure 11-13
Austin VINES configuration commands.

```
1)  Austin#show running-config [Some text has been omitted.]
2)  !
3)  vines routing 301AD204:0001
4)  !
5)  interface Ethernet0
6)    vines metric 2
7)  !
8)  interface Serial0
9)    vines metric 45
10) !
11) interface Serial1
12)   vines metric 45
13) !
14) Austin#
```

11.6   VINES Removal

We are going to leave VINES running on our test internetwork; however, if we wanted to stop the VINES routing process on a router, we could enter the following global configuration command.

```
no vines routing
```

The **no vines routing** command will remove, from the running configuration, the commands dealing with VINES routing. These commands include those that define VINES metrics.

12

Configuring Transparent Bridging

A Cisco router can be configured to perform *transparent bridging* when the router must forward frames for protocols that cannot be routed or are not being routed. Some protocols do not have logical addressing at layer 3 of their protocol stack. Since packet routing depends on layer-3 addressing, these protocols cannot be routed; they must be bridged. A bridging process forwards frames based on the destination MAC address in the frame header (layer 2), and all LAN frame headers have MAC addresses regardless of the protocol encapsulated in the frame. Some examples of nonroutable protocols are NetBEUI, LAT, and SNA.

12.1 Transparent Bridging Overview

In Chapter 2, where we covered the general operation of a bridge, we mentioned that a router running transparent bridging learns the location of hosts based on source MAC addresses, and it floods, forwards, and filters frames based on destination MAC addresses. Remember that a bridge always forwards a broadcast frame. A Cisco router running transparent bridging does one other thing—*loop avoidance,* which is done with the *Spanning Tree Protocol* (STP). To see why we need the spanning tree protocol, let us examine what happens when we do not have it.

Figure 12-1 shows three bridges (routers running bridging) configured in a loop. Host 1 has just transmitted a broadcast frame. FortWorth forwards the broadcast frame out from both of its serial interfaces. The first forwarded broadcast frame (Broadcast 1) goes to Dallas. Dallas forwards the frame out from its other two interfaces. Austin receives Broadcast 1 and forwards it out from its other two interfaces. The Broadcast 1 frame returns to FortWorth and gets forwarded yet again, including back onto the Ethernet LAN from which it originated. The second forwarded broadcast frame (Broadcast 2) from FortWorth goes to Austin where it gets forwarded onto the Austin Ethernet LAN and to Dallas. Dallas forwards the Broadcast 2 frame onto its Ethernet LAN and back to FortWorth, where it gets forwarded back onto the Ethernet LAN from which it originated. The broadcast frame has now appeared on the Ethernet LAN three times—the original time and the two times that it looped around. As a matter of fact, unless some sort of manual intervention is performed, the frame will continue looping forever while the bridges are happily doing their job. This situation is called a *broadcast storm,* which causes

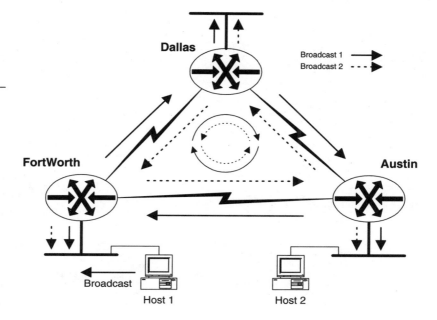

Figure 12-1
Bridged network without spanning tree protocol.

extreme congestion and can cause a network outage by using all available bandwidth.

The *spanning tree protocol* defines a form of communication to be used among the bridges of a network. The bridges use special frames called *Bridge Protocol Data Units* (BPDUs) to communicate with each other and build a logically loop-free network. The loop-free network takes the form of a tree; it has branches that extend from a root. Each bridge chooses a *Bridge ID,* which is usually the MAC address of one of its interfaces, and assigns a cost to each of its interfaces. Each bridge is also assigned a priority. The bridges transmit the BPDUs out from all of their interfaces. Using the BPDUs, the bridges select a bridge to be the root of the spanning tree. The bridge with the lowest priority becomes the root of the spanning tree; if multiple bridges have the same priority, the one with the lowest bridge ID becomes the root. The bridges then form the branches by selecting the lowest cost path from each bridge to the root bridge. A bridge's interface that is not part of the lowest cost path to the root bridge gets put into blocking mode. An interface in blocking mode cannot receive or transmit bridged frames, but it can still receive and transmit BPDUs.

Figure 12-2
Bridged network
with spanning tree
protocol.

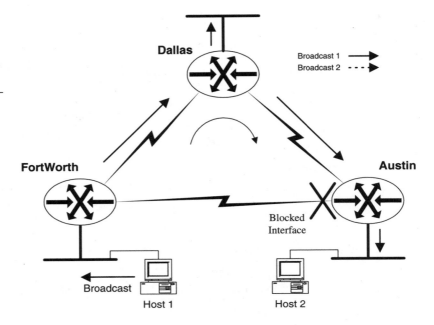

Figure 12-2 shows the three bridges in a loop formation; only this time, the spanning tree protocol has been enabled on all of the active interfaces. Dallas has been elected to be the root bridge, and one of Austin's serial interfaces is in blocking mode. Now when Host 1 sends a broadcast frame, FortWorth forwards down a nonblocked path to Dallas. Dallas forwards the broadcast frame onto its Ethernet LAN and to Austin. Since Austin's other serial interface is in blocking mode, the broadcast frame is forwarded on the Ethernet LAN. That is as far as the broadcast frame is forwarded; it shows up only once on each LAN. The spanning tree protocol has defeated the bridging loop.

A bridge's interface has three possible modes: blocking, forwarding, and learning. When a bridge configuration change occurs, the bridges must rebuild the spanning tree. While the spanning tree is being rebuilt, some of the interfaces of the bridges will get placed into learning mode. Traffic cannot be forwarded out from an interface that is in learning mode.

There are two versions of the spanning tree protocol: the DEC version and the IEEE (Institute of Electrical and Electronics Engineers) version. They work basically the same way, and it is not very important which one we use; however, all of the bridges of a network should run the same version since the versions are not compatible with each other.

There you have the bare-bones necessities of the spanning tree protocol. We are now going to cover the basic IOS commands for configuring transparent bridging.

12.2   Transparent Bridging Configuration

We are going to implement transparent bridging on our test internetwork; the configuration of transparent bridging in IOS requires running the spanning tree protocol. For our implementation, we are going to use the IEEE STP, and we are going to force Dallas to become the root bridge by setting its priority to its lowest possible value. Figure 12-3 shows the planned bridging configuration.

The general process of configuring transparent bridging involves creating a bridge group and then making a router's interfaces members of the bridge group—a *bridge group* is just a group of interfaces that have bridging enabled, and creating one starts the spanning tree protocol. We use the global configuration command **bridge protocol** to create a bridge group and the **bridge-group** interface configuration command to make an interface a member of the bridge group. A bridge group has a number, and the number must be included on just about every transpar-

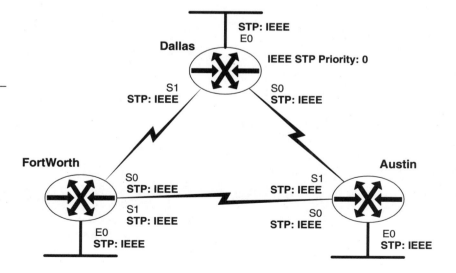

Figure 12-3
Internetwork with planned bridging configuration.

ent bridging command to uniquely identify which group we are configuring. The bridge group number is significant only on the local router.

According to Figure 12-3, we are going to run bridging on all of the active interfaces by starting the spanning tree protocol on them, and we are going to set the priority of Dallas to its lowest possible value, 0, so that Dallas will become the spanning tree root bridge. Figure 12-4 shows the configuration of Dallas, Figure 12-5 shows the configuration of FortWorth, and Figure 12-6 shows the configuration of Austin.

The IEEE spanning tree protocol is now running on all of the interfaces. If we had wanted to run the DEC spanning tree protocol, we would have used the keyword **dec** on the **bridge protocol** command. As was mentioned before, it does not really matter which spanning tree protocol we run, as long as all of the bridges run the same one.

Since we wanted to make Dallas the root bridge, we set the STP priority of the bridge group on Dallas to 0 with the **bridge priority** global configuration command (Figure 12-4, Line 4).

Figure 12-4
Transparent bridging configuration of Dallas.

```
1)   Dallas#configure terminal
2)   Enter configuration commands, one per line. End with CNTL/Z.
3)   Dallas(config)#bridge 1 protocol ieee
4)   Dallas(config)#bridge 1 priority 0
5)   Dallas(config)#interface ethernet0
6)   Dallas(config-if)#bridge-group 1
7)   Dallas(config-if)#interface serial0
8)   Dallas(config-if)#bridge-group 1
9)   Dallas(config-if)#interface serial1
10)  Dallas(config-if)#bridge-group 1
11)  Dallas(config-if)#<Ctrl-Z>
12)  Dallas#
```

Figure 12-5
Transparent bridging configuration of FortWorth.

```
1)   FortWorth#configure terminal
2)   Enter configuration commands, one per line. End with CNTL/Z.
3)   FortWorth(config)#bridge 1 protocol ieee
4)   FortWorth(config)#interface ethernet0
5)   FortWorth(config-if)#bridge-group 1
6)   FortWorth(config-if)#interface serial0
7)   FortWorth(config-if)#bridge-group 1
8)   FortWorth(config-if)#interface serial1
9)   FortWorth(config-if)#bridge-group 1
10)  FortWorth(config-if)#<Ctrl-Z>
11)  FortWorth#
```

Figure 12-6
Transparent bridging configuration of Austin.

```
1)  Austin#configure terminal
2)  Enter configuration commands, one per line. End with CNTL/Z.
3)  Austin(config)#bridge 1 protocol ieee
4)  Austin(config)#interface ethernet0
5)  Austin(config-if)#bridge-group 1
6)  Austin(config-if)#interface serial0
7)  Austin(config-if)#bridge-group 1
8)  Austin(config-if)#interface serial1
9)  Austin(config-if)#bridge-group 1
10) Austin(config-if)#<Ctrl-Z>
11) Austin#
```

The bridge group number for all of the routers is 1; we used the same number on all of the routers just for consistency—this is not a requirement. Notice that the bridge group number is specified on all of the bridging-related commands.

By default, when transparent bridging is running on a Cisco router, all traffic for protocols that are not being routed is bridged. For example, if a router did not have IPX routing enabled, it would bridge any IPX frames that it received.

12.3 Transparent Bridging Verification

We can use several **show** commands to verify the configuration and operation of transparent bridging on a router. The commands we look at in this section are as follows:

- **show bridge group**
- **show spanning-tree**
- **show bridge**

The **show bridge group** command is used to find out which bridge groups have been configured on a router and which interfaces are members of each group. Figure 12-7 shows the output of the command on Dallas. We see that bridge group 1 has been configured and is using the IEEE STP (Line 3). Ethernet0, Serial0, and Serial1 (Lines 5, 6, and 7, respectively) are all members of bridge group 1. All of the interfaces are in forwarding mode.

Figure 12-7
Show bridge
group output on
Dallas.

```
1)  Dallas#show bridge group
2)
3)  Bridge Group 1 is running the IEEE compatible Spanning Tree
    protocol
4)
5)  Port 2 (Ethernet0) of bridge group 1 is forwarding
6)  Port 6 (Serial0) of bridge group 1 is forwarding
7)  Port 7 (Serial1) of bridge group 1 is forwarding
8)
9)  Dallas#
```

Use the **show spanning-tree** command to display information about the operation of the spanning tree protocol on a router. Figure 12-8 shows the output of the command on Dallas. The Bridge ID for Dallas is the MAC address of its Ethernet0 interface, AA00.0400.0104 (Line 4). This is the MAC address that was assigned to Ethernet0 when we configured DECnet on Dallas in Chapter 10. The STP priority of Dallas is 0 (Line 4), and Dallas is the root of the spanning tree (Line 6). The output includes parameters for each interface that is running STP. We will take a look at Ethernet0, which is in forwarding mode (Line 12). The port cost for Ethernet0 is 100; this is the default cost as calculated by STP. The default cost of a port is calculated by dividing the interface bandwidth into 1,000,000,000. For example, 1,000,000,000/10,000,000 equals 100; and 1,000,000,000/1,544,000 equals 647 (Line 27). The path to the spanning tree root is maintained for each interface; since Dallas is the root, the designated root address relative to Ethernet0 is its own (Line 14).

Figure 12-9 shows the output of the **show spanning-tree** command on Austin. Austin's priority is 32768 (Line 4). This is the default priority for a bridge running the IEEE spanning tree protocol; the default priority for a bridge running the DEC spanning tree protocol is 128. The bridge ID for Austin is the MAC address of the Ethernet0 interface that was assigned by the Chapter 10 DECnet configuration, AA00.0400.0108 (Line 4). Austin knows that Dallas is the root bridge (Line 6), and the path to reach the root bridge is out from the Serial1 interface (Line 7). To defeat our bridging loop, STP has caused Austin's Serial0 interface to go into blocking mode (Line 20).

Based on the output of the **show spanning-tree** commands, a logical depiction of our example internetwork's spanning tree is shown in Figure 12-10. Dallas is shown as the root; a root bridge can never have any interfaces in blocking mode. The path between FortWorth and Austin has been pruned from the tree. This means that bridged frames will not be forwarded across the link.

Figure 12-8

Show spanning-tree output on Dallas.

```
1)   Dallas#show spanning-tree
2)
3)   Bridge Group 1 is executing the IEEE compatible Spanning Tree
     protocol
4)     Bridge Identifier has priority 0, address aa00.0400.0104
5)     Configured hello time 2, max age 20, forward delay 15
6)     We are the root of the spanning tree
7)     Topology change flag set, detected flag set
8)     Times:  hold 1, topology change 30, notification 30
9)             hello 2, max age 20, forward delay 15, aging 300
10)    Timers: hello 2, topology change 14, notification 0
11)
12) Port 2 (Ethernet0) of bridge group 1 is forwarding
13)    Port path cost 100, Port priority 128
14)    Designated root has priority 0, address aa00.0400.0104
15)    Designated bridge has priority 0, address aa00.0400.0104
16)    Designated port is 2, path cost 0
17)    Timers: message age 0, forward delay 0, hold 0
18)
19) Port 6 (Serial0) of bridge group 1 is forwarding
20)    Port path cost 3906, Port priority 128
21)    Designated root has priority 0, address aa00.0400.0104
22)    Designated bridge has priority 0, address aa00.0400.0104
23)    Designated port is 6, path cost 0
24)    Timers: message age 0, forward delay 0, hold 0
25)
26) Port 7 (Serial1) of bridge group 1 is forwarding
27)    Port path cost 647, Port priority 128
28)    Designated root has priority 0, address aa00.0400.0104
29)    Designated bridge has priority 0, address aa00.0400.0104
30)    Designated port is 7, path cost 0
31)    Timers: message age 0, forward delay 0, hold 0
32)
33) Dallas#
```

All bridges maintain a *bridging table* (or bridge forwarding table), which has a list of all of the MAC addresses that the bridge has learned. Issue the **show bridge** command to see the bridging table. An example output of the command on Dallas is shown in Figure 12-11. Dallas has allocated memory for 300 entries, of which nine are used (Line 3). A router will dynamically allocate more memory in increments of 300 entries as the bridging table grows. The MAC addresses of the nine entries are shown on Lines 9 through 17. Each of the hosts was learned from the Ethernet LAN. The *Age* column indicates the number of minutes that have elapsed since a frame to or from the host was processed. The *RX count* and *TX count* columns show the number of frames received from the host and the number of frames forwarded to the host, respectively. Our test internetwork is not very busy.

Figure 12-9
Show spanning-tree output on Austin.

```
1)  Austin#show spanning-tree
2)
3)  Bridge Group 1 is executing the IEEE compatible Spanning Tree
    protocol
4)    Bridge Identifier has priority 32768, address
      aa00.0400.0108
5)    Configured hello time 2, max age 20, forward delay 15
6)    Current root has priority 0, address aa00.0400.0104
7)    Root port is 7 (Serial1), cost of root path is 3906
8)    Topology change flag set, detected flag not set
9)    Times:  hold 1, topology change 30, notification 30
10)           hello 2, max age 20, forward delay 15, aging 300
11)   Timers: hello 0, topology change 0, notification 0
12)
13) Port 2 (Ethernet0) of bridge group 1 is forwarding
14)    Port path cost 100, Port priority 128
15)    Designated root has priority 0, address aa00.0400.0104
16)    Designated bridge has priority 32768, address
       aa00.0400.0108
17)    Designated port is 2, path cost 3906
18)    Timers: message age 0, forward delay 0, hold 0
19)
20) Port 6 (Serial0) of bridge group 1 is blocking
21)    Port path cost 17857, Port priority 128
22)    Designated root has priority 0, address aa00.0400.0104
23)    Designated bridge has priority 32768, address
       aa00.0400.0204
24)    Designated port is 7, path cost 647
25)    Timers: message age 2, forward delay 0, hold 0
26)
27) Port 7 (Serial1) of bridge group 1 is forwarding
28)    Port path cost 3906, Port priority 128
29)    Designated root has priority 0, address aa00.0400.0104
30)    Designated bridge has priority 0, address aa00.0400.0104
31)    Designated port is 6, path cost 0
32)    Timers: message age 1, forward delay 0, hold 0
33)
34) Austin#
```

Examining a bridging table is the best way of finding out if traffic from a host system is being seen and bridged by a router running transparent bridging; however, we must know the MAC address of the host before checking its status.

12.4 Transparent Bridging Configuration Summary

We generally need transparent bridging when our internetwork must carry traffic that cannot be routed. All we have to do to configure trans-

Figure 12-10

Example of inter-network spanning tree.

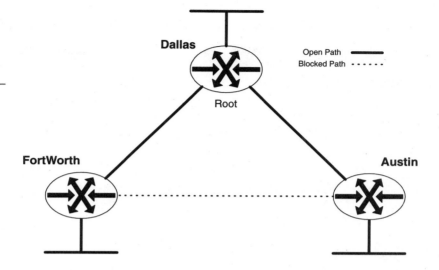

parent bridging is use the **bridge protocol** command to create a bridge group and start the spanning tree protocol; then, use the **bridge-group** command on the interfaces that are to have bridging enabled.

Figure 12-12 shows the bridging-specific commands from Dallas's running configuration, Figure 12-13 shows FortWorth's bridging-specific commands taken from the running configuration, and Figure 12-14 shows the bridging-specific commands from Austin's running configuration.

Figure 12-11

Show bridge output.

```
1)  Dallas#show bridge
2)
3)  Total of 300 station blocks, 291 free
4)  Codes: P - permanent, S - self
5)
6)  Bridge Group 1:
7)
8)      Address      Action    Interface    Age    RX count TX count
9)   00a0.c996.eef7  forward   Ethernet0     0        1        0
10)  00a0.c9dd.1804  forward   Ethernet0     2        1        0
11)  00a0.c9a5.e4c2  forward   Ethernet0     0        1        0
12)  00a0.c9a5.e4c8  forward   Ethernet0     2        1        0
13)  00a0.c9a5.e4ae  forward   Ethernet0     1        1        0
14)  00a0.c9a5.e4a9  forward   Ethernet0     0        1        0
15)  00a0.c9ce.f5ad  forward   Ethernet0     1        1        0
16)  00a0.c9a4.730f  forward   Ethernet0     0        1        0
17)  0090.273c.d93a  forward   Ethernet0     2        0        0
18)
19) Dallas#
```

Figure 12-12
Dallas transparent bridging configuration commands.

```
1)  Dallas#show running-config [Some text has been omitted.]
2)  !
3)  interface Ethernet0
4)   bridge-group 1
5)  !
6)  interface Serial0
7)   bridge-group 1
8)  !
9)  interface Serial1
10)  bridge-group 1
11) !
12) bridge 1 protocol ieee
13) bridge 1 priority 0
14) !
15) Dallas#
```

Figure 12-13
FortWorth transparent bridging configuration commands.

```
1)  FortWorth#show running-config [Some text has been omitted.]
2)  !
3)  interface Ethernet0
4)   bridge-group 1
5)  !
6)  interface Serial0
7)   bridge-group 1
8)  !
9)  interface Serial1
10)  bridge-group 1
11) !
12) bridge 1 protocol ieee
13) !
14) FortWorth#
```

Figure 12-14
Austin transparent bridging configuration commands.

```
1)  Austin#show running-config [Some text has been omitted.]
2)  !
3)  interface Ethernet0
4)   bridge-group 1
5)  !
6)  interface Serial0
7)   bridge-group 1
8)  !
9)  interface Serial1
10)  bridge-group 1
11) !
12) bridge 1 protocol ieee
13) !
14) Austin#
```

The configurations are practically identical except for the priority change on Dallas (Figure 12-12, Line 13).

Before we go on to our next topic, there is one other thing about our example configuration that should be mentioned. A bridge processes frames based on the MAC addresses in the frame headers; we are running bridging on our serial interfaces, and serial interfaces do not have MAC addresses. Our routers are actually running *encapsulated bridging* on the serial interfaces. When a router forwards a bridged frame out a serial interface, the router encapsulates the entire frame inside another frame using whatever encapsulation type has been configured on the interface. All of our serial interfaces are using HDLC encapsulation; therefore, a bridged frame gets placed inside an HDLC frame to traverse a serial link. The router on the other side of the serial link removes the encapsulated frame from inside the HDLC frame and forwards it out another interface. The Cisco router does this automatically.

12.5   Transparent Bridging Removal

We are going to leave transparent bridging running on our internetwork; however, if we wanted to stop the bridging process on a router, we could enter the following global configuration command.

```
no bridge group
```

The *group* parameter is the bridge group number that was used to create the bridge group and start STP. The **no bridge** command will remove, from the running configuration, the commands dealing with bridging and the spanning tree protocol. These commands include those that define spanning tree parameters and bridge group membership.

Configuring
Frame Relay

Frame relay is a layer-2 WAN protocol. Cisco routers can be configured for connection to frame relay networks. In this chapter, we examine the characteristics of frame relay that are important to its configuration on a Cisco router.

13.1   Frame Relay Overview

Connection to a frame relay network is done with a local loop from the serial interface of a router to one of a service provider's frame relay switches. Communication across a frame relay network uses *virtual circuits,* which are built by a service provider from a router's serial interface, through a collection of frame relay switches, to another router's serial interface. Virtual circuits that are programmed into a service provider's network to stay active all the time are called *permanent virtual circuits* (PVCs). IOS also supports *switched virtual circuits* (SVCs), which become active only when they are used; however, SVCs are not yet widely available from frame relay service providers. We use only PVCs in this chapter.

Many PVCs can be built on a single local loop. PVCs are addressed with *Data Link Connection Identifiers* (DLCIs) at layer 2. From our perspective, each PVC has two DLCIs—one at each end. From a router's perspective, each PVC needs only one DLCI—the local one. When a router wants to transmit a packet to another router across a PVC, the router must know the local DLCI of the PVC on which the packet is to be transmitted. For this reason, some people say that DLCIs are locally significant.

Figure 13-1 shows a basic frame relay network. There are three routers—Dallas, FortWorth, and Austin. Each router has a local loop to the frame relay network. There are two PVCs—one from Dallas to FortWorth and one from Dallas to Austin. Let us take a closer look at the PVC between Dallas and FortWorth. The Dallas end of the PVC has DLCI 100 and the FortWorth end has DLCI 101. These DLCIs, since they are on different local loops, do not have to be different, but they usually are, anyway. When Dallas wants to send a packet to FortWorth, Dallas must transmit the packet out the serial interface that contains the PVC, and the frame header must contain the local DLCI, 100. The switch knows that the path of the PVC with DLCI 100 on the Dallas side is supposed to go to the switch connected to FortWorth. The switch connected to FortWorth knows the path of the PVC extends across the local

Figure 13-1
Basic frame relay
network.

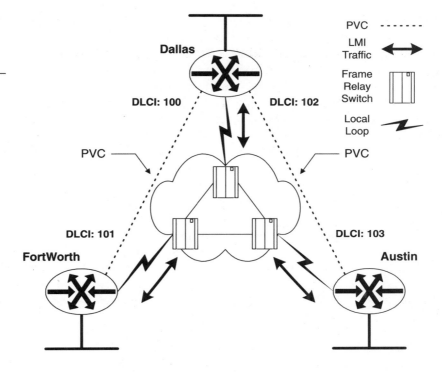

loop to FortWorth and the DLCI of the PVC on the local loop is 101. The switch puts the DLCI 101 into the frame header so the FortWorth router knows, when it receives the frame, that the frame came in on the PVC with local DLCI 101.

Dallas has two PVCs coming in on the same local loop; therefore, these PVCs must have different local DLCIs. The frame relay topology shown in Figure 13-1 is called a *partial-meshed* network because not all of the routers have PVCs to all of the other routers. We could also call this particular topology a *hub-and-spoke* network because there is one router (the hub) that has a connection to each of the other routers (the spokes), and traffic from a spoke router must go through the hub to reach another spoke router. A *fully meshed* network has PVCs running between all of the router pairs; to make the Figure 13-1 frame relay topology into a fully meshed network, we would have to add a PVC between FortWorth and Austin.

Routers and switches maintain contact with each other using *Local Management Interface* (LMI). About every 10 seconds, routers and switches send an LMI keepalive across the local loop. If a router is receiving LMI keepalives from a switch, the router makes the line protocol of its interface up so the interface state will be up/up. If a Cisco router interface is connected to a frame relay network and the state of the interface is up/up, the router has a communication path to a frame relay switch. This has nothing to do with being able to reach another router on the other end of a PVC. By default, a Cisco router uses LMI to request a status report from the switch every six keepalives (about once a minute). The status report contains a list of each of the local loop's PVCs, their DLCIs, and their status.

There are two types of LMI that are widely used between routers and switches: Annex D and Gang of Four. *Annex D* is from the American National Standards Institute (ANSI). The *Gang of Four* LMI was jointly developed by Cisco, DIGITAL, Intel, and Stratacom. The router and the local switch must agree on the type of LMI they will use between them.

13.2   Frame Relay Configuration

There are two ways of configuring frame relay on a Cisco router. The first configuration method uses the classic, frame relay *nonbroadcast multiaccess* (NBMA) model. In this configuration, the frame relay network is treated as a multiaccess network like a LAN; however, unlike a LAN, a frame relay network has no broadcast capability. There is no frame relay broadcast address. All of the routers connected to the NBMA network share a network address such as an IP subnet address or an AppleTalk cable range. The second configuration method involves treating each of the PVCs as a separate logical point-to-point network, which is done by creating a *subinterface* for each PVC. The subinterface method requires more network addresses because each PVC has its own network address.

Of the two methods, the subinterface method is usually the recommended one. Both configuration methods are briefly described in the following sections.

We are going to move our IP traffic from the point-to-point serial links to a frame relay network. To do this, we are going to do something that is not normally recommended in a production network. We are going to remove the IP addresses from the point-to-point serial links, and we are going to stop the current IP routing protocol, OSPF, which was configured in Chapter 7. Figure 13-2 shows the IP configuration changes on Dallas, FortWorth, and Austin.

Figure 13-2
Removal of IP from point-to-point serial links.

```
1)  Dallas#configure terminal
2)  Enter configuration commands, one per line. End with CNTL/Z.
3)  Dallas(config)#no router ospf 100
4)  Dallas(config)#interface serial0
5)  Dallas(config-if)#no ip address
6)  Dallas(config-if)#interface serial1
7)  Dallas(config-if)#no ip address
8)  Dallas(config-if)#<Ctrl-Z>
9)  Dallas#
10) ───────
11) FortWorth#configure terminal
12) Enter configuration commands, one per line. End with CNTL/Z.
13) FortWorth(config)#no router ospf 200
14) FortWorth(config)#interface serial0
15) FortWorth(config-if)#no ip address
16) FortWorth(config-if)#interface serial1
17) FortWorth(config-if)#no ip address
18) FortWorth(config-if)#<Ctrl-Z>
19) FortWorth#
20) ───────
21) Austin#configure terminal
22) Enter configuration commands, one per line. End with CNTL/Z.
23) Austin(config)#no router ospf 300
24) Austin(config)#interface serial0
25) Austin(config-if)#no ip address
26) Austin(config-if)#interface serial1
27) Austin(config-if)#no ip address
28) Austin(config-if)#<Ctrl-Z>
29) Austin#
```

After issuing the commands in Figure 13-2, IP is no longer being routed across our WANs. We will restore IP connectivity by configuring frame relay on the routers.

13.2.1 Frame Relay NBMA Configuration and Verification

Frame relay NBMA configuration is very easy. In a Cisco-router internetwork, the only special configuration task we really have to do is tell IOS to perform frame relay encapsulation on the serial interface to which our frame relay local loop is connected. The **encapsulation frame-relay** interface configuration command does that. We are going to implement IP routing on a frame relay network, shown in Figure 13-3, to illustrate the basics of frame relay NBMA configuration.

Since an NBMA network is treated as a single network with multiple hosts, all of the serial interfaces connected to the frame relay network

Figure 13-3

Frame relay NBMA
internetwork.

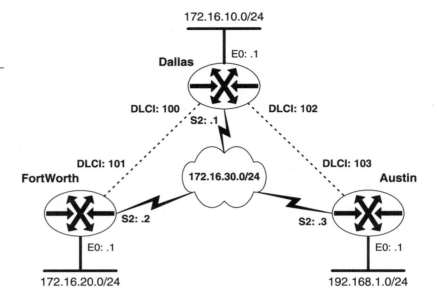

are on the same IP subnet, 172.16.30.0/24. The frame relay local loops
are connected to the Serial2 interfaces of each router. The PVCs are
arranged in a partially meshed topology; therefore, we can expect traffic
between FortWorth and Austin to go through Dallas.

Figure 13-4 shows the commands for the configuration on Dallas,
Figure 13-5 shows the FortWorth configuration commands, and Figure
13-6 shows the Austin configuration commands.

The **encapsulation frame-relay** command (Line 4) tells IOS that
the Serial2 interface is connected to a frame relay network, and any
packets that are transmitted out from the interface should be encapsulated with a frame relay header and trailer. There are two types of
frame relay encapsulation. The first type is Cisco's own encapsulation,

Figure 13-4

Frame relay NBMA
configuration on
Dallas.

```
1)  Dallas#configure terminal
2)  Enter configuration commands, one per line. End with CNTL/Z.
3)  Dallas(config)#interface serial2
4)  Dallas(config-if)#encapsulation frame-relay
5)  Dallas(config-if)#ip address 172.16.30.1 255.255.255.0
6)  Dallas(config-if)#no shutdown
7)  Dallas(config-if)#router rip
8)  Dallas(config-router)#network 172.16.0.0
9)  Dallas(config-router)#<Ctrl-Z>
10) Dallas#
```

Figure 13-5

Frame relay NBMA configuration on FortWorth.

```
1)  FortWorth#configure terminal
2)  Enter configuration commands, one per line. End with CNTL/Z.
3)  FortWorth(config)#interface serial2
4)  FortWorth(config-if)#encapsulation frame-relay
5)  FortWorth(config-if)#ip address 172.16.30.2 255.255.255.0
6)  FortWorth(config-if)#no shutdown
7)  FortWorth(config-if)#router rip
8)  FortWorth(config-router)#network 172.16.0.0
9)  FortWorth(config-router)#<Ctrl-Z>
10) FortWorth#
```

which is the default. Cisco's frame-relay encapsulation can be used when both routers on each end of a PVC are Cisco routers. The second type is defined by the Internet Engineering Task Force (IETF); we use IETF frame-relay encapsulation when we have routers from multiple vendors on a PVC. We specify IETF encapsulation with the command **encapsulation frame-relay ietf**.

Each of the Serial2 interfaces now has an IP address from the 172.16.30.0/24 subnet (Line 5), and since the interfaces were shut down, we activated them with the **no shutdown** interface configuration command (Line 6). The interfaces actually came up when they started receiving LMI traffic from the frame relay switch. Because we removed our IP routing protocol in the preceding section, we needed to start one. We started RIP with the **router rip** global configuration command (Line 7) and the appropriate **network** router configuration commands.

We now have IP configured on the frame relay network, so let us check one of the IP routing tables. Figure 13-7 shows the IP routing table on the hub router, Dallas.

The routing table entry for 192.168.1.0/24 (Line 15) has a next-hop gateway address of 172.16.30.3. Dallas learned about this route via a

Figure 13-6

Frame relay NBMA configuration on Austin.

```
1)  Austin#configure terminal
2)  Enter configuration commands, one per line. End with CNTL/Z.
3)  Austin(config)#interface serial2
4)  Austin(config-if)#encapsulation frame-relay
5)  Austin(config-if)#ip address 172.16.30.3 255.255.255.0
6)  Austin(config-if)#no shutdown
7)  Austin(config-if)#router rip
8)  Austin(config-router)#network 172.16.0.0
9)  Austin(config-router)#network 192.168.1.0
10) Austin(config-router)#<Ctrl-Z>
11) Austin#
```

Figure 13-7

IP routing table on Dallas after NBMA configuration.

```
1)  Dallas#show ip route
2)  Codes: C - connected, S - static, I - IGRP, R - RIP,
           M - mobile, B - BGP
3)         D - EIGRP, EX - EIGRP external, O - OSPF, IA - OSPF
           inter area
4)         N1 - OSPF NSSA external type 1, N2 - OSPF NSSA exter-
           nal type 2
5)         E1 - OSPF external type 1, E2 - OSPF external type 2,
           E - EGP
6)         i - IS-IS, L1 - IS-IS level-1, L2 - IS-IS level-2,
           * - candidate default
7)         U - per-user static route, o - ODR
8)
9)  Gateway of last resort is not set
10)
11)     172.16.0.0/24 is subnetted, 3 subnets
12) C      172.16.30.0 is directly connected, Serial2
13) R      172.16.20.0 [120/1] via 172.16.30.2, 00:00:04, Serial2
14) C      172.16.10.0 is directly connected, Ethernet0
15) R   192.168.1.0/24 [120/1] via 172.16.30.3, 00:00:23, Serial2
16) Dallas#
```

RIP broadcast from Austin. When Dallas wants to forward a packet to the 172.16.30.3 address, it must have a layer-2 address to put into the frame header. For frame relay, this address is a DLCI; Dallas must know the local DLCI for the PVC that leads to Austin. In most cases, routers can automatically map the layer-3 addresses on the remote ends of PVCs to the local DLCIs of those PVCs using *inverse ARP*. We can see these mappings with the **show frame-relay map** command. Figure 13-8 shows the output of the command on Dallas.

Both entries in the map table of Figure 13-8 are listed as *dynamic*; they were learned with inverse ARP. When inverse ARP is used, a router sends an inverse ARP request on a PVC asking for the layer-3 address of the device on the other end. The router learns the local DLCI of the PVC to reach the layer-3 address by reading the DLCI of the other device's inverse ARP response packet. Inverse ARP is enabled by default.

Figure 13-8

Inverse ARP mappings on Dallas.

```
1)  Dallas#show frame-relay map
2)  Serial2 (up): ip 172.16.30.2 dlci 100(0x64,0x1840), dynamic,
3)                broadcast,, status defined, active
4)  Serial2 (up): ip 172.16.30.3 dlci 102(0x66,0x1860), dynamic,
5)                broadcast,, status defined, active
6)  Dallas#
```

A frame relay network has no broadcast address; therefore, when a router wants to send a broadcast packet across a frame relay network, the router can send the packet over just one PVC at a time. Both of the PVCs on Dallas have the broadcast capability turned on, as indicated by the *broadcast* parameter in the map entries (Figure 13-8, Lines 3 and 5). Dallas must transmit all of its RIP broadcasts twice out from the Serial2 interface—once for each PVC. The display of the mappings also shows us that both PVCs are active, as indicated by the word *active* on the entries.

We can also perform manual mappings with the **frame-relay map** interface configuration command. The **frame-relay map** command allows us to statically define the local DLCI to reach a network host. Normally the network host is one that is directly connected to the other end of a PVC. If we wanted to define a static mapping for a host with the IP address 172.16.30.3, the commands to do so would look like those in Figure 13-9, and the updating mappings are shown in Figure 13-10.

A static mapping replaces a dynamic, inverse ARP mapping in the frame-relay map table. On the **frame-relay map** command, we must specify a keyword for the network protocol and a corresponding address for which we are mapping a DLCI (Figure 13-9, Line 4). In our example, we are telling Dallas that the host with IP address 172.16.30.3 can be reached from the Serial2 interface on the PVC with DLCI 102. We included the **broadcast** keyword on the command so that IOS would send any necessary broadcast message across the PVC. Without the **broadcast** keyword, IOS would not send RIP updates on the PVC to

Figure 13-9
Static mapping configuration on Dallas.

```
1)  Dallas#configure terminal
2)  Enter configuration commands, one per line. End with CNTL/Z.
3)  Dallas(config)#interface serial2
4)  Dallas(config-if)#frame-relay map ip 172.16.30.3 102
                        broadcast
5)  Dallas(config-if)#<Ctrl-Z>
6)  Dallas#
```

Figure 13-10
Show frame-relay map output on Dallas.

```
1)  Dallas#show frame-relay map
2)  Serial2 (up): ip 172.16.30.2 dlci 100(0x64,0x1840), dynamic,
3)              broadcast,, status defined, active
4)  Serial2 (up): ip 172.16.30.3 dlci 102(0x66,0x1860), static,
5)              broadcast,
6)              CISCO, status defined, active
7)  Dallas#
```

Austin because RIP updates are broadcast packets. The frame relay map table indicates that broadcasts are enabled on the PVC to Austin (Figure 13-10, Line 5).

The map table also shows that Cisco's frame-relay encapsulation is being used on the PVC to Austin (Figure 13-10, Line 6). We can change the encapsulation on a single PVC by putting either the **ietf** keyword or the **cisco** keyword at the end of a **frame-relay map** command. By default, all PVCs use the encapsulation specified on the **encapsulation frame-relay** command.

In the overview of frame relay, we mentioned that there were two major types of LMI used between routers and frame relay switches—ANSI Annex D and Gang of Four. The type of LMI depends on how our service provider has provisioned the local switch. The default LMI on a Cisco router is the Gang of Four LMI; however, as of IOS version 11.3, the router can sense the LMI type and will automatically use whichever one the switch is sending. If we wanted to manually set the LMI type, we would use the **frame-relay lmi-type** interface configuration command. The form of the command for Gang of Four LMI is **frame-relay lmi-type cisco,** and the form of the command for ANSI Annex D LMI is **frame-relay lmi-type ansi**.

We can issue the **show frame-relay lmi** command to see LMI statistics and the type of LMI being used. Figure 13-11 shows the output on Dallas. The LMI type is given at the end of the first line displayed (Line 3). Our test internetwork is using ANSI Annex D LMI. The statistics are for types of LMI messages. Two that we have already mentioned are the **Status Enquiry** message and the **Status** message (Line 9). The router transmits a **Status Enquiry** message every six LMI keepalives by

Figure 13-11
Show frame-relay LMI output on Dallas.

```
1)  Dallas#show frame-relay lmi
2)
3)  LMI Statistics for interface Serial2 (Frame Relay DTE) LMI
    TYPE = ANSI
4)     Invalid Unnumbered info 0        Invalid Prot Disc 0
5)     Invalid dummy Call Ref 0         Invalid Msg Type 0
6)     Invalid Status Message 0         Invalid Lock Shift 0
7)     Invalid Information ID 0         Invalid Report IE Len 0
8)     Invalid Report Request 0         Invalid Keep IE Len 0
9)     Num Status Enq. Sent 29          Num Status msgs Rcvd 23
10)    Num Update Status Rcvd 0         Num Status Timeouts 7
11) Dallas#
```

default, and the switch is supposed to reply with a **Status** message containing the PVC DLCIs and their status.

We can see the status of all of the PVCs ourselves by issuing the **show frame-relay pvc** command. The output of this command is shown in Figure 13-12. From the output, we can see that Dallas has two PVCs, both coming into Serial2, and their DLCIs are 100 and 102 (Lines 5 and 14); the status of both PVCs is *ACTIVE*. We also get to see some statistics on the total number of bytes and packets transmitted and received per PVC.

We have checked many things about the frame relay operation itself, but we have yet to check the most basic thing on the router—the interface. Figure 13-13 shows the output of the **show interfaces** command for Serial2 on Dallas. The interface is up/up (Line 2) and it is using frame relay encapsulation (Line 6). Since IETF is not specified with the encapsulation, Cisco's frame-relay encapsulation is being used. The output contains a few statistics for LMI messages (Lines 7 and 8) and the type of LMI being used (Line 9).

Figure 13-12

Show frame-relay PVC output on Dallas.

```
1)  Dallas#show frame-relay pvc
2)
3)  PVC Statistics for interface Serial2 (Frame Relay DTE)
4)
5)  DLCI = 100, DLCI USAGE = LOCAL, PVC STATUS = ACTIVE,
    INTERFACE = Serial2
6)
7)     input pkts 11          output pkts 10        in bytes 1084
8)     out bytes 1014         dropped pkts 1        in FECN pkts 0
9)     in BECN pkts 0         out FECN pkts 0       out BECN pkts 0
10)    in DE pkts 0           out DE pkts 0
11)    out bcast pkts 10       out bcast bytes 1014
12)    pvc create time 00:03:46, last time pvc status changed
       00:03:06
13)
14) DLCI = 102, DLCI USAGE = LOCAL, PVC STATUS = ACTIVE,
    INTERFACE = Serial2
15)
16)    input pkts 10          output pkts 10        in bytes 1054
17)    out bytes 1014         dropped pkts 0        in FECN pkts 0
18)    in BECN pkts 0         out FECN pkts 0       out BECN pkts 0
19)    in DE pkts 0           out DE pkts 0
20)    out bcast pkts 10       out bcast bytes 1014
21)    pvc create time 00:03:46, last time pvc status changed
       00:03:06
22) Dallas#
```

Figure 13-13

Show interfaces output for frame relay local loop on Dallas.

```
1)  Dallas#show interfaces serial2
2)  Serial2 is up, line protocol is up
3)    Hardware is CD2430 in sync mode
4)    Internet address is 172.16.30.1/24
5)    MTU 1500 bytes, BW 115 Kbit, DLY 20000 usec, rely 255/255,
      load 1/255
6)    Encapsulation FRAME-RELAY, loopback not set, keepalive set
      (10 sec)
7)    LMI enq sent 36, LMI stat recvd 30, LMI upd recvd 0, DTE
      LMI up
8)    LMI enq recvd 0, LMI stat sent 0, LMI upd sent 0
9)    LMI DLCI 0 LMI type is ANSI Annex D frame relay DTE
10)   FR SVC disabled, LAPF state down
11)   Broadcast queue 0/64, broadcasts sent/dropped 22/0,
      interface broadcasts 11
12)   Last input 00:00:05, output 00:00:05, output hang never
13)   Last clearing of "show interface" counters never
14)   Input queue: 0/75/0 (size/max/drops); Total output drops: 0
15)   Queueing strategy: weighted fair
16)   Output queue: 0/1000/64/0 (size/max total/threshold/drops)
17)      Conversations 0/1/256 (active/max active/max total)
18)      Reserved Conversations 0/0 (allocated/max allocated)
19)   5 minute input rate 0 bits/sec, 0 packets/sec
20)   5 minute output rate 0 bits/sec, 0 packets/sec
21)      55 packets input, 3102 bytes, 0 no buffer
22)      Received 0 broadcasts, 0 runts, 0 giants, 0 throttles
23)      0 input errors, 0 CRC, 0 frame, 0 overrun, 0 ignored, 0
      abort
24)      64 packets output, 3051 bytes, 0 underruns
25)      0 output errors, 0 collisions, 3 interface resets
26)      0 output buffer failures, 0 output buffers swapped out
27)      6 carrier transitions
28)      DCD = up DSR = up DTR = up RTS = up CTS = up
29) Dallas#
```

13.2.2 Frame Relay Subinterface Configuration and Verification

We saw our first real use of subinterfaces in Chapter 8 when we did multiple IPX encapsulations on an Ethernet interface. The concept of a subinterface is the same now with frame relay; it is just a logical interface that is directly associated with a physical interface. With frame relay subinterface configuration, we can create a subinterface for each of the PVCs coming into a serial interface.

Two types of subinterfaces can be created for frame relay—multipoint and point-to-point. A *multipoint* subinterface can handle multiple PVCs; its use is similar to that of the NBMA network that we saw in the preceding section. A *point-to-point* subinterface (the type we are going to use) effectively turns every PVC into a point-to-point network with its own network addressing. Using point-to-point subinterfaces gives us greater control over our frame relay network.

We are going to implement the configuration illustrated in Figure 13-14. Since Dallas has two PVCs, we are going to create subinterfaces on Dallas. FortWorth and Austin will continue with the original NBMA configuration since they have only one PVC each; however, Austin's Serial2 IP address will have to change since it will be connected to a different network created by the Dallas point-to-point subinterface.

Figure 13-15 shows the commands necessary to change from the NBMA configuration to a point-to-point subinterface configuration. When using subinterfaces, the physical interface normally does not have any network addressing; therefore, we removed the IP address from Serial2 (Line 4). We created the first subinterface, Serial2.1, by referencing it on an **interface** command (Line 5). The **point-to-point** keyword is used to create a point-to-point subinterface. The other option is to create a multipoint subinterface by specifying the keyword **multipoint**. Point-to-point and multipoint subinterfaces cannot be created when the physical interface's encapsulation is at its default, HDLC; therefore, we had to have the **encapsulation frame-relay** command on the Serial2 interface to be able to specify that we wanted a point-to-point subinterface. The **encapsulation frame-relay** command was issued on Serial2 during the NBMA configuration.

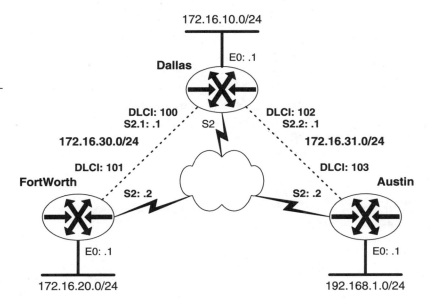

Figure 13-14

Frame-relay subinterface internetwork.

Figure 13-15
Frame-relay subin-
terface configura-
tion on Dallas.

```
1)  Dallas#configure terminal
2)  Enter configuration commands, one per line. End with CNTL/Z.
3)  Dallas(config)#interface serial2
4)  Dallas(config-if)#no ip address
5)  Dallas(config-if)#interface serial2.1 point-to-point
6)  Dallas(config-subif)#ip address 172.16.30.1 255.255.255.0
7)  Dallas(config-subif)#frame-relay interface-dlci 100
8)  Dallas(config-fr-dlci)#interface serial2.2 point-to-point
9)  Dallas(config-subif)#ip address 172.16.31.1 255.255.255.0
10) Dallas(config-subif)#frame-relay interface-dlci 102
11) Dallas(config-fr-dlci)#<Ctrl-Z>
12) Dallas#
```

Subinterface Serial2.1 has its own IP address (Line 6). Instead of mapping a remote network address to a local DLCI, we just need to tell IOS
which PVC is supposed to be processed by this subinterface. We use the
frame-relay interface-dlci subinterface configuration command to do
that. We want Serial2.1 to process the traffic for the PVC going to
FortWorth, and that PVC has the local DLCI 100 (Line 7). The second
subinterface, Serial2.2, is created and configured similarly. Notice, however, that Serial2.2 also has its own IP address (Line 9), and the IP
address is on a different IP subnet than Serial 2.1. Serial2.2 is processing traffic for the Dallas-to-Austin PVC that has DLCI 102 (Line 10).

Serial2 on Austin now needs an IP address on the same IP subnet as
that of Dallas's Serial2.2. Figure 13-16 shows the commands for changing Austin's Serial2 IP address to its new value, 172.16.31.2.

We saw the command for verifying frame relay operation after our
NBMA configuration; however, the output of the **show ip route** and
show frame-relay map commands changes slightly.

Figure 13-17 shows the new IP routing table on Dallas. The table now
shows the subinterfaces in the paths to networks. Serial2.1 is used in the
path to the FortWorth Ethernet LAN (Line 14) and Serial2.2 is used in
the path to the Austin Ethernet LAN (Line 16).

Figure 13-16
Austin IP address
change for frame-
relay subinterface
configuration.

```
1)  Austin#configure terminal
2)  Enter configuration commands, one per line. End with CNTL/Z.
3)  Austin(config)#interface serial2
4)  Austin(config-if)#ip address 172.16.31.2 255.255.255.0
5)  Austin(config-if)#<Ctrl-Z>
6)  Austin#
```

Figure 13-17

Show IP route on Dallas after subinterface configuration.

```
1) Dallas#show ip route
2) Codes: C - connected, S - static, I - IGRP, R - RIP,
         M - mobile, B - BGP
3)       D - EIGRP, EX - EIGRP external, O - OSPF, IA - OSPF
         inter area
4)       N1 - OSPF NSSA external type 1, N2 - OSPF NSSA exter-
         nal type 2
5)       E1 - OSPF external type 1, E2 - OSPF external type 2,
         E - EGP
6)       i - IS-IS, L1 - IS-IS level-1, L2 - IS-IS level-2,
         * - candidate default
7)       U - per-user static route, o - ODR
8)
9) Gateway of last resort is not set
10)
11)      172.16.0.0/24 is subnetted, 4 subnets
12) C       172.16.30.0 is directly connected, Serial2.1
13) C       172.16.31.0 is directly connected, Serial2.2
14) R       172.16.20.0 [120/1] via 172.16.30.2, 00:00:14,
            Serial2.1
15) C       172.16.10.0 is directly connected, Ethernet0
16) R    192.168.1.0/24 [120/1] via 172.16.31.2, 00:00:23,
            Serial2.2
17) Dallas#
```

Figure 13-18 shows the output of the **show frame-relay map** command on Dallas. Now that subinterfaces have been implemented, the map entries are neither dynamic nor static. Both entries are listed as point-to-point, and the subinterface is listed for each one.

The one drawback of using the subinterface configuration method for frame relay is that it requires more network address space. However, Cisco network experts still recommend using subinterfaces because of their flexibility and control. For example, if the PVC associated with a point-to-point subinterface goes down, IOS changes the status of the subinterface to down. A downed interface is a little easier to spot than a downed PVC.

Figure 13-18

Show frame-relay map on Dallas after subinterface configuration.

```
1) Dallas#show frame-relay map
2) Serial2.1 (up): point-to-point dlci, dlci 100(0x64,0x1840),
3) broadcast status defined, active
4) Serial2.2 (up): point-to-point dlci, dlci 102(0x66,0x1860),
5) broadcast status defined, active
6) Dallas#
```

13.3 Frame Relay Configuration Summary

For frame relay NBMA configuration, all we need is the **encapsulation frame-relay** command and the appropriate network protocol commands, such as **ip address** or **decnet cost**, on the physical interface connected to the frame relay network. In an NBMA environment, we may run into connectivity problems caused by split horizon (see Section 2.2.2.1, "Distance Vector Routing Protocols").

The recommended frame relay configuration makes use of subinterfaces. All we have to do is issue the **encapsulation frame-relay** command on the physical interface, create a subinterface for each PVC, use the **frame-relay interface-dlci** command to assign a DLCI to each subinterface, and issue the appropriate network protocol command(s) on each subinterface. Using point-to-point subinterfaces removes the split horizon problems sometimes experienced in an NBMA environment.

Figure 13-19 shows the frame-relay-specific commands left in Dallas's running configuration after our example work, Figure 13-20 shows those from FortWorth's running configuration, and Figure 13-21 shows those from Austin's running configuration.

Figure 13-19

Dallas frame relay configuration commands.

```
1)  Dallas#show running-config [Some text has been omitted.]
2)  !
3)  interface Serial2
4)   encapsulation frame-relay
5)  !
6)  interface Serial2.1 point-to-point
7)   ip address 172.16.30.1 255.255.255.0
8)   frame-relay interface-dlci 100
9)  !
10) interface Serial2.2 point-to-point
11)  ip address 172.16.31.1 255.255.255.0
12)  frame-relay interface-dlci 102
13) !
14) router rip
15)  network 172.16.0.0
16) !
17) Dallas#
```

Figure 13-20
FortWorth frame
relay configuration
commands.

```
 1) FortWorth#show running-config [Some text has been omitted.]
 2) !
 3) interface Serial2
 4)   ip address 172.16.30.2 255.255.255.0
 5)   encapsulation frame-relay
 6) !
 7) router rip
 8)   network 172.16.0.0
 9) !
10) FortWorth#
```

Figure 13-21
Austin frame relay
configuration com-
mands.

```
 1) Austin#show running-config [Some text has been omitted.]
 2) !
 3) interface Serial2
 4)   ip address 172.16.31.2 255.255.255.0
 5)   encapsulation frame-relay
 6) !
 7) router rip
 8)   network 172.16.0.0
 9)   network 192.168.1.0
10) !
11) Austin#
```

Frame relay is currently very popular because it is usually less expensive than normal leased lines and because it is widely available. Frame relay is usually less expensive than leased lines because when we get a leased line, our service provider provides us with dedicated bandwidth, and when we get a frame relay PVC, our service provider provides us with just a share of their bandwidth (nondedicated). Our traffic has a greater chance of being dropped traversing a frame relay network than a leased line—yet another reason for the lower cost. Most companies are willing to accept these shortcomings because of the monetary savings, and most applications are not greatly affected as long as the frame relay configuration is properly implemented on both the user side and the service provider side.

Configuring SRB and DLSw

Source Route Bridging (SRB) is a mechanism for forwarding frames across token ring LANs; it is usually needed in internetworks with mainframe host systems that use Systems Network Architecture (SNA) and internetworks with hosts that use NetBIOS.

DLSw is a way of forwarding source route bridged traffic over a WAN. SRB inherently runs only on token ring LANs. The use of DLSw allows us to enable token ring LAN-to-LAN communication across a WAN by making the devices on the LANs believe that the WAN is just another LAN.

This chapter contains just enough about these two topics to allow us to enable them on a router.

14.1   SRB Overview

SRB is a type of bridging. It is bridging because the devices that separate physical LANs forward frames are based on their layer-2 (MAC) address.

Physically, a source route bridged network consists of token ring LANs and source route bridges. Every token ring LAN has a unique number, which is assigned by the network administrator or network engineer. A token ring number can be between 1 and 4095; no two rings can have the same number. The bridges between the rings are also assigned numbers by a network administrator or network engineer. Bridge numbers range from 1 to 15, and the only limitation for uniqueness is that two bridges between the same two token rings cannot have the same bridge number. Figure 14-1 shows a source route bridge (the Waco router running SRB), Bridge 1, connected between Ring 91 and Ring 92. There could be another bridge between Ring 91 and Ring 92, but the bridge could not have the bridge number 1. On the other hand, there could be another

Figure 14-1

Simple source route bridged network.

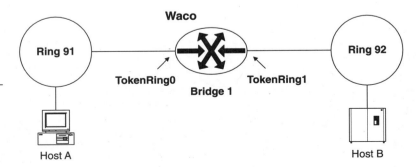

bridge with the number 1 attached to Ring 91 (as long as the second Bridge 1 did not connect to Ring 92, of course). A source route bridge can connect to only two rings.

In a source route bridged network, a source host (one that wants to start a conversation) must locate its desired destination host prior to sending any data frames to the destination host. Since the source host is responsible for locating a route to another host and frame forwarding is based on MAC addressing, we get the term *source route bridging*.

The source host locates a destination host by sending a special frame, called an *explorer,* onto the network. The explorer frame gets forwarded by the source route bridges until it has appeared on every ring of the network (sometimes more than once); hopefully, the destination host system receives at least one of the explorer frames and responds to the sending host. There are two types of explorer frames: (1) spanning-tree explorers and (2) all-routes explorers. The type used depends on the source station.

The source route bridged token ring frame header contains a special field called a *Routing Information Field* (RIF). The RIF has the path that a frame is supposed to take through a source route bridged network. The path consists of alternating ring numbers and bridge numbers. The bridges build the RIF as they forward the explorer frame from the source host. As bridges forward an explorer, they also check the explorer's RIF; the bridge will not forward a frame onto a ring if the ring's number is already in the RIF (if the explorer has already been on the ring). This keeps an explorer from circling the network forever.

Figure 14-1 shows Host A and Host B. Consider Host A to be the source host that wants to send a message to Host B, the destination host. Host A first sends a test frame looking for Host B on the local ring. Host B is on a different ring; therefore, Host A will receive no response. Host A then sends an explorer frame looking for Host B. The bridge will populate the RIF in the explorer with the values 91-1-92 because the bridge received the explorer on Ring 91, the bridge's number is 1, and the bridge forwarded the explorer onto Ring 92. Host B receives the explorer and responds to Host A using the same ring-bridge combination in the RIF. RIFs contain a *Direction bit,* which tells the bridges to read the ring-bridge entries forward or backward. Host B uses the Direction bit to tell the bridges to read the RIF in reverse. When Bridge 1 receives the frame from B, it reads the RIF in reverse so it knows that the frame should be forwarded onto Ring 91.

Cisco routers can be configured to perform the operation of the source route bridge. The configuration is pretty easy; the commands are in the following sections.

14.2 SRB Configuration

To configure source route bridging on a router, we use the interface configuration command **source-bridge**, which requires the entry of the local ring's number, the router's bridge number, and the ring number of the target ring to which token ring frames are supposed to be forwarded by the router. Figure 14-2 shows the configuration of source route bridging on the Waco router of Figure 14-1.

Source route bridging has been configured on TokenRing0 with the command **source-bridge 91 1 92** (Line 5). TokenRing0 is attached to Ring 91. The Waco router is Bridge 1, and the other token ring interface, TokenRing1, is attached to Ring 92. The configuration of source route bridging on TokenRing1 has the ring number reversed (Line 9). The **ring-speed** command sets the speed of the token ring interface. The choices are 4 (for 4 Mbps) and 16 (for 16 Mbps), and the speed of the interface must agree with the actual token ring speed. The **source-bridge spanning** command allows the router to forward spanning-tree explorers just in case an end station is using them.

Many routers have more than two token ring interfaces such as the one shown in Figure 14-3. This is Waco again; only this time, we have added a third token ring interface, TokenRing2, and we have assigned the number 80 to the new ring.

As was mentioned in the preceding section, a source route bridge is supposed to have only two token ring interfaces. This is rather limiting for us if we want to save data-center real estate by putting many interfaces into the same router. Cisco has a way of getting around this limitation. We are going to create a virtual token ring in our router. The virtual token ring is called a *ring group,* and we will assign it a ring number just

Figure 14-2

Source route bridging configuration on two-ring router.

```
1)  Waco#configure terminal
2)  Enter configuration commands, one per line. End with CNTL/Z.
3)  Waco(config)#interface tokenring0
4)  Waco(config-if)#ring-speed 16
5)  Waco(config-if)#source-bridge 91 1 92
6)  Waco(config-if)#source-bridge spanning
7)  Waco(config-if)#interface tokenring1
8)  Waco(config-if)#ring-speed 16
9)  Waco(config-if)#source-bridge 92 1 91
10) Waco(config-if)#source-bridge spanning
11) Waco(config-if)#<Ctrl-Z>
12) Waco#
```

Figure 14-3

Router with three
token ring inter-
faces.

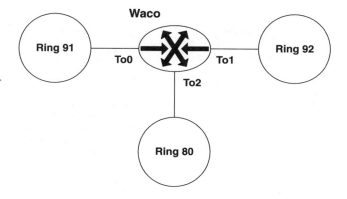

Figure 14-3

Router with three
token ring inter-
faces.

like a real token ring LAN. For each of our router's physical token ring
interfaces, we will create a virtual bridge that connects the physical ring
to the ring group. Figure 14-4 shows a depiction of this virtual source
route bridged network.

The virtual network creates the illusion that each bridge has only two
rings attached. We have assigned the number 1 to each bridge, and each
bridge has a connection to the ring group, Ring 60. The command that is
used to create the ring group is the global configuration **source-bridge
ring-group** command. Figure 14-5 shows the new configuration of
source route bridging on the Waco router.

We created the virtual ring with the **source-bridge ring-group 60**
command (Line 3). Each of the interfaces now has the ring group as its
target ring on the source-bridge command (Lines 5, 8, and 11).

Figure 14-4

Depiction of ring
group and virtual
bridges.

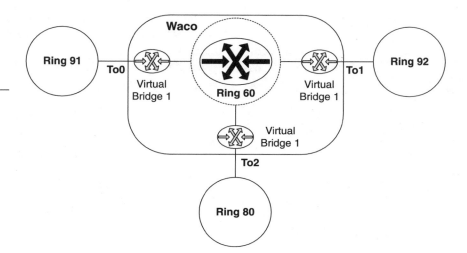

Figure 14-5

Source route bridging configuration on three-ring router.

```
 1)  Waco#configure terminal
 2)  Enter configuration commands, one per line. End with CNTL/Z.
 3)  Waco(config)#source-bridge ring-group 60
 4)  Waco(config)#interface tokenring0
 5)  Waco(config-if)#source-bridge 91 1 60
 6)  Waco(config-if)#source-bridge spanning
 7)  Waco(config-if)#interface tokenring1
 8)  Waco(config-if)#source-bridge 92 1 60
 9)  Waco(config-if)#source-bridge spanning
10)  Waco(config-if)#interface tokenring2
11)  Waco(config-if)#source-bridge 80 1 60
12)  Waco(config-if)#source-bridge spanning
13)  Waco(config-if)#<Ctrl-Z>
14)  Waco#
```

14.3 DLSw Overview

DLSw allows us to connect token ring LANs across WANs. DLSw allows this connection by sending source route bridged frames inside TCP/IP packets so that the packets can be routed over a normal IP network. DLSw performs local acknowledgment of data link layer connections—which some call *spoofing*—and termination of the SRB RIF.

Figure 14-6 shows a WAN separating two routers, each of which has a token ring interface. When Host A on Ring 37 wants to talk to Host B on Ring 38, Host A performs the same process as is normal in an SRB network. Host A sends a test frame looking for Host B on the local ring. After not finding Host B, Host A sends an explorer. The explorer is forwarded across the DLSw connection onto Ring 38.

Once Host A and Host B establish a connection, they may start exchanging data using a layer-2 protocol such as SNA or NetBIOS. When Host A transmits a frame to Host B, the router sends a layer-2 acknowledgment to Host A just as if the router were Host B. The router then puts

Figure 14-6

Two token rings separated by a WAN.

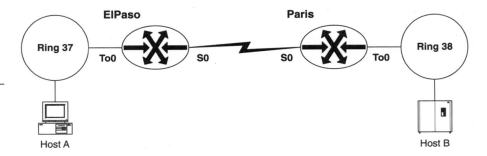

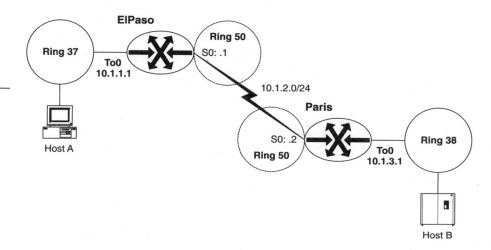

Figure 14-7
Two token rings
with DLSw ring
groups.

the frame into a TCP/IP packet and forwards the packet on the DLSw connection across the IP internetwork. This local acknowledgment of frames helps to prevent timeouts of SNA and NetBIOS sessions.

When we implement DLSw in a Cisco router internetwork, we create ring groups that looks like real token rings similarly to that shown in the preceding section. Figure 14-7 shows a depiction of the same two token rings as Figure 14-6, except now there is a ring group on each router.

We stated earlier that DLSw performs RIF termination. The RIF for frames that are forwarded across a DLSw connection are terminated at the ring group. In other words, the last ring in the RIF has the number assigned to the ring group. For example, the RIF that Host A receives back from its explorer to Host B has Ring 50 (the ring group number) as its last ring; this makes Host A believe that Host B is on Ring 50. Host A does not know that Ring 38 exists. Likewise, Host B does not know that Ring 37 exists.

14.4   DLSw Configuration

Configuration of DLSw begins with the creation of a ring group with the **source-bridge ring-group** command. We must then define the two ends of the DLSw connection, the local end first and then the remote end. The ends of the connection are called *peers*—the local peer and the remote peer—which are designated by the IP addresses of interfaces on the two end routers of the connection. If a router has multiple DLSw connections, then the router will have multiple remote peers. We use the **dlsw local-peer** global configuration command to define the local peer, and we use the **dlsw remote-peer tcp** command to define the remote end of the DLSw TCP/IP connection.

Once the ring group, the local peer, and the remote peer (or peers) are defined, we can do a normal source route bridging configuration on the interface using the ring group number as the source route bridge's target ring. We will be using the internetwork shown in Figure 14-7 in the example configurations. Figure 14-8 shows the DLSw configuration on the ElPaso router, and Figure 14-9 shows the DLSw configuration on the Paris router.

In each of the routers, the ring group has been assigned the number 50. Each router is using the IP address of its TokenRing0 interface as its local peer address and the address of the remote router's TokenRing0 interface as its remote peer address. The **dlsw remote-peer tcp** command is used when a DLSw connection relies on TCP/IP to get the datalink switched frames from one end of the connection to the other. The **0** in the command represents a ring group list, which we have not defined;

Figure 14-8
DLSw configuration on ElPaso.

```
1)  ElPaso#configure terminal
2)  Enter configuration commands, one per line. End with CNTL/Z.
3)  ElPaso(config)#source-bridge ring-group 50
4)  ElPaso(config)#dlsw local-peer peer-id 10.1.1.1
5)  ElPaso(config)#dlsw remote-peer 0 tcp 10.1.3.1
6)  ElPaso(config)#interface tokenring0
7)  ElPaso(config-if)#ring-speed 16
8)  ElPaso(config-if)#source-bridge 37 1 50
9)  ElPaso(config-if)#source-bridge spanning
10) ElPaso(config-if)#<Ctrl-Z>
11) ElPaso#
```

Figure 14-9
DLSw configuration on Paris.

```
1)  Paris#configure terminal
2)  Enter configuration commands, one per line. End with CNTL/Z.
3)  Paris(config)#source-bridge ring-group 50
4)  Paris(config)#dlsw local-peer peer-id 10.1.3.1
5)  Paris(config)#dlsw remote-peer 0 tcp 10.1.1.1
6)  Paris(config)#interface tokenring0
7)  Paris(config-if)#ring-speed 16
8)  Paris(config-if)#source-bridge 38 1 50
9)  Paris(config-if)#source-bridge spanning
10) Paris(config-if)#<Ctrl-Z>
11) Paris#
```

that is why the value is **0** (the default). Our basic DLSw configuration is complete.

14.5   SRB and DLSw Verification

The two best commands for verification of SRB and DLSw are **show source-bridge** and **show dlsw peers**. Figure 14-10 shows the output of the **show source-bridge** command on ElPaso.

The data in Figure 14-10 shows that ElPaso has one interface with source route bridging enabled. That interface is TokenRing0 (Line 5). TokenRing0 has a source ring number (*srn*) of 37 and a target ring number (*trn*) of 50, which is the ring group. Receive count and transmit count are both zero since our test network has no devices generating real traffic. Explorer statistics are also given for each interface (Line 18); again, our test network has no real traffic.

```
1)  ElPaso#show source-bridge
2)
3)  Local Interfaces:                              receive          transmit
4)            srn bn trn r p s n max hops           cnt               cnt         drops
5)  To0       37  1 50 *   f   7 7 7                 0                 0            0
6)
7)  Global RSRB Parameters:
8)   TCP Queue Length maximum: 100
9)
10) Ring Group 50:
11)   No TCP peername set, TCP transport disabled
12)   Maximum output TCP queue length, per peer: 100
13)   Rings:
14)    bn: 1 rn: 37 local ma: 4000.306e.e30b TokenRing0    fwd: 0
15)
16) Explorers: ---- input ----         ---- output ----
17)         spanning   all-rings   total   spanning   all-rings   total
18) To0        0           0         0         0           0         0
19)
20)   Explorer fastswitching enabled
21)   Local switched: 0              flushed 0            max Bps 38400
22)
23)        rings    inputs    bursts    throttles  output drops
24)        To0        0         0          0           0
25)
26) ElPaso#
```

Figure 14-10
Show source-bridge output on ElPaso.

```
1)   ElPaso#show dlsw peers
2)   Peers:            state    pkts_rx  pkts_tx  type  drops  ckts  TCP  uptime
3)    TCP 10.1.3.1    CONNECT        3        3  conf      0     0    0  00:00:39
4)   Total number of connected peers: 1
5)   Total number of connections:     1
6)
7)   ElPaso#
```

Figure 14-11 Show DLSw peers output on ElPaso.

Figure 14-11 shows the output of the **show dlsw peers** command on ElPaso. The output shows the number of DLSw connections and the addresses of the remote peers.

ElPaso has one connected peer (Line 4); the peer's address is 10.1.3.1, and it has been up for 39 minutes (Line 3). Receive and transmit counters for the connection are also shown.

14.6   SRB and DLSw Summary

To configure SRB on a token ring interface, use the **source-bridge** interface configuration command, which defines the ring number to which the interface is directly attached, the bridge number of the router, and the target ring number that the bridge is to forward source route bridged traffic. If you are using spanning-tree explorers, you should issue the **source-bridge spanning** command on the interface. Remember also that the token ring speed should be configured to be either 4 or 16 with the **ring-speed** command.

Create a ring group either when configuring SRB on more than two interfaces of the same router or when configuring DLSw. Use the **source-bridge ring-group** command to create the ring group and assign it a ring number.

To do a basic DLSw configuration over a TCP/IP connection, define the local peer with the **dlsw local-peer** command and define the remote peer with the **dlsw remote-peer tcp** command. Multiple remote peers require multiple **dlsw remote-peer tcp** commands.

Figure 14-12 shows the DLSw configuration commands from the running configuration of ElPaso and Figure 14-13 shows the DLSw configuration commands from the running configuration of Paris.

Figure 14-12
ElPaso DLSw configuration commands.

```
 8)  ElPaso#show running-config [Some text has been omitted.]
 9)  !
10) source-bridge ring-group 50
11) dlsw local-peer peer-id 10.1.1.1
12) dlsw remote-peer 0 tcp 10.1.3.1
13) !
14) interface TokenRing0
15)  ip address 10.1.1.1 255.255.255.0
16)  ring-speed 16
17)  source-bridge 37 1 50
18)  source-bridge spanning
19) !
20) ElPaso#
```

Figure 14-13
Paris DLSw configuration commands.

```
 1)  Paris#show running-config [Some text has been omitted.]
 2)  !
 3)  source-bridge ring-group 50
 4)  dlsw local-peer peer-id 10.1.3.1
 5)  dlsw remote-peer 0 tcp 10.1.1.1
 6)  !
 7)  interface TokenRing0
 8)   ip address 10.1.3.1 255.255.255.0
 9)   ring-speed 16
10)   source-bridge 38 1 50
11)   source-bridge spanning
12)  !
13)  Paris#
```

APPENDIX A

COMMAND REFERENCE

This appendix contains a list of all of the IOS commands that are used in this book. The commands are listed in alphabetical order according to their general name. The information for each command includes the following:

- Command syntax summary
- CLI mode in which the command is most used
- Common command abbreviation, if applicable
- Section number in the book where the command is used or mentioned
- Scenario for which the command is useful

appletalk cable-range

```
appletalk cable-range cable-range
no appletalk cable-range cable-range
```

cable-range   AppleTalk cable range given as two decimal numbers separated by a hyphen.

Mode: Interface Configuration
Abbrev: **app cable** *cable-range*
Section: 9.4
Usage: Assign an AppleTalk cable range to an interface. All of the routers connected to a network must agree on the cable range for the network. Use the **no** form to remove the cable range from an interface. When a cable range is removed from an interface, the zone definition and routing protocol are automatically removed.

appletalk protocol eigrp

```
appletalk protocol eigrp
no appletalk protocol eigrp
```

Mode: Interface Configuration

Abbrev: **app prot e**

Section: 9.6

Usage: Enable AppleTalk EIGRP on an interface. AppleTalk EIGRP must have already been turned on with the **appletalk routing eigrp** command. When running EIGRP, you may also want to turn off RTMP with the **no appletalk protocol rtmp** command.

appletalk protocol rtmp

```
appletalk protocol rtmp
no appletalk protocol rtmp
```

Mode: Interface Configuration

Abbrev: **app prot r**

Section: 9.6

Usage: Enable AppleTalk RTMP on an interface. RTMP is enabled on an interface by default as soon as the interface is assigned a valid AppleTalk address and zone. The **no** form of the command is used to turn off RTMP when AppleTalk EIGRP is being used instead.

appletalk route-redistribution

```
appletalk route-redistribution
no appletalk route-redistribution
```

Mode: Global Configuration

Abbrev: **app route-red**

Section: 9.6

Usage: Use to enable the redistribution of routes between AppleTalk EIGRP and RTMP. Without this command, AppleTalk routes will not get advertised across an EIGRP-RTMP boundary. Some IOS versions automatically add this command to the running configuration when AppleTalk EIGRP is enabled.

appletalk routing

```
appletalk routing
no appletalk routing
```

Mode: Global Configuration
Abbrev: **app routing**
Section: 9.4, 9.8
Usage: Use to tell IOS to route AppleTalk packets received on inter-
            faces that have a valid AppleTalk address and zone. Removing
            the AppleTalk routing process with the **no** form of the com-
            mand will remove, from the running configuration, all com-
            mands dealing with AppleTalk addresses, zones, and routing
            protocols.

appletalk routing eigrp

```
appletalk routing eigrp router-id
no appletalk routing eigrp router-id
```

router-id   A unique identifier for a router that is to run AppleTalk
              EIGRP.

Mode: Global Configuration
Abbrev: **app routing e** *router-id*
Section: 9.6
Usage: Turn on AppleTalk EIGRP and the routing of AppleTalk
            packets. Each router running AppleTalk EIGRP must have a
            unique router ID.

appletalk zone

```
appletalk zone zone-name
no appletalk zone zone-name
```

zone-name   The name of an AppleTalk zone in text format.

Mode: Interface Configuration
Abbrev: **app zone** *zone-name*
Section: 9.4
Usage: Use to make a network part of a zone. To make a network part
            of multiple zones, use multiple instances of this command. The
            zone name in the first instance becomes the primary zone. All

of the routers connected to a network must agree on the zone(s) for the network.

area stub

```
area area-id stub [no-summary]
no area area-id stub
```

area-id   An area ID in either decimal or dotted-decimal format.

no-summary   Indicates to an ABR that the stub area is a totally stubby area.

Mode: Router Configuration
Abbrev: **area** *area-id* **st[no]**
Section: 7.7.4.4
Usage: Use to tell IOS that an area of an OSPF AS is a stub area. This command sets the stub area flag in OSPF hello packets, and it must be issued on all of routers that connect to a stub area. If the area is a totally stubby area, include the **no-summary** keyword on the ABR. Use the **no** form of the command to remove the stub area definition.

auto-summary

```
auto-summary
no auto-summary
```

Mode: Router Configuration
Abbrev: **auto-sum**
Section: 7.7.1.2
Usage: Route autosummarization is enabled by default for RIPv1, RIPv2, IGRP, and EIGRP. For RIPv2 and EIGRP, it can be disabled. Use the **no** form to turn off autosummarization when a network contains noncontiguous subnets.

bandwidth

```
bandwidth bw
no bandwidth bw
```

bw   Bandwidth of an interface in kbps.

Mode: Interface Configuration
Abbrev: **band** *bw*
Section: 6.2.4, 7.5.1, 7.5.2, 7.5.3, 7.7.2
Usage: Use to assign a bandwidth to an interface. The bandwidth is used by routing protocols such as IGRP, EIGRP, and OSPF to calculate metrics for best-path determination. All interfaces have a default bandwidth. For example, the default bandwidth of a fast-serial interface is 1544, and the default bandwidth of an Ethernet interface is 10,000. Use the **no** form to remove an assigned bandwidth from an interface and restore the default bandwidth value. The bandwidth assigned to an interface can be displayed with the **show interfaces** command.

banner

```
banner {exec | login | motd} dc message dc
no banner {exec | login | motd}
```

    exec   Starts the creation of an exec banner.
    login   Starts the creation of a login banner.
    motd   Starts the creation of a motd banner.
    dc   A delimiting character. Can be any character that does not appear in the banner message. Both delimiting characters must the same.
    message Message text that should appear when the banner is displayed on a terminal.

Mode: Global Configuration
Abbrev: **ban** {**ex**| **log** | **mo**} *dc message dc*
Section: 6.1.2
Usage: Use to define a text message that will be displayed on a user's terminal at log-in time. If <Enter>is pressed after the first delimiting character, IOS will give you a blank line where you can type the text of a banner. A banner can have multiple lines and can contain any text. The next instance of the delimiting character marks the end of the message to be displayed. The motd and login banners are displayed in order when a router terminal line is accessed. The login banner is displayed only if the terminal line configuration contains the **login** command. An exec banner is displayed when a user has successfully logged in.

bridge-group

```
bridge-group group
no bridge-group group
```

    group   A bridge group number between 1 and 63.

Mode: Interface Configuration

Abbrev: **bridge-g** *group*

Section: 12.2

Usage: Use to make an interface part of a the specified bridge group, which was created with the **bridge protocol** command. Use the **no** form of the command to remove the interface from the bridge group.

bridge priority

```
bridge group priority priority
no bridge group priority
```

    group   A bridge group number between 1 and 63.

    priority A bridge priority between 0 and 65535.

Mode: Global Configuration

Abbrev: **br** *group* **pri** *priority*

Section: 12.2

Usage: Use to assign a priority to a bridge. The priority is used by the spanning tree protocol to select a root bridge. The lower a bridge's priority, the more likely it is to become the spanning tree root. Use the **no** form of the command to set a bridge's priority back to its default value.

bridge protocol

```
bridge group protocol {dec | ieee}
no bridge group
```

    group   A bridge group number between 1 and 63.

    dec   Keyword for starting the DEC spanning tree protocol.

    ieee   Keyword for starting the IEEE spanning tree protocol.

Mode: Global Configuration
Abbrev: **br** *group* **pro** { **de** | **ie**}
Section: 12.2
Usage: Use to create a bridge group and start the specified spanning tree protocol for transparent bridging. All of the bridges that communicate with each other should run the same version of the spanning tree protocol. Use the **no** form of the command to stop the spanning tree protocol for the bridge group and remove the bridge group.

cdp enable

```
cdp enable
no cdp enable
```

Mode: Interface Configuration
Abbrev: **cdp en**
Section: 6.6
Usage: Use to enable CDP on an interface. CDP is enabled by default. Use the **no** form to disable the sending and receiving of CDP packets on an interface.

cdp holdtime

```
cdp holdtime time
no cdp holdtime
```

time Number of seconds to hold an entry in the CDP neighbor table after not hearing from the neighbor.

Mode: Global Configuration
Abbrev: **cdp ho** *time*
Section: 6.6
Usage: Use to change the CDP holdtime. The default holdtime is 180 seconds. All interfaces with CDP enabled have the same holdtime. Use the **no** form of the command to set the holdtime value back to its default of 180 seconds.

cdp run

```
cdp run
no cdp run
```

Mode: Global Configuration
Abbrev: **cdp ru**
Section: 6.6
Usage: Use to turn on the CDP process on a router. CDP is running by default. CDP cannot be enabled on an interface unless the process is running. Use the **no** form of the command to stop the CDP process on a router and, effectively, disable CDP on all interfaces.

cdp timer

```
cdp timer time
no cdp timer
```

time   Time in seconds. Default is 60.

Mode: Global Configuration
Abbrev: **cdp ti**
Section: 6.6
Usage: Use to set the periodic interval for CDP packets to be transmitted out from a router's interfaces, which have CDP enabled. Use the **no** form of the command to set the periodic interval back to its default value of 60 seconds.

clear counters

```
clear counters [int-name]
```

int-name   An interface name. An interface name has the interface type along with a port number and, possibly, a slot number and a port-adapter number. See Section 3.1.3 for a description of interface naming conventions.

Mode: Privileged
Abbrev: **cle co** [*int-name*]
Section: 6.2.6

Usage: Set all of the counters associated with an interface to zero (after a confirmation). If an interface is not specified, counters on all interfaces will be cleared after a confirmation. Use this command to establish a time reference for those counters displayed with the **show interfaces** command.

clear host

`clear host` {`host-name` | `*`}

   host-name   A host name that is to be cleared from the host table.
   *   All temporary entries in host table.

Mode: Privileged
Abbrev: **cle ho** {*host-name* |*}
Section: 6.1.5
Usage: Use to clear an entry from the host table used for resolving host names to IP addresses and vice versa. Clearing a permanent entry will remove the **ip host** command associated with the entry from the running configuration. Using the asterisk (*) in the command will clear all entries that were placed in the table as a result of DNS lookups.

clear interface

`clear interface` *int-name*

   int-name An interface name. An interface name has the interface type along with a port number and, possibly, a slot number and a port-adapter number. See Section 3.1.3 for a description of interface naming conventions.

Mode: Privileged
Abbrev: **cle int** *int-name*
Section: 6.2.6
Usage: Use to reset an interface. This command is service-affecting.

clear line

```
clear line {abs-line | aux rel-line | console rel-line | tty rel-line
| vty rel-line}
```

abs-line	Absolute line number.
aux	Auxiliary terminal line.
rel-line	Relative line number.
console	Console terminal line.
tty	Terminal controller line.
vty	Virtual terminal line.

Mode: Privileged

Abbrev: **cle lin** {*abs-line* | **aux** *rel-line* | **con** *rel-line* | **tty** *rel-line* | **vty** *rel-line*}

Section: 6.3.3

Usage: Use to disconnect a session from a terminal line. The numbering of terminal lines is covered in Section 5.2.4.

configure memory

```
configure memory
```

Mode: Privileged

Abbrev: **conf mem**

Section: 6.4.2.2

Usage: Use to merge the commands in the startup configuration into a router's running configuration. This command is the predecessor of the **copy startup-config running-config** command.

configure network

```
configure network
```

Mode: Privileged

Abbrev: **conf net**

Section: 6.4.2.3

Usage: Use to merge the commands in a text file on a TFTP server into a router's running configuration. This command is useful for performing repetitive configuration tasks on multiple routers. For example, building a host table on multiple routers can be done by entering the necessary **ip host** commands into a text file and then using this command to put the text file into the routers' running configurations. The **configure network** command is the predecessor of the **copy tftp running-config** command.

configure overwrite-network

`configure overwrite-network`

Mode:	Privileged
Abbrev:	**conf over**
Section:	6.4.5.2
Usage:	Use to copy a file from a TFTP server to a router's startup configuration in NVRAM. This command is useful for restoring a backup configuration to a router just before the router is to be rebooted. The file that is copied to NVRAM is not checked for valid commands; in other words, IOS will allow any file to be copied to NVRAM with this command. The **configure overwrite-network** command is the predecessor of the **copy tftp startup-config** command.

configure terminal

`configure terminal`

Mode:	Privileged
Abbrev:	**conf t**
Section:	4.2.3.1, 6.4.2.1
Usage:	Use to enter configuration commands from a terminal line. Issuing this command will place a terminal session into global configuration mode for the acceptance of configuration commands. Commands can either be typed manually or entered automatically via a terminal emulator "paste" operation.

copy flash running-config

`copy ` *`flashdev:filename`* `running-config`

flashdev	The name of a flash device such as flash: or slot0:.
filename	Name of a file.

Mode: Privileged
Abbrev: **copy** *flashdev:filename* **run**
Section: 6.4.2.5
Usage: Use to merge the commands from a flash-memory text file into a router's running configuration.

copy flash startup-config

`copy` *flashdev:filename* `startup-config`

> *flashdev*   The name of a flash device such as flash: or slot0:.
> *filename*   Name of a file.

Mode: Privileged
Abbrev: **copy** *flashdev:filename* **start**
Section: 6.4.5.4
Usage: Use to replace the contents of a router's startup configuration with the commands from a flash-memory text file.

copy rcp running-config

`copy rcp running-config`

Mode: Privileged
Abbrev: **copy rcp run**
Section: 6.4.2.4
Usage: Use to merge the commands in a text file on an rcp server into a router's running configuration. The rcp application uses a TCP connection, which requires authentication. See also, **copy tftp running-config**.

copy rcp startup-config

`copy rcp startup-config`

Mode: Privileged
Abbrev: **copy rcp start**
Section: 6.4.5.3
Usage: Use to copy a file from an rcp server into a router's NVRAM; this will replace the router's startup configuration. The rcp

application uses a TCP connection, which requires authentication. See also, **copy tftp startup-config**.

copy running-config flash

```
copy running-config flashdev:filename
```

flashdev	The name of a flash device such as flash: or slot0:.
filename	Name of a file.

Mode: Privileged
Abbrev: **copy run** *flashdev:filename*
Section: 6.4.3.4
Usage: Use to copy the running configuration to a file in flash memory.

copy running-config rcp

```
copy running-config rcp
```

Mode: Privileged
Abbrev: **copy run rcp**
Section: 6.4.3.3
Usage: Use to copy the running configuration to a host using rcp. You will be prompted for the address of the host and the name of the destination file.

copy running-config startup-config

```
copy running-config startup-config
```

Mode: Privileged
Abbrev: **copy run start**
Section: 5.4.2, 6.4.3.1, 6.4.5.1, 6.9
Usage: Use to copy the running configuration to NVRAM where it becomes the startup configuration. Issue this command after configuration changes have been made and tested so the configuration changes will be intact the next time the router boots. This command is the replacement for the **write memory** command.

copy running-config tftp

`copy running-config tftp`

Mode: Privileged
Abbrev: **copy run tftp**
Section: 6.4.3.2
Usage: Use to back up the running configuration file on a TFTP server. You will be prompted for the address of the server and the name of the destination file. This command is the replacement of the **write network** command.

copy startup-config flash

`copy startup-config` *flashdev:filename*

flashdev   The name of a flash device such as flash: or slot0:.
filename   Name of a file.

Mode: Privileged
Abbrev: **copy start** *flashdev:filename*
Section: 6.4.6
Usage: Use to copy the startup configuration to a file in flash memory (for example, **copy start flash:config.txt**).

copy startup-config rcp

`copy startup-config rcp`

Mode: Privileged
Abbrev: **copy start rcp**
Section: 6.4.6
Usage: Use to copy the startup configuration to a host using rcp. This command will prompt for the host address and destination file name.

copy startup-config running-config

`copy startup-config running-config`

Mode: Privileged
Abbrev: **copy start run**

Section: 6.4.2.2

Usage: Use to merge the commands in the startup configuration into a router's running configuration. This command is the replacement of the **configure memory** command.

copy startup-config tftp

```
copy startup-config tftp
```

Mode: Privileged

Abbrev: **copy start tftp**

Section: 6.4.6

Usage: Use to copy the startup configuration to a host using TFTP. This command will prompt for the host address and destination file name.

copy tftp running-config

```
copy tftp running-config
```

Mode: Privileged

Abbrev: **copy tftp run**

Section: 6.4.2.3

Usage: Use to merge the commands in a text file on a TFTP server into a router's running configuration. This command is useful for performing repetitive configuration tasks on multiple routers. For example, building a host table on multiple routers can be done by entering the necessary **ip host** commands into a text file and then using this command to put the text file into the routers' running configurations. This command is the replacement of the **configure network** command.

copy tftp startup-config

```
copy tftp startup-config
```

Mode: Privileged

Abbrev: **copy tftp start**

Section: 6.4.5.2

Usage: Use to copy a file from a TFTP server to a router's startup configuration in NVRAM. This command is useful for restoring a

backup configuration to a router just before the router is to be
rebooted. The file that is copied to NVRAM is not checked for
valid commands; in other words, IOS will allow any file to be
copied to NVRAM with this command. This command is the
replacement of the **configure overwrite-network**
command.

debug

```
debug description | all
no debug description | all
undebug description | all
```

    description   Keyword(s) for type of debug activity or information to
                be displayed.

    all   All possible debugging activity and information (not rec-
                ommended).

Mode: Privileged
Abbrev: **deb** *description* | **al**
Section: 6.8
Usage: Use to have IOS display details about a particular type of activ-
        ity. This command is normally used only during troubleshoot-
        ing or experimenting. By default, output produced by the
        debug command is sent to the console and all other terminal
        lines that have the monitor capability. Use the **terminal**
        monitor command during a telnet session to give your VTY
        the monitor capability. Multiple debug activities can be enabled
        simultaneously, but the more that are enabled, the more diffi-
        cult the output is to read. Use the **no** form of the command to
        disable a debug activity. Use the **no debug all** command or the
        undebug all command to disable all debugging activity that
        has been enabled. Some versions of IOS have the alias **u**
        defined for **undebug**; in those versions, the **u al** command
        abbreviation can be used to turn off all debug activity.

decnet cost

```
decnet cost cost
no decnet cost
```

    cost   A value between 1 and 63 to be used by DRP to select the best
             route to a destination DECnet node.

Mode: Interface Configuration
Abbrev: **dec cos** *cost*
Section: 10.3
Usage: Use to enable DECnet on an interface and to assign an outbound cost metric to the interface. When this command is issued on a LAN interface, the MAC address of the interface is changed to the value that is translated from the router's DECnet address. Use the **no** form of the command to remove DECnet traffic processing from an interface.

decnet node-type

```
decnet node-type {area | routing-iv}
no decnet node-type
```

area   Indicates that the router is a Level-2 routing node.
routing-iv Indicates that the router is a Level-1 routing node.

Mode: Global Configuration
Abbrev: **dec nod {ar | ro}**
Section: 10.3
Usage: Use to define the type of routing node that a router is to be. A node type must be defined for DECnet to function. A Level-1 routing node knows only about DECnet nodes within its area, and a Level-2 routing node knows about all DECnet areas and, also, DECnet nodes within its area. Use the **no** form of the command to remove the node type.

decnet routing

```
decnet routing area.node
no decnet routing
```

area   A DECnet area number between 1 and 63.
node   A DECnet node number between 1 and 1023.

Mode: Global Configuration
Abbrev: **dec routi** *area.node*
Section: 10.3
Usage: Use to start the DECnet routing process on a router. After issuing this command, a node type should be set, and costs should be assigned to the appropriate interfaces. Use the **no** form of the command to stop the DECnet routing process.

delay

```
delay dly
no delay
```

dly   Delay value in tens of microseconds (μsec).

Mode: Interface Configuration
Abbrev: **del** *dly*
Section: 7.7.2
Usage: Use to assign a throughput delay to an interface. The delay is used by the routing protocols IGRP and EIGRP to calculate their composite metric for best-path determination. All interfaces have a default delay. The delay assigned to an interface is given in microseconds (μsec) when it is displayed with the **show interfaces** command. For example, the default delay of a fast-serial interface is 20,000 μsec, and the default delay of an Ethernet interface is 1000 μsec. Note that the displayed value is 10 times greater than the value entered in the command. Use the **no** form to remove an assigned delay from an interface and restore the default delay value.

description

```
description descr
no description
```

descr   Text description.

Mode: Interface Configuration
Abbrev: **desc** *descr*
Section: 6.2.5
Usage: Use to document an interface. The text description is displayed in the output of the **show interfaces** command. Use this command to include information such as circuit identifier and location to an interface's configuration.

dir

```
dir flashdev
```

flashdev   The name of a flash device such as slot0: or slot1:.

Mode: User, Privileged
Abbrev: **dir** *flashdev*
Section: 5.2.1
Usage: Use on 7x00-series routers to view list of files in flash memory.

disable

```
disable
```

Mode: Privileged
Abbrev: **disa**
Section: 4.2.2
Usage: Use to get from privileged mode to user mode.

disconnect

```
disconnect [conn-num | conn-name]
```

    conn-num   A connection number, which can be obtained with the **show sessions** command.

    conn-name   A connection name, which can be obtained with the **show sessions** command.

Mode: User, Privileged
Abbrev: **disc** [*conn-num* | *conn-name*]
Section: 6.5
Usage: Use this command to disconnect a connection that has been suspended. When the **disconnect** command is typed without a connection number or name, the session that appears with an asterisk in the **show sessions** output is disconnected after a confirmation.

distance

```
distance distance
no distance distance
```

    distance   Administrative distance value between 1 and 255.

Mode: Router Configuration
Abbrev: **dista** *distance*
Section: 7.7.1.1

Usage: Use to set the administrative distance for all routes learned from a specific IP routing protocol. The routing protocol is specified with a **router** command. The **no** form of the command sets the administrative distance to its default value.

dlsw local-peer

```
dlsw local-peer peer-id addr
no dlsw local-peer peer-id addr
```

addr   The IP address of a local interface on a router.

Mode: Global Configuration
Abbrev: **dls loc pee** *addr*
Section: 14.4
Usage: Use to define the local end of a DLSw connection. Use the **no** form of the command to remove the local peer definition.

dlsw remote-peer tcp

```
dlsw remote-peer list tcp addr
no dlsw remote-peer list tcp addr
```

list   Ring group list number. Use 0 as the default.
addr   The IP address of an interface on another router to which a DLSw connection should be established.

Mode: Global Configuration
Abbrev: **dls rem** *list* **tcp** *addr*
Section: 14.4
Usage: Use to define the remote end of a DLSw connection. Issue one of these commands for each DLSw connection to be established from a router. Use the **no** form of the command to remove the remote peer definition.

enable

```
enable
```

Mode: User
Abbrev: **en**
Section: 4.2.2, 6.1.3.2

Usage: Use to get from user mode to privileged mode. When connected to the console, you will be prompted for a password if an enable secret password or an enable password exists; otherwise, privileged mode access will be granted without the entry of a password. When connected to one of a router's VTYs, you will be prompted for a password if one exists. The possible passwords are, in order of precedence, enable secret password, enable password, and console password. If none of these passwords has been configured, you will not be allowed to enter privileged mode when connected to a VTY. If you type the correct password at the password prompt after entering the **enable** command, IOS will grant you access to privileged mode. Use the **disable** command to return to user mode.

enable password

```
enable password pwd
no enable password
```

   pwd   Text password that will be the enable password.

Mode: Global Configuration
Abbrev: **ena pass** *pwd*
Section: 6.1.3.2, 7.5.3
Usage: Use to define an enable password. The enable password is entered at the password prompt after the **enable** command to gain access to privileged mode, if an enable secret password has not been defined. The enable password is shown in clear text in the configuration file unless the password-encryption service is enabled with the **service password-encryption** command. Reissue the **enable password** command with a new password to change the enable password. Use the **no** form of the **enable password** command to remove an enable password.

enable secret

```
enable secret pwd
no enable secret
```

   pwd   Text password that will be the enable secret password.

Mode: Global Configuration
Abbrev: **ena sec** *pwd*
Section: 6.1.3.2, 7.5.3
Usage: Use to define an enable secret password. The enable secret password is entered at the password prompt after the **enable** command to gain access to privileged mode. The enable secret password is encrypted in the configuration file.

encapsulation

```
encapsulation {frame-relay [ietf] | hdlc | ppp | x25 [dte | dce]}
no encapsulation
```

frame-relay   Use when connected to a frame relay network.

ietf   Use when the other router on a PVC is not a Cisco router.

hdlc   Use on a point-to-point leased line when the other router is a Cisco router. This is the default.

ppp   Use on a point-to-point leased line when the other router is not a Cisco router.

x25   Use when connected to an X.25 network.

dte   Use when connected to an X.25 switch.

dce   Use when doing X.25 switching.

Mode: Interface Configuration
Abbrev: **enc {fr [ie] | hd | ppp | x25 [dt | dc]}**
Section: 6.2.3, 13.2.1, 13.2.2
Usage: Use when changing the layer-2 encapsulation of a serial interface. This book does not cover the tasks for configuring WANs that use encapsulations other than HDLC or PPP. The other encapsulation options are shown for illustration. Use the **no** form of the command to restore the default encapsulation, HDLC.

end

```
end
```

Mode: Global Configuration, Any Subconfiguration Mode.
Abbrev: **end**
Section: 4.2.3.1

Usage: Use to exit any configuration mode and return to privileged mode. This command performs the same function as **<Ctrl-Z>** when used in any configuration mode.

erase startup-config

```
erase startup-config
```

Mode: Privileged
Abbrev: **er st**
Section: 6.4.5.5
Usage: Use to erase the contents of NVRAM, which normally contains the startup configuration. If NVRAM is empty when a router boots, IOS will ask you if you want to start the Initial (System) Configuration Dialog. Use this command when you want to start from scratch with a router's configuration. This command is the replacement of the **write erase** command.

exec-timeout

```
exec-timeout min sec
no exec-timeout
```

min Number of minutes. Default is 10.
sec Number of seconds. Default is 0.

Mode: Line Configuration
Abbrev: **exec-t** *min sec*
Section: 6.3.2
Usage: Use to define how long a terminal session can be inactive before IOS disconnects it. The default time is 10 minutes. Use the **no** form of the command to disable the inactivity timeout. The timeout can also be disabled by setting it to 0 minutes, 0 seconds, for example, **exec-timeout 0 0**.

exit (Configuration)

```
exit
```

Mode: Global Configuration, Any Subconfiguration Mode
Abbrev: **ex**

Section: 4.2.3.1, 4.2.3.2
Usage: Use to return to privileged mode from global configuration mode, or use to return to global configuration mode from any subconfiguration mode.

exit (User, Privileged)

```
exit
```

Mode: User, Privileged
Abbrev: **ex**
Section: 4.4
Usage: Use to log out of a terminal session. Performs the same function as the **logout** and **quit** commands.

frame-relay interface-dlci

```
frame-relay interface-dlci dlci
no frame-relay interface-dlci dlci
```

dlci   The local DLCI of the PVC processed by a subinterface.

Mode: Subinterface Configuration
Abbrev: **fr int** *dlci*
Section: 13.2.2
Usage: Use this command to tell IOS which PVC is associated with a frame relay subinterface. A point-to-point subinterface can be associated with one PVC; a multipoint subinterface can be associated with multiple PVCs to create an NBMA network. Use the **no** form of the command to disassociate a PVC from a subinterface.

frame-relay lmi-type

```
frame-relay lmi-type {ansi | cisco}
no frame-relay lmi-type
```

ansi   Indicates that ANSI Annex D LMI should be used to communicate with the frame relay switch.

cisco Indicates that Gang of Four LMI should be used to communicate with the frame relay switch. This is the default.

Mode: Interface Configuration
Abbrev: **fram lmi {an | ci}**
Section: 13.2.1
Usage: Use to define the LMI type that is to be used to communicate with the local frame relay switch. This command is not needed in IOS version 11.3 and later because those versions automatically sense and use the LMI type that the switch is using. Use the **no** form of the command to set the LMI type to its default, Gang of Four.

frame-relay map

```
frame-relay map protocol addr dlci [broadcast] [cisco | ietf]
no frame-relay map protocol addr
```

protocol	A protocol name keyword such as **ip**, **ipx**, **appletalk**, **decnet**, and **vines**.
addr	A host address for the specified protocol.
dlci	The local DLCI of the PVC, which can be used to reach the host with the specified address.
broadcast	Keyword indicating that IOS should send normal broadcast traffic, such as routing protocol updates, over the specified PVC.
cisco	Use Cisco's frame relay encapsulation on the specified PVC.
ietf	Use the IETF frame encapsulation on the specified PVC.

Mode: Interface Configuration
Abbrev: **fram map** *protocol addr dlci* [**br**] [**ci** | **ie**]
Section: 13.2.1
Usage: Use to statically map a remote network address to the PVC, which can be used to reach the network address. Usually, this command is not needed since inverse ARP, which is enabled by default, performs dynamic mappings. The default encapsulation of a PVC is the one specified with the **encapsulation frame-relay** command; this can be overridden with the **cisco** or **ietf** keywords. Use the **no** form of the command to remove a static mapping.

hostname

```
hostname name
no hostname
```

    name   Text string to be assigned as a router's host name.

Mode: Global Configuration
Abbrev: **host** *name*
Section: 4.2.3.2, 6.1.1, 7.5.3
Usage: Use to set the host name of a router. The host name appears in the IOS command line prompt. The host name should be descriptive, and each router should have a unique name. Use the **no** form of the command to set the host name to its default value of *Router*.

interface (Logical)

```
interface int-name
no interface int-name
```

    int-name Interface name including interface type and interface number, for example, Loopback0.

Mode: Global Configuration
Abbrev: **int** *int-name*
Section: 4.2.3.2, 6.2
Usage: Use to create a logical interface or enter interface configuration mode for an existing interface. Use the **no** form to remove the logical interface from the running configuration. The logical interface will not be completely removed until the router is rebooted.

interface (Physical)

```
interface int-name
```

    int-nam Interface type and interface number, for example, Serial0.

Mode: Global Configuration
Abbrev: **int** *int-name*
Section: 4.2.3.2, 6.2, 7.5
Usage: Use to enter interface configuration for a physical interface.

interface (Subinterface)

```
interface int-name.subint-num
no interface int-name.subint-num
```

    int-name   Interface name including interface type and interface number.

    subint-num   Subinterface number.

Mode: Global Configuration
Abbrev: **int** *int-name.subint-num*
Section: 6.2, 8.7
Usage: Use to create a subinterface or enter subinterface configuration mode for an existing subinterface. Use the **no** form to remove the subinterface from the running configuration. The subinterface will not be completely removed until the router is rebooted.

interface (Subinterface, Frame Relay)

```
interface int-name.subint-num {multipoint | point-to-point}
no interface int-name.subint-num
```

    int-name   Interface name including interface type and interface number.

    subint-num   Subinterface number.

    multipoint   Create a multipoint subinterface.

    point-to-point Create a point-to-point subinterface.

Mode: Global Configuration
Abbrev: **int** *int-name.subint-num* {**mu** | **po**}
Section: 13.2.2
Usage: Use to create a subinterface of a physical interface using frame relay encapsulation. The physical interface configuration must already have the **encapsulation frame-relay** command before IOS will allow the creation of a multipoint or point-to-point subinterface. Use the **no** form to remove the subinterface from the running configuration. The subinterface will not be completely removed until the router is rebooted. Once a subinterface has been created as either multipoint or point-to-point, its type cannot be changed unless it is removed and the router is rebooted.

ip address

```
ip address addr netmask
ip address addr netmask [secondary]
no ip address
no ip address addr netmask [secondary]
```

addr	IP address in dotted-decimal notation.
netmask	Network mask in dotted-decimal notation.
secondary	Keywork that designates an additional IP address to be assigned to an interface.

Mode: Interface Configuration, Subinterface Configuration
Abbrev: **ip addr** *addr netmask* [**sec**]
Section: 6.2.1.1, 7.4, 7.5
Usage: Assign an IP address to an interface. The first IP address assigned to an interface is the interface's primary IP address. Use the **secondary** keyword to assign a secondary IP address to an interface. An interface can have multiple secondary addresses. Use the **no** form of the command to remove all IP addresses from an interface. Use the **no secondary** form of the command to remove a specific secondary address.

ip domain-lookup

```
ip domain-lookup
no ip domain-lookup
```

Mode: Global Configuration
Abbrev: **ip domain-lo**
Section: 6.1.5
Usage: Use to tell IOS to use DNS for IP address resolution. IOS uses DNS by default. Use the **no** form of the command to turn off DNS lookups.

ip host

```
ip host name [port] addr [addr2 - addr8]
no ip host name
```

name	Text string with name of host to put into local host table.

port	TCP port number that is accessible on the host. The default value is 23 (telnet).
addr	Primary IP address of the host.
addr2 - addr8	Other IP addresses that the host has (separated by spaces).

Mode: Global Configuration
Abbrev: **ip host** *name* [*port*] *addr* [*addr - addr8*]
Section: 6.1.5
Usage: Use to make an entry into a router's host table, which is used for address resolution. Up to eight IP addresses can be assigned for each host name. When performing a ping or trace using the host name, only the primary address is used. When performing a telnet using the host name, IOS attempts to establish a telnet session to each of the addresses in order until either a telnet session is established or all of the attempts fail. Use the **no** form of the command to remove a host table entry.

ip name-server

```
ip name-server addr [addr2 - addr6]
no ip name-server [addr] [addr2 - addr6]
```

addr	IP address of a host running a DNS server process. The default DNS server is 255.255.255.255.
addr2 - addr6	IP addresses of other hosts running DNS server processes.

Mode: Global Configuration
Abbrev: **ip nam** *addr* [*addr2 - addr6*]
Section: 6.1.5
Usage: Use to define the IP address of the server to which DNS requests are to be sent. Up to six addresses can be assigned.

ip rcmd remote-username

```
ip rcmd remote-username user
no ip rcmd remote-username user
```

user   Text string representing a user name on a host.

Mode: Global Configuration

Abbrev: **ip rc remote-u** *user*

Section: 6.4.2.4

Usage: Use this command to define the name of the remote user that will be used for authentication and file location during rcp copy operations. Use the **no** form of the command to remove the user name definition.

ip rip

```
ip rip {send | receive} version {1 | 2}
no ip rip {send | receive } version {1 | 2}
```

send   Transmission of RIP updates using packets formatted according to specified version.

receive   Receive and process RIP updates for specified version.

1   RIP version 1.

2   RIP version 2.

Mode: Interface Configuration

Abbrev: **ip rip** {**se** | **re**} **ver** {1 | 2}

Section: 7.7.1.3

Usage: Use this command to define the version of RIP that will be used on an interface. RIP must already be enabled on the interface before the command will have an effect. The **router rip** and **network** commands are used to enable RIP on an interface. The default RIPv1 behavior is to send version 1 updates and receive both version 1 and version 2 updates. The default RIPv2 behavior is to send and receive only version 2 updates. Use this command to override the default behavior.

ip route

```
ip route netaddr netmask {gwaddr| int-name} [distance]
no ip route netaddr netmask
```

netaddr   Prefix, in dotted-decimal notation, representing a network or location to which a route is being defined.

netmask   Network mask that tells IOS how much of the prefix is significant for routing.

gwaddr   IP address of the next-hop gateway.

> *int-name*   Interface name that includes interface type and interface port number.
>
> *distance*   Administrative distance. The default value is 1.

Mode: Global Configuration
Abbrev: **ip route** *netaddr netmask* {*gwaddr* | *int-name*} [*distance*]
Section: 7.6, 7.6.2, 7.6.3
Usage: Use to create an IP static route, which is a manual entry into the IP routing table. If the next-hop gateway address is specified, its address should be on a directly connected network. When an interface name is specified, the route is treated as directly connected. Generally, the interface name should be used when the interface is point-to-point such as a serial interface. Specifying the interface name to be a LAN interface may cause excessive ARP traffic and ARP cache memory utilization. Use the **no** form of the command to remove a static route.

ipx maximum-paths

```
ipx maximum-paths paths
no ipx maximum-paths
```

> *paths*   A decimal value between 1 and 64 that specifies the number of equal-cost paths over which IPX traffic may be load shared. The default value is 1.

Mode: Global Configuration
Abbrev: **ipx maximum-p** *paths*
Section: 8.4
Usage: Use to specify the number of equal-cost paths over which IOS may load share IPX traffic. Use the **no** form of the command to disable equal-cost path load sharing.

ipx network

```
ipx network netnum [encapsulation encap [secondary]]
no ipx network [netnum]
```

> *netnum*   IPX network number in hexadecimal.
>
> **encapsulation** Use to change the default encapsulation of an interface.

| *encap* | Encapsulation keyword. Some possibilities are **arp**, **novell-ether**, **sap**, **snap**, **token**, **token-snap**. |
| **secondary** | Use when assigning another IPX network number and encapsulation to an interface. |

Mode: Interface Configuration, Subinterface Configuration
Abbrev: **ipx netw** *netnum* [**enc** *encap* [**sec**]]
Section: 8.4, 8.7
Usage: Use this command to assign an IPX network address to an interface and enable the interface to send and receive IPX packets. The node part of the interface's IPX address becomes the interface's MAC address or, if the interface does not have a MAC address, the address specified on the **ipx routing** command. The first IPX network number assigned to an interface is that interface's primary IPX network number. Use the **secondary** keyword to add other IPX network addresses to an interface when multiple encapsulations are required. Use the **no** form of the command to remove an IPX network number from an interface. Removing the primary network number will also remove any secondary network numbers from an interface.

ipx router eigrp

```
ipx router eigrp asn
no ipx router eigrp asn
```

asn Autonomous system number. All routers sharing routes with IPX EIGRP must use the same ASN.

Mode: Global Configuration
Abbrev: **ipx router ei** *asn*
Section: 8.6
Usage: Use to enable IPX EIGRP on a router. Use the **network** command to enable IPX EIGRP on specific interfaces. Use the **no** form of the command to disable IPX EIGRP on all interfaces.

ipx router rip

```
ipx router rip
no ipx router rip
```

Mode: Global Configuration
Abbrev: **ipx router ri**
Section: 8.6
Usage: Use to enable IPX RIP on a router. IPX RIP is enabled by
          default on all interfaces that have been assigned an IPX net-
          work number with the **ipx network** command. This com-
          mand is used mostly when disabling IPX RIP on interfaces
          when both IPX EIGRP and RIP are being used. Use the **no**
          form of the command to disable IPX RIP on all interfaces.

ipx routing

```
ipx routing [address]
no ipx routing
```

   address   A MAC address in the form *xxxx.xxxx.xxxx,* where *x* is a
              hexadecimal digit.

Mode: Global Configuration
Abbrev: **ipx routi** [*address*]
Section: 8.4, 8.9
Usage: Use to enable the routing of IPX packets on a router. The
          address becomes the node part of all IPX addresses on inter-
          faces that do not have a MAC address. If an address is not
          entered, IOS automatically selects one and places it in the
          running configuration with the command. The address
          selected is the MAC address of the router's first LAN inter-
          face, with the first Ethernet interface taking precedence. If a
          router has no LAN interfaces, IOS chooses an address at ran-
          dom. We should verify that the address is unique among
          directly connected routers. Use the **no** form of the command to
          disable the routing of IPX packets.

line

```
line {abs-line | aux rel-line | console rel-line | tty rel-line | vty
{rel-line | rel-line-beg rel-line-end}}
```

   abs-line   Absolute line number.
   aux   Auxiliary terminal line.
   rel-line   Relative line number.
   console   Console terminal line.

tty	Terminal controller line.
vty	Virtual terminal line.
rel-line-beg	Beginning relative line number of a range.
rel-line-end	Ending relative line number of a range.

Mode: Global Configuration
Abbrev: **lin** {*abs-line* | **aux** *rel-line* | **con** *rel-line* | **tty** *rel-line* | **vty** {*rel-line* | *rel-line-beg rel-line-end*}}
Section: 6.3, 7.5.3
Usage: Use to get to line configuration mode for configuring a terminal line. The numbering of terminal lines is covered in Section 5.2.4. We can create additional VTYs by referencing their relative line numbers with the **line vty** form of the command. We can reference multiple VTYs with a range (two relative line numbers separated by spaces), for example, **line vty 0 4** references the first five VTYs.

login

```
login
no login
```

Mode: Line Configuration
Abbrev: **logi**
Section: 6.1.3.1, 6.3.1, 7.5.3
Usage: Use to enable login authentication on a terminal line. Once this command has been issued on a line, a password should be assigned to the line with the **password** command. Use the **no** form of the command to disable authentication.

logout

```
logout
```

Mode: User, Privileged
Abbrev: **logo**
Section: 4.4
Usage: Use to log out of a terminal session. Performs the same function as the **exit** and **quit** commands.

mtu

```
mtu bytes
no mtu bytes
```

    bytes   Number of bytes that will be assigned as the MTU for an interface.

Mode: Interface Configuration
Abbrev: **mt** *bytes*
Section: 7.7.2
Usage: Use to change the MTU for an interface. All interfaces have a default MTU. Use the **no** form of the command to restore the default MTU to an interface.

network (IP)

```
network net
no network net
```

    net   An IP class-A, class-B, or class-C network address.

Mode: Router Configuration (RIP, IGRP, EIGRP)
Abbrev: **netw** *net*
Section: 7.7, 7.7.1.1, 7.7.1.3, 7.7.2.1, 7.7.3.3
Usage: Use to enable an IP routing protocol on a router's interface(s) after the routing protocol has been specified with one of the **router** commands. The routing protocol will be enabled on all interfaces with IP addresses within the network specified. IOS requires that at least one **network** command be entered before the RIP, IGRP, or EIGRP process is started. If a subnet address or host address is entered with this command, IOS will convert the entered address to the major, classful network address to which it belongs. If a supernet address, such as 192.0.0.0, is entered, the command will have no effect. Use the **no** form of the command to disable a routing protocol on the interfaces belonging to an IP network.

network (IPX)

```
network netnum
no network netnum
```

netnum   An IPX network number in hexadecimal.

Mode: IPX Router Configuration
Abbrev: **netw** *netnum*
Section: 8.6
Usage: Use to enable an IPX routing protocol such as EIGRP on an interface. The routing protocol will be enabled on the interface that has the specified IPX network number. By default, IPX RIP is enabled on all interfaces that have a defined IPX network number. Use the **no** form of the command to disable an IPX routing protocol on an interface. For example, use the **no network** command to disable IPX RIP on an interface after using the **network** command to enable IPX EIGRP on an interface.

network area

```
network ipaddr wildcard-mask area area-id
no network ipaddr wildcard-mask area area-id
```

ipaddr   An IP address in dotted-decimal notation. This address can be a network address, a subnet address, a host address, or any other type of IP address.

wildcard-mask   A wildcard mask in dotted-decimal notation. A wildcard mask has bits with the reverse definitions as a network mask. In a wildcard mask, a significant bit is a binary zero (0), and a bit that should be ignored is a binary one (1).

area-id   The ID of the area in which an interface should be placed. The area ID can be written in decimal or dotted-decimal notation.

Mode: Router Configuration (OSPF)
Abbrev: **netw** *ipaddr wildcard-mask* **ar** *area-id*
Section: 7.7.4.2
Usage: Use to enable OSPF on a router's interface(s). All interfaces with addresses that match the address-mask pair are enabled for the OSPF process and are placed in the specified area. The **network area** commands that are part of an OSPF process's configuration are processed from the top to the bottom; therefore, the order of the commands can be significant. An interface can be part of a single OSPF process and a single OSPF

area. Use the **no** form of the command to disable OSPF on an interface.

passive-interface

```
passive-interface int-name
no passive-interface int-name
```

    int-name   The name of an interface including the interface type and interface port number.

Mode: Router Configuration
Abbrev: **pas** *int-name*
Section: 7.7.1.3, 7.7.2.1, 7.7.3.3
Usage: Use to stop routing protocol updates from being transmitted out from the specified interface. The routing protocol should already have been enabled on the interface with a **network** command. The interface will still be able to receive updates. Use the **no** form to allow an interface to transmit updates.

password

```
password [encrypt-type] pwd
no password
```

   encrypt-type   A decimal value indicating the type of encryption that has been applied to the password being entered. Possible values are 0 for no encryption and 5 for Cisco encryption. Used in configuration files when encryption has been done to prevent an encrypted password from being reencrypted when a configuration file is copied from one router to another or back to its original router. Not normally used when directly typing a password.

   pwd   A password text string.

Mode: Line Configuration
Abbrev: **pass** [*encrypt-type*] *pwd*
Section: 6.1.3.1, 6.3.1, 7.5.3
Usage: Use to assign a password to a terminal line. For password to be checked, the terminal line configuration should also contain the **login** command. Use the **no** form of the command to remove a password. If a router's VTYs do not have a password, telnet will not be allowed to the router.

ping (Extended)

`ping`

Mode: Privileged
Abbrev: **pi**
Section: 7.6.1, 8.5, 9.5, 10.4, 11.4
Usage: Use to test connectivity from a router to a host using echo packets according to the specified protocol. The extended ping application prompts for the protocol name. The extended ping provides more flexibility in troubleshooting by allowing us to change ping parameters such the number of echoes, the size of echo packets, and the echo reply timeout. Sample extended ping output is shown in the sections referenced above.

ping (Simple)

`ping` [`protocol`] `addr`

   protocol   A protocol name keyword such as **ip**, **ipx**, **appletalk**, **decnet**, and **vines**.
   addr   A host address.

Mode: User, Privileged
Abbrev: **pi** *addr*
Section: 7.6.1, 8.5, 9.5, 10.4, 11.4
Usage: Use to test connectivity from a router to a host using echo packets according to the specified protocol. When the protocol name is not specified, IOS attempts to determine the desired protocol by address or name format. For example, an address in dotted-decimal format is interpreted as an IP address, and IOS will use ICMP echoes to test connectivity.

prompt

`prompt` *prompt*
`no prompt`

   prompt   Text string to be the user mode and privileged mode command line prompt. Maximum displayed length is 30 characters.

Mode: Global Configuration
Abbrev: **pro** *prompt*
Section: 6.1.4
Usage: Use the **prompt** command to define the command line prompt for user mode and privileged mode. This command does not affect the configuration mode prompts. The default prompt is the first 29 characters of the router's host name followed by a prompt character (> or #), which indicates user mode or privileged mode. Use the **no** form of the command to set the prompt to its default value.

quit

`quit`

Mode: User, Privileged
Abbrev: **q**
Section: 4.4
Usage: Use to log out of a terminal session. Performs the same function as the **exit** and **logout** commands.

reload

`reload`

Mode: Privileged
Abbrev: **rel**
Section: 6.9
Usage: Use the **reload** command from a terminal line session to reboot a router. IOS will prompt for confirmation after this command is entered. If the terminal session user entered a configuration mode and did not copy the running configuration to NVRAM prior to issuing this command, IOS will prompt to perform the copy before it prompts for reload confirmation.

resume

`resume` [*conn-num* | *conn-name*]

> *conn-num*   A connection number, which can be obtained with the **show sessions** command.

conn-name   A connection name, which can be obtained with the **show sessions** command.

Mode: User, Privileged
Abbrev: **res** [*conn-num* | *conn-name*]
Section: 6.5
Usage: Use this command to resume a connection that has been suspended. When the **resume** command is typed without a connection number or name, the session that appears with an asterisk in the **show sessions** output is resumed. The session with the asterisk is called the next active session. The next active session can also be resumed by simply pressing **<Enter>**on a blank command line.

ring-speed

`ring-speed` *speed*

speed   Number specifying the speed of the token ring LAN to which an interface is attached. Possible values are 4 and 16.

Mode: Interface Configuration
Abbrev: **ring** *speed*
Section: 14.2
Usage: Use this command to set the speed of a token ring interface. Verify that the speed entered is the same as that of the LAN itself; otherwise, an outage may occur.

router eigrp

`router eigrp` *asn*
`no router eigrp` *asn*

asn   Autonomous system number. All routers that are using EIGRP to share route information must use the same ASN.

Mode: Global Configuration
Abbrev: **router ei** *asn*
Section: 7.7.3.3, 7.7.3.6
Usage: Use to start an EIGRP process or configure an existing EIGRP process. Typing this command will put the user into router configuration mode where commands for configuring the

EIGRP process can be entered. After typing this command the first time, at least one **network** command must be entered before the EIGRP process will start. Use the **no** form of the command to stop the EIGRP process and remove all of its configuration commands.

router igrp

```
router igrp asn
no router igrp asn
```

asn Autonomous system number. All routers that are using IGRP to share route information must use the same ASN.

Mode: Global Configuration
Abbrev: **router ig** *asn*
Section: 7.7.2.1, 7.7.2.5
Usage: Use to start an IGRP process or configure an existing IGRP process. Typing this command will put the user into router configuration mode where commands for configuring the IGRP process can be entered. After typing this command the first time, at least one **network** command must be entered before the IGRP process will start. Use the **no** form of the command to stop the IGRP process and remove all of its configuration commands.

router ospf

```
router ospf pid
no router ospf pid
```

pid A process ID. The process ID identifies the local OSPF process; it has no relationship to OSPF processes on other routers.

Mode: Global Configuration
Abbrev: **router os** *pid*
Section: 7.7.4.2, 7.7.4.6
Usage: Use to start an OSPF process or configure an existing OSPF process. Typing this command will put the user into router configuration mode where commands for configuring the OSPF process can be entered. After typing this command the

first time, at least one **network area** command must be entered before the OSPF process will start. Use the **no** form of the command to stop the OSPF process and remove all of its configuration commands.

router rip

```
router rip
no router rip
```

Mode: Global Configuration
Abbrev: **router rip**
Section: 7.7.1.1, 7.7.1.2, 7.7.1.5
Usage: Use to start the IP RIP process or configure the existing RIP process. Typing this command will put the user into router configuration mode where commands for configuring the RIP process can be entered. After typing this command the first time, at least one **network** command must be entered before the RIP process will start. Use the **no** form of the command to stop the RIP process and remove all of its configuration commands.

send

send {***** | *abs-line* | **aux** *rel-line* | **console** *rel-line* | **tty** *rel-line* | **vty** *rel-line*}

*	All terminal lines.
abs-line	Absolute line number.
aux	Auxiliary terminal line.
rel-line	Relative line number.
console	Console terminal line.
tty	Terminal controller line.
vty	Virtual terminal line.

Mode: Privileged
Abbrev: **send** {***** | *abs-line* | **aux** *rel-line* | **con** *rel-line* | **tty** *rel-line* | **vty** *rel-line*}
Section: 4.3.3, 6.7

Usage: Use to send a message to a terminal line. The numbering of terminal lines is covered in Section 5.2.4. After typing this command, the user will get a blank line on which a message can be typed. After typing the message, pressing **<Ctrl-Z>**, and confirming the operation, the message is sent to the specified terminal line on the router. Pressing **<Ctrl-C>** prior to confirmation aborts the operation. Use the **send *** command to send a message to all active terminal lines.

service password-encryption

```
service password-encryption
no service password-encryption
```

Mode: Global Configuration
Abbrev: **se pas**
Section: 6.1.3.3
Usage: Use this command to enable the service that encrypts the terminal line passwords and the enable password with Cisco's encryption algorithm. This algorithm is not secure and is easily broken; it is meant to hide passwords from accidental, casual exposure. When passwords have been encrypted with this algorithm, the **password** and **enable password** commands in the configuration files will be followed by the numeral 5 signifying that the password to follow is encrypted. Use the **no** form of the command to disable the service. Disabling the service will not unencrypt the passwords; however, when the passwords are reentered after the service is disabled, they will appear in the configuration files in clear text format.

show appletalk eigrp neighbors

```
show appletalk eigrp neighbors
```

Mode: User, Privileged
Abbrev: **sh app ei n**
Section: 9.6
Usage: Use to display the contents of the AppleTalk EIGRP neighbor table.

show appletalk eigrp topology

```
show appletalk eigrp topology
```

Mode: User, Privileged
Abbrev: **sh app ei to**
Section: 9.6
Usage: Use to display the contents of the AppleTalk EIGRP topology
          table.

show appletalk interface

```
show appletalk interface [int-name]
```

   int-name   An interface name that includes an interface type and
               interface port number.

Mode: User, Privileged
Abbrev: **sh app int** [*int-name*]
Section: 9.5
Usage: Use to display the status of AppleTalk on an interface. If no
          interface is specified, the AppleTalk status of all interfaces is
          displayed.

show appletalk route

```
show appletalk route
```

Mode: User, Privileged
Abbrev: **sh app rou**
Section: 9.3, 9.5
Usage: Use to display the contents of the AppleTalk routing table.

show appletalk zone

```
show appletalk zone
```

Mode: User, Privileged
Abbrev: **sh app zo**
Section: 9.3, 9.5
Usage: Use to display the contents of the AppleTalk ZIT (zone infor-
          mation table).

show bridge

```
show bridge
```

Mode: User, Privileged
Abbrev: **sh br**
Section: 5.3.5, 12.3
Usage: Use to display the contents of the transparent bridge forwarding table.

show bridge group

```
show bridge group
```

Mode: User, Privileged
Abbrev: **sh br gr**
Section: 12.3
Usage: Use to display a router's bridge groups and the spanning tree mode of the interfaces that are members of each bridge group.

show buffers

```
show buffers
```

Mode: User, Privileged
Abbrev: **sh buf**
Section: 5.3.3
Usage: Use to display the status of the IOS buffer pools.

show cdp

```
show cdp
```

Mode: User, Privileged
Abbrev: **sh cdp**
Section: 6.6
Usage: Use to display the status of CDP and the CDP global timer values.

show cdp interface

`show cdp interface [int-name]`

    int-name An interface name that includes an interface type and interface port number.

Mode: User, Privileged
Abbrev: **sh cdp int** [*int-name*]
Section: 6.6
Usage: Use to display the status of CDP on an interface. If no interface is specified, the CDP status of all interfaces is displayed.

show cdp neighbors

`show cdp neighbors [detail]`

    detail Indicates that details of table entries should be shown.

Mode: User, Privileged
Abbrev: **sh cdp n [d]**
Section: 6.6
Usage: Use to display the contents of the CDP neighbor table. A one-line summary of each entry is displayed unless the **detail** keyword is included.

show clock

`show clock`

Mode: User, Privileged
Abbrev: **sh clo**
Section: 5.3.7
Usage: Use to display the current time on a router.

show config

`show config`

Mode: Privileged
Abbrev: **sh conf**
Section: 6.4.4

Usage: Use to display the contents of NVRAM, which usually contains the startup configuration. This command is the predecessor of the **show startup-config** command.

show controllers

```
show controllers [all | [int-type [int-num]]]
```

all   Keyword meaning all controllers.
int-type   Interface type keyword such as ethernet, serial, tokenring.
int-num   Interface port number.

Mode: User, Privileged
Abbrev: **sh cont [all** | [*int-type* [*int-num*]]]
Section: 5.2.2
Usage: Use to display information about controllers on a router. If a specific controller or a specific controller type is not entered, the default behavior of this command is to display information about all controllers. When displaying information about serial controllers, this command shows the type of cable (DTE, DCE, V.35, RS-232) that is connected to the serial interfaces.

show decnet interface

```
show decnet interface [int-name]
```

int-name An interface name that includes an interface type and interface port number.

Mode: User, Privileged
Abbrev: **sh dec int** [*int-name*]
Section: 10.4
Usage: Use to display DECnet parameters for an interface. If no interface is specified, DECnet global parameters are displayed along with DECnet parameters for all interfaces.

show decnet neighbors

```
show decnet neighbors
```

Mode: User, Privileged
Abbrev: **sh dec nei**

Section: 10.4
Usage: Use to display the adjacencies being maintained by a DECnet router.

show decnet route

`show decnet route`

Mode: User, Privileged
Abbrev: **sh dec rou**
Section: 10.4
Usage: Use to display the contents of the DECnet routing table.

show dlsw peers

`show dlsw peers`

Mode: User, Privileged
Abbrev: **sh dls pe**
Section: 14.5
Usage: Use to display the status of the DLSw peer connections.

show environment

`show environment [all]`

Mode: User, Privileged
Abbrev: **sh env [all]**
Section: 5.3.9
Usage: Use to get information about the environmental parameters on a router. Use the **all** keyword to display details such as voltage levels and temperatures.

show flash

`show flash`

Mode: User, Privileged
Abbrev: **sh fla**
Section: 5.2.1
Usage: Use to get a directory of a router's primary flash memory device. The directory should contain a list of the files in flash,

their sizes, the total amount of flash, and the amount of flash in use (or free).

show frame-relay lmi

```
show frame-relay lmi
```

Mode: User, Privileged
Abbrev: **sh fram lmi**
Section: 13.2.1
Usage: Use to display the LMI type and LMI traffic statistics.

show frame-relay map

```
show frame-relay map
```

Mode: User, Privileged
Abbrev: **sh fram map**
Section: 13.2.1, 13.2.2
Usage: Use to display a router's known associations (mappings) between network protocol addresses and DLCIs.

show frame-relay pvc

```
show frame-relay pvc
```

Mode: User, Privileged
Abbrev: **sh fram pvc**
Section: 13.2.1
Usage: Use to display the status of the frame relay PVCs coming into a router.

show history

```
show history
```

Mode: User, Privileged
Abbrev: **sh hi**
Section: 4.3.1.1, 4.3.3
Usage: Use to display the contents of the command history buffer, which, by default, should show the last 10 commands that were typed during the current terminal line session.

show hosts

`show hosts`

Mode: User, Privileged
Abbrev: **sh ho**
Section: 6.1.5
Usage: Use to display the contents of a router's host table. The display contains both permanent and temporary entries. A permanent entry is one that is made with the ip host command, and a temporary entry is one that IOS makes dynamically after performing a DNS lookup.

show interface

`show` *protocol* `interface` [*int-name* | `brief`]

protocol   The name of a protocol, for example, **ip**, **ipx**, **appletalk**, **decnet**, and **vines**.

int-name   The name of an interface including the interface type and interface port number.

brief   Keyword used to request a display showing a summary of all interfaces.

Mode: User, Privileged
Abbrev: **sh** *protocol* **int** [*int-name* | **brie**]
Section: 5.2.3, 5.3.8
Usage: Use to display detailed, protocol-specific information about a router's interfaces. If no interface name is entered, the display includes all interfaces on which the specified protocol is enabled. Use the **brief** keyword to get a summary that includes the status of all interfaces on a single page (unless, of course, the router has more interfaces than a page has lines), for example, **sh ip int brie**.

show interfaces

`show interfaces` [*int-name*]

int-name   The name of an interface including the interface type and interface port number.

Mode: User, Privileged
Abbrev: **sh int** [*int-name*]
Section: 5.2.3, 7.7.2, 13.2.1
Usage: Use to display information about a router's interfaces. The information includes interface status, input counters, output counters, and error counters. The counters can be reset to zero with the **clear counters** command. If no interface name is entered, the display includes all interfaces on the router.

show ip eigrp neighbors

```
show ip eigrp neighbors
```

Mode: User, Privileged
Abbrev: **sh ip ei n**
Section: 7.7.3.4
Usage: Use to display the contents of the IP EIGRP neighbor table.

show ip eigrp topology

```
show ip eigrp topology
```

Mode: User, Privileged
Abbrev: **sh ip ei to**
Section: 7.7.3.4
Usage: Use to display the contents of the IP EIGRP topology table.

show ip eigrp traffic

```
show ip eigrp traffic
```

Mode: User, Privileged
Abbrev: **sh ip ei tr**
Section: 7.7.3.4
Usage: Use to display statistics for IP EIGRP. The statistics include counters for the input and output of each type of EIGRP packet.

show ip ospf

`show ip ospf`

Mode: User, Privileged
Abbrev: **sh ip os**
Section: 7.7.4.3
Usage: Use to display global information about OSPF processes on a
            router. The information includes the router ID, the number of
            areas connected, and the number of interfaces in each area.

show ip ospf database

`show ip ospf database` [*lsa-type*]

   lsa-type   Keyword for type of LSAs to view in detail, for example,
           router, **summary**, **network**.

Mode: User, Privileged
Abbrev: **sh ip os d** [*lsa-type*]
Section: 7.7.4.3
Usage: Use to display the contents of the OSPF link state database. If
            no LSA type is specified, the output is a summary of all the
            records in the database.

show ip ospf interface

`show ip ospf interface` [*int-name*]

   int-name   An interface name consisting of an interface type and an
           interface port number.

Mode: User, Privileged
Abbrev: **sh ip os i** [*int-name*]
Section: 7.7.4.3
Usage: Use to display information about the interfaces that have
            OSPF enabled. The information includes the interface's net-
            work type (for example, broadcast or point-to-point) and timer
            values (such as hello interval and dead interval). If no inter-
            face name is specified, all interfaces are displayed.

show ip ospf neighbor

`show ip ospf neighbor`

Mode: User, Privileged
Abbrev: **sh ip os n**
Section: 7.7.4.3
Usage: Use to display the contents of the OSPF neighbor table. The
           neighbor table contains the router IDs of all OSPF neighbors
           and the state of each neighbor's connection.

show ip protocols

`show ip protocols`

Mode: User, Privileged
Abbrev: **sh ip prot**
Section: 7.7.1.1, 7.7.2.2, 7.7.3.4, 7.7.4.3
Usage: Use to display general information about all of the IP routing
           protocols running on a router. This command tells us quickly
           which IP routing protocols have been configured.

show ip route

`show ip route [summary]`

summary   Keyword used to indicate that a summary of the contents
              should be displayed.

Mode: User, Privileged
Abbrev: **sh ip rou [sum]**
Section: 5.3.5, 7.3, 7.5.4, 7.7.1.1, 7.7.2.2, 7.7.3.4, 7.7.4.3
Usage: Use to display the contents of the IP routing table. Each
           routing table entry usually consists of a prefix, a prefix length
           (or network mask), an administrative distance, a metric, a
           next-hop gateway, and a local interface. The summary display
           shows how many of each type of route are in the routing table.

show ipx eigrp neighbors

`show ipx eigrp neighbors`

Mode: User, Privileged
Abbrev: **sh ipx ei n**
Section: 8.6
Usage: Use to display the contents of the IPX EIGRP neighbor table.

show ipx eigrp topology

`show ipx eigrp topology`

Mode: User, Privileged
Abbrev: **sh ipx ei to**
Section: 8.6
Usage: Use to display the contents of the IPX EIGRP topology table.

show ipx interface

`show ipx interface` [*int-name*]

int-name   An interface name that includes an interface type and
             interface port number.

Mode: User, Privileged
Abbrev: **sh ipx int** [*int-name*]
Section: 8.5
Usage: Use to display the status of IPX on an interface. If no interface
           is specified, all interfaces that have IPX enabled are displayed.
           This command is useful for obtaining an interface's full IPX
           address.

show ipx route

`show ipx route`

Mode: User, Privileged
Abbrev: **sh ipx rou [sum]**
Section: 8.3, 8.6
Usage: Use to display the contents of the IPX routing table. Each
           routing table entry usually contains a network number, a met-
           ric (ticks and hops), a next-hop gateway, and a local interface.

show ipx servers

```
show ipx servers [detailed]
```

    detailed   Keyword that indicates more details should be displayed.

Mode: User, Privileged
Abbrev: **sh ipx ser [det]**
Section: 8.3
Usage: Use to display the Novell service table that was built by listening to SAP updates. Each service table entry usually contains a service type, a service name, an address, a hop count, and a local interface name.

show ipx traffic

```
show ipx traffic
```

Mode: User, Privileged
Abbrev: **sh ipx tr**
Section: 8.5
Usage: Use to display statistics for IPX. The statistics include counters for the input and output of each type of IPX packet. The number of routes in the routing table and the number of services in the service are given in the output.

show line

```
show line {abs-line | aux rel-line | console rel-line | tty rel-line
| vty rel-line}
```

    abs-line   Absolute line number.
    aux   Auxiliary terminal line.
    rel-line   Relative line number.
    console Console terminal line.
    tty   Terminal controller line.
    vty   Virtual terminal line.

Mode: Privileged
Abbrev: **sh li** {*abs-line* | **aux** *rel-line* | **con** *rel-line* | **tty** *rel-line* | **vty** *rel-line*}
Section: 5.2.4

Usage: Use to show terminal line characteristics. If no terminal line is specified, the display is a summary of all terminal lines.

show logging

`show logging`

Mode: User, Privileged
Abbrev: **sh log**
Section: 5.3.6
Usage: Use to display the logging levels that have been configured for the console, monitor, syslog, and buffer locations. The contents of the buffer location are also displayed.

show memory

`show memory`

Mode: User, Privileged
Abbrev: **sh mem**
Section: 5.3.2
Usage: Use to show the characteristics of all IOS memory blocks. This command also displays total memory utilization.

show processes cpu

`show processes cpu`

Mode: User, Privileged
Abbrev: **sh proc cpu**
Section: 5.3.1
Usage: Use to display CPU utilization statistics. The output contains total CPU utilization along with CPU utilization statistics for each IOS process.

show processes memory

`show processes memory`

Mode: User, Privileged
Abbrev: **sh proc mem**
Section: 5.3.2

Usage: Use to display memory utilization statistics. The output contains total memory utilization along with memory utilization statistics for each IOS process.

show protocols

`show protocols`

Mode: User, Privileged
Abbrev: **sh prot**
Section: 4.3.6, 5.3.8, 8.5, 9.5, 10.4, 11.4
Usage: Use to find out the routed protocols that are running on a router. The output contains the status of each interface and the primary characteristic of the enabled routed protocols on each interface.

show route

`show` *protocol* `route`

protocol A protocol name keyword such as **ip**, **ipx**, **appletalk**, **decnet**, and **vines**.

Mode: User, Privileged
Abbrev: **sh** *protocol* **rou**
Section: 5.3.5
Usage: Use to display the contents of the routing table for the specified protocol.

show running-config

`show running-config`

Mode: Privileged
Abbrev: **sh run**
Section: 5.4.1
Usage: Use to display the contents of the running configuration file, which contains the commands that are currently being used by a router. This command is the replacement of the **write terminal** command.

show sessions

```
show sessions
```

Mode: User, Privileged
Abbrev: **sh ses**
Section: 6.5
Usage: Use to show the suspended sessions for the current terminal session. The sessions can be resumed with the **resume** command and disconnected with the **disconnect** command.

show source-bridge

```
show source-bridge
```

Mode: User, Privileged
Abbrev: **sh sour**
Section: 14.5
Usage: Use to show information about the configuration of source route bridging. The output includes the source and target ring numbers and statistics for each interface that has SRB configured.

show spanning-tree

```
show spanning-tree [group]
```

group A bridge group number between 1 and 63.

Mode: User, Privileged
Abbrev: **sh sp** [*group*]
Section: 12.3
Usage: Use to display information about a spanning tree bridge group and its member interfaces. If no bridge group number is specified, information about all spanning tree bridge groups is displayed.

show stacks

```
show stacks
```

Mode: User, Privileged
Abbrev: **sh stac**

Section: 5.3.4
Usage: Use to display the status of the IOS process stacks. This command is most useful in determining the cause of a crash.

show startup-config

```
show startup-config
```

Mode: Privileged
Abbrev: **sh start**
Section: 5.4.2, 6.4.4
Usage: Use to display the contents of a router's NVRAM, which usually contains the startup configuration file. This command is the replacement of the **show config** command.

show tech-support

```
show tech-support
```

Mode: Privileged
Abbrev: **sh tech**
Section: 5.5
Usage: Use in conjunction with a terminal emulator's log feature to capture the output of many important **show** commands for router documentation and Cisco TAC. The **show** commands include **show interfaces**, **show running-config**, and **show controllers**.

show terminal

```
show terminal
```

Mode: User, Privileged
Abbrev: **sh term**
Section: 5.2.4
Usage: Use to display the characteristics for the current terminal session. These characteristics can be modified with the **terminal** command.

show users

`show users`

Mode: User, Privileged
Abbrev: **sh us**
Section: 5.2.4, 6.7
Usage: Use to see a list of all active terminal lines and the source of the terminal line sessions. Most versions of IOS have the undocumented command **who**, which performs the same operation as this command.

show version

`show version`

Mode: User, Privileged
Abbrev: **sh ver**
Section: 5.1
Usage: Use to display the version of IOS that a router is running. The output also includes the boot location, the elapsed time since boot time, the router model (series), the type of interfaces in the router, and the value of the configuration register. This command performs the same operation as the **show hardware** command.

show vines interface

`show vines interface` [*int-name*]

int-name   An interface name that includes an interface type and interface port number.

Mode: User, Privileged
Abbrev: **sh vi int** [*int-name*]
Section: 11.4
Usage: Use to display VINES parameters for an interface. If no interface is specified, VINES global parameters are displayed along with VINES parameters for all interfaces, which have an assigned VINES metric.

show vines neighbor

`show vines neighbor`

Mode: User, Privileged
Abbrev: **sh vi ne**
Section: 11.4
Usage: Use to display the VINES 0-hop neighbors that have been learned by hearing VINES keepalives.

show vines route

`show vines route`

Mode: User, Privileged
Abbrev: **sh vi rou**
Section: 11.4
Usage: Use to display the contents of the VINES routing table, which contains a list of all of the VINES servers and routers in an internetwork.

shutdown

`shutdown`
`no shutdown`

Mode: Interface Configuration, Subinterface Configuration
Abbrev: **shut**
Section: 4.3.5, 6.2.7, 7.5
Usage: Use to disable an interface by placing it into administratively down state. Use the **no** form of the command to enable an interface. The **no** form is the default form of this command, and it does not appear in a router's configuration files.

source-bridge

`source-bridge` *srn bridge trn*
`no source-bridge`

   srn   Source ring number between 1 and 4095. The number assigned to an interface's token ring LAN.

bridge   Bridge number between 1 and 15. The number assigned to the router acting as a bridge.

trn   Target ring number between 1 and 4095. The number assigned to the ring on the other side of the bridge with the specified number.

Mode: Interface Configuration
Abbrev: **sou** *srn bridge trn*
Section: 14.2, 14.4
Usage: Use to enable source route bridging on a token ring interface. Issuing this command also initializes a token ring interface. Use the **no** form of the command to disable SRB on an interface.

source-bridge ring-group

```
source-bridge ring-group rn
no source-bridge ring-group
```

rn   Ring number between 1 and 4095 to be assigned to the virtual token ring (ring group) of a router.

Mode: Global Configuration
Abbrev: **sou ring** *rn*
Section: 14.2, 14.4
Usage: Use to create a virtual ring in a router to be used either for DLSw or for SRB, when more than two token ring interfaces in the same router are to run SRB. Use the **no** form of the command to remove a ring group.

source-bridge spanning

```
source-bridge spanning
no source-bridge spanning
```

Mode: Interface Configuration
Abbrev: **sou spa**
Section: 14.2, 14.4
Usage: Use to enable the use of spanning-tree explorers on a token ring interface running SRB. Use the **no** form of the command to disable the use of spanning-tree explorers on an interface.

telnet

```
telnet {ipaddr | host-name}
```

ipaddr	IP address in dotted-decimal notation.
host-name	The name of a host that can be resolved to an address using DNS or a host table.

Mode: User, Privileged
Abbrev: **tel** {*ipaddr* | *host-name*}
Section: 6.5
Usage: Use to access a remote host by the establishment of a telnet connection. When a host name is specified, IOS must perform address resolution to get an IP address before attempting the telnet.

terminal

```
terminal {parameter}
terminal no {parameter}
```

parameter   One or more keywords and values used to define characteristics for the current terminal line session.

Mode: User, Privileged
Abbrev: **term** {*parameter*}
Section: 4.3
Usage: Use to change the characteristics for the current terminal line session. Type **terminal ?** to get a list of the options. Most of the terminal session characteristics can be applied directly to a terminal line device by typing the parameter keywords and values (without the word *terminal*) in line configuration mode.

terminal editing

```
terminal editing
terminal no editing
```

Mode: User, Privileged
Abbrev: **term edit**
Section: 4.3.1.1

Usage: Use to enable command line editing control and escape sequences. They are enabled by default. Use the **no** form of the command to disable the command editing function.

terminal history

```
terminal history
terminal no history
```

Mode: User, Privileged
Abbrev: **term hist**
Section: 4.3.1.1
Usage: Use to enable the use of the command history function, which causes IOS to save entered commands in a command history buffer. This function is enabled by default. The size of the command history buffer is defined with the **terminal history size** command. Use the **no** form of the command to disable the command history function.

terminal history size

```
terminal history size number
terminal no history size
```

   number The number of lines in the command history buffer. The default is 10.

Mode: User, Privileged
Abbrev: **term hist size**
Section: 4.3.1.1
Usage: Use to change the number of lines that IOS keeps in the user mode and privileged mode history buffer and the configuration mode history buffer. Use the **no** form of the command to set the number of lines back to its default value of 10.

terminal length

```
terminal length len
terminal no length
```

   len The length, in lines, of a terminal screen. The default is 24.

Mode: User, Privileged
Abbrev: **term len** *len*
Section: 4.3.6
Usage: Use this command to change the number of lines that IOS will display on a terminal screen before stopping the display and presenting the More prompt. Setting the terminal length to zero (0) will disable the More function. Use the **no** form of the command to set the number of lines back to its default value of 24.

terminal monitor

```
terminal monitor
terminal no monitor
```

Mode: Privileged
Abbrev: **term mon**
Section: 5.3.6, 6.8
Usage: Use to give a terminal line the monitor capability that enables the line to receive logged messages according to the monitor logging level. The monitor logging level can be displayed with the **show logging** command. When accessing a remote router via a telnet connection, the **terminal monitor** command must be entered to view **debug** command output. Use the **no** form of the command to disable the monitor function.

terminal width

```
terminal width width
terminal no width
```

  width   The width, in characters, of a terminal screen. The default is 80.

Mode: User, Privileged
Abbrev: **term wid** *width*
Section: 4.3.6
Usage: Use this command to change the number of characters that IOS should display on a line before wrapping. This command has no effect on most command output. So why bother? Use the **no** form of the command to set the width to its default value of 80.

trace

`trace` [*ipaddr* | *host-name*]

ipaddr   IP address in dotted-decimal notation.
host-name   The name of a host that can be resolved to an address
             using DNS or a host table.

Mode: User, Privileged
Abbrev: **tr** [*ipaddr* | *host-name*]
Section: 7.7.2.3
Usage: Use **trace** to discover the path that IP packets are taking from
           the local router to a remote host. The **trace** command is actu-
           ally an abbreviation of **traceroute.** The trace application uses
           a combination of UDP packets and ICMP packets to trace the
           desired route. Typing **trace** with no address or name will start
           an extended trace that allows the changing of trace parameters
           such as source address (like an extended ping), initial TTL
           (time to live), and probe count. An extended trace can be done
           only in privileged mode. When a host name is specified, IOS
           must perform address resolution to get an IP address before
           attempting the telnet. A trace can be aborted with the IOS
           escape sequence, which has a default value of <Ctrl-Shift-6>.

transport preferred none

`transport preferred none`

Mode: Line Configuration
Abbrev: **tr pr no**
Section: 6.5
Usage: Use this command to stop IOS from assuming that a noncom-
           mand word typed on the command line is the name of a host to
           which it should attempt to establish a telnet session.

version 2

`version 2`
`no version 2`

Mode: Router Configuration (RIP)
Abbrev: **ver 2**
Section: 7.7.1.2

Usage: Use to enable RIP version 2 (RIPv2) on a router. The default is RIP version 1 (RIPv1). This command will enable RIPv2 on all interfaces that have addresses matching one of the **network** commands. Use the **ip rip** command to override the RIP version on an individual interface. Use the **no** form of the command to disable RIPv2 and reenable RIPv1.

vines metric

```
vines metric [number]
no vines metric
```

number   A value to become the VINES metric on an interface. The metric is used by RTP and SRTP to determine the best path to a network.

Mode: Interface Configuration
Abbrev: **vi me** [*number*]
Section: 11.3, 11.5
Usage: Use to enable VINES on an interface and to assign a metric to the interface. If the metric value is not included on the command, IOS automatically calculates one and puts it into the running configuration. VINES RTP starts on an interface when a metric is assigned to the interface. Use the **no** form of the command to remove VINES traffic processing from an interface.

vines routing

```
vines routing [address]
no vines routing
```

address   A VINES address in the form *xxxxxxxx:xxxx*, where *x* is a hexadecimal digit. The network part of the address must be greater than or equal to hexadecimal 20000000, and the subnetwork (host) part of the address must be 1 (or hexadecimal 0001).

Mode: Global Configuration
Abbrev: **vin routi** [*address*]
Section: 11.3, 11.5, 11.6
Usage: Use to enable the routing of VINES packets on a router. If an address is not entered, IOS automatically selects one and

places it in the running configuration with the command. The address selected is based on the MAC address of the router's first LAN interface, with the first Ethernet interface taking precedence. If a router has no LAN interfaces, IOS chooses an address at random. We should verify that the address is unique among routers. Use the **no** form of the command to disable the routing of VINES packets.

vines srtp-enabled

```
vines srtp-enabled
no vines srtp-enabled
```

Mode: Global Configuration
Abbrev: **vi sr**
Section: 11.3
Usage: Use to enable the support of VINES SRTP. When SRTP is enabled, the router will use either RTP or SRTP (or both) after it determines which one the other hosts on a network are using. Use the **no** form of the command to disable VINES SRTP and return to RTP only.

write erase

```
write erase
```

Mode: Privileged
Abbrev: **wr e**
Section: 6.4.5.5
Usage: Use to erase the contents of NVRAM, which normally contains the startup configuration. If NVRAM is empty when a router boots, IOS will ask you if you want to start the Initial (System) Configuration Dialog. Use this command when you want to start from scratch with a router's configuration. This command is the predecessor of the **erase startup-config** command.

write memory

`write memory`

Mode: Privileged
Abbrev: **wr** (or **wr mem**)
Section: 6.4.3.1, 6.4.3.2, 6.4.5.1
Usage: Use to copy the running configuration to NVRAM where it becomes the startup configuration. Issue this command after configuration changes have been made and have been tested so the configuration changes will be intact the next time the router boots. This command is the predecessor of the **copy running-config startup-config** command.

write terminal

`write terminal`

Mode: Privileged
Abbrev: **wr t**
Section: 6.4.1
Usage: Use to display the contents of the running configuration file, which contains the commands that are currently being used by a router. This command is the predecessor of the **show running-config** command.

APPENDIX B

ACRONYM GLOSSARY

AARP	AppleTalk Address Resolution Protocol
ABR	Area Border Router
AEP	AppleTalk Echo Protocol
ANSI	American National Standards Institute
ARP	Address Resolution Protocol
ARPA	Advanced Research Projects Agency
ASBR	Autonomous System Boundary Router
ASCII	American Standard Code for Information Interchange
ASN	Autonomous System Number
AUX	Auxiliary port on a Cisco router
BDR	Backup Designated Router
BPDU	Bridge Protocol Data Unit
BRI	Basic Rate Interface
BVI	Bridge-group Virtual Interface
BW	Bandwidth
CCO	Cisco Connection Online (*http://www.cisco.com*)
CDP	Cisco Discovery Protocol
CLNS	Connectionless Network Service
CON	Console port on a Cisco router
CTY	Console port on a Cisco router
DB25	Data Bus connector with 25 pins
DCE	Data Circuit-terminating Equipment (or Data Communications Equipment)
DDP	Datagram Delivery Protocol
DEC	Digital Equipment Corporation
DLCI	Data Link Connection Identifier
DLY	Delay
DNA	Digital Network Architecture
DNS	Domain Name System (or Domain Name Service)
DR	Designated Router
DRP	DECnet Routing Protocol
DTE	Data Terminal Equipment

DUAL	Diffusing Update Algorithm
ED	Early Deployment
EIA/TIA	Electronic Industries Association/Telecommunications Industry Association
EIGRP	Enhanced Interior Gateway Routing Protocol
FDDI	Fiber Distributed Data Interface
GD	General Deployment
GMT	Greenwich Mean Time
GNS	Get Nearest Server
HDLC	High-level Data Link Control
HSSI	High-Speed Serial Interface
HTTP	HyperText Transfer Protocol
I/O	Input/Output
IBM	International Business Machines Corporation
ICMP	Internet Control Message Protocol
IEEE	Institute of Electrical and Electronics Engineers
IETF	Internet Engineering Task Force
IGRP	Interior Gateway Routing Protocol
IOS	Internetwork Operating System
IP	Internet Protocol
IPX	Internetwork Packet eXchange
ISDN	Integrated Services Digital Network
ISO	International Organization of Standardization
kbps	Kilobits per second
LAA	Locally Administered Address
LAN	Local Area Network
LAPB	Link Access Procedure Balanced
LAT	Local Area Transport
LD	Limited Deployment
LMI	Local Management Interface
LSA	Link State Advertisement
MAC	Media Access Control
MB	Megabyte
Mbps	Megabits per second
MOTD	Message Of The Day
MTU	Maximum Transmission Unit
NBMA	Nonbroadcast Multiaccess
NBP	Name Binding Protocol
NCP	NetWare Core Protocol
NDS	Novell Directory Services
NetBEUI	NetBIOS Extended User Interface

NetBIOS	Network Basic Input/Output System
NLSP	Novell Link Services Protocol
NTP	Network Time Protocol
NVRAM	Non-volatile RAM
OSI	Open Systems Interconnection
OSPF	Open Shortest Path First
OUI	Organizational Unique Identifier
PC	Personal Computer
PCMCIA	Personal Computer Memory Card International Association
PID	Process Identifier
PPP	Point-to-Point Protocol
PVC	Permanent Virtual Circuit
RAM	Random Access Memory
RFC	Request For Comment
RID	Router Identifier
RIP	Routing Information Protocol (or Rest In Peace)
RIPv1	RIP version 1
RIPv2	RIP version 2
RJ45	Registered Jack connector with eight wires
ROM	Read-Only Memory
RSP	Route Switch Processor
RTMP	Routing Table Maintenance Protocol
RTP	Routing update Protocol
SAP	Service Access Point (or Service Advertisement Protocol)
SIMM	Single In-line Memory Module
SNA	Systems Network Architecture
SNAP	Subnetwork Access Protocol
SNMP	Simple Network Management Protocol
SPF	Shortest Path First
SPX	Sequenced Packet eXchange
SRTP	Sequenced Routing update Protocol
STP	Spanning Tree Protocol
SVC	Switched Virtual Circuit
TAC	Technical Assistance Center
TACACS	Terminal Access Controller Access Control System
TCP	Transmission Control Protocol
TCP/IP	Transmission Control Protocol/Internet Protocol
TFTP	Trivial File Transfer Protocol
TTY	Teletype terminal. An asynchronous terminal
UDP	User Datagram Protocol
UTC	Coordinated Universal Time

VINES	Virtual Networking System
VIP	Versatile Interface Processor
VTY	Virtual teletype (or virtual terminal)
WAN	Wide Area Network
XNS	Xerox Network Systems
ZIP	Zone Information Protocol
ZIT	Zone Information Table

APPENDIX C

REFERENCES

Cisco Systems, Inc. *Cisco IOS 11.3 Configuration Guides, Command References. http://www.cisco.com*; 1989-1998.

Cisco Systems, Inc. *Internetworking Technology Overview. http://www.cisco.com*; 1989-1999.

Cisco Systems, Inc. *Router Products Configuration and Reference. http://www.cisco.com*; 1989-1998.

Cisco Systems, Inc. *Software Naming Conventions for IOS.* Version 1.32. *http://www.cisco.com*; 1997.

Cisco Systems, Inc. *Types of Cisco IOS Software Releases.* Product Bulletin #537. *http://www.cisco.com*; 1992-1999.

Comer, Douglas E. *Internetworking with TCP/IP, Vol. 1: Principles, Protocols, and Architecture.* 2d ed. Englewood Cliffs, NJ: Prentice-Hall, Inc.; 1991.

Dickie, Mark. *Routing in Today's Internetworks: The Routing Protocols of IP, DECnet, NetWare, and AppleTalk.* New York, NY: Van Nostrand Reinhold; 1994.

Doyle, Jeff. *CCIE Professional Development: Routing TCP/IP, Volume I.* Indianapolis, IN: Macmillan Technical Publishing; 1998.

Huitema, Christian. *Routing in the Internet.* Englewood Cliffs, NJ: Prentice-Hall, Inc.; 1995.

Naugle, Matthew. *Network Protocols.* Signature ed. New York, NY: The McGraw-Hill Companies, Inc.; 1999.

Perlman, Radia. *Interconnections: Bridges and Routers.* Reading, MA: Addison-Wesley Publishing Company; 1992.

Stevens, W. Richard. *TCP/IP Illustrated, Volume 1: The Protocols.* Reading, MA: Addison-Wesley Publishing Company; 1994.

Tanenbaum, Andrew S. *Computer Networks.* 2d ed. Englewood Cliffs, NJ: Prentice-Hall, Inc.; 1988.

APPENDIX D

FINAL CONFIGURATIONS

It might be nice to see the final product of the configuration we have been doing. Most of our configuration examples through Chapter 13 used the same three-router internetwork. This internetwork is shown once again in Figure D-1.

The hardware setup is provided as a courtesy of MentorLabs (*http://www.mentorlabs.com*). For each of the router-to-router serial connections, the routers' serial interfaces are connected directly to each other with a DTE-to-DCE cable. The DCE end of each cable is connected to a Serial1 interface; therefore, the Serial1 interfaces have the responsibility of providing the clock for the link. For example, there is a single

Figure D-1
Final three-router internetwork.

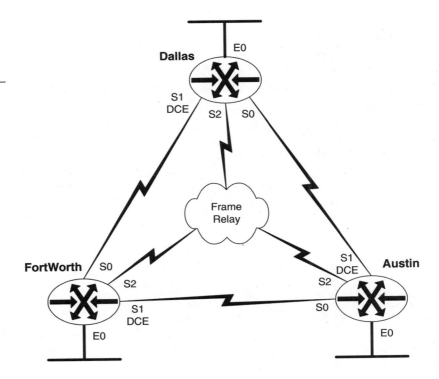

cable between Dallas's Serial0 interface and Austin's Serial1 interface; the DCE end of the cable is connected to Austin's Serial1; therefore, Austin's Serial1 must provide the clock for the serial network. The clocking is set with the **clockrate** command; you can see this in the final configurations below.

Our internetwork ended up routing IP on the frame relay network and routing IPX, AppleTalk, DECnet, and VINES on the point-to-point serial links. We also threw bridging in just for grins.

The final configurations are being shown with no edits; everything is included so you can see exactly what each router has. Figure D-2 shows the final running configuration on Dallas; Figure D-3 shows the final running configuration on FortWorth; and Figure D-4 shows the final running configuration on Austin. These configurations were saved immediately after Chapter 13 where we did frame relay.

On FortWorth, we simulated a NetWare server by creating a loopback interface (Figure D-3, Line 27), assigning it an IPX address (Line 29), and then creating static SAP entries to look like services (Lines 99 through 103). The configurations should hold no other surprises for you.

Figure D-2

Dallas final configuration.

```
1)    Dallas#show running-config
2)    Building configuration...
3)
4)    Current configuration:
5)    !
6)    version 11.3
7)    service timestamps debug uptime
8)    service timestamps log uptime
9)    no service password-encryption
10)   !
11)   hostname Dallas
12)   !
13)   enable secret 5 $1$S.px$gAcVrJaShGu2x6Rvu/F1C/
14)   enable password enableme
15)   !
16)   no ip domain-lookup
17)   appletalk routing eigrp 100
18)   appletalk route-redistribution
19)   !
20)   decnet routing 1.1
21)   decnet node-type area
22)   !
23)   ipx routing 0010.7b3a.d4bf
24)   ipx maximum-paths 2
25)   vines routing 301AD4BF:0001
26)   !
27)   !
28)   interface Ethernet0
```

```
29)     description Dallas Ethernet LAN
30)     ip address 172.16.10.1 255.255.255.0
31)     no lat enabled
32)     appletalk cable-range 100-109 100.10
33)     appletalk zone Headquarters
34)     decnet cost 5
35)     ipx network AC100A00
36)     vines metric 2
37)     no mop enabled
38)     bridge-group 1
39)  !
40)   interface Serial0
41)     description 256k Line to Austin
42)     no ip address
43)     bandwidth 256
44)     appletalk cable-range 1002-1002 1002.1
45)     appletalk zone WAN
46)     appletalk protocol eigrp
47)     no appletalk protocol rtmp
48)     decnet cost 25
49)     ipx network C0A80200
50)     vines metric 45
51)     bridge-group 1
52)  !
53)  interface Serial1
54)     description T1 to FortWorth
55)     no ip address
56)     appletalk cable-range 1001-1001 1001.100
57)     appletalk zone WAN
58)     appletalk protocol eigrp
59)     no appletalk protocol rtmp
60)     decnet cost 15
61)     ipx network AC100B00
62)     vines metric 35
63)     clockrate 1300000
64)     bridge-group 1
65)  !
66)  interface Serial2
67)     no ip address
68)     encapsulation frame-relay
69)  !
70)  interface Serial2.1 point-to-point
71)     ip address 172.16.30.1 255.255.255.0
72)     frame-relay interface-dlci 100
73)  !
74)  interface Serial2.2 point-to-point
75)     ip address 172.16.31.1 255.255.255.0
76)     frame-relay interface-dlci 102
77)  !
78)  interface Serial3
79)     no ip address
80)     shutdown
81)  !
82)  interface BRI0
83)     no ip address
84)     shutdown
```

Figure D-2
Dallas final config-
uration.

```
85)  !
86)  router rip
87)    network 172.16.0.0
88)  !
89)  ip classless
90)  !
91)  !
92)  !
93)  !
94)  !
95)  ipx router eigrp 500
96)    network AC100B00
97)    network C0A80200
98)  !
99)  !
100) ipx router rip
101)   no network C0A80200
102)   no network AC100B00
103) !
104) !
105) !
106) bridge 1 protocol ieee
107) bridge 1 priority 0
108) !
109) line con 0
110)   exec-timeout 0 0
111)   password letmein
112)   login
113) line aux 0
114) line vty 0 4
115)   password letmein
116)   login
117) !
118) end
119)
120) Dallas#
```

Figure D-3
FortWorth final
configuration.

```
1)   FortWorth#show running-config
2)   Building configuration...
3)
4)   Current configuration:
5)   !
6)   version 11.3
7)   service timestamps debug uptime
8)   service timestamps log uptime
9)   no service password-encryption
10)  !
11)  hostname FortWorth
12)  !
13)  enable secret 5 $1$LKJD$eQwhzhNEr4LsUFCwrJ8eG0
14)  enable password enableme
15)  !
16)  no ip domain-lookup
17)  appletalk routing eigrp 200
```

Figure D-3

FortWorth final
configuration.

```
18)    appletalk route-redistribution
19)    !
20)    decnet routing 1.2
21)    decnet node-type routing-iv
22)    !
23)    ipx routing 0010.7b3a.d4af
24)    vines routing 301AD4AF:0001
25)    !
26)    !
27)    interface Loopback0
28)     no ip address
29)     ipx network AC101401
30)    !
31)    interface Ethernet0
32)     description FortWorth Ethernet LAN
33)     ip address 172.16.20.1 255.255.255.0
34)     no lat enabled
35)     appletalk cable-range 200-209 200.20
36)     appletalk zone Twilight
37)     decnet cost 5
38)     ipx network AC101400
39)     vines metric 2
40)     no mop enabled
41)     bridge-group 1
42)     !
43)    interface Serial0
44)     description T1 to Dallas
45)     no ip address
46)     appletalk cable-range 1001-1001 1001.200
47)     appletalk zone WAN
48)     appletalk protocol eigrp
49)     no appletalk protocol rtmp
50)     decnet cost 15
51)     ipx network AC100B00
52)     vines metric 35
53)     bridge-group 1
54)    !
55)    interface Serial1
56)     description 56k Line to Austin
57)     no ip address
58)     bandwidth 56
59)     appletalk cable-range 1003-1003 1003.1
60)     appletalk zone WAN
61)     appletalk protocol eigrp
62)     no appletalk protocol rtmp
63)     ipx network C0A80300
64)     vines metric 45
65)     clockrate 56000
66)     bridge-group 1
67)     !
68)    interface Serial2
69)     ip address 172.16.30.2 255.255.255.0
70)     encapsulation frame-relay
71)     !
72)    interface Serial3
73)     no ip address
74)     shutdown
```

Figure D-3
FortWorth final configuration.

```
75)  !
76)  interface BRI0
77)   no ip address
78)   shutdown
79)  !
80)  router rip
81)   network 172.16.0.0
82)  !
83)  ip classless
84)  !
85)  !
86)  !
87)  !
88)  !
89)  ipx router eigrp 500
90)   network AC100B00
91)  network C0A80300
92)  !
93)  !
94)  ipx router rip
95)   no network AC100B00
96)   no network C0A80300
97)  !
98)  !
99)  ipx sap 4 FW_Server AC101401.0000.0000.0001 451 1
100) ipx sap 47 FW_Printer AC101401.0000.0000.0001 8060 1
101) ipx sap 107 FW_Server AC101401.0000.0000.0001 8104 1
102) ipx sap 26B FW_Server AC101401.0000.0000.0001 5 1
103) ipx sap 278 FW_Server AC101401.0000.0000.0001 4006 1
104) !
105) bridge 1 protocol ieee
106) !
107) line con 0
108) exec-timeout 0 0
109) password letmein
110) login
111) line aux 0
112) line vty 0 4
113) password letmein
114) login
115) !
116) end
117)
118) FortWorth#
```

Figure D-4
Austin final configuration.

```
1)   Austin#show running-config
2)   Building configuration...
3)
4)   Current configuration:
5)   !
6)   version 11.3
7)   service timestamps debug uptime
```

Figure D-4
Austin final config-
uration.

```
8)    service timestamps log uptime
9)    no service password-encryption
10)   !
11)   hostname Austin
12)   !
13)   enable secret 5 $1$NtPU$4sdeFDrV4nD6kAsdrWI0s.
14)   enable password enableme
15)   !
16)   no ip domain-lookup
17)   appletalk routing eigrp 300
18)   appletalk route-redistribution
19)   !
20)   decnet routing 2.1
21)   decnet node-type area
22)   !
23)   ipx routing 0010.7b3a.d204
24)   vines routing 301AD204:0001
25)   !
26)   !
27)   interface Ethernet0
28)    description Austin Ethernet LAN
29)    ip address 192.168.1.1 255.255.255.0
30)    no lat enabled
31)    appletalk cable-range 300-309 304.219
32)    appletalk zone Strike
33)    decnet cost 5
34)    vines metric 2
35)    no mop enabled
36)    bridge-group 1
37)   !
38)   interface Ethernet0.1
39)    ipx encapsulation SAP
40)    ipx network C0A80100
41)   !
42)   interface Ethernet0.2
43)    ipx network C0A801FF
44)   !
45)   interface Serial0
46)    description 56k Line to FortWorth
47)    no ip address
48)    bandwidth 56
49)    appletalk cable-range 1003-1003 1003.2
50)    appletalk zone WAN
51)    appletalk protocol eigrp
52)    no appletalk protocol rtmp
53)    ipx network C0A80300
54)    vines metric 45
55)    bridge-group 1
56)   !
57)   interface Serial1
58)    description 256k Line to Dallas
59)    no ip address
60)    bandwidth 256
61)    appletalk cable-range 1002-1002 1002.2
62)    appletalk zone WAN
63)    appletalk protocol eigrp
64)    no appletalk protocol rtmp
```

```
65)    decnet cost 25
66)    ipx network C0A80200
67)    vines metric 45
68)    clockrate 250000
69)    bridge-group 1
70)  !
71)  interface Serial2
72)    ip address 172.16.31.2 255.255.255.0
73)    encapsulation frame-relay
74)  !
75)  interface Serial3
76)   no ip address
77)   shutdown
78)  !
79)  interface BRI0
80)   no ip address
81)    shutdown
82)  !
83)  router rip
84)    network 172.16.0.0
85)    network 192.168.1.0
86)  !
87)  ip classless
88)  !
89)  !
90)  !
91)  !
92)  !
93)  ipx router eigrp 500
94)    network C0A80300
95)    network C0A80200
96)  !
97)  !
98)  ipx router rip
99)   no network C0A80300
100)  no network C0A80200
101) !
102) !
103) !
104) bridge 1 protocol ieee
105) !
106) line con 0
107)  exec-timeout 0 0
108)  password letmein
109)  login
110) line aux 0
111) line vty 0 4
112)  password letmein
113)  login
114) !
115) end
116)
117) Austin#
```

INDEX

A

AARP (*see* AppleTalk Address Resolution Protocol)

Abbreviations (on command line), 74–75

ABR (Area Border Router), 234

Absolute line numbering schemes, 100

Active configuration (*see* Running configuration)

Address resolution, 133–136

Address Resolution Protocol (ARP), 14, 181, 182

Addresses:
  broadcast, 14, 174
  interface, 38–39
  locally administered, 301
  MAC (*see* Medium Access Control addresses)
  multicast, 15
  unicast, 14

Addressing, 8–9
  DECnet, 300–301
  IP, 172–179
  IPX, 254–255
  LAN, 13–15
  layer-2, 12–15
  layer-3, 15–16
  VINES, 316–318
  WAN, 15

Administrative distance, 186

Advanced Research Projects Agency (ARPA), 96

Advertised distance, 224

AEP (AppleTalk Echo Protocol), 283

AFP (AppleTalk Filing Protocol), 283

All-ones subnet, 178

American Registry for Internet Numbers (ARIN), 179

Annex D, 346

AppleTalk, 14, 38, 280–298
  addressing with, 280–281
  configuration of, 285–288, 293–298
  and OSI model, 282–283

AppleTalk (*Cont.*):
  removal of, 298
  routing with, 283–285
  verification with, 288–293

AppleTalk Address Resolution Protocol (AARP), 280–281

AppleTalk Echo Protocol (AEP), 283

AppleTalk EIGRP, 293–295

AppleTalk Filing Protocol (AFP), 283

Applications layer (layer 7), 10
  AppleTalk, 283
  IP, 184
  IPX, 257–258

Area Border Router (ABR), 234

ARIN (American Registry for Internet Numbers), 179

ARP (*see* Address Resolution Protocol)

ARPA (Advanced Research Projects Agency), 96

ARPA encapsulation, 142

ASBR (Autonomous System Boundary Router), 234

ASN (*see* Autonomous system number)

Asynchronous serial ports, 99

Austin (sample router), 188–189, 191–193

Autonomous System Boundary Router (ASBR), 234

Autonomous system number (ASN), 217, 270

Autosummarization, 202

Auxiliary port, 32–33, 99

B

Backup configuration, 34

Backup Designated Router (BDR), 237

Bandwidth setting, 143–144

Banners, 125–128

Banyan VINES, 14

Basic Rate Interface (BRI), 44

457

ABOUT THE AUTHOR

JOHN ALBRITTON (CCIE #2833) is Principal Consultant for Wit Consulting in Dallas, Texas. He teaches Cisco router configuration for a Cisco Training Partner, Chesapeake Computer Consultants, Inc. He has performed many jobs in IT, including software development, network design, network implementation, network management, and the administration of NetWare, Windows NT, VMS, and Unix systems.